# INFORMATION SYSTEMS
## PROJECT MANAGEMENT

*To Thomas and Sabrina, with love—David*
*To my mother, my wife, and my daughter, with love—Reza*

# INFORMATION SYSTEMS
## PROJECT MANAGEMENT

**DAVID AVISON**
*ESSEC Business School, Paris, France*

**GHOLAMREZA TORKZADEH**
*University of Nevada Las Vegas*

Los Angeles • London • New Delhi • Singapore

*For information:*

SAGE Publications, Inc.
2455 Teller Road
Thousand Oaks, California 91320
E-mail: order@sagepub.com

SAGE Publications Ltd.
1 Oliver's Yard
55 City Road
London EC1Y 1SP
United Kingdom

SAGE Publications India Pvt. Ltd.
B 1/I 1 Mohan Cooperative Industrial Area
Mathura Road, New Delhi 110 044
India

SAGE Publications Asia-Pacific Pte. Ltd.
33 Pekin Street #02-01
Far East Square
Singapore 048763

Printed in the United States of America

*Library of Congress Cataloging-in-Publication Data*

Avison, D. E.
Information systems project management/David Avison, Gholamreza Torkzadeh.
    p. cm.
Includes bibliographical references and index.
ISBN 978-1-4129-5702-1 (pbk.)
    1. Information resources management. 2. Information technology—Management. 3. Project management.
I. Torkzadeh, Gholamreza. II. Title.

T58.64.A985 2009
004.068′4—dc22                          2008011837

This book is printed on acid-free paper.

08   09   10   11   12   11   10   9   8   7   6   5   4   3   2   1

| | |
|---|---|
| *Acquisitions Editor:* | Al Bruckner |
| *Editorial Assistant:* | MaryAnn Vail |
| *Production Editor:* | Diane S. Foster |
| *Copy Editor:* | Tony Moore |
| *Typesetter:* | C&M Digitals (P) Ltd. |
| *Indexer:* | Molly Hall |
| *Cover Designer:* | Candice Harman |
| *Marketing Manager:* | Jennifer Reed Banando |

# Brief Contents

# Detailed Contents

# Preface

**T**here are a number of books out there on project management. What is different and specific about this book?

There is a balance between **sociocultural** and **technical** aspects, and there is a balance between **qualitative** and **quantitative** aspects—project management is seen as both an **art** and a **science**.

It provides an **information systems** orientation for project management: neither information technology oriented on the one side nor production and operations oriented on the other, but applicable to both within an **organizational-wide** view.

It stresses **information systems as a whole**, not just software development—no project is successful if only software aspects are considered.

It gives a truly **international** view of the domain—examples and experiences from different parts of the world add richness as well as context to the material. Globalization has ensured that most projects take on an international dimension.

It provides a coherent explanation of the concerns of the project manager as the project develops through the **project life cycle**—it does not follow a "kitchen sink" approach.

Each chapter has the following **consistent structure:** introduction and outline, an exhibit, the main text with examples, interview with a project manager, chapter summary, discussion questions, exercises, and appendix—this structure provides coherence and consistency.

1. The exhibit, interview, and appendix contain **real-world** examples, experiences, case studies, discussion material, software descriptions, and professional codes. These provide material for **class discussion** and **group work.**

2. There is an **accompanying CD** with further material, including PowerPoint slides for each chapter.

3. The material has been used on our courses in the United States, Europe, and Australia, given to **practitioners** as well as **students** (both undergraduate and postgraduate)—it has been well tested as part of our own project management!

The book has the following structure (see the overall diagram on the following page, which provides a "road map" of the whole book). In Chapter 1, the introduction, we provide an outline of the stages of an information systems project and set the scene. We also describe the roles and importance of the various stakeholders. Chapter 2

Information Systems Project Management—Overall Book Structure

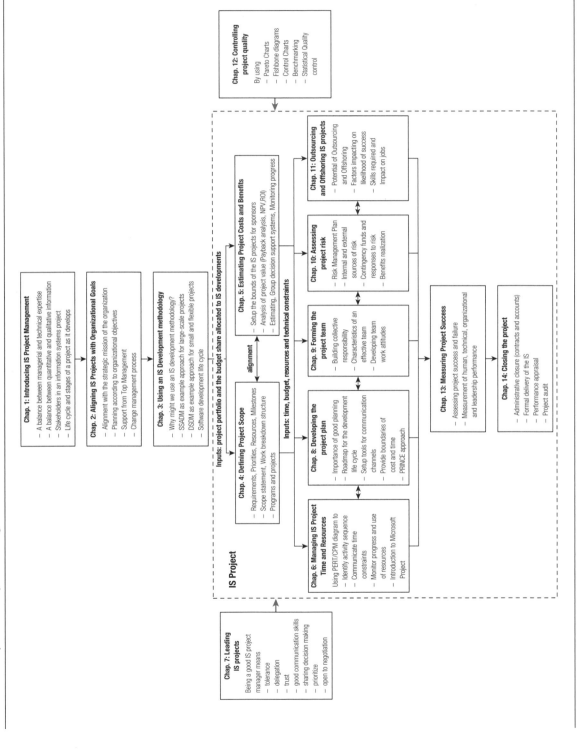

**Chap. 1: Introducing IS Project Management**
– A balance between managerial and technical expertise
– A balance between quantitative and qualitative information
– Stakeholders in an information systems project
– Life cycle and stages of a project as it develops

**Chap. 2: Aligning IS Projects with Organizational Goals**
– Alignment with the strategic mission of the organization
– Planning according to organizational objectives
– Support from Top Management
– Change management process

**Chap. 3: Using an IS Development methodology**
– Why might we use an IS development methodology?
– SSADM as example approach for large-scale projects
– DSDM as example approach for small and flexible projects
– Software development life cycle

**Chap. 4: Defining Project Scope**
– Requirements, Priorities, Resources, Milestones
– Scope statement, Work breakdown structure
– Programs and projects

**Chap. 5: Estimating Project Costs and Benefits**
– Setup the bounds of the IS projects for sponsors
– Analysis of project value (Payback analysis, NPV, ROI)
– Estimating, Group decision support systems, Monitoring progress

alignment

Inputs: project portfolio and the budget share allocated to IS developments

Inputs: time, budget, resources and technical constraints

**IS Project**

**Chap. 6: Managing IS Project Time and Resources**
Using PERT/CPM diagram to
– Identify activity sequence
– Communicate time constraints
– Monitor progress and use of resources
– Introduction to Microsoft Project

**Chap. 8: Developing the project plan**
– Importance of good planning
– Roadmap for the development life cycle
– Setup tools for communication channels
– Provide boundaries of cost and time
– PRINCE approach

**Chap. 9: Forming the project team**
– Building collective responsibility
– Characteristics of an effective team
– Developing team work attitudes

**Chap. 10: Assessing project risk**
– Risk Management Plan
– Internal and external sources of risk
– Contingency funds and responses to risk
– Benefits realization

**Chap. 11: Outsourcing and Offshoring IS projects**
– Potential of Outsourcing and Offshoring
– Factors impacting on likelihood of success
– Skills required and impact on jobs

**Chap. 12: Controlling project quality**
By using
– Pareto Charts
– Fishbone diagrams
– Control Charts
– Benchmarking
– Statistical Quality control

**Chap. 13: Measuring Project Success**
– Assessing project success and failure
– Measurement of human, technical, organizational and leadership performance

**Chap. 14: Closing the project**
– Administrative closure (contracts and accounts)
– Formal delivery of the IS
– Performance appraisal
– Project audit

**Chap. 7: Leading IS projects**
Being a good IS project manager means
– tolerance
– delegation
– trust
– good communication skills
– sharing decision making
– prioritize
– open to negotiation

shows how the project fits in with the organizational goals, and we begin to understand the importance of planning and the role of the project manager in the change management process. Chapter 3 looks at some information systems development methodologies that can support the project manager in developing the project. Chapter 4 looks at the scope of the project and discusses requirements, priorities, and resources, while Chapter 5 discusses not only the potential benefits of these requirements and resources but ways of estimating the cost of providing them. Chapter 6 shows how an effective project manager needs to manage resources such as people, time, and materials. In the diagram above we have placed Chapter 7 to show its relevance to the project development as a whole, because good leadership needs to be apparent throughout. Planning skills are particularly important, and developing the project plan is discussed in Chapter 8. Forming the project team concerns not only ensuring all skills are represented, but as shown in Chapter 9 we need to create a good synergy between team members. Assessing project risk and ensuring that project benefits are realized is the concern of Chapter 10. Chapter 11 considers the particular issues involved when a project or part of the project is outsourced or offshored. Controlling project quality is the concern of Chapter 12. Like Chapter 7, this is placed in the diagram to show that quality is an issue of concern in all aspects of project development. Finally, Chapters 13 and 14 discuss how we assess whether the project is a success or a failure and how we close the project.

As seen above, the design of the book is such that it can be read from beginning to end as we look at the role of the project manager as the information system progresses in chronological fashion. However, it can also be read in other ways. The most obvious is to pick and choose chapters as appropriate to your course. Each chapter can be read and understood in itself. However, it is also useful to read the book iteratively, by which we mean rereading the exhibits, interviews, and cases following further reading, as this greater knowledge can provide further insights on this material in particular.

We hope that you enjoy using this book. Please email us if you have any suggestions for improvement.

—David Avison,
Formiguéres, France (avison@essec.fr)

—Gholamreza Torkzadeh,
Las Vegas, United States (reza.torkzadeh@unlv.edu)

July 2008

# Acknowledgments

We wish to thank many colleagues and friends who have helped us with this book. The book was originally reviewed by several colleagues in the United States, Europe, and Australia who kindly took time to examine the text and its orientation and to give us detailed feedback and suggestions. Many, if not most, of these have been assimilated in this first edition, and we therefore thank the following reviewers in particular:

- Gary Hackbarth – Northern Kentucky University
- James E. Whitworth – Georgia Southern University
- James Moody – George Mason University
- Ardeshir Lohrasbi – University of Illinois at Springfield
- Philip F. Musa – University of Alabama at Birmingham
- Kuan-Chou Chen – Purdue University–Calumet
- Fatemeh Zahedi – University of Wisconsin–Milwaukee
- Weidong Xia – University of Minnesota in Minneapolis
- Emmanuel Monod – Paris Dauphine University
- Gezinus Hidding – Loyola University of Chicago
- David Wilson – University of Technology Sydney
- Philip Powell – University of Bath
- Jon T. Blue – University of Delaware

The following practitioners and research students also helped us with many comments, criticisms, and suggestions in the text: Ingrid Lee, Julien Malaurent, Kashif Mehmood, Ando Ratsimanohatra, Mohammad Hosseyn Vahdat, and Mahmood Zargar.

We are also particularly grateful to the following people:

- Guy Fitzgerald for the LASCAD case and the AAHelp exhibit
- Terry Young for Exhibit 6.1
- Gary Pan, Shan L. Pan, Michael Newman, and Donal Flynn, authors of the "How to Transform a Failing Project" case
- David Wilson and Shirley Gregor, co-authors of the One.Tel case
- Rudy Hirshheim, who suggested that we include a separate chapter on outsourcing and offshoring.

We have also been greatly influenced by our many students in the United States, France, England, and Australia, but we would like in particular to mention the following students who carried out some of the interviews and helped us to write several of the cases, in particular:

- Julien Malaurent, co-author of the "ERP in a Chinese Subsidiary" exhibit
- Leslie Owen, co-author of the Hendrich Electronics case
- Greg Hanson, co-author of the MedicalCo case
- Dean Hurst, co-author of the NGC case
- Howard Harris, co-author of the "A Conversation With a Student: Whose Side Are You On?" exhibit
- Ela Young, co-author of the Sarbanes–Oxley appendix
- Roy Lewis, co-author of the Beltech case
- Matthew Stephenson, co-author of the A-BANK cases.

Most of the names of the organizations have been made anonymous, but the cases are based on real situations in real companies.

We are also grateful to GroupSystems for permission to use *ThinkTank* material in Chapter 5. We are also appreciative of the assistance that we received from Helen Gerth of the Department of Management Information Systems at the University of Nevada, Las Vegas. Finally, we would like to thank the staff at Sage Publications, especially Al Bruckner, Diane Foster, Tony Moore, and MaryAnn Vail, for their support in helping us develop this book.

# Introducing Information Systems Project Management

**T**his chapter introduces many of the themes that will be discussed fully later in the book. It looks first at our application domain of information systems projects and then describes what project management is and what the characteristics of an effective project manager are. It points out the skill set needed by a project manager for the successful completion of an information systems project. It outlines principles and techniques that are important for a project manager to succeed. The information systems project development life cycle is defined in five stages, and its usefulness for successful project development is described. The various stakeholders who play key roles to a successful information systems project are also described. These stakeholders include the technologists and the various types of user, both internal and external to the organization. This chapter also describes why there is a need for good project managers in the information age and the ethical values that such project managers need to have. Finally, this chapter describes what is presented in the rest of the book and how the content of this text is designed to provide a balance between sociocultural and technical aspects of information systems project management. In the book we will look at cases coming from Unites States, United Kingdom, Australia, and elsewhere, describing information systems successes and failures (we learn from both) and sometimes projects that have been turned around into successes. First we look at Exhibit 1.1, which is a brief account of a successful project.

---

### Exhibit 1.1    AAHELP: A Successful Project

You will not have heard much if anything about the computer project described here for the British Automobile Association (AA). Why? Because it was a success, not newsworthy at all—indeed, perhaps commonplace. The system nevertheless won the British Computer Society's Information Systems Management award. The system proved itself excellent in three categories: the impact of the information systems (IS) on the performance of the organization; the quality of the relationships with customers, users, and systems providers; and the management of the development and operation of the system.

The AA provides roadside assistance to its 9 million members and has the world's largest patrol force of 3,600 people. To support members who require assistance, it developed a PC system known as AAHELP at a cost of 35 million British pounds (US$70 million). The system has delivered quicker help to members, improved customer satisfaction, and led to better resource planning.

Much of its success can be attributed to the change management program. Indeed AA sees the system as part of an ongoing process of change. Another point to its success was that the AA sees IS and the business working closely together. There is no need to "build bridges." IT and IS are well integrated in the organizational structure.

It was a large ongoing project, and it was divided into several phases. As the first phase proved successful, they got the board's support for the next phase and so on. None of these phases lasted longer than 6 months. This added cost to the project but also gave flexibility so that results from each phase could lead to changes in the next. Prototyping was used to check the validity of designs before further major development work. All of this concerned the management of risk, which was seen as a crucial issue.

The project management methodology called PRINCE was used to develop AAHELP. Quality was assessed by a project assurance team. The project was overseen by a project board and supporting teams. The IS/IT team was 70 strong, with most work done in-house (with some outsourcing). Everyone was seen as "owning" the system, with problem solving and brainstorming *together* leading to an excellent team spirit.

Teams were assigned for infrastructure acquisition and installation, design, programming, configuration management, testing, user acceptance, and maintenance. User involvement was also seen as key, so relevant business managers chose five representatives from the user population who became full-time members of the team. They included patrols, call handlers, and dispatchers. User requirements were translated through a joint application development (JAD) workshop, in which users and technologists worked together. When the system was implemented, participants at the workshop acted as champions of the new system.

The system can handle 6 million calls a year, and 80% of these are dispatched automatically to patrols without manual intervention. Only a proportionally few calls required the intervention necessary in the previous system. The system includes a geographical information system (an electronic map of the UK with important reference points), a diagnostics system (to identify the problem for any motor breakdown), automatic deployment of the patrols to the customer, and a system to handle communications between the patrol and the operations center.

But the media are not very interested in AAHELP—it is a story of a successful IT project, and thus is not newsworthy!

Adapted from IT at the Heart of Business, by G. Fitzgerald, 2000, London: BCS. (Note that the explanations to the technical terms used here will be given in the book.)

## 1.1. What Is an Information System?

Before addressing the question "What is project management?" we look first at information systems, as in this book we are concerned with the project management of information systems projects. The growth and preponderance of information systems—i.e., the applications of information and communication technology (ICT)—affect every aspect of our daily work life in one way or another. Information systems have greatly influenced the individual and society as a whole, and this process will continue and grow even further.

We will look at *information* and *system* separately before defining an information system. *Information* comes from selecting, summarizing, and presenting facts in such a way that it is useful to the recipient. Information is therefore meaningful and significant in a particular context and is useful to support decision making in that context. An information system in an organization provides information useful to its members and clients. This information should help it operate more effectively. The *system* part of "information system" represents a way of seeing the set of interacting components, such as people (e.g., systems analysts, business users, and line managers), information and communications technology (e.g., computer hardware devices, a user interface, communications networks, and the World Wide Web), and procedures (e.g., business processes and business rules for good project management). We can now define an *information system*:

> An **information system** is a system that assembles, stores, processes, and delivers information relevant to an organization (or to society) in such a way that the information is accessible and useful to those who wish to use it, including managers, staff, clients, and citizens. An information system is a human activity (social) system that is supported by information and communications technology.

The information might concern an organization's customers, suppliers, products, equipment, procedures, operations, and so on. Information systems in a bank, for example, might concern the payment of its employees, the operation of its customer accounts, or the efficient running of its branches.

There is almost no activity in our daily life that has not been affected by information systems. Nowadays, information systems are normally reliant on ICT—that is, the hardware, software, and communications elements—but information systems are more than that. They are the combination of IT and its application in organizations, including human aspects (the users and other stakeholders) that make the technology into something applied and useful for the organization. This is illustrated in Figure 1.1 for a sales order processing system.

❖ **Figure 1.1**    An Information System Supporting Sales Order Processing

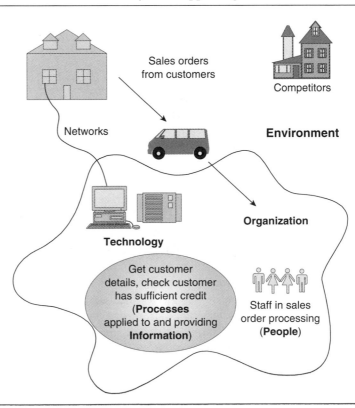

Think for a moment about communication, travel, banking, shopping, entertainment, education, privacy, security, and the like, and consider how in the last decade or two we have changed the way we deal with these or even perceive them because of the impact of information systems and information and communications technology.

For example, the Internet has changed the way we think of shopping. It enables us to search, find, order, and pay for a product in a few minutes without having to leave the home or the office. Even enthusiasts for technology such as software engineers and systems designers did not expect so much progress in such a short time. It is now no longer a matter of whether you will adopt a new tool but when and how. Information systems pervade all aspects of life, at home as well as in the office, school, and hospital.

## 1.2. What Is Project Management?

We are concerned in this book with information systems projects. We have already defined an information system, and a *project* can be defined as follows:

> A **project** is a non-routine, one-time job limited by time and budget to meet a specified need of the customer.

Thus a project is temporary (although the time span may be from a few days to a few years), it has a particular purpose for the customer (sometimes referred to as the project sponsor), and it requires resources (the budget allocated will be for people, technology, and other resources).

Computers were first used in scientific projects, then for business applications, and later on for tasks in the home. Information system applications that initially were intended to handle specific tasks have increasingly become more complex and sometimes now involve integrating multiple systems. The development of these large and complex information systems demands more sophisticated processes for planning, scheduling, and controlling. The demand on resources, including human, financial, structural, and organizational resources, for the development of these systems has also increased. However, information systems executives are increasingly challenged to justify huge expenditures for information systems development in value-added terms. They are also required to comment on the likelihood that the information system will be delivered on time and within budget, performing the functions expected of it. Information systems projects are notorious for budget overrun and delay and not delivering the functional promises. In other words, the challenges of satisfying rising expectations for information systems require excellent *project management.*

Whether the domain of the project is information systems, production, operations management, or whatever, project management remains the same in principle. The following definition is provided by the Project Management Institute (PMI):

> **Project management** is the application of knowledge, skills, tools, and techniques to project activities to meet project requirements.

The topic of project management has been traditionally covered under the discipline of production and operations management, but it is relevant in many disciplines. Because of the potential organizational impact of information systems and its mixed record of success, good project managers are in very high demand in that field of practice because they play such a critical role in the development and delivery of quality information systems. In recent years, therefore, disciplines such as information systems have recognized the importance of project management skills for information systems *and* management professionals (and sometimes engineers) involved in developing information systems projects. Information systems curricula have been increasingly revised to incorporate courses that deal with project management principles. Project management skills are necessary for a team leader who is responsible for channeling collective team activities to produce an effective information system within budget and in a timely manner with the required functionality.

Think of a typical information systems project: It could involve Web development, an online checkbook, a travel organizer, an accounts receivable system, an inventory control system, or a flight simulator.

For any of these systems to be developed or modified successfully, several activities must take place to varying degrees. Although there are different terminologies applied to these stages, the activities relate to the *initiating, planning, developing, implementing*, and *closing* of a project. These five stages, shown in Figure 1.2, will be detailed further in Section 1.6.

The quality and usefulness of the outcome will depend on how well these activities are performed. The project manager is the person who is responsible for making sure that these activities occur on time and with the right emphasis. An effective information systems project manager must not only understand the technology and its impact but also the role that each of these activities plays in the successful development and implementation of an information system. Thus this book emphasizes the impact of an information system on people and the organization—it is concerned with the sociocultural aspects of technical change and not just limited to the technical change itself. Again, it is also concerned with the role of and impact on general managers in an information systems project, and not just the technologists.

Interestingly, most books on the subject concentrate on the technical side, yet our interviews of project managers as well as our experience indicate that the bigger concern to project managers are the nontechnical aspects. In this book we have a balance of the two.

## 1.3. Why "Information Systems" Project Management?

Although the concept of project management has been around for some time and it has been a part of the curricula of other disciplines, the principles of project management

❖ **Figure 1.2**    Life Cycle of an Information Systems Project—A First Approximation

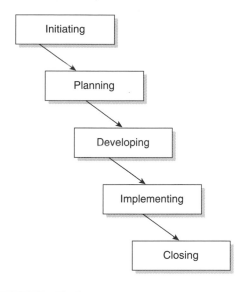

and related techniques and tools are particularly important for the design, development, and implementation of information systems projects. Further, the management of an information systems project requires additional knowledge and abilities that are expected of information systems professionals. Rapid changes in technology and enhancements require continual self-training and self-learning. Newly identified potential uses of information systems seem to be discovered almost daily, affecting all levels in the organization. This rapid change also means that the project description and its features may change before the project is complete—not to mention the user expectations of the project outcome. It is important to understand this dynamic aspect of information systems project management relative to the traditional project management function.

This is a recent dimension even in the domain of information systems. Information systems have traditionally been developed on the assumption that systems requirements are defined at the beginning of the project and will not change. This would now be considered naïve and unacceptable. The business environment might change as the information system is developed, and there may be changes in the organizational structure (of customers and suppliers as well). Project managers must be aware that the information systems application can and will change during its development. Changes to requirements are the norm, and this is reflected in Figure 1.3. This suggests that in the "real world" it is not simply a process of requirements being communicated and simply incorporated into the new system as a "one off" exercise. The requirements may change as the project develops. The process is much more sophisticated.

❖ **Figure 1.3**   The Old and More Up-to-Date Views of Requirements in an
Information Systems Project

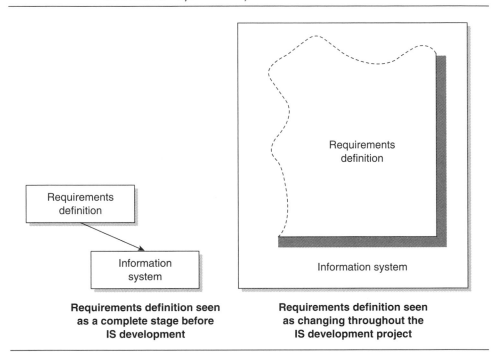

**Requirements definition seen
as a complete stage before
IS development**

**Requirements definition seen
as changing throughout the
IS development project**

All this requires a project manager of an information systems project to have a
clear understanding of information: how it is generated, how it is used, how it is
maintained, and how it is integrated to serve different functions within an organization. End-users and other stakeholders often become a part of developmental
activities in addition to the project team members who have specific responsibilities.
An effective information systems project manager must have qualities and skills that
relate to the management of the information systems function as well as principles
and concepts that relate to managing a project. It is clear that without a project manager there may be many more arguments due to sectional interests that could slow
down, or perhaps stop, the project, and should the project finish it is likely to be
much less directed to the interests of the organization as a whole. Exhibit 1.2 summarizes important project management skills that are required to make a successful
project much more likely.

However, it is unlikely that all these can be covered adequately by any one
person, and hence we can understand the advantage of the team approach to project
management.

**Exhibit 1.2    Project Management Skills for an Information Systems Project**

- Ability to communicate project information effectively
- Ability to document the flow of project information effectively
- Ability to manage human resources for a project effectively
- Ability to define project scope clearly
- Ability to understand the technical aspects of a project
- Ability to manage the project within the fiscal budget
- Ability to manage changes in requirements for a project
- Ability to maintain support for a project
- Ability to provide leadership
- Ability to manage time effectively
- Ability to solve problems
- Ability to close a project correctly

## 1.4. Project Management in Modern Organizations

Information systems using information and communications technology (ICT) can empower workers by enabling them to be more productive and by giving them greater control of their tasks. This means organizations reevaluate job descriptions frequently and add management responsibility to what was traditionally considered end-user-level work. As a result, separate and distinct tasks in the traditional work environment are now integrated and managed by the same person through the use of ICT. This trend has gradually reduced the need for some middle-level managers who were primarily responsible for work planning as well as horizontal and vertical communication with other middle-level managers, subordinates, and superiors. These middle-level managers also made sure that "the left hand knew what the right hand was doing," thus avoiding overlap and confusion and also controlling the work flow. This essential function must not be lost in the change process.

As technology reshaped the role and definition of the work unit, it made ordinary tasks more abstract and in need of instant coordination with other tasks that were infeasible to accomplish without technological help. In other words, technology has played a role in its own creation. More and more, jobs have become increasingly abstract and involve sense-making with an increased number of variables influencing decision outcome. This has created the need for more specialized careers that did not exist before. These new careers involve the need for greater technology application in the context of the business mission, goals, and objectives. Integration of technology across functions and organizations has increasingly become a norm. Technology has influenced career options in different ways. On the one hand it has increased the responsibility, influence, and complexity of most jobs, and on the other hand it has created opportunities for those with the know-how to use and manage it effectively.

However, the growth of ICT and its increased application created the challenge of keeping up with information systems development needs. Delayed and over-budget information systems projects became the norm rather than the exception. A 2-year backlog for the development of an information system was considered almost normal in many organizations. This could not go on. Fortunately, rapid development methodologies, techniques, and tools may have helped to ensure a more timely response to information systems development needs. Here technology itself is being used to help technology applications.

The traditional information systems development process involved a dichotomous relationship between developers and systems analysts on the one hand and users on the other. Figure 1.4 is a reflection of Figure 1.3, but with the recognition of user involvement in information systems development activities. Users and other stakeholders are now playing an increasingly critical role in any IS development project. We will say more about what we mean by the "user" in Section 1.7.

With the increased need for integrated information systems that closely align with organizational goals and objectives and address the user expectations came the job of information systems project management. While project management principles and

❖ **Figure 1.4** The Changing Relationship Between Users and the Project Manager

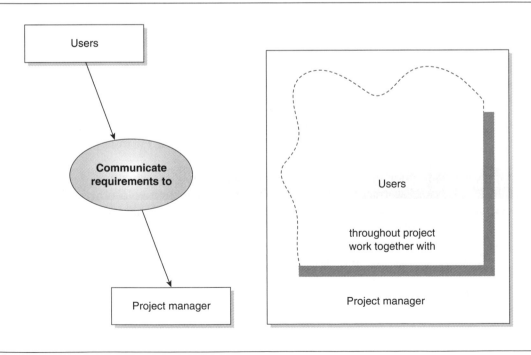

techniques have been used elsewhere, such as in the construction industry (and discussed in the discipline of operations management), its application for the development of information systems is newer, rapidly growing and becoming more sophisticated.

Project management has become one of the most sought-after positions in service as well as in manufacturing industries and in private as well as public organizations. The traditional job of the information systems analyst has been gradually redefined to go beyond the responsibilities of requirements analysis, design, development, and implementation. Project management has gradually replaced the traditional middle-management position. By its nature, the job of the information systems project manager combines a set of responsibilities that span from understanding the technology to managing human resources to addressing organizational needs. Its primarily role involves managing all aspects of an information systems development project from beginning to end and delivering it *as specified, on time,* and *within budget.* Therefore, critical project management dimensions relate to project scope, time, and budget.

## 1.5. Principles, Techniques, and Tools

An information systems project starts when someone within an organization initiates the idea of a new information system or suggests the modification of an existing one. Initiation is the first step among many steps necessary for the development and implementation of a successful information system. Whether the initial idea is carried forward into design, development, and implementation is influenced by a variety of factors, some of which are tangible and easier to measure (such as the cost of hardware, software, and personnel), and some of which are intangible and harder to assess (such as organizational and political support).

Large organizations often employ some form of *information systems portfolio committee* that evaluates and recommends information systems project proposals. The portfolio committee will normally follow a priority scheme that includes, among other things, the elements shown in Exhibit 1.3 (the question of priorities is raised further in chapter 2):

---

### Exhibit 1.3    Prioritization Factors

- The strategic and operational needs of the organization as determined by top management
- User requests for information systems increasing the efficiency of operations or providing information not presently available
- Views of all stakeholders and their "political" force
- Particular issues, such as "customer value," "improved processes," or concentration on particular performance measures
- Major revisions to existing applications owing to changes in the organization or its environment
- New opportunities, perhaps owing to the availability of new technology
- Competitive pressure—a matter of "keeping up with the competitors"

In smaller organizations, senior management or the "owner" usually makes that decision.

Once a project is recommended for development and its budget is approved it will go through the project development life cycle that ends with the implementation of the proposed idea and the formal closure of activities, contracts, and documents. An *information systems development project* can therefore be defined as follows:

> An **information systems development project** is a non-routine, one-time job limited by time and budget involving the application of information and communications technology by people in an organization to meet the specified needs of a customer.

The triple constraints of *scope, time,* and *cost* affect all information systems projects regardless of size or type and will be reflected through the necessity of defining the project as specified, on time, and within budget. These triple constraints directly and proportionally affect each other like three sides of a triangle, as shown in Figure 1.5. For example, increasing the scope of a project will increase its cost and/or the time to develop it. Reducing the time to delivery is likely to increase the cost of the project.

The project manager is responsible for the successful delivery of this one-time job within the limits of allocated resources. To be successful, the project manager must

❖ **Figure 1.5** The Triple Constraints of Scope, Time, and Cost

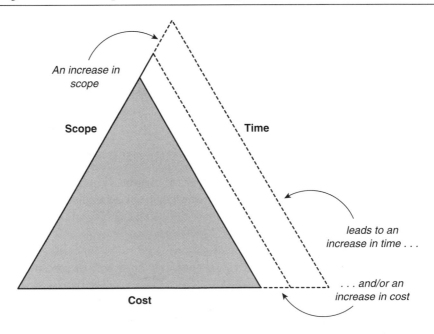

start by getting answers to some important questions relative to the issues listed in Exhibit 1.4. Without the project manager there will be real problems, as there will be no one to galvanize the team together toward the goals of the project.

---

### Exhibit 1.4    The Issues for the Project Manager to Consider

- Specific objectives of the project
- The expected delivery time for the project
- The limit on resources
- The extent of available talent pool
- Key stakeholders—people who initiated the idea and those who will be recipients of the final product
- Top management support
- Interorganizational relationships, especially for large projects

---

Let us look at these issues. A particularly important function of the project manager concerns project scope. The project scope is a key success indicator, as it defines objectives, is essential to evaluating resources, and is critical to achieving customer satisfaction. One of the persistent problems in information systems projects is the phenomenon known as *creeping scope*. This problem occurs when stakeholders or proponents of the project gradually expand their requests, adding new features or modifying initial specifications. They may expect these improvements at the same cost. If not controlled, this creeping process will eventually affect customer expectations— they will be too high—and thereby the evaluation of the project outcome leads inevitably to disappointment.

To save time and get the project underway, inexperienced project managers often spend too little time on developing a clear and agreed-upon description of the project scope and detailed requirements and start development activities prematurely. This will eventually haunt the project team in general and the project manager in particular as the project gets closer to the finishing line and customers have a clearer understanding of the project functions and can come up with even more requests. Not only is the due date affected by the scope creep, but also resources and other projects will be affected. After completing a project, team members and the project manager may have been assigned to another project that has been scheduled to start when the current project was due to finish.

However, there is a balance to be struck here. Scope needs to be clearly defined, but within that, some change in requirements has to be expected and dealt with. The world does not stand still! Thus there needs to be some built-in flexibility regarding changes in requirements. We will return to this problem later.

Once the scope is clearly defined, resources are estimated and the completion time for the entire project is established. A clearly defined scope helps the project manager estimate the time, cost, and human resources required. The available talent pool is often a key factor in deciding whether to outsource some aspects of the project. *Outsourcing* refers to the procurement of talent, such as consultants and suppliers, outside the organization, sometimes overseas. The latter is frequently referred to as *offshoring.* This is such an important topic nowadays that we devote the whole of chapter 11 to outsourcing and offshoring.

The project manager must evaluate carefully what resources are available and for how long and with what flexibility. Highly qualified individuals and domain experts may be scheduled to work on separate projects, and as a result their time is allocated based on what was initially agreed upon. In such cases, the project manager must make sure that adequate human expertise with necessary flexibility is allocated to the project for the project to be completed in a timely manner. Estimating resources is an important responsibility for a project manager, and it is extensively discussed later in the book (see Section 5.3, for example).

The next two issues in Exhibit 1.4 relate to key stakeholders of the project and top management support, both of which are considered critical for the success of any project although in different ways. It is important to know how to communicate and understand why communication skills are critical. Information systems professionals have proved much better in this role than ICT experts, who are more geared to the technology than people and organizations. This is only one reason why we emphasize information systems project management rather than software project management in this book. Another reason is the fact that the software and technology aspects represent only one aspect of an information systems development project.

The project manager must be able to communicate properly with key stakeholders of the project throughout the project development life cycle. The stakeholders of a project include individuals at all levels with interest in the project and its final product (Exhibit 1.5). We look at stakeholders in more detail in Section 1.7.

---

**Exhibit 1.5    Some of the Stakeholders of an IS Development Project**

- Top management
- Those who fund the project, such as functional area managers
- Those who directly work on the project, such as team members
- Primary customers
- Users of the project outcome
- Suppliers

---

Some key users may be included in the development team. User involvement in information systems development activities is strongly recommended because it gives users the opportunity to take part in the project development, feel responsible for the project outcome, and provide continual feedback. They will feel that they have a real "stake" in the project and are therefore more likely to cooperate and help to ensure the success of the project.

Top management support is also critical to the success of a project for reasons of support as well as recognition. The project manager must initially succeed in convincing top management that the proposed system has organizational value and serves the overall business strategy that the organization has adopted. Without initial support by top management the project will not start, and without the continued *full* (that is, not lip-service) support of top management its development will be hampered. If it is not seen as a top management priority, it will not be a project that people in the organization need to care about much or give the time and effort necessary for its success. It is therefore also important for the project manager to update top management continually with the developmental activities of the project and to make sure that top management support for the project is sustained. A key vehicle for obtaining continued support is clear and timely communication that informs top management as well as other key stakeholders about project progress and status. In particular, stakeholders would like to know whether the project is making timely progress (that it is on schedule) and is within budget. *It is important to communicate and explain, as early as possible, delays and unexpected costs.* It is the top management that will eventually have to approve additional funds and/or to extend the deadline. Therefore, it is critical to minimize the element of surprise before requesting additional support if it becomes necessary.

Interorganizational relationships are important particularly for large information systems development projects. Increasingly, information systems are developed to integrate functions and eliminate application redundancy (where the same process is done more than once). The success of such **integrated** applications depends on the broad participation of people in those functions that will be affected by the outcome. Further, globalization means that many—if not most—projects have the additional international design considerations to take into account in their scope.

We will look in more detail at the human qualities required by a project manager, but good communication skills are an obvious prerequisite. The project manager should understand and establish appropriate communication modes to inform all interested parties effectively. Early in the project development life cycle, the project manager should identify what works best and establish the process and means of good communications. For example, if email seems to work effectively and with ease for all concerned, then that could be the main mode of communication. However, there are situations or environments in which email systems exist but they are not used for one reason or another. In that case, this communication medium may not be effective unless some behavioral changes take place. What is important is that the message gets communicated effectively by whatever means. But establishing the mode of communication early in the project development life cycle is important.

## 1.6. Information Systems Project Life Cycle

Every project goes through several distinct stages before it is complete. A typical information systems project involves a spectrum of activities that starts from the initiation phase when the project idea is formed to the delivery phase when the project is complete and team members and management can move on to other projects. The project life cycle gives a useful viewpoint to the project manager to plan activities, allocate

❖ Figure 1.6 Life Cycle of an Information Systems Project—More Detailed

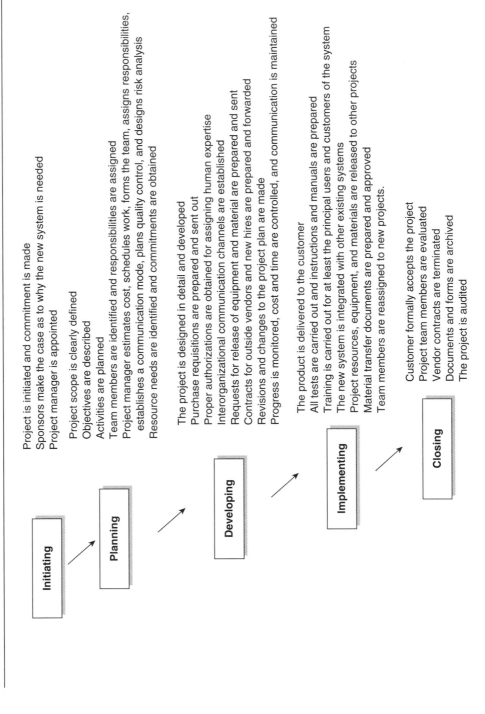

**Initiating**

Project is initiated and commitment is made
Sponsors make the case as to why the new system is needed
Project manager is appointed

**Planning**

Project scope is clearly defined
Objectives are described
Activities are planned
Team members are identified and responsibilities are assigned
Project manager estimates cost, schedules work, forms the team, assigns responsibilities, establishes a communication mode, plans quality control, and designs risk analysis
Resource needs are identified and commitments are obtained

**Developing**

The project is designed in detail and developed
Purchase requisitions are prepared and sent out
Proper authorizations are obtained for assigning human expertise
Interorganizational communication channels are established
Requests for release of equipment and material are prepared and sent
Contracts for outside vendors and new hires are prepared and forwarded
Revisions and changes to the project plan are made
Progress is monitored, cost and time are controlled, and communication is maintained

**Implementing**

The product is delivered to the customer
All tests are carried out and instructions and manuals are prepared
Training is carried out for at least the principal users and customers of the system
The new system is integrated with other existing systems
Project resources, equipment, and materials are released to other projects
Material transfer documents are prepared and approved
Team members are reassigned to new projects.

**Closing**

Customer formally accepts the project
Project team members are evaluated
Vendor contracts are terminated
Documents and forms are archived
The project is audited

resources, set milestones, monitor progress, and communicate developments. While there are many different project life cycle models, a typical generalized one was introduced in Section 1.2. Figure 1.6 is a more detailed version of Figure 1.2. In chapter 3 we will also look at more formalized methodologies to develop information systems.

- **Initiation stage:** At this stage a project is initiated and commitment is made. A person, group, unit, or units within the organization may initiate the need for a system. This might have been identified when a problem arises in the organization or a need for change is recognized. Usually a process is then followed to determine whether the idea should be supported or not. Sponsors of the idea must make the case as to why the new system is needed and how it helps organizational objectives. This is a challenging task since there are often competing proposals for limited resources. Proposals that are closely aligned with organizational strategic objectives have a better chance of receiving top management support. At this stage, someone is appointed as the manager of the project who will be responsible to carry out the project through the development life cycle and deliver the final product, assuming the project comes to fruition. This is the project manager.

- **Planning stage:** At this stage the project scope is defined as clearly as possible, objectives are described, and activities are planned. Team members are identified and responsibilities are assigned. If the project manager was not appointed at the initiation stage, someone will be assigned at the early stage of planning. At this stage, the project manager needs to estimate cost, schedule work, form the team or teams, assign responsibilities, establish a communication mode, plan quality control, and design risk analysis. If there are different information systems proposals for achieving the objectives, a choice needs to be made between alternatives. Sometimes there are constraints that limit choice, but the solution agreed on needs to be technologically reliable, reasonable to schedule, economically worthwhile, and organizationally acceptable. Specific and unique resource needs are also identified and commitments are obtained. For example, depending on the scope and nature of a project, specialized know-how and expertise may be necessary. The project manager must in such cases determine whether in-house expertise is adequate to satisfy the project needs or whether arrangements need to be made to obtain external assistance. Planning activities are critical to the success of project management since they map out what needs to be accomplished, how they are accomplished, how progress is monitored, how quality is controlled, and—in short—how the project is managed. Since estimates of resources and activities are not always projected accurately, planning must allow for some flexibility in this respect. Things are not cast in stone. A project plan may need adjusting during the development phase. However, changing the plan *must* be done following an agreed-upon process. For large projects, a committee is usually responsible for the evaluation and approval of proposed plan changes.

- **Development stage:** This stage, sometimes known as the executing phase, encompasses the detailed design through to, but excluding, the final implementation of the plan. It is important that the design is detailed as it is difficult to estimate accurately if we are unsure of the design. As we will see later, prototyping may be helpful here. The executing stage as a whole is the stage in which mental and physical activities take place. Activities are coordinated with the aim of delivering the specified information system on time and within budget to the satisfaction of the customer. Here are a few examples that illustrate activity types at this stage of the project development life cycle: Purchase requisitions are prepared and sent out; proper authorizations are obtained for assigning human expertise; interorganizational communication channels are established; requests for release of equipment and material are prepared and sent; contracts for outside vendors and new hires are prepared and forwarded; revisions and changes to the project plan are made following an established process; progress is monitored; cost and time are controlled; and communication is maintained. Regular monitoring that helps to determine that the product is being developed according to specification is critical at this stage. *Quality assurance* is obtained through quality control that is built into the process with responsibilities clearly assigned.

- **Implementation stage:** At this stage, sometimes known as the control phase (although we would argue that "control" features throughout the project), the product is delivered to the customer. All tests are carried out and instructions and manuals are prepared. Training is planned and carried out for at least the principle users of the system. The level of user involvement during the system development life cycle will influence the success of these training programs. Such training programs may be specific and limited to certain users or may be more general to include a wide range of users. In any case, training programs must be designed to facilitate the effective use of the system by the customer. Success of the system is directly linked to the effective use and satisfaction of the customer. Poorly designed and badly developed systems are very likely to fail regardless of the implementation efforts. It is important also to take onboard the fact that information systems that are well designed and developed may also fail because of inadequate and improper use. Sometimes, the implementation phase includes integration of the new system with other existing systems. The project manager must be careful not to disrupt other information systems development projects or operational systems and make every effort to minimize downtime. Project resources, equipment, and materials are released and redeployed to other projects. Material transfer documents are prepared and approved. Team members are reassigned to new projects.

- **Closing stage:** At this stage the project is closed from an administrative point of view. Activities at this stage include formalizing customer acceptance of the project; evaluating the project team members; terminating vendor contracts as well as employment of those hired specifically for the duration of the project; archiving all documents and forms relative to the project; and conducting the project audit by individuals other than the project manager or project team. The primary intent for the project audit is to formalize and document the lessons learned, to generate a report that summarizes experiences gained, and to suggest ideas beneficial to future projects. The intent of this project audit is not to point a finger at individuals or to punish anyone. It is a review of facts relative to events, activities, and processes for the purpose of *organizational learning*. Organizations need to learn from their successes and failures through this knowledge sharing (its *organizational memory*) and build on this past experience to improve future performance.

❖ Figure 1.7 Indicating the Potential Added Complexity of a Real Project

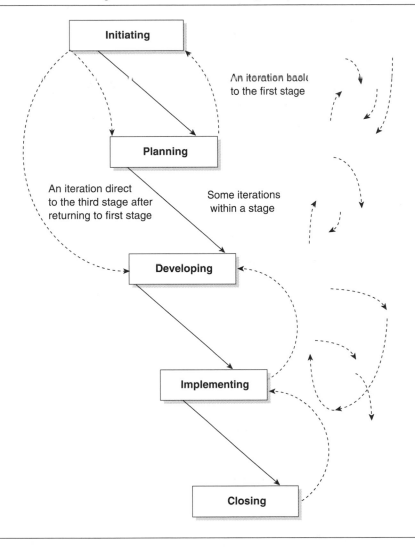

However, Figure 1.6 represents an idealistic view of project management. In fact in any project this is likely to be much more complex, with many iterations and jumps. Figure 1.7 attempts to show the complexity of a real project.

## 1.7. Stakeholders

Here we look at the people who will probably be involved in the development of a computer information system. Following the analysis of David Avison and Guy Fitzgerald, we identify a number of stakeholder groups or individual stakeholders. However, in this text we start with those in the business or organization for whom the information system is required rather than the technical people. This group is often generically known as the "users," but this is misleading as they are not homogeneous and there is a range of different types of user. Indeed, "users" can also be "developers." We break this category down as shown in Exhibit 1.6.

---

### Exhibit 1.6    Who Are the "Users"?

- **End users** use the system in an operational sense. They may be intermediaries between the system and the business users.
- **Business users** are people in the particular business function that have a need for the system. They might or might not physically interact with the system itself. They are interested in its functions and output, as support for achieving their business objectives.
- **Business management** have responsibility for the business function that the information system addresses and may have been responsible for commissioning the system and financing it from their budget. They are responsible for the strategic use of IT in their business unit.
- **Business strategy management** are those responsible for the overall strategy of the organization and the way that information systems can both support and enable the strategy.

---

Again, we are describing roles for people here. They may be combined or separated. Sometimes, different categories of user are identified—for example, regular user and occasional or casual user. This categorization is important for determining what type (or types) of user interface may be required in a system or what type of training is needed. Clearly, these will be different for regular users and occasional users. A regular user may not require a lot of help and explanation and just the minimum of interactions, whereas an occasional user will require detailed help and guidance when using the system.

Our next category is external users. These are stakeholders outside the boundaries of the company in which the system exists (Exhibit 1.7).

---

### Exhibit 1.7    External Users

- **Customers or potential customers** use the system to buy products and services or to search for information relating to products. They are generally not employees of the company and thus have a different relationship to the earlier categories of user. Too often, customers are ignored when systems are being designed and developed, even though they are obviously important stakeholders with specific requirements. In some Internet applications this is particularly important.
- **Information users** are people external to the organization who may use the system but are not customers, in that they do not buy anything. Users of a government Web site may just be looking for information on building regulations, for example. This category of user is also often ignored when the system is designed.

- **Trusted external users** have a particular relationship with the organization and may be given special privileges in the system. Suppliers are examples of such users. There are likely to be specific design requirements and security implications for this category of user.
- **Shareholders, other owners, or sponsors** are people who have invested in the organization and have a financial interest. They may be only peripherally concerned with the information systems in the organization, but they will want to ensure that they are contributing to the financial development and success of the organization.
- **Society** includes those people who may be affected by the system without necessarily being traditional customers or users in any way. This is a broad category and relates to people, or society as a whole, who may be potentially affected by the system in some way. People may be put out of work by a system or it may disseminate inaccurate or personal information. Society is an important stakeholder in information systems development, and societal impacts also need to be considered.

Exhibit 1.8 identifies those stakeholders on the information systems development side.

## Exhibit 1.8    Stakeholders on the Information Systems Development Side

- **Software engineers or programmers** code and develop programs in an information system using a computer programming language.
- **Systems analysts** specify the requirements for a system and the outline designs and solutions that will meet the requirements. Typically, they are the interface or liaison between the business users/analysts and the programmers.
- **Business analysts** understand the complexities of the business and its needs and liaise with the systems analysts. They are typically from the business side of the organization but adopt this role in the context of a particular development project for a specific period.
- **Project managers** manage the project with particular emphasis on schedules and resources.
- **Senior IT management members** are responsible for IT and managing it overall within the organization.
- **Chief information officer (CIO)** is responsible for IT, IS, and information strategy and aligning them to the needs of the business as a whole. Although usually a member of the IT department, it is essential that the CIO is part of the organization's top management team.

The above groups may not exist as discrete groups in all organizations. The boundaries between them have undoubtedly become blurred over the years. In some circumstances one person may undertake a number of roles, or a group may flexibly undertake all roles as needed. The situation is even more confused by the tendency of the IT industry to have a wide and varied range of overlapping job titles for these roles. Further, many organizations no longer have a rigid separation between the IT systems development side and the business. Often multi-skilled development teams, capable in both business and IT, are formed for a particular development project, often managed and led by the business units themselves.

In general, we believe that it is desirable that all stakeholders of a system are involved in the whole development process. It is important that an "us and them" attitude does not exist between stakeholders on the information systems development side (Exhibit 1.8) and the other stakeholders. They all have some kind of stake in the success of the information system and need to work together toward a common goal. Good communications will help to make such an atmosphere feasible. In the information systems development process, some users might be part of a group, such as the information systems strategy group, the steering committee, and the development team.

However, if we accept this wider view of the stakeholders of an information systems project, it might be difficult for the project manager to decide how to proceed. For example, how does the project manager evaluate the relative importance of each stakeholder if there is conflict? *Stakeholder analysis* is a technique to help project managers in such circumstances (Table 1.1).

Stakeholder analysis is often done in a kind of brainstorming session (see Section 9.2) and then documented as a list or a set of interconnecting circles, sometimes known as a *stakeholder map*. These stakeholders are then considered as having some relevance or potential input to a system under development, and they then might be consulted and involved. We might consider stakeholders as having higher and lower power (and influence) and higher and lower interest. We may simply monitor those stakeholders who are on the low power/low interest quadrant but involve those stakeholders on the high power/high interest quadrant. Other stakeholders warrant at least to be kept informed. The stakeholder map might look at the needs of each group or individuals. Some practitioners argue that *interest* is too narrow a term and use *attitude* and *confidence* instead. Usually each stakeholder group is considered to have some specific requirement that needs to be considered and addressed in the system. They are seen as groups who have diverse requirements that need to be addressed by the system for it to be successful. Indeed, a project manager might hold a workshop with the key

❖  Table 1.1   Stakeholder Map

| Stakeholder | Attitude | Power/Influence | Actions |
|---|---|---|---|
| Tom (clerk) | Negative—concerned about job | Little | Keep informed and try to reassure job is safe |
| Doris (manager) | Positive—sees potential increase in status | Medium—but key member of new system | Manage closely and ensure satisfied with potential of new system and her role in it |

stakeholder groups at the beginning and at other times in a project. Stakeholder analysis provides a way to make explicit, or give a voice to, the claims of all those stakeholders involved.

## 1.8. Project Management and Ethics

The discussion of ethics in business courses often generates interesting reactions. Some students see ethical issues less relevant to the business domain. Some consider ethics an individual trait that is formed early in life and influenced by family environment and values and that it is less likely to change later in life. As our thought process evolves through learning, experience, and interaction with others, our values are reaffirmed or reformed. In reality, ethics influences our decisions continually as we try to distinguish right from wrong. Ethical issues in information systems project management are prevalent as we provide estimates of time and cost, evaluate individual performance, communicate completion date, and so on. We estimate project cost and time to the best of our abilities, trying to use our professional expertise and experience. It is unacceptable to falsify these estimates or to exaggerate benefits. Ethical issues are more acute in situations in which there is pressure on the project manager to give "good" news about the due date, progress, safety, accuracy, and the like. It is important to distinguish mistakes from misrepresentation or falsification.

Many companies have codes of conduct to guide employee behavior. Professional organizations have in place codes of ethics that they publicize and make available for their members as well as the public. The appendix at the end of this chapter looks at the Project Management Institute (PMI) member code of ethics and the joint Institute of Electrical and Electronic Engineers and Association of Computing Machinery (IEEE/ACM) code of ethics and professional practice for software engineers. Similar codes are available for other organizations, and many are available on the Web (see, for example, that of the British Computer Society at www.bcs.com). There is a great deal of overlap in professional and ethical codes for different organizations because they share core principles. Decisions have consequences. Information systems project managers must always contemplate the impact of their decisions and continually ask themselves how their decisions affect the stakeholders and how their decisions will be judged by everyone in the organization.

An individual's ethical conduct is influenced by education, family, religion, and work environment to varying degrees. Organizational environment, culture, decision processes, and reward systems also influence employees' belief in doing the "right" thing. The organizational environment is also affected by individuals' conduct. Organizations benefit from the ethical behavior of their employees, and they have a vested interest to promote it. Information systems projects as mechanisms for implementing organizational goals and objectives also benefit from ethical conduct. The ultimate success of an information systems project is based not only on the actual outcome but also on the way it is accomplished. Good means and good deeds go hand in hand; falsifying one leads to falsification of the other.

It is important that the information systems project manager can be trusted and is trusted. Team members are prepared to go the extra mile and put in the extra effort for leaders they trust and respect. It is hard to define *trust* but we know that individuals are trusted depending on their character, competency, and ethical standing. Project managers who are perceived as political animals or manipulators may succeed for a while by pulling rank or enforcing rules, but they will eventually face resistance and non-cooperation. The project manager leadership should be free of "game play." When team members feel that games are being played or there are hidden agendas, then their interaction will be affected and soon the entire environment will be changed. Project managers need also to build trust among team members, and trusted project managers have an easier job of doing that.

There are situations when all facts are not known and ambiguity may exist. Effective project managers are up front about these situations and explain what they know and what they do not know about a situation. It is important to realize that trust is built over time, and trusted individuals are given the benefit of the doubt in unusual situations. For project managers who have not been on the job or have not worked with their team long enough to build the necessary level of trust, unusual situations may prove more challenging. On the other hand, ambiguous and unusual situations provide unique opportunities for the project manager to demonstrate competency and built trust. It is very important that your team members feel that you want to do the right thing.

In his book *Seven Habits of Highly Effective People,* Stephen Covey suggests that effective managers have ethical characteristics evidenced by respect for the individual, dignity, fairness, pursuit of truth, and helpfulness (see also chapter 7). In situations where there is sufficient funding, support, hardware, software, equipment, and the like and you still see resentment and lack of full cooperation, ask yourself the few questions, seen in Exhibit 1.9.

---

### Exhibit 1.9   Reflections on Ethics

- Have you been true to the purpose of the project?
- Have you treated everyone alike, giving everyone a chance?
- Have you been consistent (do people know where you stand)?
- Have you been fair in your evaluation of others?
- Have you been open to suggestions and opinions?
- Have you accepted responsibilities and admitted mistakes?

---

These are not ambiguous questions that require a great deal of analysis. You may even be able to ask some of your key team members for feedback on some of these questions. If you have been open about your mistakes and have shown that you respect opinions and suggestions expressed by others, you will get valuable feedback.

If you ask people what they like about their boss, you will be surprised how simple things make a difference: "I like working with my boss because she listens carefully and explains things clearly," "I like my boss because you always know what he expects from you," "I like my boss because she treats everyone the same," or "I like my boss because he is reasonable." These comments indicate both trust and competency. You cannot develop trust in people who do not know their field and cannot promote confidence in those they work with. Competency must be evident in technical as well as business domains. A software engineer who is well trained to design and develop complex information systems may not necessarily be able to manage an information systems development project. Developing a project involves more than knowing the technical dimension alone. It involves human resource management, conflict resolution, confidence building, networking, coordination, control, and the like. Indeed, a technical deficiency can be made up through the support of the experts, but an ethical deficiency is much more difficult to fix.

## 1.9. Text Content and Objectives

The intent of this text is threefold. First, to study and understand the *job* of information systems project management, one must know the following:

- What kind of subject area it is
- What it entails
- How it relates to other subject areas
- What opportunities and challenges it provides
- Why it is important for information system professionals

Second, to study and understand what makes a *person* successful as an information systems project manager, one must know the following:

- What kind of skills are needed
- How much technical expertise is required
- How much management talent is necessary
- What individual traits are important to be successful at this job

Third, to study and understand the *techniques, tools*, and *processes* that are necessary for the success of information systems project management, one must know the following:

- How to manage time
- What software tools are available and how to use them
- How to measure quality
- How to measure performance
- What techniques are available for quality control
- What methods are most useful to the project manager for keeping track of events and activities

This text, therefore, focuses on what information systems project management is, what type of person will make a successful information systems project manager, and

❖ Figure 1.8  Information Systems Project Management—Overall Book Structure

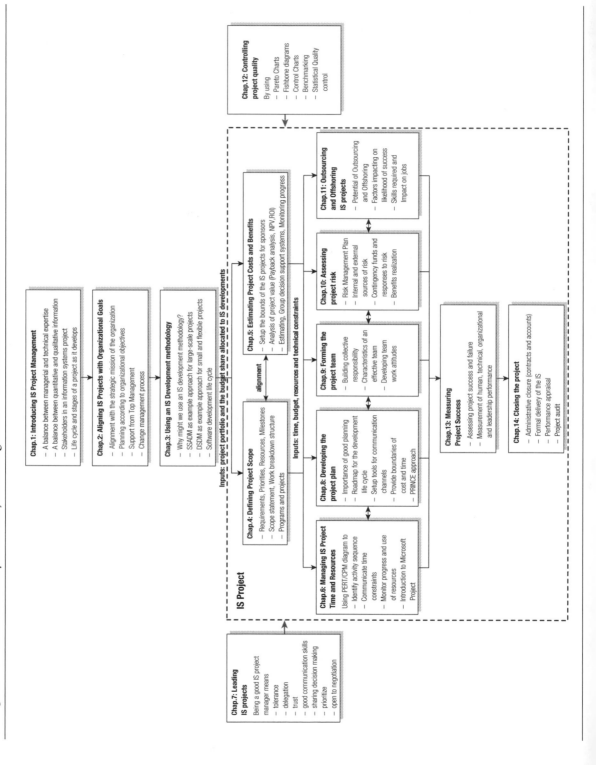

what helps to be successful. Although these three themes run throughout the text, the chapters are not arranged under three modules. That is because it is important to learn about all three areas concurrently. It is also because it is not always practical or useful to deal with one concept in isolation without referring to the others. Therefore, while some chapters may discuss only one theme, others combine multiple themes.

However, these three aspects of project management are seen in the context of how information systems project management affects the organization as a whole, and especially those stakeholders affected by an information systems project.

This text is also written with a broad spectrum of information systems project managers in mind. In other words, the intent is to make this text valuable to a wide range of information systems professionals and be relevant to management students and information technology students as well as students studying information systems. Thus, the type and coverage of each topic is determined and evaluated with the intent to create a balance between the science and the art of information systems project management. Management issues such as evaluation, planning, and strategy are combined with analytical and software skills such as understanding networks, techniques, and tools such as PERT-CPM, perhaps using Microsoft Project to create an appropriate balance so that individuals with backgrounds in either areas of management or technology are able to benefit from the text. This balance is important since most information systems project management careers require both technical and managerial competencies. However, even if you are not planning a career as an information systems project manager, all those interested in both management and information technology need to know about the issues discussed in this book.

Even if you have no intention to become a project manager in the near future, in work you are very likely, nevertheless, to be a member of a project team, and therefore the interests of the book are still very relevant. Figure 1.8 provides the overall structure of the book.

In Chapter 1 we have introduced the topic of project management and as well as its principles and tools along with information systems, our domain of application. It has introduced many of the concepts and themes that are discussed more fully in the chapters that follow. This chapter also outlined the intent and focus of the text and has set the tone for the remaining chapters. Chapter 2 describes why projects must be aligned with organizational goals and objectives to serve the overall mission. We also show the importance of planning the project and dealing with change management. Chapter 3 provides an overview of the potential of formalized information systems development methodologies (including software aspects) in supporting the work of the project manager. It looks at an approach suitable for larger projects and one suitable for situations in which speed and flexibility are particularly important. Chapters 4 and 5 describe the initial but important stages of information systems project development. They show how to define project scope at the early stage to help development and implementation of a system meeting the project requirements, and how to estimate cost in order to be able to carry out project activities and deliver the final product that delivers the benefits predicted.

Once a project is identified and costs are projected the task of scheduling activities starts. Chapter 6 describes the essentials of project time management and scheduling.

This is an important chapter since it describes how activities depend on one another and how progress is monitored through proper scheduling. Time management tools such as PERT, which assist project managers in monitoring progress, are described. Reliable estimates are essential for setting and controlling activities and schedules. Chapter 7 describes project management leadership and its importance to the success of any project. As we see in Figure 1.8, it is affecting the IS project as a whole. We also discuss the role of team members and provide information about project management careers in this chapter. Chapter 8 describes the project plan and the steps involved in developing a functional and workable plan for the entire project. The PRINCE approach to planning is described.

Chapter 9 describes project team formation. Identifying competent and reliable individuals as team members is an important activity for the project manager. We discuss characteristics of an effective team. Chapter 10 describes how project risks are identified and planned for. It describes the need for contingency planning in the event that changes become necessary or additional resources are required. Continuous monitoring of project activities is a critical function of project management.

Outsourcing and offshoring are now key elements of any decision on project management. Will some of the project be developed by another company, perhaps in another country? This issue is discussed in Chapter 11. Chapter 12 describes standards and quality-control methods that help delivery of the desired outcome. As for chapter 7 on project leadership, the theme of quality has an impact throughout the project's development, and therefore is seen in Figure 1.8 as affecting the whole IS project.

Projects are evaluated from different perspectives: top management, the customer, team members, and the triple constraints of cost, time, and quality of outcome. Chapter 13 shows why measuring project success is important and describes approaches that help an organization evaluate the final product effectively. Chapter 14 describes the final step in the information systems project life cycle—i.e., administrative closure. Formal closure helps tie loose ends and create archive documents for future use.

Each chapter starts with an "exhibit," a piece taken from the views or experience of practitioners that sets the scene for the chapter topic, and ends with a summary, discussion questions, exercises, and a short bibliography for further study. Each chapter has an appendix, which might be a case study, other reading material, or another exhibit for further study, discussion, group work, or class work.

Real-world situations do not always correspond with what is covered in textbooks, so in each chapter we have included a section called "Interview With a Project Manager." Textbooks tend to be comprehensive, covering all aspects of a subject area. Besides, there is always something unique about any situation that makes it different from others. To understand the career of information systems project management better and get a perspective of real-world issues, we conducted numerous interviews with qualified individuals. All these individuals were information systems professionals who either started their career managing IT projects or grew into such a career. Some of these individuals have had formal training in project management, and many learned through practice and experience. Some planned their career toward project management, and some were drawn into it because of demand and company needs. In any case, they all find the experience both challenging and rewarding at the same time.

We will share examples of these interviews here and elsewhere in this text to complement, not replace, the material. We did not plan the study to capture everyone's response to the same questions. We rather asked each respondent a somewhat different set of questions, although the more important questions were repeated. Repeated questions relate to opportunities and challenges, successes and failures, personality traits and skills, and so on. We are indebted to all interviewees and thank them for sharing their insights and experiences with us.

The interview in each chapter does not necessarily directly relate to the material covered in the chapter, but the issues and lessons can be appreciated at that point.

Most of our interview transcripts represent part of an interview with an information systems project manager who learned the career through practice and experience. Our first one, however, is now an owner–manager of a small company, and we wondered whether he thought that his issues were different from that of a project manager in a larger firm.

### 1.10. Interview With a Project Manager

Tell me about your background.

"I am now owner of a small company of 15 full-time employees and several part-time staff working at home, and we develop niche software products. I am effectively project manager for all projects in the business. Previously I was at a large company as a senior analyst developing software products."

How are the project management concerns different?

"You have no idea. All the books and courses seem to be for large companies. At my previous company we had strategies, plans, and objectives all worked out. We had groups representing user interests. We had formal procedures for justifying and evaluating our projects. It was very bureaucratic. Mind you, we still got it wrong a lot of the time. So they should still learn a lot from you. But in a smaller company like ours there is much less need for a formal procedure, and we cannot afford it in any case."

How can you justify that statement?

"Look, there are relatively few people involved, and I know them all—even people working at home. It is much easier to judge things. Accountability is clear, we know whose fault it is if things go wrong, and in any case everybody involved is working to ensure the success of the project. My staff are much more flexible than the unwieldy project teams I had to deal with before. And in any case, things are usually much simpler."

Well, let me put a few arguments to you. For example, your approach may lead to you overlooking things, or you jump on the first solution, which may not be the best, as you haven't discussed the issues fully.

"There may be some truth in what you say, but we don't have the resources or the time to do what big companies can do. The danger that I see most is a bit different, and that is I basically own the company, and although I think I am a nice man, I am seen as the boss. People don't challenge me as they should even though I ask to be contradicted. Yes, that is a concern and I am not infallible.

Actually when I think about it, I do many of the things a large company does, even if I do it less formally. For example, I make sure our important customers get what they want, and I work out risk factors, costs, and benefits and the rest."

Finally, how do you work out your priorities?

"First I know what our key business needs are, and I start with the most critical. I am interested most in the bottom line, and projects with the highest potential payoff gets the highest priority. Finally, I give priority to those projects that have the lowest risk of failure—at least how I see it!"

## 1.11. Chapter Summary

The rapid growth of information systems using information technology has created clear opportunities and challenges for today's executives. Increasingly, some middle managers of the past who managed routine tasks and functions are replaced with project managers who are responsible for non-routine, one-time developmental projects within specified time and budget to deliver a system to the satisfaction of the customer. This has caused a significant demand for quality information systems project managers. Information systems project management competency requires a balance of managerial and technical expertise. Successful information systems project managers are able to plan work activities, manage people, communicate with all stakeholders effectively, monitor progress, plan and manage change, deal with the unexpected, understand organizational processes, and so on. They must understand the project development life cycle and have competency in initiating, planning, developing, implementing, and closing a project but also behave ethically throughout. Career opportunities for individuals with such qualifications and traits have never been stronger. All managers and IT professionals, as well as those in information systems, need to be aware of the issues discussed in this book.

## DISCUSSION QUESTIONS

1. Project management competency skills include managerial and technical expertise. It has been suggested that technical aspects represent the "science" of project management, and the sociocultural aspect represents the "art" of managing a project. What do you think of this statement?

2. Information systems development has grown over the last couple of decades in terms of volume and complexity. Discuss the role of project management in information systems development and success. How does information systems project management differ from the job of the systems analyst?

3. This chapter defines the information systems project life cycle in terms of initiation, planning, development, implementation, and closure. Discuss how this multiple-stage perspective helps the success of information systems project management.

4. In your opinion, what are the most important individual traits for a successful information systems project manager? What would be your three most important traits? Would the list change from project to project?

5. It may be argued that it is not the individual traits that make a successful project manager but the knowledge of all aspects and the understanding of how they interact and influence each other that matters. Would you agree with this statement and, if so, why?

6. Do you agree with the small firm company director that his project management concerns are totally different from larger companies?

7. Do you think students who cheat (in exams or by copying coursework) are likely to continue this habit in the business domain?

## EXERCISES

1. Distinguish between information systems (IS) and information technology (IT).

2. In your own words, describe an information systems project and identify major components and activities for it. What is unique about the project that you have described?

3. What makes an information systems project different from other projects, such as constructing a bridge, planning a conference, planning a holiday, or developing a new degree program? Do you expect skill differences across different projects? If so, list these differences.

4. For an organization that you know (your university, for example) identify the stakeholders of any information systems project (student records, for example). Do you think that the stakeholders were consulted about the project?

5. You are scheduled to interview an information systems project manager. Prepare, for your interview, a list of eight questions that would further enhance what you have learned in this chapter. For example, ask about opportunities and challenges of a project management career or the most important skill based on the experience of the person you will interview.

6. You are scheduled to interview another information systems project manager. This time your assignment is to write a short report that describes a day in the life of an information systems project manager. Try to point out things that are specific to this career that make it different from any other management job.

7. Search the project management literature on the Web and print an article that you find interesting and that relates to the topic in this chapter. Read and prepare a short presentation describing the content of that article.

8. Write an exam question based on the content of this chapter. Ask the person sitting next to you for an answer to your question. Share with the class your question and the response and point out whether you would agree with the response or not and why.

## APPENDIX TO CHAPTER 1: CODES OF BEHAVIOR

As we saw in Section 1.8, project managers are expected to behave in an ethical way. Indeed, they are expected to behave in accordance to good standards generally. Many of these standards are obvious and represent good codes of behavior in all walks of life. But some are more specific, related to the role of project management in general or project management of information systems projects more specifically.

The Project Management Institute (PMI) is a professional organization dedicated to the development and promotion of the field of project management. Its Web site is www.pmi.org. Its Member Code of Ethics can be found at www.pmi.org/prod/groups/public/documents/info/ap_memethstandards.pdf, and it attempts to define and clarify the ethical responsibilities for present and future PMI members.

The code begins with this statement: "In the pursuit of the project management profession, it is vital that PMI members conduct their work in an ethical manner in order to earn and maintain the confidence of team members, colleagues, employees, employers, customers/clients, the public, and the global community." It goes on by asking members to pledge to uphold and abide by the following:

- I will maintain high standards of integrity and professional conduct.
- I will accept responsibility for my actions.
- I will continually seek to enhance my professional capabilities.
- I will practice with fairness and honesty.
- I will encourage others in the profession to act in an ethical and professional manner.

There follows sets of member standards of conduct. These are more detailed. We will pick on a few of these for discussion. For example, for professional behavior, it asserts: "PMI Members will fully and accurately disclose any professional or business-related conflicts or potential conflicts of interest in a timely manner." Is it reasonable to expect project managers to disclose all potential conflicts? What happens if the disclosure is against the interest of the company or the department that the person is working?

"PMI Members are asked to refrain from offering or accepting payments [that] may provide unfair advantage for themselves, their business or others they may represent." Is this reasonable if they work for a consulting firm—are they not looking for further work for their business (at the cost of work for other businesses)?

Can you ascertain what happens if the PMI member fails to carry out one or more of the codes?

These guidelines are rather general. Start to add additional pages to this guide, where you provide clauses that give more specifics and examples for project managers. You can add to this as you read further chapters of this book.

Along with professional societies for project managers in general, project managers developing information systems projects might be expected to belong to one of the professional associations related to computing and information systems. The most well known are the Institute of Electrical and Electronics Engineers (IEEE; www.ieee.org), which describes itself as the "the world's leading professional association for the advancement of technology," and the Association of Computing Machinery (ACM; www.acm.org), "the world's first educational and scientific computing society" in North America; with their equivalents elsewhere, for example, the British Computer Society (BCS; www.bcs.org), "the leading professional body for those working in IT," and the Australian Computer Society (ACS; www.acs.au.org), which describes itself as "the public voice of the ICT profession and the guardian of professional ethics and standards in the ICT industry, with a commitment to the wider community to ensure the beneficial use of ICT."

The IEEE/ACM have a joint code of ethics and professional practice for software engineers who are described as

> those who contribute by direct participation or by teaching, to the analysis, specification, design, development, certification, maintenance and testing of software systems. Because of their roles in developing software systems, software engineers have significant opportunities to do good or cause harm, to enable others to do good or cause harm, or to influence others to do good or cause harm. To ensure, as much as possible, that their efforts will be used for good, software engineers must commit themselves to making software engineering a beneficial and respected profession. In accordance with that commitment, software engineers shall adhere to the following Code of Ethics and Professional Practice.

The code contains eight principles related to the behavior of and decisions made by professional software engineers, including practitioners, educators, managers, supervisors, and policy makers, as well as trainees and students of the profession. The principles identify the ethically responsible relationships in which individuals, groups, and organizations participate and the primary obligations within these relationships. The clauses of each principle are illustrations of some of the obligations included in these relationships. These obligations are founded in the software engineer's humanity, in special care owed to people affected by the work of software engineers, and the unique elements of the practice of software engineering. The code prescribes these as obligations of anyone claiming to be or aspiring to be a software engineer.

Look carefully through the code and address the same questions that we suggested for the PMI code. In your view, does the statement "ethical tensions can best be addressed by thoughtful consideration of fundamental principles, rather than blind reliance on detailed regulations" provide an opt-out to good practice?

The first "public" principle asks that software engineers "accept full responsibility for their own work." What happens if the member was following the orders of his/her manager who required the work to be done in this way, even if that conflicted with the individual's way?

With regard to the second principle on the relationship between the client and employee, the client is asked to provide "service in their areas of competence, being honest and forthright about any limitations of their experience and education." Are all consultants honest in this respect? Would they get work if they were "totally honest"?

On the fourth principle, about product, the engineer is asked to "strive for high quality, acceptable cost and a reasonable schedule, ensuring significant tradeoffs are clear to and accepted by the employer and the client, and are available for consideration by the user and the public." Why is it, then, that so many projects fail in some way?

Regarding Principle 5 "management," we are asked to "ensure good management for any project on which they work, including effective procedures for promotion of quality and reduction of risk" and later to "ensure realistic quantitative estimates of cost, scheduling, personnel, quality and outcomes on any project on which they work or propose to work, and provide an uncertainty assessment of these estimates." Of course, these aspects are fully discussed in this book, amongst other concerns.

Another aspect where this book could be key concerns the requirement that members "further their knowledge of developments in the analysis, specification, design, development, maintenance and testing of software and related documents, together with the management of the development process." Reading this text is a major step in that direction!

The BCS and ACS also suggest codes of professional conduct and practice, but they are meant to apply to any professional involved in developing an information system, so they apply to all the stakeholders listed in Exhibit 1.6. However, there is considerable consistency throughout these professional codes. The professional ethics page of the Association of Information Systems (www.fb.cityu.edu.hk/is/research/ISWorld/ethics) contains advice pertinent to academics in information systems and many links to other Web sites relating to ethical issues.

## APPENDIX TO CHAPTER 1: DISCUSSION QUESTIONS

1. Read the appendix and address the questions asked.

2. Regarding the code of ethics provided in the appendix, prepare a short report that outlines your opinion and comments on the subject. Does it make sense to you? Which part of this code do you agree with, and which parts do you question?

3. Search the Web for other examples of codes of conduct relevant to any of the stakeholder types mentioned in Section 1.7. What consistencies and inconsistencies do you see with those for the software engineers described in the appendix?

4. Suggest a code of ethics for students. Are you and your colleagues consistent with your code of ethics?

## BIBLIOGRAPHY

Avison, D., & Fitzgerald, G. (2006). *Information systems development: Methodologies, techniques and tools* (4th ed.). Maidenhead, UK: McGraw-Hill.

Cadle, J., & Yeates, D. (2004). *Project management for information systems.* Upper Saddle River, NJ: Prentice Hall.

Dejoie, R., Fowler, G., & Paradice, D. (1991). *Ethical issues in information systems.* San Francisco: Boyd & Fraser.

Fitzgerald, G. (2000). *IT at the heart of business.* British Computer Society.

Kerzner, H. (2003). *Project management: A systems approach to planning, scheduling, and controlling.* New York: Wiley.

Kemerer, C. (1996). *Software project management.* New York: McGraw-Hill.

Marchewka, J. T. (2003). *Information technology project management: Providing measurable organizational value.* New York: Wiley.

McLeod, G., & Smith, D. (1996). *Managing information technology projects.* San Francisco: Boyd & Fraser.

Meredith, J. R., & Mantel, S. J., Jr. (2000). *Project management: A managerial approach.* New York: Wiley.

Olson, D. L. (2004). *Information systems project management.* New York: Irwin McGraw-Hill.

PMI. (2004). *A guide to the project management body of knowledge* (3rd ed.). Newtown Square, PA: Project Management Institute.

Rosenau, M. D. J. (1998). *Successful project management.* New York: Wiley.

Reynolds, G. (2007). *Ethics in information technology.* Boston: Thomson Course Technology.

Schwalbe, K. (2006). *Information technology project management.* Boston: Thomson Course Technology.

Tedesco, P. A. (2006). *Common sense in project management.* Thomson Course Technology.

Yourdon, E. (1997). *Death march: The complete software developer's guide to surviving "Mission Impossible" projects.* Upper Saddle River, NJ: Prentice Hall.

# 2

# Aligning the Information Systems Project With Organizational Goals

**Themes of Chapter 2**

- ❖ What is the information systems portfolio?
- ❖ How can information systems support decision making?
- ❖ How can information systems support the long-term goals of an enterprise?
- ❖ Why was early thinking on information systems so short term in scope?
- ❖ What do we mean by strategic alignment?
- ❖ What is meant by the governance issue?
- ❖ What is meant by the expectations gap?
- ❖ What is the role of the information systems project manager?
- ❖ How can change be best managed in the organization?

**T**his chapter describes the importance of establishing an information systems portfolio that in turn drives information systems project management efforts. It describes how growth in the applications of information technology has frequently influenced decision-making processes to respond only to short-term and immediate needs. It outlines principles and concepts behind an effective information systems development portfolio. The portfolio idea is based on the principle that any investment, including information technology investment, must be assessed from the point of view of the organization and how it will benefit the long-term goals and objectives of the organization and therefore be more effective. This chapter describes the importance of obtaining project proposal support through goal alignment and management recognition and shows the importance of the planning process. It also discusses how top management support can be encouraged and the importance of public relations more generally. Finally it discusses aspects of change management in organizations. We start with a brief comment on a huge present-day project.

---

### Exhibit 2.1 Challenges for the IT Initiative of the UK National Health Service

Healthcare in the UK has been exploring the role of information and communications technology for over 50 years and has had both successful and less successful experiences. The UK National Health Service (NHS) is currently going through a nationwide information systems overhaul that was originally estimated to cost £6.2bn, or about US $12 billion. It is a 10-year project and the largest non-military IT program in the world. However, cost estimates seem to have already risen two or even three times these original estimates.

The NHS's National Program for IT (NPfIT) is a huge project, and the UK government of Tony Blair hoped that it would help solve the problems in the much-criticized UK health service. Its aim is to provide "cradle to grave" healthcare for all. The project includes secure email, patient e-bookings, e-prescriptions, integrated care records, picture archiving, and communications systems, alongside a service for general practitioners and a public health Web site.

Such an ambitious and large project is bound to be difficult. There have already been a number of setbacks to patient administration systems. A failure at a data center caused systems at 80 hospitals to collapse for about 4 days, which is the NHS's biggest IT failure ever. A data-recovery system also failed to provide backup. Polls among some NHS staff have suggested reducing support for NPfIT.

On the other hand, another application is "Choose and Book," a national service that, for the first time, combines electronic booking and a choice of place, date, and time for first outpatient appointments. A Web site has been developed so that patients can book their own appointments online—at a time that suits them. Nearly 2.5 million patients have been referred to specialist care through Choose and Book. This represents approximately 40% of all referrals, representing nearly 65,000 patients a week. Feedback suggests that the electronic booking of referrals to specialist care improves patient experience and reduces costs.

There are bound to be "teething problems" in such projects, and while some pundits suggest that it is a "giant failure waiting to happen," others argue that with good project management, the prospects for a much improved UK National Health Service, supported by information systems, are positive.

## 2.1. Project Management Portfolio

The rapid progress of information technology and the need for applications development have caused many organizations to adopt, often by default, a strategy that might be described as a short-term operational-level response. In the fusion of learning and managing new technologies, many organizations focused more on the logistical and operational aspects of technology transfer rather than its alignment with the organizational goals and objectives. *Technology transfer* refers to the diffusion of technology in organizations. Concerns include these:

- What types of technologies are available?
- How can these technologies help management and decision makers with pressing issues of cost and efficiency?
- What is the best way to develop and implement applications?

This growth inertia that pushed developmental activities in response to immediate needs led to the following:

- Less planning and more action
- Less strategic alignment and more implementation
- Less attention to an information systems development portfolio approach and more emphasis on operational response activities

This trend meant more technology transfer in organizations. But this only occurred at the level of task and unit rather than the organization as a whole. Ideas for new application development would often be initiated by individuals with technical skills who knew how the technology worked and how it could help solve problems at hand. However, these individuals were not necessarily able to assess the impact of technology at the organizational level. In other words, initiators and planners were too close to the action, "seeing the trees rather than the forest." This does not necessarily mean that individual applications did not help or that they did not accomplish their purpose. In fact, they often helped experimentation with technology fit, end-user training, and know-how at the functional level. However, the effort to align information systems selection and developmental activities with the overall organizational goal and objectives was lacking. Thinking about information systems was short term. This led to an underperformance in the application of technology.

Some time later, when demands and requests for resources to develop and implement new technologies became a significant budget item, some high-ranking executive would pose a simple but important question: "What does all this technology investment mean to our bottom line?" That is a difficult question to answer and has appropriately led to a significant and enduring stream of research in this field. This question is important because the impact of information technology is broad. It influences all levels of management decision making and all types of activity, and therefore investment in information technology and information systems must be evaluated with an encompassing approach.

*Evaluation* concerns the process of assessing whether an information system has met its objectives. Traditionally, information systems executives measured success through the evaluation of system features such as ease of use, accuracy, integrity, speed, format, and so on. This approach is appropriate for identifying strengths and weaknesses of an application and to that extent is useful to information systems development activities. However, it defines success narrowly and ignores broader issues of impact.

Nowadays, information systems executives are increasingly required to explain and justify technology expenditure from a broader perspective that includes impact on work, the customer, and the organization (see Exhibit 2.2). As a result, the evaluation of information systems success has been expanded over recent years to include systems use, task productivity, task innovation, management control, and the like. We look later in Section 13.2 in more detail at both quantitative and qualitative means of evaluating information systems.

---

### Exhibit 2.2 Narrow and Wider Views of Evaluating an Information Systems Project

**Narrow View of Evaluation**

- Ease of use
- Accuracy
- Integrity
- Speed
- Format

**Wider View of Evaluation**

- Impact on work
- Impact on the customer
- Impact on the organization
- Impact on the environment

---

The first business activities that were computerized tended to be the basic transaction processing systems such as payroll, sales order processing, stock control, and invoicing. Thus early information systems in businesses affected mostly the accounting domain. Activities were computerized to make them more efficient. Payroll, for example, previously required large numbers of manual payroll clerks to perform the activity. When computerized, it did not need all these clerks. Early computerization therefore aimed to promote efficiency and in particular to reduce labor costs. Cost-displacement savings are relatively easy to quantify, and a clear financial case for investment can be demonstrated, using any of the available financial analysis techniques discussed in Chapter 5.

However, in more recent times, the opportunities for further information systems investments based on efficiency and labor-displacement criteria have been limited.

First, the number of opportunities is reduced, as more and more projects are implemented, and, second, the returns are declining, as the most clear-cut efficiency-improving opportunities have already been addressed. In most large organizations almost all the activities are now computerized or supported by computers in some way. So, overall, the propensity for reducing traditional labor costs via information systems has been declining.

Over the years, computing and technology investment has moved from just being about cost savings and efficiencies to more strategic information systems aimed at effectiveness rather than efficiency. In particular, this sees the use of information systems and information technology as a direct way of obtaining *competitive advantage*. The basic objectives of effectiveness projects are not simply to reduce the costs of performing existing tasks but to identify ways of doing different things that achieve the required results better, leading to increased revenues and better service. Information systems can be used to improve the business in the marketplace and in this way to help the following:

- Redefine the boundaries of particular industries.
- Develop new products or services.
- Empower the workforce to be innovative and to come up with new ideas.
- Change the relationships between suppliers and customers.
- Provide intrinsic value and task learning opportunities to the user.
- Establish barriers to deter new entrants to marketplaces.
- Enhance organizational design, intelligence, and decision making.

The basic objective of this type of information system is to identify better ways of doing things, leading to increased revenues, greater functionality, better products and services, improved presentation or image, and improved competitive positioning of the organization.

Increasingly, organizations have developed technology selection and information systems implementation processes using priorities that aim to ensure congruity and alignment with organizational strategy. The strategic goals of most organizations are tightly linked with customer needs and customer satisfaction. Simple but important questions help set the course for identifying, selecting, and developing information systems that will satisfy the expectations of modern organizations (see Exhibit 2.3).

---

**Exhibit 2.3    Questions to Guide the Identification, Selection, and Development of Information Systems**

- Who is initiating the project?
- Who is sponsoring the project?
- How does the project support the mission of the organization?
- What is the relative position of a project on the priority list of the organization?
- How does the project contribute value to the strategic goals of the organization?
- How does the project help meet current and future needs of the customer?

Responses to these questions help the information systems project manager evaluate the contribution of a project to the organization. Questions concerning whether the project is doable or whether there are sufficient resources to accomplish project goals are also valid, and they will be discussed later. First, we will address the issues concerned with the organizational strategy and information systems.

## 2.2. Setting Priorities for Project Management

This topic has already been introduced in Section 1.5. In today's organizations, all management levels have come to be involved with strategic planning and strategic issues. This is in contrast with the past, when only top executives and senior management would be concerned with strategic issues. Creating and maintaining a strong link between the organizational strategic plan and information systems projects is an increasingly important role for the project manager—indeed, it is important for all stakeholders. Everyone in the organization needs to "buy into" the mission statement and the strategic plan at the most broad context to help ensure the success of each stage of the project at the lowest levels. This is a difficult task that requires cooperation from all levels of management. The larger the organization, the more challenging this task will be.

An important factor that facilitates this cooperation is a process that defines how a project is to be aligned with organizational goals and objectives. This process can also be useful to the project manager in evaluating and verifying the extent, if any, to which a project meets organizational goals. Using this process, the project manager can then go ahead with the task of allocating project resources—people, equipment, and facilities.

Project managers are increasingly involved with the process of setting organizational priorities for technology selection, development, and implementation. Therefore, project managers have become a part of strategic planning and the organizational decision-making process. They are also affected by these processes since all projects should follow these criteria. The involvement of project managers with this process offers several advantages:

- Project manager insights and expertise help develop realistic priority plans.
- Project managers can develop a high-level organizational perspective for projects.
- Project manager involvement helps networking and communication opportunities.
- Project managers gain an interorganizational perspective for projects.

These are two-way benefits that help the project manager and the organization alike. The net result is that the project manager brings know-how into the planning process and gains an organizational and strategic perspective.

## 2.3. What Is a Strategic Plan?

A strategic plan provides an organizational *road map* that suggests directions for resources and activities for the future. In setting a strategic plan, organizations need to analyze the three questions shown in Exhibit 2.4 very carefully. These are concerned with where they are now, where they want to be, and how to get there.

---

| **Exhibit 2.4    Three Questions Concerning the Strategic Plan** |
|---|

1. **Where are they now?** Organizations need to ask where they are at any point in time by assessing how they are perceived—what their position within the industry is, what their strengths and weaknesses are, and what lessons have been learned.

2. **Where do they want to be?** Organizations need to ask where they want to go in the future by describing what they aspire to become—what position they want to secure in the environment or in the industry in which they compete.

3. **How can they get there?** Organizations need to ask how to get there by evaluating and outlining necessary resources, opportunities, challenges, and risks.

Answering the first question helps self-assessment and self-realization. It provides the foundation for formulating a realistic plan for the future. Answering the second question helps organizations see themselves in the next 5 or 10 years. It provides criteria and guidelines to evaluate the extent to which accomplishments have been made. Answering the third question helps set success measures and outlines criteria for monitoring progress.

It is important to realize how these three steps are interdependent. Careful definition and description of any one of these steps directly benefits the others. It is difficult to develop a workable and realistic strategic plan without a sound foundation—a clear understanding of what we are about and where we are at.

There are two important characteristics of a strategic plan. One is the fact that it looks into the future and maps directions. Another is that it is inclusive and broad, covering internal as well as external entities and resources. A strategic plan supports the organizational mission and is influenced by the organizational culture. Internally, it considers talents and skills, facilities, interorganizational issues, and the like. Externally, it considers competition, partnership, government, environmental issues, and the like. It creates consistency across functions, across projects, and over time. An effective strategic plan is a critical success factor for the survival of the organization.

## 2.4. A Strategic Plan and Information Systems Project Management

As shown in Exhibit 2.5, an effective strategic plan influences information systems project management in several ways.

Information systems can help the firm follow its strategy in a number of ways:

1. Information systems provide information. This information can, for example, inform the organization about whether it is on track with its business strategy.

2. Certain types of information systems can provide decision support to help managers and executives decide how the organization can get back on track or to plan its strategy in the first place.

---

| Exhibit 2.5    The Influence of the Strategic Plan |
| :--- |

- **It creates consistency across projects:** All projects are assessed to ensure they support organizational goals and objectives.
- **It reduces redundancy:** Cross-functional resource sharing and interorganizational communication are facilitated.
- **It helps prioritize projects:** Integrated information systems projects that affect large user groups and those that affect critical functions are ranked higher.
- **It provides a long-term perspective for needs assessment of the customers:** The needs of future customers as well as the future needs of current customers are considered.
- **It provides criteria to measure project success:** Projects that do not support organizational goals and objectives can be discontinued. It can be helpful to a project audit and in evaluating the project outcome.

3. The influence of information systems may be strong enough to help dictate the strategy. This is most obvious in high-tech companies—for example, those leading the way in electronic commerce. Here, information systems might be leading company strategy, not merely supporting it or aligning with it.

It is only through its implementation that a strategic plan is effective and useful. *Information systems projects, in general, are tools and mechanisms for the implementation of a strategic plan.* In other words, a collection of projects when implemented realizes goals and objectives formulated in the strategic plan. Without implementation, the plan remains just a written document. Information systems projects are therefore instrumental in implementing the strategic plan. This is a major contribution toward accomplishing organizational goals and objectives, and that is why it is critical for information systems projects to be aligned with these goals and objectives.

## 2.5. Organizational Mission, Goals, and Objectives

Organizations are defined through their ***mission statement.*** In other words, an organization exists for a purpose, and that purpose is described in its mission. A mission statement therefore guides decisions and directs collective efforts. It is expressed in broad terms and is widely communicated so that all employees, customers, stakeholders, and the public are aware of what the organization strives for. Everyone working for the organization must know and understand the mission. It is not unusual for an organization to expect its employees to memorize the mission. The international accreditation body for colleges of business, for example, requires that all schools have a clearly defined and understood mission and that all faculty and staff are able to describe their college's mission.

Organizational success and performance in the long term can be assessed through a mission statement. A mission statement generally describes what product and services the organization wants to provide, in what region, and for whom. Further, it positions the organization relative to competitors and within the industry. For example, a software engineering firm may include in its mission statement that they want "to be the primary provider of information systems security in the western region of the United States within 5 years." Or the statement could mention that the primary mission is "to provide the most reliable information systems security."

Can you describe your organization's mission? Does it correspond to any written statement that you can find for the organization in the foyer or in written documentation, such as a company report?

Notice that the first mission statement for our company is silent on the issue of quality, suggesting that the firm's primary mission is growth. The second statement is silent on growth and volume, suggesting that the firm's primary mission is quality related. Both statements could belong to the same firm at different times since an organizational mission can be reviewed and changed if the purpose of the firm is modified. A specific mission statement provides clear direction to the employees, but it also limits the scope. A firm must strike a balance between the specifics and the scope in the mission statement that serves its purpose.

A firm's philosophy and culture are also described through the mission statement. Although the management style and decision-making processes are more indicative of organizational culture, a mission statement is also used by organizations to create public image by linking it to contributions to society.

As Figure 2.1 suggests, a mission statement implies ***goals and objectives*** to be achieved; conversely, achieving these goals and objectives will make alignment with the mission statement more likely.

Goals and objectives must be clearly ***defined, measurable,*** and ***doable.*** Relative to a mission statement, goals and objectives describe in more concrete terms what organizations like to do. While a mission statement sets the direction for the entire organization, goals and objectives define what specifically needs to be done in order to accomplish the mission. Therefore, goals and objectives are more specific and as a result they are more appropriate as measures of success. Functional areas and work units often set their own goals and objectives in accordance with the overall mission of the organization. Managers at all levels use goals and objectives to create targets for themselves and their employees. These targets are used to evaluate performance outcomes.

❖ **Figure 2.1**   Mission Statement and Goals and Objectives

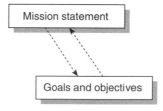

You may come across organizational goals and objectives that mostly relate to the type and quality of products and services. As part of these goals and objectives, customer satisfaction is described and planned for. That is why you often see organizations refer to customer satisfaction as an important goal. Lower-level units develop goals and objectives in support of higher-level units. The hierarchy of goals and objectives exist in order to define responsibilities of the management hierarchy more clearly. For example, if a firm's goal is to have all internal communication paperless in 2 years, then that becomes one of the Information Systems Department's goals to accomplish. The Information Systems Department needs to formulate strategies that describe how this goal can be achieved. As we move down the hierarchy path, goals and objectives become more specific and more closely linked with individuals and their skills.

❖ **Figure 2.2**   A Hierarchy of Goals and Objectives Relating to Customer Satisfaction

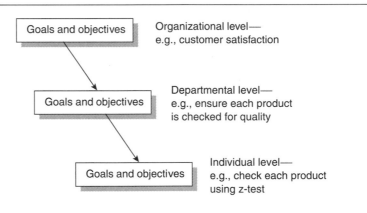

While goals and objectives conceptualize the organizational mission, *operational strategies* facilitate the implementation of these goals and objectives. As mentioned earlier, projects—including information systems projects—are implementation tools for strategies. Take the example of the firm that wants to convert all internal communications from paper to online. This may involve a combination of several information systems. The Information Systems Department will need to develop strategies for how best to accomplish this goal. The process may include developing several project proposals, obtaining approval for them, selecting a project manager, and finally authorizing development. Without *goals* we would not know what to pursue. Without *strategies* we would not know how to get what we want.

## 2.6. Planning

Planning approaches are designed to counteract the possibility that information systems will be implemented in a piecemeal fashion, a criticism often made of applications in the past. A narrow function-by-function approach could lead to the various

❖ **Figure 2.3**   Strategies: Ways of Achieving Goals and Objectives

subsystems failing to integrate satisfactorily. Further, it fails to align information systems with the business strategy. Both top management and information systems personnel should look at organizational needs in the early stages and develop a strategic plan for information systems development as a whole so that information systems are integrated and compatible. This becomes a framework for more detailed plans. Individual information systems are then developed within the confines of these plans. Another way, therefore, of looking at planning is to consider the three layers in Figure 2.3 as bounds for planning: long term, medium term, and short term.

1. **Long-term planning** of information systems considers the objectives of the information systems function and provides rough estimates of resources required to meet these needs. It will normally involve producing a mission statement for the information systems group, which should reflect the mission statement of the organization as a whole. The information systems plan at this stage will be an overview document—for example, providing only prospective project titles.

2. **Medium-term planning** concerns itself with the ways in which the long-term plan can be put into effect. It considers the present information requirements of the organization and the information systems that need to be developed or adapted to meet these needs. Information about each potential information system will be spelled out in detail, including the ways in which they address the overall strategic objectives of the organization. The ways in which the information systems are to be integrated will be stated. Priorities for development will also be established, and again these will reflect the long-term plan and mission statement. A planning document that shows the current situation along with an action plan for future development will usually be produced.

3. **Short-term planning**, perhaps covering the next 12 months, will provide a further level of detail. It concerns the schedule for change, assigning resources to effect the change, and putting into place project control measures to ensure effectiveness. As well as detailing the resources required for each application in terms of personnel, hardware, and budget, it will contain details of each stage in the development process as suggested in the systems development life cycle outlined in Section 1.6.

## 2.7. Achieving Alignment

Raymond Papp offers managers a method by which they may assess or achieve alignment. This involves assessing the firm's perspectives, learning to recognize and lever information systems to maximum efficiency, incorporating financial measurements suitable for the particular industry, giving everyone a role to facilitate synergy between information systems and the business, and, finally, continuous review of alignment and assessment.

❖ **Figure 2.4**    Alignment With Information Systems

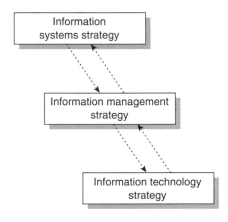

As we see from Figure 2.4, there are other aspects to strategic alignment. We have tended to concentrate on the most important alignment between the business strategy and the information systems strategy. However, there needs to be alignment between the information systems strategy and the information management strategy. By the latter we mean the stakeholders on the information systems development side (see Exhibit 1.8 and Section 1.7), in particular, the senior IT management, the chief information officer, and of course the project manager. They—indeed the sentiment can be extended to all the stakeholders—need to be positive and committed to the information systems strategy so that the IS strategy is more likely to be fulfilled. If the stakeholders are not fighting in the same direction as the information systems strategy, then that is unlikely to succeed, which will have negative implications on the potential success of the business strategy itself.

Similarly, the information technology strategy needs to be aligned with the information systems strategy. Thus the hardware, software, and communications technologies need to support the information systems being developed. Investment should not be in technology "for its own sake." Together, the three strategies seen as Figure 2.4 need to provide the information, how required, when required, at the appropriate level of detail, and to the appropriate individuals to support the business strategy. It is vital that there is this alignment of these three strategies as they are high expenditure activities, critical to many organizations, affecting all levels of management, involving many stakeholders. As we shall see in the next section, there may be severe repercussions if projects fail.

## 2.8. Project Proposal and Management Support

Regardless of how well strategies are formulated and communicated, they need to be supported. As mentioned in Section 1.5, the most critical support for any project is provided by top management. It is critical to obtain management support for information systems projects at the time of proposal development and to maintain that support throughout the information systems development life cycle. Initial management support must come through the recognition that the project is aligned with organizational goals and objectives. It is important that the project proposal clarify how the ultimate outcome supports these goals and objectives. It is also critical that top management support does not wane as the project progresses. Such support is even more critical if a project is overdue and behind schedule, since that is (or, to be more generous, has often been) the case with information systems projects.

The appendix to this chapter shows what can go wrong if top management does not give its full support and care and attention. A major element of good practice concerns *governance*. This is the patterns of authority for key information systems activities in organizations, including IT infrastructure, information systems use, as well as project management. The three case studies discussed all show that senior management sometimes lacks awareness of the importance of information systems and its governance on the success of information systems projects, and some senior managers may even argue that "IT doesn't matter" (we disagree strongly with this view and discuss this suggestion in the appendix to Chapter 3).

In the One.Tel example described in the appendix, the auditors saw a failure to plan comprehensively and to apply governance arrangements—including senior management involvement and support—to ensure the project was properly managed. Other problems indicated a lack of sound project management. The auditor's criticisms of the second example covered governance, project management, and contractor selection. The project was managed by an executive steering committee, whose governance charter was not spelled out in detail; there were problems with project management and the auditors also found that planning was inadequate; testing was neither timely nor comprehensive; and risk management was ineffective. In addition, it found that the project team lacked some necessary skills. In the third example, the traditional principles of good project management practice were not in place. Top management saw the information system as unglamorous and technically unchallenging and therefore did not show support of a key information system to the company.

Senior management in all three organizations had not ensured that prudent checks and balances were in place to enable them to monitor either the progress of the projects or the alignment and impact of the new information systems on their business. Proper governance, particularly with respect to financial matters, auditing, and contract management, was not evident. Furthermore, project-level planning and control were notably absent or inadequate—with the result that project status reports to management were unrealistic, inaccurate, and misleading.

But communication is a two-way process. The information systems project manager is responsible for communicating project progress to stakeholders including top management. If a project is not making adequate progress or if a project runs into unanticipated difficulties (for example, sudden turnover among key team members) top management must be informed of the situation as early as possible. This proactive approach helps prepare management for eventual requests for additional resources. It also suggests openness on the part of the project manager and team members. It is important to realize that top management has to deal with a plethora of decisions, some of which relate to supporting information systems projects. Project managers must try to minimize the element of surprise by providing timely, accurate, and relevant information.

Managing expectations is a challenging task for information systems project managers. Expectations vary and are not always easy to predict. Top management expectations differ from those of users. Changes occur in the work environment that may lead to changes in functional needs that in turn may lead to changes in expectations. This leads to an *expectation gap*—that is, the difference between what the project outcome is expected to be and what it actually is. Timely, accurate, and relevant information about project progress helps reduce this expectation gap. It enables top management and other stakeholders to adjust their expectations based on new and current developments.

## 2.9. Public Relations

In the past, duties and responsibilities of information systems project managers were more narrowly defined and primarily included project activities, team performance, deadlines, and the like. In other words, the project manager and the project team worked to deliver what was planned for "on time and within budget."

Increasingly, this scope has widened to include constant communication, negotiation, and public relations across functional areas. In the past, the list of stakeholders only included groups that were directly affected by or were involved with the project such as sponsors, team members, customers, and users. However, as we saw in Section 1.7, this list has broadened to include support staff, suppliers, and can even include opponents of the project. The project manager is responsible to communicate continually with and update these groups about the status of the project and whether the project is making progress as planned.

As we will see in the next section, change management is an important aspect of the project manager's role. Other abilities that help with these challenging responsibilities include organizational skills, leadership skills, and coping skills. We will look at these in Chapter 7. All these help the project manager survive in increasingly integrated work environments where information systems affect productivity and the performance of several units and functions. Sometimes it affects the entire organization. Organizational politics is another factor that influences project selection priorities, funding arrangements, and eventually the outcome. The faith in a project is not decided by facts alone but also by convincing management that it aligns with the mission and helps organizational goals and objectives. Therefore, project initiators must be *persuasive, consistent,* and *flexible.* Experienced project managers recognize the importance of organizational networking and public relations.

Most large-scale information systems projects involve multiple functions. Team members of these projects have different backgrounds and loyalties. They belong to functional areas that may or may not benefit from the proposed deliverables. The project manager must work with these individuals and must keep a good relationship and good communications with their functional managers. Often, individuals who work on a project are evaluated and rewarded not by the project manager but by their functional manager. This obviously makes the situation more complicated for a project manager because of reduced influence over these team members. Good relationships with functional managers will help the management of these team members.

## 2.10. Change Management

There are many themes to project management, but one that needs to be high on the agenda throughout concerns how we manage change. Inadequate attention to change management is a primary reason for project failures. Indeed, change management should be part of the strategic planning process, not merely just a succeeding event. People's long-term roles, responsibilities, and reporting structures, as well as the way processing is handled and functions are carried out, will change as a result of the new information system.

Change management is another dimension added to the responsibilities of the information systems project manager. Constant negotiation and communication is essential for the success of these interorganizational activities. That is why communication is ranked very high on the list of skills for information systems project managers. The project manager must make sure that information that is communicated to stakeholders is accurate, timely, and relevant. Too little or too much information can prove to be dysfunctional. Individuals tend to pay less attention when they feel information provided to them is repetitive or redundant.

One approach to dealing with change is called *force field analysis.* In this approach understanding of the change process is gained by identifying the forces working *for* and *against* the change being successful by analyzing the change from the point of view of people, resources, time, external factors, and corporate culture and formulating a change strategy that is a good fit with these forces. The change can be *transformational,* that is, quick and dramatic, or *incremental,* that is, a much more gradual process. The latter is normally preferable as it allows time for training, reflection, adaptation, and consolidation, but sometimes transformational change is necessary because of environmental circumstances (government requirements or reacting quickly to a competitor's move, for example) but may encounter greater resistance. As previously suggested, all people need to "buy into" the plans, and this requires everyone being fully trained, to give one practical example. But this buy-in is also reflected in the organizational culture.

The organizational culture will affect strategies for planning the information system development project. Charles Handy suggests that there are four types of organization. In those where *power is centralized,* the project manager needs a member of the power base to sponsor or champion the project. In a *bureaucratic structure,* it will be difficult to effect the change without following the rules and norms of that organization. Some organizations are more *individualistic,* and consensus is needed. Change is likely to be easiest to implement in organizations where *project teams* work on tasks as the norm.

Many organizations have undergone total change through a process referred to as *business process reengineering (BPR).* Firms undergoing BPR look at all aspects of the company and changing many if not most aspects, sometimes "reinventing" the company in another market, with a different product mix, processing methods, and staff. It is inevitable that new information systems will be required in these circumstances.

However, in general, change is easiest to implement in organizations where *change is the norm* in the organization. In such *organic* organizations, people accept change, indeed embrace it, and regard it as a positive thing. Although a project might be a "one off," change is not. Successful change and change strategies should be replicated elsewhere in the organization so that there is a diffusion of best practice. Repeated change seems to be part of modern life and essential for business survival, partly due to globalization and the widespread use of communication technologies.

We will return to the issue of change management in different guises throughout this book, because it is so interconnected with project management.

## 2.11. Interview With a Project Manager

When you started with the company did they expect any type of project management?

"They expected us to manage the project but not like they do today."

Can you clarify what you mean? How is it different today?

"When I started with computers, I would go in with a sales team and we would discuss what computers did, and how they would benefit a business. Since computers were still fairly young, we had to do more than just sell the product. We had to set the computers up for installation, program them, and train the customer's employees on how to use them and more. Now when we sell the product to people they have teams that sit down and figure out how to put these systems in with minimal disruption to the end-user. Back in '72 we just sort of put the machines in; we didn't sit down and figure out how long it would take using charts like we do today. The company just expected to finish when we got done.

Today, we have to show progress to managers and customers. They want to see charts showing expected completion times. They want to know how much disruption they should expect. They want all sorts of details. You simply cannot make the sale without having some idea as to how the project should be managed."

Would you say then that project management has become more than just a tool used by project managers?

"Absolutely. I would say that if people expect to be successful in whatever field they are in they must learn at least the basics of how project management works. If they don't, they're in for a tough time. For example, if you and I went to XYZ Corp. trying to sell them some widgets, let's say for $10 million. If you walk in and show XYZ management how long it will take you to install the widgets, and what phases they can expect you to be in at different times of the project, and I walk in with nothing more than a sales pitch of what widgets do, then you will certainly get the sale over me. Project management is a skill, and it puts managers' minds at ease. They like to know where everything is at any given time, especially when dealing with large sums of money."

Would you say that interpersonal communication is a key part of project management?

"Interpersonal communication is *the* key to project management. It may be the most important part of it. The software will keep you on track with scheduling, but you'll get nowhere if you can't communicate with people what is required out of them and/or their departments."

At what point do you think a project has finished successfully?

"Usually, it becomes apparent that a project is finished because all the tasks are completed on the list. If we finish our project within budget and on time we call the project a success. If we have been forced to crash a project, meaning we were forced to maybe add more money in order to finish the project on time or finish early, then we go back and look at two things before we call it a success. Did we make money and did we meet the new deadline? If the answer to both of these questions is yes, then we still call it a success. Although, we will return to the project later and try to identify what caused us to have to crash the project in the first place."

If you could offer one piece of advice concerning project management to students, what would that be?

"Learn it! You will use it more than you think, and it applies to so many areas that no matter what you find yourself doing, you will use it. You don't have to be an engineer or a scientist to use project management. It will only make you more valuable to your company and to your customer."

## 2.12. Chapter Summary

Arguably the most important factor influencing the management decision to fund or not to fund an information systems project relates to whether the system is aligned with the strategic mission of the organization and whether it supports organizational goals and objectives and may also suggest developing a portfolio of projects. Organizations define their existence through a mission statement. Goals and objectives collectively define what needs to be done to accomplish the mission. Strategies help map out how to operationalize goals and objectives. Projects are tools that make goals and objectives happen. It is therefore important that information systems projects are selected based on what they do to help organizational goals and objectives become a reality. This broadens the responsibilities of information systems project managers in that they need to coordinate activities across functional areas, negotiate and obtain support from top management, be mission driven, communicate and maintain a good relationship with decision makers and other stakeholders, and so on. Stakeholders need to work together toward a common objective, requiring a "buy in" to this common goal through good communications, training, and other means. In addition, they are responsible for delivering project deliverables on time and within budget. Project management success has much to do with the change management process as a whole, and again this depends to a large extent on how the organization has effected change in the past.

## DISCUSSION QUESTIONS

1. What comes first, business strategy or information systems strategy (or are they developed together)? What is the relationship between information systems strategy and information technology strategy?

2. Discuss the pros and cons of the portfolio approach to information systems development. In your opinion, what is the most important point in favor of this approach? What is the least attractive point in favor of this approach?

3. Discuss the information systems development portfolio approach in the context of information system success. The ultimate question about any project is linked to whether it meets specifications and whether it is done within specified resources. How would a portfolio approach help accomplish this objective?

4. How might you encourage all the stakeholders to "buy into" both the high-level strategy of the organization and each of the development projects?

5. It is suggested that an integrative approach to project management is important in today's environment. An integrative approach includes two parts. *First*, projects must have a strong link to the organizational strategic plan which is directed toward meeting the customers' needs. This linkage is reinforced by a project priority system that prioritizes projects by their contribution to the strategic plan and allocates resources based on this priority system. *Second*, an integrative approach provides an integrated system within a sociocultural environment for the actual implementation of the system. This creates a positive and active environment for the team members responsible for completing the project. Discuss pros and cons of an integrative approach to project management.

6. This chapter suggests that the expectation gap can be addressed and improved through timely, relevant, and accurate information. Discuss how information overload or redundant information might affect the expectation gap.

7. You are on the information technology steering committee in your organization that approves funding support for information systems development. You have been asked to analyze and recommend two of the three systems proposals that have been proposed for development by user departments. Proposal 1 intends to improve **interorganizational communication**. Proposal 2 intends to improve **information system security and privacy**. Proposal 3 intends to improve **customer satisfaction**. Your preliminary analysis of these proposals suggests the following:

   - All three proposals support organizational strategy in different ways.
   - Sufficient technical expertise exists to develop any of these systems.
   - Economic, political, and environmental reasons exist for each proposal.
   - The three user departments feel strongly positive about their proposals.

   What steps would you take to make a recommendation and to rationalize your decision-process?

8. Many students think ethical choices are irrelevant to computer science, engineering, and information systems and that their job is simply to do their employers' will. However, information systems professionals enter the realm of ethical choice in design whenever they make decisions affecting people. Ethical reflection begins with the assumption that all designs and all implementations involve value choices. Comment.

## EXERCISES

1. Search the project management literature on the Web and find what you can learn about the history of project management. How did it start? When did it start? Who used it first? How did it become a part of the information systems development process? Prepare a short presentation describing your findings.

2. For an organization of your choice, sketch out lists of long-term, medium-term, and short-term plans concerning information systems.

3. Search the project management literature in the library or on the Web and write a short paper about ethical issues of information systems project management. Conclude your paper with a paragraph about your own opinion and describe why ethical issues are (or are not) important to the discipline of information systems.

4. Search the Web for examples of mission statements and "goals and objectives." Compare the two and describe how they differ.

5. Write an exam question based on the content of this chapter. Ask the person sitting next to you to provide you with an answer to your question. Share with the class your question and the response and point out whether you would agree with the response. Give reasons for your answer.

## APPENDIX TO CHAPTER 2: IT FAILURE IN AUSTRALIA

In this appendix, we look at an IT failure in Australia and see what lessons we can draw. It makes a useful comparator to the AA case that we looked at in the beginning of Chapter 1 and the mixed results so far from the NHS program discussed at the beginning of this chapter, although we are not asserting that the success rates in the UK and Australia are very different! We look at aspects of the collapse of the Australian telecommunications company One.Tel (and more briefly at two other related cases). There are many interpretations of the One.Tel collapse, but one relates to the failure of IT, in particular the invoicing system.

The One.Tel Company was founded in 1995 and ceased trading in 2001. The company grew at a very substantial rate and accomplished a great deal in a short time. From 1996 to 2000, sales revenue grew from $65 million to $653 million Australian (the U.S. dollar and the Australian dollar are near parity at the time of this writing), and the number of subscribers

*(Continued)*

(Continued)

grew from 80,000 to 1,840,000. The strategy in these early years was "customers not cables" (One.Tel Annual Report, 1999). In other words, One.Tel positioned itself as a marketer and reseller of services and not as a provider of hardware infrastructure. The company perceived a market opportunity presented by the deregulation of the telecommunications industry within Australia, which took place in the early 1990s. Although fixed wire services expanded during this time, One.Tel also wanted to build a presence in the massive take-up of mobile phones that was occurring during these years. Another growth area that One.Tel correctly anticipated was the increasing demand for Internet services. Thze company grew at a very fast pace.

One.Tel prided itself on its enlightened management techniques. The company operated a flat, non-bureaucratic organizational structure and was organized into small functional teams. It described itself as the "can do" company. Within the IT group, a number of quite sophisticated systems were developed in an unusually short time frame.

Systems development at One.Tel seemed to exemplify the "Initial" level of maturity described by Carnegie Mellon's Capability Maturity Model. The characteristics of this level are "chaotic, ad hoc, heroic, unorganized, uncoordinated, high variance, unpredictable, crisis management." The teams of young and highly paid technicians at One.Tel thrived in this environment. Systems were delivered in quick time for billing, call center, dealer management, and debt collection, among many others. Only two significant systems were outsourced: the financial system and a data warehouse used to generate key performance indicators.

The One.Tel billing system was one of the first systems to be developed when the new company commenced trading in 1995. The billing system was designed and developed entirely in-house by a team of young and enthusiastic programmers and it was a classic representation of the One.Tel approach to building systems. In the euphoric atmosphere that prevailed within One.Tel in the early years, the systems developers acquired a high reputation and status. Every time some critical new functionality was required, the development team produced a champion who would work night and day to deliver a result. However, specifications, documentation, and standards suffered in this atmosphere. This lack of discipline was understandable and not unusual at this stage in the growth of the firm and its IT systems, but it was problematical, particularly in the case of the billing system. Companies depend on the unfailing timeliness and accuracy of this system for their cash flow, and One.Tel was no exception. In the long term, some serious flaws in the billing system at One.Tel revealed themselves:

**A long-term dependence on an inadequate design.** The original system was designed and developed by developers, including programmers, under conditions of great stress and urgency. It should have been viewed as only a short-term solution. However, the basic system remained in production, relatively unchanged, until the termination of business in 2001. The system lacked flexibility and was supported by inadequately designed database tables. It became impossible to accommodate, within the database, the complex sales plans, which were an important part of One.Tel's marketing strategy. The system became increasingly dependent on hard-coding to provide functionality. Consequently, the individual programs became exceedingly complex and the system increasingly difficult to maintain.

**A lack of checks and balances.** The system failed to provide the most basic financial integrity checks. It was impossible to reconcile the value of bills produced in a billing run, either backward to the calls loaded from the carriers or forward to the value finally posted to the general ledger. There were no checks at each stage of value loaded, value billed, or value posted. In the final year of its operation, the system was producing 600,000 bills per month, and, apart from the most basic visual checking, the company had no means to verify their accuracy.

**Lack of prioritization and forward planning.** Proper priority was not given to major enhancements required to the billing system. Two conspicuous examples of this were the implementation of the Goods and Services Tax (GST) and the introduction of the NextGen mobile service, both in 2000. In the case of GST, not only were these changes implemented a month late, but they were so poorly executed that it caused billing run times to increase by about 50%. The changes to accommodate NextGen mobile were implemented 3 months behind schedule, which caused the first users of the new phones to wait 3 months for their first bill. It would appear that sufficient resources were not allocated in time to meet critical deadlines. On each occasion the billing system suffered from these failures to plan, and the result was large numbers of seriously delayed bills.

As we have seen, there was a failure to recognize the weaknesses within the billing system in sufficient time to take effective corrective action. It is true that a great deal of remedial work took place in the last 9 months of the system's life, but this was "too little, too late." The principal strategic failure took place in 1999 when One.Tel received a massive injection of funding and went from being a junior local telecommunications company to a full-service international operation. At this time, when funds were plentiful and substantial change and growth was in prospect, it was necessary to develop a long-term plan. However, no such planning took place, the assumption presumably being that a management-by-crisis approach could continue to deliver systems to serve the company.

In 1999 the One.Tel business plan for the next several years must have been formulated at boardroom level as much of it was published in the Annual Reports for 1999 and 2000. For example, the following events were all clearly on the horizon:

Significant growth on all business fronts: fixed wire, mobile, and ISP

Introduction of cut-price local call plans

Introduction of NextGen mobile

Introduction of GST from July 2000

All of these changes were to have a significant impact on the billing system, which was unable to cope with substantial increases in volume and complexity. As described above, the billing system survived relatively intact until the introduction of GST in July 2000, but this caused run times to expand by around 50%. The billing system depended on one cycle being processed every 3 days. If the cycle processing time exceeded 3 days, bills were inevitably produced late. After GST, it was taking 6–7 days to complete a bill cycle. Further, large numbers of bills were calculated incorrectly and needed to be reprinted.

*(Continued)*

(Continued)

While a rectification team was trying to improve throughput, two further complications were added to the system. Firstly, the data-replication team launched their solution, which further increased the load on the struggling system. Secondly, the NextGen mobile team finally completed their input to the billing system, 3 months behind schedule. This introduced yet more loading and another round of incorrect bills, which needed recalculation.

At this point, late in the year 2000, the company realized that it had a crisis on its hands, and maintenance and improvement of the billing system became the absolute priority. However, the system never recovered from the GST problems in July 2000, and from that time onward the production of bills was always from 3 to 6 weeks behind schedule.

The progressive failure of the One.Tel billing system affected the business in a number of ways. First, the delay of up to 6 weeks in dispatching bills had a dramatic effect on cash flow. Second, One.Tel's billing system had a great propensity for producing incorrect bills, for reasons already described. While these were sometimes identified and corrected, often they were not. The One.Tel call center was constantly besieged with callers making complaints about their bills, and caller waiting times became intolerable. Customers with incorrect bills are not inclined to pay them. Perhaps the most damning effect of the failure of the billing system was that it brought the company into serious disrepute. For many customers, the bill is the only regular contact that they have with their telecommunications supplier, and frequently it is all the contact they need or want. If the bills do not appear, or are suspected to be inaccurate, then there will be a general loss of confidence in the business. The media then fueled this loss of confidence with many derisory articles about One.Tel and its problems.

One.Tel was a very open company, and no attempt was made to hide the very obvious problems in the billing team, the call center, or the cash flow problems that became increasingly apparent. Paul A. Strassman observed, "The history of IT can be characterized as the overestimation of what can be accomplished immediately and the underestimation of the long term consequences." We might ask: If the billing system had been redeveloped, or outsourced, in 1999 would One.Tel still be in business? There are other issues consequential from the One.Tel case—for example, ethical ones, which also need to be investigated fully.

In an article published in 2006, David Avison, Shirley Gregor, and David Wilson argue that this case, along with two other Australian cases, shows that companies can display a phenomenon that they call "managerial IT unconsciousness." They represent a major failure of IT governance—that is, the patterns of authority for key IT activities in business firms, including IT infrastructure, IT use, and project management. The case studies show that senior management often exhibits a lack of awareness of the importance of IT and its governance to the success of large IT projects.

In the RMIT case, a university attempted to implement an academic management system using the PeopleSoft platform. The system went live late in 2001, but the original attempt at implementation was deemed a failure. There was extensive corruption of the student database and difficulties in billing fee-paying students. The state auditor general's report suggests problems with meeting statutory and legislative reporting requirements. The original project budget was AU$12.6 million. The anticipated cost to the end of 2003 has since increased nearly four times to AU$47.3 million. These monies are significant and would threaten the equivalent private company's existence.

In the RMIT case, the auditors directly attributed the failings in the student system to governance:

> We found that RMIT did not plan comprehensively and apply the governance arrangements—including senior management involvement and support—to ensure the project was effectively managed. As a result the current system does not provide the desired functionality and RMIT faces significant challenges in moving to a higher quality student administration system.

The auditor's report examines the implementation of the project, the system's functionality, and the financial consequences in detail. The software was complex and needed tight governance for the information system to be implemented successfully. The report lists numerous problems with the project. The project steering committee that was responsible for the management of the project was viewed as ineffective. This committee included a representative of senior RMIT management, the overall project director, and project managers from both RMIT and PeopleSoft separately. The auditors found that weekly project status reports to this committee were inadequate, with an absence of information on the overall status of the project, milestones, and key deliverables.

Related to this was a lack of sound project management. Business users were not involved sufficiently. The Web portal was not tested properly, leading to extensive corruption of the student database during initial system operation. The system became operational at a critical processing period, and there was no pilot or parallel conversion. In addition, a series of poor technical decisions led to undersized application servers and inappropriate operating system configuration. The auditors also noted that project staff lacked relevant experience, and there was poor control of their performance. These deficiencies were all too evident because of the extent of customization, which made the system very complex to implement.

In the third case, at Sydney Water, the auditors' review of the customer information and billing system covered issues of governance, project management, and contractor selection. Auditors noted problems with governance in this project. They concluded that the board of Sydney Water did not oversee the project as effectively as it might have, and its understanding of the project, in light of its complexity, was limited. The project was managed by an executive steering committee, which had an unclear governance charter. The project may not have proceeded if there had been a timely analysis of the technical proof of contract. Contract administration was also found to be deficient.

The auditors also concluded that Sydney Water had problems with project management. Planning was found to be inadequate, testing was neither timely nor comprehensive, and risk management was not effective. In addition, the project team lacked some necessary skills. When the Sydney Water project team was formed in 1999 the members had minimal experience with large and complex IT projects such as this, and concern was also expressed that the project manager was "young and inexperienced."

One major worrying factor in the RMIT case was that the director was reported in a newspaper as saying, "The project reports that came through to me and then went on to the council showed that the project was on time, on budget, and meeting its milestones. We all thought that this project was actually going OK."

These case studies are developed further in two articles: Avison, D., & Wilson, D. N. (2002). IT failure and the collapse of One.Tel. In R. Traunmuller (Ed.), *Information systems: The e-Business challenge*. Amsterdam: Kluwer; and Avison, D., Gregor, S., & Wilson, D. N. (2006, July). Managerial IT unconsciousness. *Communications of the ACM*.

*(Continued)*

(Continued)

## APPENDIX TO CHAPTER 2: DISCUSSION QUESTIONS

1. Do you think there might be other explanations for the failure of One.Tel, such as "bad management," "poor business strategy," or "poor accounting standards"? State any assumptions that you make.

2. What is the link (if any) between governance issues and project management issues?

3. Do you think that the "chaotic, ad hoc, heroic, unorganized, uncoordinated, high variance, unpredictable, crisis management" can ever be justified as a basis for developing information systems? For example, can it be justified for a small but growing company?

4. Should One.Tel have scrapped the old invoicing system and started again with a new project developed under more conventional project management standards, or would maintaining the system with good project management standards have been appropriate?

5. At the end of the piece, the director of RMIT seems totally unaware that the project was failing. Why could this be so?

6. Search the Web for cases that provide counter-studies to the three cases discussed, where good governance and project management led to successful information systems.

7. Textbooks and courses tend to emphasize an ideal, such as an ideal way of doing project management. Starting with the One.Tel case, construct a table showing how the ideal and the reality might differ. Develop the table through later case studies in the book and through other cases found in the Web.

## BIBLIOGRAPHY

Avison, D., Powell, P., & Wilson, D. (2004). Using and validating the strategic alignment model. *Journal of Strategic Information Systems, 13*(3), 223–246.

Edwards, B. (1989). *Project sponsors: Their contribution to effective IT implementation.* Paper presented at the Oxford/PA Conference, Templeton College, Oxford.

Gary, C. F., & Larson, E. W. (2000). *Project management: The managerial process.* New York: Irwin McGraw-Hill.

Handy, C. (1995). *The gods of management: The changing work of organizations.* Oxford, UK: Oxford University Press.

Jurison, J. (1999). Software project management: The manager's view. *Communications of the Association for Information Systems, 2*(17).

Marchewka, J. T., & Keil, M. (1995). A portfolio theory approach for selecting and managing IT projects. *Information Resources Management Journal, 8,* 5–14.

McFarlan, F. W. (1981, September–October). Portfolio approach to information systems. *Harvard Business Review.*

Papp, R. (2001). *Strategic information technology: Opportunities for competitive advantage.* Hershey, PA: IGI Publishing.

Strassmann, P. A. (1997). *The squandered computer: Evaluating the business alignment of information technologies.* New Canaan, CT: http://www.strassmann.com/iep/iep.html

Torkzadeh, G., Chang, J. C. J., & Hansen, G.W. (2006). Identifying issues in customer relationship management at Merck-Medco. *Decision Support Systems, 42*(2), 1116–1130.

# Using an Information Systems Development Methodology

---

**Themes of Chapter 3**

❖ What is an information systems development methodology?

❖ What are the functions of an information systems development methodology?

❖ What aspects of a methodology are particularly aimed at project management?

❖ How can we compare methodologies?

❖ What are the costs and benefits of using a methodology?

❖ Does the use of an information systems development methodology guarantee project success?

---

This chapter describes more formal ways of developing an information system through the use of a methodology designed for this purpose. Information systems development methodologies are usually based on the generalized life cycle that we have introduced in Chapter 1. Although the use of a methodology does not guarantee success, if used appropriately, methodologies should make major problems less likely.

We look here at two of the many information systems development methodologies available: structured systems analysis and design method (SSADM) and dynamic systems development method (DSDM), which typify two major types of methodology. SSADM is particularly appropriate for large projects and was designed for government applications and is somewhat bureaucratic in style. DSDM is much more flexible; indeed, it can be used for applications where speed of development is particularly important. It also emphasizes the role of the stakeholders. We also look at software development and again we look at the more traditional engineering approach alongside a less formal approach that aims at rapid production. But first we look at the views from two practitioners giving reasons for their support (or otherwise) for using information systems development methodologies. Read this first and reconsider the debate after reading the chapter.

---

### Exhibit 3.1    Methodologies: Whose Side Are You On?

**Why We Don't Use Methodologies**

1. They fail to deliver any productivity benefits; indeed, to conform to the documentation standards, they increase the time taken to develop a project.

2. They add to the cost of a project, and this includes purchase costs of the materials, consultancy costs for training, and the cost of tools supporting the methodology.

3. Methodologies are very complex and unnecessarily complex as they contain many features we will not require in our organization. However, methodologies seem to be designed so that you have to follow every step even if inappropriate for us.

4. Methodologies require significant skills. These skills are often difficult for methodology users and end-users to learn and acquire.

5. The tools that the methodology advocates are difficult to use and do not generate enough benefits. They increase the focus on the production of documentation rather than lead to better analysis and design.

6. Methodologies overemphasize the narrow, technical development issues, and there is not enough emphasis given to the social and organizational aspects of information systems development.

7. My colleagues don't like conforming to the methodology's straitjacket—information systems development is an art, not a science.

**Why We Use Methodologies**

1. Using a methodology enables us to control the development process and identify the outputs (or deliverables) at each stage.

2. We can build systems faster and cheaper because we are experienced in using the methodology and the level of new skills required is reduced.

3. Everyone knows the standards so that if people leave and others join the project there is much less of a problem than otherwise.

4. Similarly the new system is more likely to be compatible with other applications that are already operational.

5. Good documentation helps communications between all the stakeholders.

6. In brief, although the use of a methodology doesn't guarantee a successful project, it makes it much more likely.

## 3.1. What Is an Information Systems Development Methodology?

In this book we have argued that information systems are generally developed following a life cycle consisting of five phases (initiating, planning, developing, implementing, and closing). In this chapter we do not detract from this generalized approach to developing computer applications; however, many organizations follow a particular information systems development methodology. We could call these "brand name" methodologies. They are usually based on our life-cycle model but provide a more rigorous and step-by-step approach and/or other benefits. Although there are possibly over a hundred very distinct methodologies, we look here only at two: SSADM and DSDM.

> An **information systems development methodology** can be defined as a collection of procedures, techniques, tools, and documentation aids that will help the systems developers in their efforts to implement a new information system. A methodology will consist of phases, themselves consisting of subphases, which will guide the systems developers in their choice of the techniques that might be appropriate at each stage of the project and also help them plan, manage, control, and evaluate information systems projects.

The above definition from David Avison and Guy Fitzgerald suggests that a methodology provides a lot of support to the project manager. Each of the five phases in the life cycle is divided into more detailed subphases. Within each of these, the methodology suggests procedures to be followed, techniques that can be used, software tools that may make the work easier, and so on. In this text, we will discuss techniques such as CPM-PERT, brainstorming, mind mapping, work breakdown structure, structured walkthroughs, return on investment, CoCoMo, and SWOT; tools such as MS Project and *ThinkTank*; and documentation such as the project proposal, project plan, and project scope. The methodology will guide the project manager as to when the use of these techniques, tools, and documentation aids are appropriate. It may even have particular versions of the tools and documentation aids that make following the methodology and doing the work much easier.

Many methodologies emphasize project management aspects. In this chapter we draw attention to these aspects in methodologies. A methodology may have a number of objectives, which may include those listed in Exhibit 3.2.

---

### Exhibit 3.2　Objectives of Information Systems Development Methodologies

1. *To record accurately the requirements for an information system.* The methodology should help users specify their requirements or systems developers investigate and analyze user requirements, otherwise the resultant information system will not meet the needs of the users.

2. *To provide a systematic method of development so that progress can be effectively monitored.* Controlling large-scale projects is not easy, and a project that does not meet its deadlines can have serious cost and other implications for the organization. The provision of checkpoints and well-defined stages in a methodology should ensure that project-planning techniques could be applied effectively.

3. *To provide an information system within an appropriate time limit and at an acceptable cost.* Unless the time spent using some of the techniques and other aspects included in methodologies is limited, it is possible to devote an enormous amount of time attempting to achieve perfection.

4. *To produce a system that is well documented and easy to maintain.* The need for future modifications to the information system is inevitable as a result of changes taking place in the organization and its environment. These modifications should be made with the least effect on the rest of the system. This requires good documentation.

5. *To provide an indication of any changes that need to be made as early as possible in the development process.* As an information system progresses from analysis through design to implementation, the costs associated with making changes increase. Therefore, the earlier changes are effected, the better.

6. *To provide a system that is liked by those people affected by that system.* The people affected by the information system—that is, the stakeholders—may include clients, managers, auditors, and users. If a system is liked by the stakeholders, it is more likely that the system will be used and be successful.

---

One of the goals of an information systems development methodology is to manage information systems development projects efficiently and effectively. As we have seen, in order to help the process of application development, a methodology further divides our five phases (initiating, planning, developing, implementing, and closing) into subphases, with the activities to be carried out in each of the subphases spelled out clearly in the methodology documentation, usually found in manuals. The outputs (or "deliverables") of each subphase are usually also detailed carefully. These deliverables may include documents, plans, or computer programs. Some of the deliverables of one stage will form the inputs of another.

Of course the use of a methodology does not guarantee a successful resultant information system. Despite following an approach carefully, the information system product may fail to meet the needs of management, may be overtaken by events occurring out of its control, may be inflexible, may not be satisfactory in the eyes of the users, may be developed over time and over budget, and may not even provide the required functionality and quality. Project management should not be seen as a mechanical process where the project manager merely applies the rules of a methodology with a perfect system guaranteed at the end of the process. Good project management has a lot to do with people management, change management, and other factors discussed in this book. However, if a methodology is appropriate for the application, the people developing the system, the stakeholders affected by the system, and the culture of the organization, then the use of a methodology *should* make major problems less likely.

In the next few sections we provide an overview of two information systems development methodologies that are exemplars of different approaches, and we will highlight those aspects that have particular relevance to the themes of this book. Further detail of these and other information systems development methodologies and the issues concerning them can be found in the book by David Avison and Guy Fitzgerald (see the bibliography).

## 3.2. Structured Systems Analysis and Design Method (SSADM)

SSADM is a traditional methodology stemming from the UK that is still used on large projects—for example, for UK government projects. Methodologies such as Information Engineering, Yourdon Systems Methodology, and Merise are not too dissimilar to SSADM, all four stemming from around the 1980s, though they have changed much since. The SSADM methodology provides project development staff with very detailed rules and guidelines to work to. As the name implies, it is highly structured. Another reason for its success has been in the standards provided (often exercised by completing preprinted documents or through using supporting software tools). The SSADM framework consists of a number of modules made up of stages. Each of these stages is itself made up of a series of steps that use appropriate techniques for the tasks involved. The stages and steps have defined inputs and outputs. In addition, there are a number of forms and documents that are completed to record specific items of relevant information. The overall stages of SSADM are shown in Exhibit 3.3.

If we compare SSADM with our generic structure of initiating, planning, developing, implementing, and closing, we can clearly see that the earlier phases are covered in much detail, but not all of implementation and closure. It is also assumed that most of the planning has been completed (this is covered in much more detail in some of the alternative IS development methodologies, such as Information Engineering) and that many aspects of the stages following design are installation specific and therefore not covered by the methodology in detail. However, the stages do show the phases and subphases that are required within our generic structure. Indeed this detail provided by the approach is a source of criticism. In the present times, when quick development is often seen as essential, SSADM is described by some as slow and bureaucratic—almost too thorough!

## Exhibit 3.3   The Overall Stages of SSADM

### • Feasibility Study

*0 Feasibility*

- Prepare for the feasibility study
- Define the problem
- Select feasibility options
- Create feasibility report

### • Requirements Analysis

*1 Investigation of current environment*

- Establish analysis framework
- Investigate and define requirements
- Investigate current processing
- Investigate current data
- Derive logical view of current services
- Assemble investigation results

*2 Business systems options*

- Define business system options
- Select business system options
- Define requirements

### • Requirements Specification

*3 Definition of requirements*

- Define required system processing
- Develop required data model
- Derive system functions
- Enhance required data model

- Develop specification prototypes
- Develop processing specification
- Confirm system objectives
- Assemble requirements specification

### • Logical System Specification

*4 Technical system options*

- Define technical system options
- Select technical system options
- Define physical design module

*5 Logical design*

- Define user dialogues
- Define update processes
- Define enquiry process
- Assemble logical design

### • Physical Design

*6 Physical design*

- Prepare for physical design
- Create physical data design
- Create function component implementation map
- Optimize physical data design
- Complete function specification
- Consolidate process data interface
- Assemble physical design

The feasibility stage is concerned with ensuring that the project that has been suggested in the earlier planning phase is feasible—that is, it is technically possible and the benefits of the information system will outweigh the costs. This phase has four steps: Prepare for the study, which assesses the scope of the project; define the problem, which compares the requirements with the current position; select feasibility option, which considers alternatives and selects one; and assemble feasibility report. Systems investigation techniques, such as interviewing, using questionnaires, reading reports, sampling, and so on are used in this stage, amongst other techniques such as data-flow diagramming and entity models, which are specific to systems analysis.

The second module of SSADM, requirements analysis (see also Section 4.1), has two stages: investigation of current requirements and business system options. This module sets the scene for the later stages, because it enables a full understanding of the requirements of the new system to be gained and establishes the direction of the rest of the project. The results of the feasibility study are examined, the scope of the project is reassessed, and the overall plan is agreed upon with management. The requirements of the new system are examined along with investigating the current processing methods and data of the current system, again in more detail than that carried out at the feasibility stage. There is a complete description of the results of this stage assembled and reviewed as the deliverable. SSADM suggests that decisions be made at this stage regarding customization of steps and techniques used for the particular problem situation. Customization factors include risk assessment, application type, situational factors, project objectives, available technology, control procedures, and organizational constraints.

In the second stage of requirements analysis, the functionality of the new system is determined and agreed. The user requirements were set out in Stage 1, but it is at Stage 2 that only those requirements that are cost justified are carried forward (using standard cost–benefit analysis techniques—see Section 5.1), and these requirements are specified in greater detail. Function point analysis is recommended for estimation (see Section 5.4). A number of business system options are outlined, all satisfying this minimum set of user requirements, and a few of these are presented to management so that one can be chosen (or a hybrid option chosen, taken from a number of the options presented). Each of these will have an outline of its cost, development timescale, technical constraints, physical organization, volumes, training requirements, benefits, and impacts on the organization. The option chosen is documented in detail and agreed upon as the basis of the system specification, which is the next stage of SSADM.

The third stage leads to the full requirements specification and provides clear guidance to the design stages, which follow. It is at the center of SSADM, where investigation and analysis are replaced by specification and design. For example, stress is placed on the required system design rather than the functionality of the current system. Each required function is documented in detail. This stage in SSADM also has an optional prototyping phase. The methodology suggests demonstrating prototypes of critical dialogues and menu structures to users, and this will verify the analysts' understanding of the users' requirements and their preferences for interface design. As well as verifying the specification, this phase can have other benefits, such as increased user commitment.

The next stage and the following logical design stage are carried out in parallel. In the technical system options stage, the environment in which the system will operate, in terms of the hardware and software configuration, development strategy, organizational impact, and system functionality, is determined. The definition of technical options will be implementation specific, because there are so many alternative hardware, software, and implementation strategies. The analysts need to identify constraints; for example, the hardware platform may be "given" along with time and cost maxima and minima. System constraints might include performance, security, and service level requirements that must be met, and these will limit choice. Technical system options need to meet all these constraints, and a chosen option has to be agreed upon with management. The analysts may perform an impact analysis of the various technical system options, focusing on organizational, personnel and operating changes, training requirements, systems documentation, savings, and testing requirements.

The logical design is a statement of what the system is required to do rather than a statement about the procedures or program specifications to do it. The latter is the realm of the final stage (Stage 6), the physical design. In Stage 5 the dialogue structures, menu structures, and designs are defined for particular users or user roles. User involvement is important at this stage (as it is in others), and the prototypes developed in Stage 3 are referenced. Furthermore, the update processes and operations are defined along with the processing of inquiries, including the sequence of processing. All the requirements to start designing the physical solution are now in place. At the final stage the logical design is mapped onto a particular physical environment. The phase provides guidelines regarding physical implementation, and these should be applicable to most hardware and software configurations. However, this stage will be carried out with the actual configuration in mind. Along with the well-defined tasks, and guidance with the techniques, the methodology defines the outputs expected from the stage and gives time- and resource-management guidelines.

The proponents of the methodology recommend *Quality Assurance Reviews* (see chapter 12) based on structured walkthroughs (see Section 4.7). They are meetings held to review identifiable end products of the various phases of the methodology. Usually, the end product is presented by the authors and reviewed by personnel from related project teams (helping good communications between project teams and ensuring a common standard of work), specialist quality-assurance teams, or groups of users. The purpose of the meetings is to identify errors in the product. Post-implementation feedback is also encouraged, and there is an audit at this time.

The successful implementation of the methodology relies on the skills of key personnel being available, although the techniques and tools are widely known and the project team method of working, along with structured walkthroughs, encourages good training procedures and participation. SSADM emphasizes good documentation standards, clear and detailed guidelines, and thorough quality assurance.

## 3.3. Dynamic Systems Development Method (DSDM)

In the mid 1990s, the need was apparent for a less bureaucratic, more flexible approach to developing information systems. DSDM came about from an independent and not-for-profit consortium to define a standard for developing applications rapidly. The consortium includes IBM, the British Ministry of Defense, British Telecom, and British Airways but has an international mix of users. It is to some extent the other extreme from SSADM, being much more flexible, much less bureaucratic and complex.

Rapid application development is fundamental to DSDM. **Rapid Application Development (RAD)** is seen by the consortium as a project-delivery framework that actually works. It aids the development and delivery of business solutions to tight timescales and fixed budgets (www.DSDM.org).

The DSDM approach not only addresses the developer's view of RAD but also that of all the other parties who are interested in effective information systems development, including the users and quality-assurance personnel and, of course, project managers. The consortium readily admit DSDM is not appropriate for all situations, and therefore many organizations use a methodology like SSADM for some larger applications development and DSDM for others. As seen in Exhibit 3.4, it has nine principles which should be followed by all adherents.

---

### Exhibit 3.4    The Nine Principles of DSDM

1. Active user involvement is imperative.

2. Teams must be empowered to make decisions. The four key variables of empowerment are authority, resources, information, and accountability.

3. Frequent delivery of products is essential.

4. Fitness for business purpose is the essential criterion for acceptance of deliverables.

5. Iterative and incremental development is necessary to converge on an accurate business solution.

6. All changes during development are reversible—i.e., you do not proceed further down a particular path if problems are encountered; you backtrack to the last safe or agreed point and then start down a new path.

7. The high-level business requirements, once agreed upon, are frozen. This is essentially the scope of the project.

8. Testing is integrated throughout the life cycle—i.e., "test as you go" rather than testing just at the end, where it frequently gets squeezed.

9. A collaborative and cooperative approach between all stakeholders is essential.

---

Many of these principles are encompassed in the following characteristics of its practice:

• *Incremental development.* It is understood that not all the requirements can be identified and specified in advance. Some requirements will only emerge when the users see and experience the system in use; others may not emerge even then, particularly complex ones. Requirements are also never seen as complete but evolve and change over time with changing circumstances. So DSDM starts with a high-level, rather imprecise list of requirements, which are refined and changed during the process. The easy, obvious requirements and those providing the most impact are used as the starting point for development.

- *Timeboxing.* The information system to be developed is divided up into a number of components, or timeboxes, which are developed separately. The most important requirements, and those with the largest potential benefit, are developed first and delivered as quickly as possible in the first timebox. Some of its proponents argue that no single component should take more than 90 days to develop, while others suggest a maximum of 6 months. Whichever timebox period is chosen, the point is that it is quick compared with the more traditional systems development timescale of SSADM, for example. The aim is to deliver quick and often. This rapid delivery of the most important requirements also helps to build credibility and enthusiasm from the users and the business—indeed, all the stakeholders. Obviously such an approach requires a radically different development culture from that required for traditional or formalized methodologies, such as SSADM. The focus is on speed of delivery, the identification of the absolutely essential requirements, implementation as a learning vehicle, and the expectation that the requirements will change in the next timebox.

- *Pareto principle.* This is essentially the 80/20 rule and is thought to apply to requirements. The belief is that around 80% of an information system's functionality can be delivered with around 20% of the effort needed to complete 100% of the requirements. This means that it is the last, and probably most complex, 20% of requirements that take most of the effort and time. Thus the question is asked, "why do it?" Instead, choose as much of the 80% to deliver as possible in the timebox. The rest, if it proves necessary, can be delivered in subsequent timeboxes (or not at all).

- MoSCoW rules. This is a form of prioritizing of requirements according to four categories:

> M: the Must Haves. Without these features the project is not viable (i.e., these are the minimum critical success factors fundamental to the project's success).
> S: the Should Haves. To gain maximum benefit, these features will be delivered, but the project's success does not rely on them.
> C: the Could Haves. If time and resources allow, these features will be delivered, but they can easily be left out without affecting the project.
> W: the Won't Haves. These features will not be delivered. They can be left out and possibly, although not necessarily, be done in a later timebox.

The MoSCoW rules ensure that a critical examination is made of requirements and that no large "wish lists" are made by users. All requirements have to be justified and categorized. Normally in a timebox, all the "must haves" and at least some of the "should haves" and a few of the "could haves" would be included. Of course, as has been mentioned, under pressure during the development, the "could haves" may well be dropped and even possibly the "should haves" as well.

• *JAD workshops.* DSDM requires high levels of participation from all stakeholders in a project as a point of principle and achieves this partly through the JAD (joint application development) workshop. This is a facilitated meeting designed to overcome the problems of traditional requirements gathering, where users feel they have no real say on decision making. A JAD workshop will help establish and reach agreement on the initial requirements, the length of the timebox, what should be included in the timebox, and manage expectations and gain commitment from the stakeholders. Later workshops will firm up the detail.

• *Prototyping.* A prototype is a rough approximation of the application (or part of it) that can be used to test some designs and other features of the final product and gain user reaction at an early stage in the development process. Prototyping is an important part of DSDM and is used to help establish the user requirements, and in some cases the prototype evolves to become the system itself. Prototyping helps speed up the process of eliciting requirements, and although speed is obviously important in DSDM, it also fits the DSDM view of evolving requirements and users not knowing exactly what they want until they see or experience using the system.

• *Agile programming.* Although speed of delivery is not specifically mentioned in its principles (Exhibit 3.4), only alluded to, it is clearly a key principle of DSDM, and many practitioners use the agile approach to developing software. Indeed version 4.2 of DSDM suggests a joint approach with XP. The agile approach could be described as a separate methodology itself, but its principles align themselves with those of DSDM. There is an emphasis on the following:

○ Individuals and interactions over processes and tools

○ Working software over comprehensive documentation

○ Customer collaboration over contract negotiation

○ Responding to change over following a plan

Extreme Programming, or eXtreme Programming (XP) (see Section 3.4), is one agile approach that stresses the role of teamwork and open and honest communication between managers, customers, and developers with concrete and rapid feedback. The customer must define their requirements in *user stories*; these are the things that the system needs to do for its users and therefore replaces the requirements document. An *architectural spike* is an aid used to figure out answers to tough technical or design problems. This is usually a very simple program to explore the potential solutions; it builds a system, which only addresses the problem under examination, and ignores all other concerns. *Paired programming*—two programmers per workstation—reduces the potential risk when a technical difficulty threatens to hold up the system's development. While one programmer is keying in the best way to perform a task, the other is "thinking more strategically" about whether the whole approach will work, tests that may not work yet, and ways of simplifying.

Historically, there have been problems concerning speed of delivery in information systems practice, and DSDM recognizes that the business often needs solutions faster than they can be delivered. It is recognized that deadlines are frequently set with no reference to the work involved—that is, the deadline is outside of the control of those tasked with the delivery of the project. In situations of tight deadlines it is tempting to introduce extra resources and people to a project. However, as Fred Brooks has observed, this frequently makes things worse, as there is a considerable learning curve for new people joining a project, and existing people are diverted to help bring the new people up to speed. Thus if the deadline of a late-running project cannot be altered, the only thing left is to reduce functionality. This is the RAD solution and the one that DSDM adopts.

The phases and the main products that need to be produced in each phase together with the various pathways through the process are seen in Figure 3.1. As can

❖ **Figure 3.1** DSDM in Overview

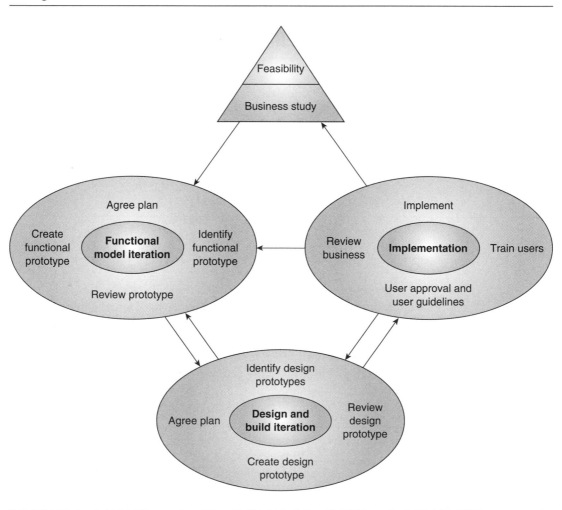

be seen, the feasibility and business studies are performed sequentially and before the rest of the phases because they define the scope and justification for the subsequent development activities. The arrows indicate the normal forward path through the phases, including iteration within each phase, although they also indicate the possible routes back for evolving and iterating the phases. In fact, the sequence that the last three phases are undertaken in or how they are overlapped is not defined but left to the needs of the project and the developers.

As can be seen there are five main phases in the DSDM development lifecycle:

## Feasibility Study

This includes the usual feasibility elements—for example, the cost–benefit case for undertaking a particular project—but also, and particularly important, it is concerned with determining whether DSDM is the correct approach for this project. DSDM recognizes that not all projects are suitable for RAD and DSDM. This is concerned with the maturity and experience of the organization with DSDM concepts. Further, where engineering, scientific, or particularly computationally complex applications apply, DSDM is not usually advised. Projects in which all the requirements must be delivered at once may also not be suitable for DSDM. General business applications, especially where the details of the requirements are not clear but time is critical, are particularly suitable for DSDM. The feasibility study is "a short, sharp exercise," taking no more than a few weeks, in dramatic contrast to SSADM feasibility studies, which take much longer. Thus it is not particularly detailed but highly focused on the risks and how to manage them. A key outcome is the agreement that the project is suitable and should proceed.

## Business Study

This is also supposed to be quick and is at a relatively high level. It is about gaining understanding of the business processes involved, their rationales, and their information needs. It also identifies the stakeholders and those that need to be involved. It is argued that traditional requirements-gathering techniques, such as interviewing, take too long. Facilitated joint application development (JAD) workshops are recommended, involving all the stakeholders. The high-level major functions are identified and prioritized as is the overall systems architecture definition and outline work plans. These plans include the Outline Prototyping Plan, which defines all the prototypes to be included in the subsequent phases. These plans get refined at each phase as more information becomes available. DSDM advocates using "what you know" and is not prescriptive concerning analysis and design techniques.

## Functional Model Iteration

Here the high-level functions and information requirements from the business study are refined. Standard analysis models are produced followed by the development of prototypes and then the software. This is described as a symbiotic process with feedback from prototypes serving to refine the models and then the prototypes moving toward first-cut software, which is then tested as much as is possible given its evolving nature.

## System Design and Build Iteration

This is where the system is built ready for delivery to the users. It should include at least the "minimum usable subset" of requirements. Thus the "must haves" and some of the "should haves" will be delivered, but this depends on how the project has evolved during its development. As indicated above, testing is not a major activity of this stage because of the ongoing testing principle. However, some degree of testing will probably be needed as in some cases this will be the first time the whole system has been available together.

## Implementation

This is the cut-over from the existing system or environment to the new. It includes training, development, and completion of the user manuals and documentation. The term completion is used because, like testing, these should have been on-going activities throughout the process. Ideally, user documentation is produced by the users rather than the specialist developers. Finally a project review document is produced, which assesses whether all the requirements have been met or whether further iterations are required.

DSDM emphasizes the key role of people in the process and is described as a "user centered" approach. Overall, there is a project manager, requiring all the skills of traditional project managers and more, as the focus is on speed! The project manager is responsible for project planning, monitoring, prioritization, human resources, budgets, module definition, re-scoping, etc. The use of software project management and control tools are recommended. Some people see the use of such project control tools to be in conflict with the dynamic nature of DSDM, but most DSDM users argue that this is not the case.

On the user side there are two key roles. The first is that of Ambassador User. This is someone (or more than one person) from the user community who understands and represents the needs of that community. The second is the Visionary User. This is the person that had the original idea or vision as to how the project might help in the business or organization. As well as defining the original vision, they have a responsibility to make sure that the vision stays in focus and does not become diluted. In other contexts this might be described as the project champion.

On the IT side, although they are crucial, there are in general no particular specialist roles—i.e., no distinction is made between different IT roles, such as analysts, designers, and programmers. Everyone has to have flexible skills and be capable of turning their hand to whatever is required at any particular time. Of course in practice particular skills may have to be imported at times, but the key IT team members are generalists and do not change. One exception to this is the specific role of technical coordinator, responsible for the technical architecture, technical quality, and configuration management. A particular requirement for all is good communication skills.

DSDM recommends small development teams composed of users and IT developers. A large project may have a number of teams working in parallel, but the minimum team size is two, as at least one person has to be from the IT side and one from the business or user side. The recommended maximum is six, as it has been found that above this number the RAD process can prove difficult to sustain.

## 3.4. Software Development

We have shown that information systems development projects involve much more than software. However, software is nevertheless an important component, and therefore we discuss this frequently in the book but devote this section to these aspects. We have argued that project management is both an art as well as a science, but software development is much more the latter. Indeed, methodologies emphasizing quality software tend to use the term *software engineering*. Those tempted not to use a formalized software engineering approach may think about the findings of the study of Dietmar Pfahl and colleagues, which suggests that *finding and fixing a software problem after delivery is 100 times more expensive than finding and fixing it during the requirements and early design phases*. This is because after early design the programs will have been written, tested, implemented, and operational.

Software engineering concerns the use of sound engineering principles, good management practice, applicable tools, and methods for software development. This was thought to be the solution to the software crisis—that is, the ability to maintain programs, fulfill the growing demand for larger and more complex programs, and the increased potential of hardware, which has not been exploited fully by the software. The principles established in software engineering have now generally been accepted as a genuine advance and an improvement to programming practice, primarily by achieving better designed programs and hence making them easier to maintain and more reliable. This has led to improved software quality.

Software engineering offers a more disciplined approach to programming that is likely to increase the time devoted to program design but will greatly increase productivity through savings in testing and maintenance time. A good design is one achievement of the "software engineering school" and a second is good documentation, which greatly enhances the program's "maintainability." One of the main techniques is that of functional decomposition, where a complex task is broken down into its elements for full understanding and good design. We will see this process in Section 3.3 when discussing the work breakdown structure and elsewhere in the book. Thus a large software project can be broken down into separate programs, programs to modules, and modules to statements. Some of these components might be used on other software projects.

The most well-known general model for developing software is that of Barry Boehm, who proposed the spiral model in 1988 (see Figure 3.2), which adopts the concept of a series of incremental developments or releases. As can be seen, development spirals outward from the center in a clockwise direction with each cycle of the spiral resulting in successive refinement of the system.

❖ **Figure 3.2**     Spiral Model (Modified From "A Spiral Model For Software Development and Enhancement," by B. W. Boehm, 1988, *IEEE Computer, 21*[5])

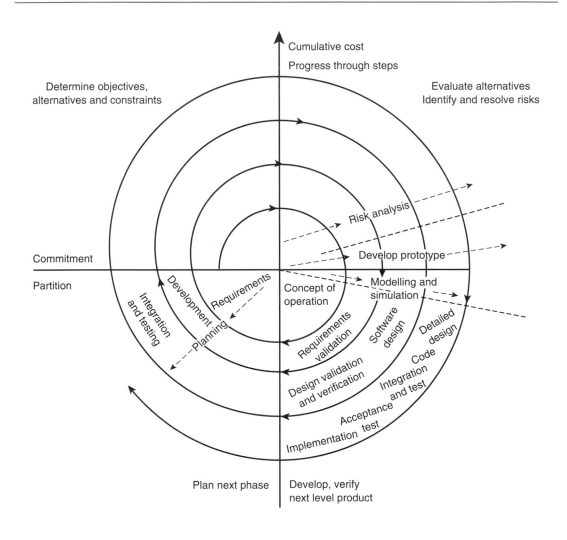

In each cycle of the spiral there are four main activities, represented by the four quadrants. First, there is planning (bottom left quadrant), and at each cycle around the spiral this is about planning the next part or phase, and different elements will be involved depending on what stage the project has reached. Second, there is an objectives phase (top left), then, third, a risk-analysis stage (top right) concerned with the identification and resolution of risks in the software aspects of the system. Risks, such as design flaws, failing to meet user needs, escalating costs, and losing sight of the perceived benefits, are detected early in the development process.

The fourth stage is development (bottom right). In the early stages this might concern the development of manual or paper models, but it might later involve the development of a prototype. The prototype might be used for a number of reasons:

Help define and understand the requirements

Illustrate a user interface for users to react to

Demonstrate, test, and evaluate the functionality of a program

Demonstrate, test, and evaluate the program design

Test response times, loads, volumes, etc.

The prototypes may then evolve into the delivered software components, and in later cycles they become more complete software systems until finally they are the fully tested and engineered releases of the software.

However, some experts have argued that prototypes are inadequate, or partial, software designs and that they are not properly engineered. In effect, they just emerge and lead to poor operational software. If that is the case, prototypes are best seen as a model on which the operational software is built rather than potential operational software.

The exact number of cycles is not defined by Boehm. It depends on the nature and characteristics of the particular project and the difficulties encountered in the cycles. The vertical axis in the model represents the cumulative cost of the development project, which increases with each cycle. Similarly, the horizontal axis represents the commitment to the project, also increasing with each cycle. Prototyping is an important element of the spiral model, but some commentators regard this aspect as its main characteristic, often forgetting the importance of the other quadrants. It is noticeable that many of the strengths of the model are reflected in project management as a whole, developed in this text, but of course Boehm's model emphasizes the software aspects of the project.

As shown in Figure 3.3, ISO12207 suggests a more conventional life cycle for software development. In fact it looks at development in terms of the "system" as well as the information and communications technology—in particular, the software—components. However, the "system" is seen as somewhat narrower in vision than that portrayed in this book. For example, it includes the specification of the users' tasks and training required but not the roles and power structures of all the stakeholders discussed in the book. Although the diagrammatic description of the approach shown as Figure 3.3 appears step-by-step in sequence, some degree of iteration is expected— indeed, the repetition of some of the terminology would imply some iteration as well as further detail as one proceeds through the life cycle.

Thus "real world" software development might well turn out to be a mix of the approaches described in Figures 3.2 and 3.3, where the latter is seen as an "ideal type." The iterations and variations in detail of the former impinge on this "ideal type" in the messy reality of each situation as the project develops.

One of the main features of today's world of information systems is the requirement to implement them quickly, particularly obvious when developing Web applications, but

❖ **Figure 3.3**   Software Development Life Cycle (ISO 12207)

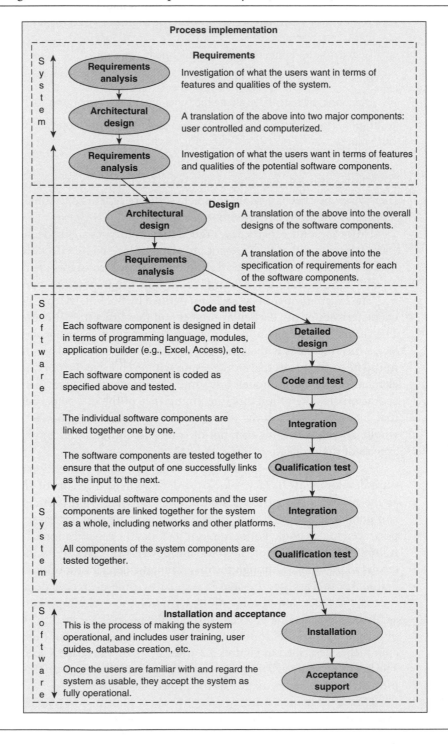

a noticeable movement elsewhere. This has impacted greatly on the software aspects and, as seen above, the methodology DSDM incorporates agile software development methods in its framework for rapid application development as a whole. The market requires low-volume, high-quality, custom, and specific products. These products have very short life cycles, and very short development and production lead times are required. Many traditional software engineers may not like some of the practices that agile development embodies. Further, there is a concern that agile development might lead to poor software because not enough time has been spent on requirements, design, development, and testing. Writing in 2002, Barry Boehm argued that both approaches have importance, but what is critical is getting the balance right between agility and discipline.

Different variants on the agile software development theme include Extreme Programming (XP), SCRUM, Adaptive Software Development, Crystal, Feature-Driven Development, and Pragmatic Programming. One of their themes is "working software over comprehensive documentation"—in other words, the "bureaucratic" components of SSADM, for example, are dispensed with. This is about frequent delivery of working software to keep the customer involved and providing regular and rapid benefits and is seen as being much more important than producing the detailed documentation usually required in traditional software development (as IS development).

The originators of this approach (see, for example, Jim Highsmith's book, which stresses project management aspects) suggested a "manifesto" for agile development including the following:

The highest priority is to satisfy the customer through early and continuous delivery of valuable software.

Changing requirements are welcome, even late in development. Agile processes harness change for the customer's competitive advantage.

Working software is delivered frequently, from a couple of weeks to a couple of months, with a preference to the shorter timescale.

Working software is the primary measure of progress.

Continuous attention to technical excellence and good design enhances agility.

Simplicity, the art of maximizing the amount of work not done, is essential.

The best architectures, requirements, and designs emerge from self-organizing teams.

At regular intervals, the team reflects on how to become more effective and then tunes and adjusts its behavior accordingly.

## 3.5. Issues

As we have seen by our descriptions "brand name" methodologies, such as SSADM and DSDM, following a particular methodology can guide the project manager in the development process. Exhibit 3.5 suggests how a methodology can be expected to provide this support, and Exhibit 3.6 suggests products that might be provided as part of the "methodology package." However, some methodologies—for example, DSDM—are far less prescriptive than ones such as SSADM. However, one question often posed relates to whether project managers are guaranteed successful information systems as a result of using any methodology, and the answer is clearly "no." A methodology is only a guide, and in any case it needs to be applied for an appropriate application, in an appropriate environment, by an appropriate project manager, with an appropriate set of stakeholders. However, one of its main functions is to enable better control and thereby improved information systems. These issues are discussed fully by Avison and Fitzgerald, where further detail can be found about information systems development methodologies.

---

**Exhibit 3.5    Methodology Guidance for the Project Manager**

- What tasks are to be carried out at each stage?
- What outputs are to be produced?
- When, and under what circumstances, are they to be carried out?
- What constraints are to be applied?
- Which people should be involved?
- How should the project be managed and controlled?
- What support tools may be utilized?
- What will be the training needs for the IS professionals?
- What will be the training needs of users and other stakeholders?

---

**Exhibit 3.6    Potential Methodology Components**

- Manuals
- Education and training (including videos)
- Consultancy support
- Tools and toolsets
- Pro forma documents
- Model-building templates

---

### 3.6. Interview With a Project Manager

What information systems development methodology do you use, or don't you use one?

"The answer is something in between. I expect my team not to have "anarchical development" of course, but I have found methodologies much too restrictive, inflexible, and not appropriate for many projects. Thus within the company we have devised what I like to call a "framework" to guide us— neither a free-for-all nor a restrictive methodology."

### What do you mean by a framework?

"In some respects, everything that is in a methodology, but we can pick and choose what we think appropriate for each project and we can change the sequence in which we do things. But it is not "anarchy"! We have certain agreed upon standards and techniques, which we all know. We all use them in agreed-upon ways. But some developments really are required quickly, and this pressure often overrides extensive documentation, for example. But I agree upon all with the stakeholders before-hand. It is essential to be honest and say what can be achieved in such time-pressured situations. Some applications are more long term and large, and they will require many of the features that using a methodology can give us—for example, good control over budget and timekeeping, even if the project takes several months, and delivery of documentation, etc."

### You say several months, but projects can take years

"Not ours! We would call that a program and it would consist of several projects. Things change and we would develop what the management wants first and review the situation every so often, and maybe some of the projects would not start and others would change greatly. The days are far gone of "projects" that take years—at least here—and in fact most of our projects really take only a few weeks and are expected to be tossed away after a time and be replaced by something else. Today's environment is one that changes consistently, and we don't have the time to think so much about the medium or long-term future."

### Tell me more about your framework

"When such an approach was described to me many years ago it was said to be a contingent frame-work rather than a highly prescriptive methodology, because the techniques described were to be used as necessary according to the different situations that cropped up. It was not like an old-fashioned methodology that had to be followed step-by-step. We can use data-flow diagrams, data-modeling techniques, and the rest, but we use them if we think they are appropriate. We tend to use techniques and other standards for larger projects. We think prototyping is a good way for requirements elicitation, and we use a software package that helps us develop one quickly to show the user interface so the users can guide us toward a good design.

I remember the days when everyone was supposed to use one of these huge methodologies that required so much work for the methodology's sake, not us nor the user, but these are not appropriate for our situation. The documentation we produce is essential and kept at a minimum. The word is *speed*. But we also deliver reasonable quality and systems that can be maintained until no longer viable or useful."

## 3.7. Chapter Summary

This book as a whole provides a generalized approach to managing projects. However, this chapter has gone from the general to the specific, giving an outline of two information systems development methodologies. In the first example, that of SSADM, we looked at a typical methodology for large-scale IS projects. It emphasizes a rigorous and generalized approach that stresses control, standardization, and documentation. Its detailed step-by-step approach reminds us of an extraordinarily complex recipe that has to be followed exactly if the "dish" is to taste good.

DSDM, on the other hand, is far more flexible in the way it sees project development. But the project cannot be very large (or at least each "chunk" known as a timebox is comparatively small). It may take only days to develop and implement each timebox. Documentation and standardization are seen as less important than delivering the essentials of what the users want as quick as possible, and the users' involvement in the process should help to ensure that this goal comes about.

DSDM is frequently used with a rapid software development approach, known as XP. Although software development is only part of information systems development, it is an important part nevertheless. Good practice here is therefore also essential, and we discussed good software engineering principles. There are different models for software development, but most, like ISO12207, suggest a life-cycle approach. Thus we have a software life cycle within our overall information systems development life cycle. Again, we looked at rapid approaches like XP along with the more conventional software engineering ones.

## DISCUSSION QUESTIONS

1. "Using a systems development life cycle approach such as SSADM is a waste of time. Most effort is expended on the approach rather than the information system." Discuss.

2. Search the Web for an IS failure or success. Was the project outcome a result of using (or not using) an information systems development methodology? Explain your answer.

3. Is there a need for a methodology to develop information systems? If the response is affirmative, why do you think that many organizations do not use them for the projects?

4. In what ways, if any, does DSDM potentially sacrifice quality for speed?

5. Why do you think that cultural change might be particularly important for an organization thinking about changing from SSADM to DSDM as its principle approach for developing information systems?

6. In what respects is software development a subset of information systems development? What parallels can you draw between the two?

## EXERCISES

1. For the objectives of using methodology discussed in this chapter, suggest which ones are particularly important in relation to project management aspects.

2. Construct a table with four columns covering the key elements of the three methodologies discussed in this chapter along with the generalized life-cycle approach discussed previously in this book. Discuss the reasons for similarities and differences that you have revealed.

3. If you were a project manager developing a new Web application, lay out the issues for using an information systems development methodology or not.

4. Do you think the project manager should leave software development to the technologists and simply wait for them to deliver the software?

## APPENDIX TO CHAPTER 3: DO IS AND IT MATTER—WHOSE SIDE ARE YOU ON?

In May 2003, the *Harvard Business Review* published an opinion piece by Nicolas Carr entitled *IT Doesn't Matter*. Because the *Harvard Business Review* published it, the opinion piece had considerable impact. Carr argued that organizations gave IT a misplaced importance, spending huge sums on IT (about half their capital expenditure) to gain competitive advantage. But he argued that this does not bring strategic value because IT is ubiquitous—it is not a scarce resource. Indeed Carr compares IT to the spread of the railways, electricity, and telephones—no one really gains competitive advantage from them because everyone has them, as they now have IT. He admits that companies can gain *short-term* advantage through the use of IT, but this can be copied and thus the advantage will not last long. Indeed, he goes on, the time between innovation, emulation, and infusion, including that of the competition, is shortening, partly because the Internet enables such developments even more. The present time, he argues, is one of overinvestment in IT, just as there was a period of overinvestment in the railways.

Although still using the term *IT*, Carr develops this argument to information systems, as he argues that not only can companies reproduce the hardware and software infrastructure, but they can also replicate the applications. Enterprise resource planning systems such as SAP and Oracle provide a case in point, as they embed many of the basic applications of most companies. From most points of view, he argues, as prices are falling all the time, it is best for companies to wait and invest later—be a "follower" rather than a technology "leader." For one thing, followers can learn from the mistakes of leaders as well as gain from the price differential. Even then, the argument continues, most companies already have what IT they need.

Where, then, might Carr think IT spending is worthwhile? The headline "from offense to defense" answers this question. He argues that companies are vulnerable to IT failure, so it is important to spend on such things as backup and security and protection against obsolescence or unreliable vendors. So, in conclusion, his "new rules for IT" are: spend less; follow, don't lead; and focus on vulnerabilities, not opportunities.

At first sight, these appear to be compelling arguments! It is evident that the project manager needs some responses, otherwise she may not be able to motivate the stakeholders, and if there is a negative atmosphere then any information system is liable to fail. ***What counterarguments can the project manager make?*** Here we present some arguments used by opponents of Carr. Many were expressed in the subsequent June 2003 issue of the *Harvard Business Review*.

The first response is to make clear that the project manager must be able to justify the IT spending. The days of accepting what the project manager asks for without proper review are over. In that sense Carr has articulated a basic requirement, and readers of this text should, we hope, agree with this view and, having read the text, be able to fulfill this requirement by, for example, explaining in detail the costs and benefits of the project.

A second response, also discussed throughout this book, is to argue that information systems are not just about IT, nor indeed just about ICT, information and communications technology. Information systems are about the applications, not just the infrastructure to which Carr devotes

*(Continued)*

(Continued)

most of his article. IT relates to capital expenditure, but information systems are about effective management and highly skilled and motivated people in an organizational context. Stakeholders will be affected through information systems, and we have also stressed impacts on the whole organization.

Further, electricity and the railroad, for example, each have only one basic use—that is, energy and transport, respectively—whereas ICT has so many uses and potential. Information systems, in any case, is not just about hardware and software (where comparisons with the railways, telephone, and electricity might be apt), and whereas train drivers will be limited in what they can do by the technology, information systems people, including project managers, will only be limited by their intelligence and resourcefulness.

Third, there is something fundamentally different about information and communications technology. With the railroads, electricity, and the like, the pace of change—once a good level of standard had been reached—was slow. That is not the case with ICT. As one respondent to the Carr article points out, whereas the speed of trains increased from 15 mph to 80 mph in 40 years, the speed of computing—just to give one example—had increased 10 million times from the 1960s to the year 2000. More important, however, the use of a railway line has been fairly stable, whereas the uses and potential uses of IT have grown exponentially and into so many different fields of activity. Here the pace of change is relentless, and the new innovations do provide new and great opportunities for companies.

A good project manager must, nevertheless, be realistic and thorough in ensuring that the opportunity is realized. Further, if the potential competitive advantage is more short-lived than was previously the case, then the project manager may consider advocating flexible and rapid development approaches discussed in this chapter rather than the more bureaucratic approaches more appropriate to long-term and fundamental applications.

Fourth, and a development of the previous arguments, IT might be a commodity, but information systems applications can be made unique to each firm. The information held—and more important, perhaps, the organizational knowledge and experience contained within the information system—and the uses that can be made of such knowledge are individual to the firm and can therefore be used to gain competitive advantage. Thus this book has not been about "software project management" (although as we saw in this chapter software is an important and integral part) but about *information systems* project management.

Fifth, and again this is demonstrated frequently in this book through discussions in our exhibits, project manager interviews, and appendices, information systems projects can be successes as well as failures, and while the former can well lead to competitive advantage, the opposite is also true of failures. There are cases of failure discussed in this book, like One.Tel, where an information systems failure did have disastrous consequences, but there are many examples, such as AAHELP, also discussed in the book, which have led to competitive advantage for the organization. Yet again, some systems, like LASCAD, were turned around from being failures to successes. The principles for good project management discussed in the book will make successes for project managers much more likely.

Sixth, competitive advantage does not come usually from one application—although as we have seen, it can happen—but the good practices discussed in this book if applied to all information systems developments in the firm will lead to sustained competitive advantage through a company's portfolio of successful applications. It will be seen as a leading firm in the *use* of IT, not in the IT investment per se.

It is interesting to note that Carr's later publication is entitled *Does IT Matter?* This suggests that he later had doubts! However, whether IT matters depends on the interpretation of "information technology." One thing is certain: ***Information systems do matter***, and project managers need to convince their doubting colleagues. You have the weapons to convince in this book!

## APPENDIX TO CHAPTER 3: DISCUSSION QUESTIONS

1. Read the relevant articles in the *Harvard Business Review* of May and June 2003. Whose side are you on?

2. Prepare a group presentation, giving the points to the debate. If possible have some members of the group supporting Carr and others against the views of Carr.

3. Read what Nicolas Carr has argued since that original article. Have his views changed?

4. Some stakeholders of the information system for which you are project manager have read the article by Carr, "IT Doesn't Matter." Prepare a presentation that argues the contrary case and try to convince them that "IT does matter."

5. Make a case that IT does not matter but that IS does matter.

6. What particular aspects of the project manager's role will help to gain the support of managers who are skeptical about the impact of information systems?

## BIBLIOGRAPHY

Avison, D., & Fitzgerald, G. (2006). *Information systems development: Methodologies, techniques and tools* (4th ed.). Maidenhead, UK: McGraw-Hill.

Bennatan, E. M. (2000). *On time within budget* (3rd ed.). New York: Wiley.

Boehm, B. W. (1988). A spiral model for software development and enhancement. *IEEE Computer, 21*(5).

Boehm, B. W. (2002, January). Get ready for agile methods with care, *Computer,* 64–69.

Brooks, F. P. (1995). *The mythical man–month and other essays on software engineering.* Reading, MA: Addison-Wesley.

DSDM (2007). *DSDM business-focused development.* DSDM Consortium. Retrieved from www.dsdm.org/webshop.

Eva, M. (1994). *SSADM version 4: A user's guide* (2nd ed.). New York: McGraw-Hill.

Highsmith, J. (2004). *Agile project management: Creating innovative products.* Reading, MA: Addison Wesley.

Hughes, B., & Cotterell, M. (2006). *Software project management* (4th ed.). New York: McGraw-Hill.

Pfahl, D., Klemm, M., & Ruhe, G. (2000). *Using system dynamics simulation models for software project management education and training.* The Software Process Simulation Modeling Workshop, London. Retrieved from www.prosim.pdx.edu/prosim2000/paper/ProSim EA24.pdf.

Stapleton, J. (2002). DSDM: *A framework for business focused development.* Harlow, UK: Pearson.

Weaver, P., Lambrou, N. C., Walkley, M. (2002). *Practical business systems development using SSADM* (3rd ed.). Harlow, UK: Prentice Hall.

Whitehead, P. (2001). *Leading a software development team.* Harlow, UK: Pearson.

# 4

## Defining Project Scope

> **Themes of Chapter 4**
>
> ❖ How can we determine requirements?
> ❖ How can we prioritize?
> ❖ How can we produce a scope statement?
> ❖ How can we cope with changes in requirements as the project develops?
> ❖ How can we develop a work breakdown structure?

**D**etermining exactly what customers and sponsors of a project need is not always easy. Priorities change and perceptions of what technology can do on the one hand and what the business problem is on the other create uncertainty in the minds of users and sponsors of a project. Experienced project managers save a great deal of time and effort down the road by spending time up front to specify the user expectations as clearly as possible. A scope statement goes a long way toward establishing this objective. It becomes a means of communication with all stakeholders, particularly team members, users, and sponsors. It is possible that some changes to the requirements become necessary as the project develops. The project manager must plan and manage change within the broad scope of the project. This chapter describes what the project scope is and why it is important to define it carefully before any project activity starts. It describes how to develop and manage project scope. It describes how to develop a useful work breakdown structure as an important step for any project development. It also describes how to plan and manage change if and when it is necessary. We first look at the question of stakeholder requirements as these issues reflect on all the topics of this chapter. However, before doing so, we look at Exhibit 4.1, the story of a project where project managers failed to take account of cultural differences.

### Exhibit 4.1   Potential Problems When Introducing Information Systems

Information and communications technology applications pervade organizations everywhere. Some applications might be developed "tailor made" for the organization, but most nowadays are generic. Since the mid 1990s, enterprise resource planning (ERP) applications, such as those developed by SAP and Oracle, have been implemented widely. ERP systems form a complex series of software modules used to integrate many business processes covering information, people, money, products and services, equipment, and more recently modules for e-commerce, customer relationship management, and call centers. In this way ERP systems have an impact outside the organization as well as within it, as they allow for communication with suppliers and customers, all along a global supply chain. Indeed, they attempt to provide a complete IT solution for businesses.

It is therefore not surprising that organizations running successful ERP systems in the United States and Europe wish to extend their ERP systems to include foreign subsidiaries and other linked companies. Without such links, managers have only partial control and a subset of information. Adding the overseas companies to the overall system will give managers the total picture, and it is surely a simple task—"if it works here, it will work there." If only!

One European company that has successfully implemented an ERP system in their European, North American, and South American companies expected similar success in their Chinese companies. The global ERP system was to be implemented in the Chinese units by using a worldwide template designed by teams of information systems practitioners based in the European headquarters. Whatever could go wrong did go wrong, but we wish to mention here those factors that relate particularly to project management, in particular cultural aspects.

The usual procedure for this kind of ERP implementation was to send ERP consultants from headquarters to the local site for just a 2-week period in order to communicate the basics of the global template to the local project team. The consultants then managed the project from Europe through daily conference calls. The local project team was composed of project managers (three European expatriates), key users (local staff), and also external local ERP consultants.

One of the first difficulties that we saw in this project was limited employee involvement due to poor communications. Local employees did not feel involved in the project. They had the feeling that only top management (meaning primarily European expatriates) was concerned with this project. Not enough time was spent with locals to ensure the backing of the whole company staff. The support and "buy in" of the local staff are vital to the project's success: They are the future users of the system.

A second problem concerned language difficulties. The official language of the project team was English, but for some Europeans on the project, English was a second or third language and came with accents that were difficult for the Chinese to comprehend, especially when their own level of English was not good. It is another obvious pitfall, but one that seems to have been ignored, since "officially" everyone spoke English. This oversight led to many key people being pushed to the margins of the project.

Even worse, the ERP worldwide template had not been translated into Chinese, and the English version was implemented. The company's technical team determined that the current version of the ERP system would not support Chinese characters. They made this discovery only after the project was launched, making a difficult situation almost intolerable for those key users whose English was poor. Local suppliers, customers, and administrators required documents in Chinese only. The only way to address the need for Chinese-language documents was to keep using the legacy system in addition to the new ERP system. This necessitated a double-entry procedure for the operational staff.

Not only did this imply that many advantages of the ERP system were lost, but it meant that additional errors were likely to enter the data.

Yet another pitfall related to the assumption that laws and regulations were standard. In fact, there were local laws and regulations, with those relating to accounting and bidding processes proving particularly difficult. Once again, the only solution was to keep using the legacy system to be consistent with local administration requirements.

Other cultural differences that made an impact concerned attitudes and values concerning control, management, and communications. One aspect that proved important concerned "losing face." European headquarters staff did not hesitate to expose weaknesses of Chinese managers in front of the managers' subordinates. In China, respect for the hierarchy is still strong, and external consultants have to understand this to avoid crises. This potential pitfall is well known, indeed almost a cliché, yet seemed to be ignored in this case. Another attitudinal factor concerns the "patience" required by Chinese culture. The European staff expected problems to be raised, whereas Chinese staff adopted a fairly passive attitude. The Asian "yes" may also not be as frank and wholehearted as was assumed by headquarters staff.

In all the above, the parties assumed (and we have assumed to some extent) that there are "Chinese characteristics" that are held by all, whereas of course there are many differences within both Chinese and European peoples that complicated communications even further. One of the weaknesses of Geert Hofstede's famous study on cultural differences at IBM and his cultural dimensions theory is its assumption of generalized national characteristics. The assumption that cultures are separate, distinct entities that identify and distinguish one group form another is too simplistic. Cultures are contested, ever changing, and emergent; they are invented and reinvented in social life.

As the following figure shows, cultural problems are likely to be more marked as the company attempts to implement the system further away from the company's home base (in this case, France).

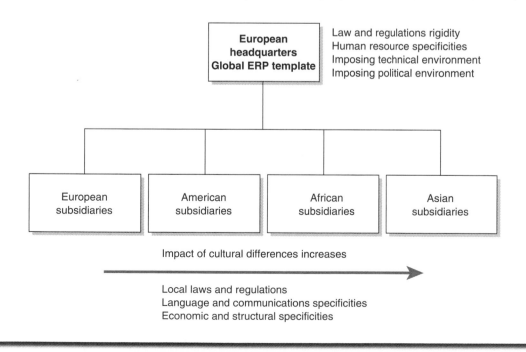

As a result of the problems encountered in this case, it is not surprising that the attempt to extend the ERP system to Chinese subsidiaries was seen by the company as largely a failure, with a parallel legacy system still running. What conclusions can we draw from the case?

- Good communication is essential—spending time with the local employees and managers is a considerable expense, but one that cannot be left aside.
- Top managers need to be involved and esteemed for their potential contribution.
- Governance issues require special attention for international ERP implementation.
- Training needs to be well planned and effective and potential language difficulties must be addressed.
- Most of all, parties to an international partnership need to be aware of cultural differences and difficulties and ensure that they are addressed.

From "ERP Introduction by Foreign Firms: Impact of Cultural Difference," by D. Avison and J. Malaurent, 2007, Association of Information Management (AIM) Conference, Lausanne.

## 4.1. Requirements Definition

The definition of requirements can be problematic, but in relation to information systems, it can be said to be a balance of what can reasonably be provided between everything that the set of relevant stakeholders (Section 1.7) want from a system on the one hand and the various cost, time, and other resource constraints on the other. Issues associated with identifying, gathering, analyzing, documenting, and communicating requirements are at the heart of project management. Incorrect requirements, changes to requirements, misunderstood requirements, and many other requirement problems are an ongoing problematic theme. Requirements are obviously important because they determine what the system will do and to some extent how it will do it. They are also important because of the costs in both time and money of getting them wrong. According to Dean Leffingwell, requirement errors account for between 70% and 85% of rework costs. Further, there exist a number of studies that suggest that the costs of fixing errors at the planning stage are around 80 to 100 times less than if an error is discovered at the later controlling stage.

But it is not easy to define requirements early. At the beginning, stakeholders may only have a vague notion of what the project should achieve. Worse, these notions will vary between stakeholders. These problems need to be resolved, and this process is difficult and time-consuming and may involve interviews, meetings, surveys, workshops, prototypes, storyboards, and so on. Traditionally, a specification is then fed back to the stakeholders (or their representatives) for agreement and they "signed off" the specification document which was then "frozen." If the project was delivered to the stakeholders delivering this specification, then the project could be deemed a "success." Unfortunately, this term may be misleading.

Since the time of user sign-off, the environment may have changed so that this specification may no longer be appropriate. Further, the stakeholders at that early stage may not have fully understood the issues, and they may have been "signing in the dark." Some stakeholders may not have been willing to devote much time to the project at that early stage and paid lip-service to participation while others may have been so interested that they suggested large and inappropriate "wish lists" that became firm deliverables. Further, stakeholders may have been inconsistent and the compromises reached might also have led to inappropriate decisions.

Clearly, changing and evolving requirements create a problem for the requirements process. Requirements can and do change while the system is being developed, and this is a major issue because the specification may have been "frozen" at user sign-off.

However, somehow the designers of the scope statement need to go from general requirements to *measurable objectives*. As one of our referees put it, "It cannot be just touchy-feely." You can say "improve customer service by 7%," but you must also have numbers that measure the task groups leading to this major objective. This objective may require a 50% improvement in the speed by which customer complaints are sent to the marketing manager for action. It is very desirable and even necessary for there to be a strong underlying understanding of the project with specific and measurable objectives before completing the scope statement because it is the blueprint for the work breakdown structure. This will require back and forth communication until the scope statement is finalized.

The traditional requirements process also embodies an assumption that requirements are conceptually able to be "discovered" from stakeholders. However, some requirements are so complex and so obscure that they are not easy to capture in this way, no matter how diligent and hard-working the participants. In the early days of Web applications, for example, suppliers, users, customers, and technologists were not sure what a good Web site would be like, and much was discovered by a trial-and-error process, often at the expense of the customer. Further, terms like "reliable," "available," "flexible," and "easy to use" are often difficult to specify to information systems developers in meaningful and measurable ways. Also, if the project is one that is more strategic, perhaps designed to give the company competitive advantage, requirements will be much more difficult to ascertain than standard efficiency projects (see Section 2.1).

One response might be to try to somehow build *flexibility* into the "philosophy" of the project manager so that the requirements are flexible, the nature of the change process is flexible, and the information system itself is flexible. But even if these are feasible, there are likely to be tradeoffs—for example, between flexibility and other system characteristics. These tradeoffs may be with political realities within an organization, system complexity, efficiency, effectiveness in relation to particular objectives, the need for standardization, ability to integrate with other information systems, and other factors. There may also be a tradeoff between organizations' needs to have uniform data standards and the need for local discretion in the face of unpredictable demands.

Flexibility is nearly always seen as a "good thing." It appears to have three broad advantages:

1. It improves the *quality* of internal processes in ways that may offer a variety of performance improvements. Advantages accruing might include higher staff morale.

2. It may give firms a *competitive edge*—for example, through the speed of response to an unexpected increase in sales orders, which other firms could not meet.

3. It is part of the *"survival kit"* of an organization. It may be that a measure of flexibility is necessary in a turbulent world: "be flexible or cease operating."

As a number of writers have noted, the acquisition of flexibility is not without costs, and these need to be compared with the likely benefits. In terms of information systems, real costs may include hardware, software, training, reorganization, and ongoing costs.

In this section we have illustrated the difficulties inherent in only one aspect of project scope. This provides a useful backdrop to the discussion on project scope as a whole and the procedures that follow.

## 4.2. Project Scope

The principal questions for any system development project relate to *where* you want to go and *how* you intend to get there. Both questions are equally important. However, without a clear understanding of the first question there will be little or no progress made on the second. It is equally important for the developers (project manager and team members) and recipients (users and sponsors) of the project outcome to have the same understanding of what the project intends to accomplish. The convergence between these two understandings is critical:

- For obtaining support throughout the project development life cycle
- For effective allocation of resources during the project development life cycle
- For the success and final evaluation of project outcome

A *project scope statement* is critical for obtaining support because it gives sponsors confidence that the developers know exactly what the project is expected to accomplish. It is important for effective allocation of resources because it helps developers plan expenditures according to what is needed and save time and energy by eliminating/reducing features that have little value to the customer. The success of any project is closely associated with whether it meets user expectations, and user expectations are closely tied with user needs specification. Therefore it is important to understand the cause-and-effect relationship between these two aspects of "what" is to be done and "how" to accomplish it.

The project scope specifies outcome as it relates to customer expectations. It defines the limits of the project and within that it describes deliverables for the customer. An experienced project manager values a scope statement and spends time up front to define the mission of the project clearly. The project scope is the source for developing the project plan, and that in turn becomes the guide for project execution. There is a clear association between a good *project plan* and a clearly defined *project scope*. Research studies report that a successful project is more likely to have a clearly defined scope statement. It is also reported that a poorly defined project scope statement leads to inadequate project planning.

The project manager is responsible for developing the project scope but should do so through close collaboration and interaction with the customer. The scope clearly describes deliverables that should be both *realistic* and *obtainable*. They should also be *measurable* where appropriate, as vague and poorly described scope statements not only do not help project planning and execution but also become sources of confusion. As mentioned earlier, both developers and recipients must be clear on what the project intent is and what the deliverables are. The project scope statement is published and shared by the project manager and the customer and is a source for measuring progress and quality of the operational information system. The project scope specifically includes the following four aspects:

1. The overall objectives of the project based on customer needs.

This is essential as it provides a legitimate background for the rest of the document. For example, consider a firm that wants to integrate the inventory systems of all its suppliers with its own and make it accessible through the Web. The overall objective of this information system can be stated as the *development and implementation of a Web-based inventory system that integrates all suppliers within 18 months at an approximate cost of $100,000*. It is clear from this statement **what** is expected, **when** it is expected, and at **what cost**.

2. The specific deliverables in support of the overall objectives.

The overall objectives act as a base for the development of a deliverable list.
*Deliverables* may be expected during the development life cycle or at the completion of the project. If a project specification defines deliverables to include, for example, a prototype of the information system at an early stage, then delivery of the prototype system is expected before the development of the actual system. Other usual deliverables for information systems projects include the development and delivery of user manuals, development and implementation of training programs, and testing of the final system.

Every deliverable must have a time, cost, and specification associated with it. In other words, the outcome must be delivered on time, within budget, and as specified. Specifying cost and time for deliverables that are due during the information systems development life cycle informs sponsors and the top management of the likelihood that the entire project will be complete on time and within budget.

Consider our example of the prototype system as an early deliverable. If this prototype system takes significantly longer than expected to develop and costs significantly more than what was initially estimated then management may need to decide whether it is viable to continue with the project or abandon the idea. Based on the list of deliverables, it may be necessary to reevaluate the entire project plan and reallocate resources to obtain a timely outcome. Deliverables are also used as a basis on which to assign responsibilities and evaluate performance. Deliverables often become bases for setting project milestones.

3. The milestones that help control quality and monitor progress.

A *milestone* is a point in the life of a project when a significant piece of work has been accomplished. It indicates a major event in the project development life cycle. The milestone is a clear help to the project manager to determine whether the necessary progress is being made and if the whole project is on schedule for completion. Once the deliverables of a project are defined, then milestones are developed toward achieving those deliverables.

For example, consider a company that sells outdoor gear and sporting goods through retail stores and chains. An information system has been proposed for this company that would replace the current sales function with an online version, eliminating face-to-face contact with customers. This proposal has been evaluated through a cost–benefit analysis (see Section 5.1) and has been determined to meet organizational goals and objectives.

A prototype of this system has been included as part of the information system development life cycle. The development of this prototype system is an example of a milestone. Once user feedback and experience with the prototype system is gathered and used to modify project plans, activities begin for the development of the actual system. Another milestone can be set for when the actual system is developed and it is ready to be tested. The next milestone can be set for when the information system is tested, modified, and is ready for implementation. A training and implementation phase can be considered, and the end of which is seen as another milestone. The final milestone can be set for when the project is administratively closed.

These milestones should be easy to recognize by all team members and sponsors. They indicate a logical point in the development life cycle of the information system and an appropriate point in time when progress can easily be assessed. Setting milestones is critical to the quality-control process as well as to progress assessment, especially for large systems.

4.  The resources that are needed to complete the project.

The list of resources could be divided into three main components of human resources, facilities and equipment, and organizational resources. *Human resources* refer to the talent and skills of the project team members. The project scope must describe special talents that are required for project success. For example, individuals with skills such as network design or network security may be included as project resources. Examples of *facilities and equipment* may include high-speed communication channels or specific testing tools or software. *Organizational resources* can be critical, especially when multiple functions and departments are involved or when outsourcing or other collaboration with outside organizations is necessary.

An experienced project manager foresees unique requirements and special resources that are critical to the fulfillment of the project objectives and includes them in the project scope. Extensive demand on user training time may be necessary for large and complex information systems projects. User departments are usually reluctant to free up large groups of users for training for an extended period of time. In such cases, organizational support may help these user departments with their human resource needs (for example, by hiring temporary help).

These four components define (a) what the project is about, (b) what it intends to accomplish, and (c) what it needs to accomplish its goals. They help to set the boundaries for the project and in that sense protect the project manager from excessive demands or unrealistic expectations. Additional statements can be added to the project scope to limit the project manager's responsibilities within reasonable boundaries. These *exclusion* or *exemption* clauses also help the customer develop realistic expectations. It is similar to a disclaimer that communicates to the customer what should or should not be expected from the project. Examples of statements of limitations for information systems development projects include the extent and length of training programs and system maintenance.

It is important that the customer agrees and signs off on the scope statement. One practical way to achieve this is to get all stakeholders to sign or initial the scope statement and in that way confirm what is agreed upon by all. If necessary, the project manager must go over issues with the customer to make sure the focus of the project and its objectives are clearly understood and the customer is satisfied with the deliverables. By doing this, the project manager makes one more attempt to form realistic expectations with the customer. The project manager must also make sure that the customer understands limitations and exclusions included in the project scope, as they influence expectations in the same way that deliverables do.

In summary, the development of project scope provides a useful forum to eliminate misunderstandings at the early stage of the information systems development life cycle and to create a document that is used to clarify future questions.

The scope statement should be short and to the point but cover important issues as described above. The scope statement may vary depending on the size and the type of the project. In most cases, the scope statement is between one and three pages. Most companies use a document known as a ***project charter*** to formally support the project and to authorize the project manager to start planning developmental activities. The project charter is itself often about one page and includes the following items (an example project charter is shown as Exhibit 4.2):

- Title of the project
- Sponsor or sponsors of the project
- Name of the project manager
- Project start date
- Project objectives
- Project cost and resources
- Due date for the entire project

A project charter does not replace the project scope statement, and it is not always used. Some companies authorize project responsibilities more informally through verbal communication. However, where a project charter is written, it provides a basis for the development of the project scope. As described above, the project scope is more comprehensive than a project charter. As we see in the next section, the project scope is operationalized through the development and implementation of the ***work breakdown structure***.

---

**Exhibit 4.2    Example Project Charter**

*Project title:* OS migration from Windows XP to Vista

*Project sponsors:* IT Support Services

*Project manager:* Misty Blue

*Start date:* November 1, 2008

*Project objectives:* Upgrade operating systems to Vista for all employees within 6 weeks. See attached page for the list of eligible employees.

*Project cost:* Budgeted $50,000 for labor costs and $25,000 for software.

*Completion date:* December 15, 2008

*Comments:* We expect Dew Berry and Jip Nipa from the Instructional Development Office to work on this project. See attached for the list of team members.

---

## 4.3. Work Breakdown Structure

The work breakdown structure (WBS) is an important document for project management in that it defines specifics for each part of the project in terms of what needs to be done, who is responsible for that task, how much it costs, and when it is due. The WBS breaks down the entire project into manageable pieces. Each piece is a work unit assigned to an individual or individuals to be done within allocated time and budget. The WBS looks somewhat similar to an organizational chart (see Figure 4.1).

A quick glance at an organizational chart will tell you the number of divisions or departments that exist in that organization, the hierarchical relationship between those divisions (divisions and subdivisions), the title and responsibility of each division (for example, services, marketing, sales), the person in charge of each division, and the size of each division (number of employees in that division). This is a generic description of an organizational chart, and some organizational charts may provide more information. However, there is a tradeoff between the amount of information included in an organizational chart and its usefulness as a quick, big-picture reference source.

A WBS works in a similar way to an organizational chart in that it provides an overview of how the project is broken down, who is responsible for which part, and so on. Consider a simple information systems project that has the objective to develop a Web page for a small business. You may break this project down to three phases—*design, develop,* and *implement.* The design phase consists of (a) needs analysis determined through interviews with the business owner and employees, and (b) a review and selection of software and languages. The development phase includes the

❖ **Figure 4.1**    Company Organizational Chart

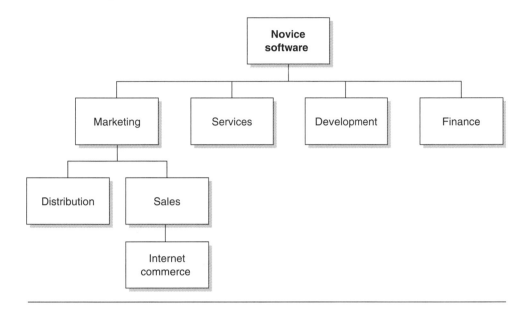

following: (a) purchase software, (b) write programs and test, (c) review the product with the user, and (d) make revisions based on feedback from the user. Finally, the implementation phase consists of: (a) select server site, (b) obtain permission, and (c) install and test. Activities for each phase are further defined in Exhibit 4.3.

A quick look at this simple breakdown of the Web page project as listed above or depicted in Figure 4.2 shows the three main parts to developing this project as well as the list of activities for each part. It also provides the hierarchical relationships between main activities (design, development, and implementation) and sub-activities (needs analysis, software selection, and review).

Further information on due dates for each activity as well as who is responsible for each activity can be provided in a table (see Table 4.1). Each activity can be referred to by the number associated with it (for example, 2.1, 3.2) to allocate costs or add measures of quality and assessment.

The same information can be given in a tabular form with the same numbering system giving the information in hierarchical form (see Exhibit 4.3). Levels of hierarchy are identified by the numbering system as well as the indentation. Level 1 in this WBS represents the main activities of design, development, and implementation. Level 2 represents activities such as needs analysis, write program, and select server. This WBS also shows level 3 items for the "design" activity. The numbering system with its levels and sublevels, depicted in Exhibit 4.3, is sometimes referred to as a *WBS coding scheme* and is used for reference purposes. Accounts, budget, and cost information for

❖ **Figure 4.2**   Breakdown for Web Page Project

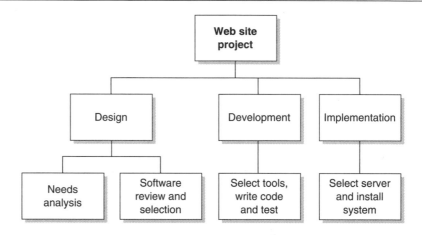

❖ **Table 4.1**   Web Page Project Task and Responsibilities

| Phase | Activity Description | | Due date | Team member |
|---|---|---|---|---|
| 1. Design | 1.1 | Needs analysis | 2 days | Greg |
| | 1.2 | Software selection | 2 days | Fred |
| 2. Development | 2.1 | Purchase software | 1 day | Fred |
| | 2.2 | Write program | 4 days | Matt |
| | 2.3 | Review with user | 1 day | Matt |
| | 2.4 | Make revisions | 1 day | Matt |
| 3. Implementation | 3.1 | Select server | 1 day | Jennifer |
| | 3.2 | Obtain permission | 1 day | Jennifer |
| | 3.3 | Install system | 2 days | Matt |

**Exhibit 4.3   Hierarchical Information for Web Page Project Task**

1. Design
   1.1. Needs analysis
      1.1.1. Define owner needs
      1.1.2. Define user needs

   1.2. Software selection
      1.2.1. Define system needs priorities
      1.2.2. Survey available software
      1.2.3. Recommend software choice

2. Development
   2.1. Purchase software
   2.2. Write program
   2.3. Review with user
   2.4. Make revisions
3. Implementation
   3.1. Select server
   3.2. Obtain permission
   3.3. Install system

each activity are identified using these numbers. This coding scheme helps communication, documentation, and accuracy of information. It is in effect used for the project and work unit identification.

A word of caution is appropriate here. Most information systems projects go through several changes before they are complete. It is possible that users may change their minds, project outcome may be needed sooner than initially planned, priorities may change due to reorganization or cost saving ideas, and the like. When a change is made in a level or a work unit number, all records must be updated for consistency. Frequent change makes this task more difficult. Further, since the project manager and team members are often preoccupied with deadlines and project progress, they may ignore or forget documenting changes. Fortunately, the use of a software package like MS Project will automatically adjust any changes throughout the WBS document (just as a spreadsheet program will work out all the repercussions of a single change to the whole worksheet). We give an initial description of MS Project in Chapter 6.

## 4.4. Work Breakdown Structure as a Management Tool

The work breakdown structure (WBS) provides management with a tool to monitor and evaluate cost, time, and quality. Consider our example Web page project described earlier. Management can allocate and control cost for each phase or if necessary for each activity. In a large project, the project manager can appoint a key individual to be responsible for each phase of the project, and in turn these key individuals will allocate tasks and activities to team members who report to them. In that way management does not need to be concerned about each sub-activity, and management is not expected to know the details of each sub-activity. Individuals must be given responsibilities that correspond with their competency and experience.

Large and complex projects involve more activities, resources, and communication and therefore need a more elaborate WBS that corresponds to the project scope. There is no hard-and-fast rule to determine how many levels are appropriate in a WBS. As a rule of thumb, however, the lowest level in a WBS must be easily defined as a *work unit* or *work package.* A work unit or a work package should be easy to assign to an individual and is easy to evaluate. In the example of our Web page project, *review and selection of software* is a work unit. It is easy to understand what it is, how long it might take to complete, the extent of the resources it might take, who might be a good candidate for the job, and whether it is successfully performed. A well-defined work unit should be possible to complete within a week or two. If it takes too long to complete a work unit, it might be necessary to further break down that work unit.

Work units identified by the WBS document are useful to the project manager for quality-control purposes. Again, consider the work unit, review and selection of software, in our earlier example. It is relatively easy for the project manager to assess the outcome of this task. The outcome of this work unit not only identifies which software should be used but it also describes how that decision is reached and the rationale for that choice. This would suggest to the project manager whether a wide range of software was considered and whether the reasons behind the selection include consideration of the overall project outcome, such as ease of use and maintenance.

Another benefit of WBS is that the quality can be checked at each work unit, and, if necessary, adjustments can be made to avoid adverse effects on subsequent activities. If, for example, very few team members know about the software or if users may ultimately have difficulty using that software, then it might be more cost effective to reconsider the decision to purchase that software in the early stage of the information systems development life cycle and choose another. Therefore, each work unit defined at the lowest level of a WBS is a *control point* assisting project management. Completion of work units are usually reported in reports and meetings that are scheduled about once a week for a progress status update. Brief progress reports and meetings should be scheduled frequently so that adjustments can be made and quality can be controlled before it is too late or too costly to address them.

Each work unit usually includes a deliverable that makes it possible to allocate resources, define time, and monitor progress. It is possible to have more than one work unit per deliverable and to have more than one deliverable per work unit. Some work units may include workers from different departments. In such cases, performance evaluations and monitoring of progress and quality is more challenging and may require further breakdown of the task. For small projects it may be more cost effective and practical for team members and individuals from different departments to participate in different work units.

In any event, a WBS must be developed with the outcome of the project in mind. In other words, the approach must be outcome oriented. Once the first draft of a WBS is complete, the project manager and team members should ask themselves, "Does this WBS lead us to the desired outcome?" or "Is each work unit easily understood?" "Is each work unit independent of other work units?" and "Is it easy to monitor the progress for each work unit?" A useful and functional WBS has clear deliverables and leads the project to the specified outcome. The project manager must be outcome oriented and consider these issues as they design and develop work breakdown structures.

## 4.5. Work Breakdown Structure Approach

The development of a useful and practical WBS is time-consuming and challenging. This is particularly true for large and complex information systems that involve multiple organizational units and include internal and external entities. Experience is the most important asset in developing an effective WBS. Large organizations, such as the U.S. Department of Defense or Boeing, that regularly deal with information systems development, use well-practiced guidelines that are suitable for their own purposes. Once a WBS is developed and tested through practice, it can be used as a generic version, and, with minor modification, it can be used in subsequent information systems development projects.

For a totally new system with no similar prior experience, project managers and team members often start either from the highest level and work their way down to the lowest level or start from the lowest levels and work their way up toward the overall project level. The first method is called the ***top-down approach*** and the second one is called the ***bottom-up approach.*** The top-down approach progressively refines activities, providing greater detail for each until it reaches the level of work units. This approach is effective when the project manager can visualize the big picture and is able to identify key components to start the breakdown process.

The bottom-up approach is less structured. Team members and sometimes users with ideas about activities that are necessary to complete the project will prepare brief descriptions of all possible work units. Next, these work unit descriptions can be placed on a wall or a large board and through an *iterative process* the team will group them in several logical categories. These categories are then combined to create higher level activities and to form the hierarchical information necessary for the WBS. This approach is time-consuming and tedious, but because it involves broad participation and because it requires consensus building among team members about work units and groupings, it provides valuable learning experience as well as commitment among participants. For an entirely new system, the bottom-up approach for developing WBS may be the more effective one.

One technique that can be valuable in documenting the bottom-up discussions (indeed it can be useful to document many complex situations) is ***mind mapping.*** This is often used to document the discussions before creating a WBS when confusion exists or the situation is particularly complex. Tony Buzan developed the mind-mapping technique, which is based on the workings of the human mind. The technique adopts a holistic approach to note taking and memory recall. Mind maps are simple to create: The main idea is first written in the center of a piece of paper. Branches are then added from the main idea labeled with keywords. Creativity is the key for developing successful mind maps. The use of color, illustrations, and symbols assists in improving the recall of the material and detail discussed. An example of a mind map is illustrated in Figure 4.3.

The power and yet simplicity of mind maps has many applications beyond note-taking. Mind maps can be used, for example, in brainstorming sessions, project planning, structuring material to assist in report writing and for the preparation of presentations. Mind maps are very flexible and one of their strengths is the ability to assist in the identification of relationships between concepts in the material.

In summary, it must be stated that developing practical and useful work breakdown structures is challenging and time-consuming. Even experienced project managers will go through several iterations before they finalize a WBS. As stated earlier, there is no hard-and-fast rule about how many levels or which approach to use. Often experience is the best guide, but even that is not enough for unique and specific cases. The checklist in Exhibit 4.4 can be used as a guide for developing an effective WBS.

❖ **Figure 4.3**   Mind Mapping

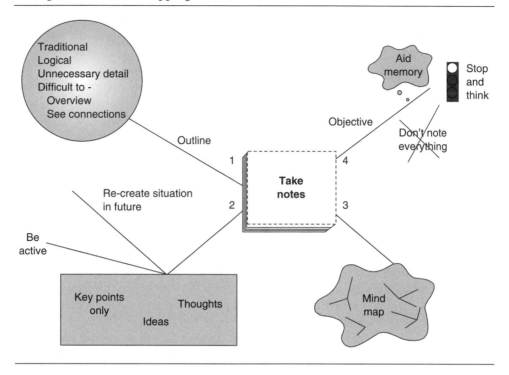

---

**Exhibit 4.4   The WBS Checklist**

- A work unit must be clearly defined and understood by those responsible for it.
- A work unit must be independent of other work units for ease of allocating cost and responsibility.
- Each work unit must have one person responsible for it even if multiple individuals work on it.
- The sum of work units must result in the project outcome.
- Involvement of the project team members in WBS development is essential to learning and commitment.

## 4.6. Assigning Responsibility

Responsibilities assigned through the development of the work breakdown structure need to be documented and communicated. A simple tabular form can be used to do this. The partially complete Table 4.2 illustrates key (principal) and support individuals for each work unit for the Web page project. A work unit, as described earlier, may have one or more individuals working on it. However, for ease of accountability and communication, there must be one person responsible for

❖ Table 4.2   Responsibility Assignment for Web Page Project

| Deliverables | Greg | Matt | Jennifer | Fred |
|---|---|---|---|---|
| Define owner needs | Principal | | | |
| Define user needs | Principal | | Support | |
| Define system needs priorities | | Support | | Principal |
| Survey available software | | Support | | Principal |
| Recommend software choice | | | | |
| . . . . . | | | | |
| . . . . . | | | | |

that work unit. The responsibility chart or table must include all work units identified in the WBS. For larger tables, symbols may be used to identify key individuals from support members or footnotes may be added regarding a specific role or a specific work unit. In any case, the responsibility chart must be self-explanatory and easy to interpret.

In large projects where there are very many work units it might not be feasible to include all work units in one responsibility chart. Multiple tables and charts can be used in such cases to avoid information overload and confusion. However, there must be a logical grouping of responsibilities. One way is to break down the responsibility chart at higher activity levels (for example, level 1, level 2). It is also possible to use functions as a basis to prepare the responsibility chart. For example, important functions in a typical information systems project include requirement analysis, prototyping, coding, testing, and so on. Consider testing of a large system that involves multiple sites and multiple user groups at each site. We can see that major functions can act as a basis for the development of the responsibility chart. The project manager must decide on a form of communication that is practical, easy, and is free from departmental politics.

Responsibility charts not only identify who is responsible for what, but they also suggest authority. Each member of the team that is responsible for a work unit needs to know the line of communication as well as the extent of their personal responsibility. This also helps coordination between work units. Lack of clarification on individual responsibility and authority is often the source of misunderstanding, poor coordination, and discontent. In small projects where it is easy to see the entire project and it is clear what activities are needed, the responsibility chart may be sufficient, thus eliminating the need for a work breakdown structure. It is simpler, quicker, and does the job.

## 4.7. Structured Walkthroughs

Another useful technique that can be used at any stage of the project to ascertain views and point out errors is the *structured walkthrough.* This is a review of aspects of the information system and can be held at various stages of project development. Structured walkthroughs are intended to be team-based reviews of a product but are not intended to be management reviews of individuals or their performance.

Walkthroughs are (normally) informal peer reviews of any product—for example, the scope document. Normally the person responsible presents the product and may raise areas of difficulty—it is not a process of "selling" the product, but one of ensuring the best product is eventually produced in the process. As the document or other product is looked at in detail and step-by-step, the reviewers are expected to be critical in a positive way, providing feedback to help in improving the product that is being reviewed.

---

### Exhibit 4.5    Potential of Structured Walkthroughs

- The overall quality of each aspect of the project under scrutiny is improved, since more than one person is responsible for it and the analysis and design are exposed to the scrutiny of others at every appropriate opportunity.
- There is the opportunity to detect errors earlier in the development of a project than might otherwise be possible, avoiding the errors propagating throughout the rest of the information systems development process.
- All team members have the opportunity to be "educated" in the total system, resulting in a much better understanding of the total system by a greater number of organizational personnel. This means that team members can take over work from each other more easily. Potentially, all stakeholders have the opportunity to familiarize themselves with the overall system as well as particular components.
- Technical expertise is communicated through discussion that is often generated as a result of a structured walkthrough. More experienced staff will spot common sources of potential problems and discuss these with other staff members, thereby transferring their own knowledge and skills. This means that the technical knowledge is dispersed more widely than would otherwise be the case.
- Technical progress can be more readily and easily assessed, and the walkthroughs provide ideal milestones and opportunities to do this.
- If carried out in the correct spirit and atmosphere, structured walkthroughs can provide an opportunity for less experienced people to gain experience and enable them to work on complex problems more quickly because of their contact with other more experienced team members and also because of the opportunity of having walkthroughs on their work where they receive specific comments and feedback in a nonthreatening environment.

If used at this stage, the team can have separate walkthroughs—for example, to see if all the requirements have been documented, that the project scope is realistic and obtainable, the plan encompasses progress monitoring, the resources committed to the project are appropriate, the WBS is consistent and there are no aspects omitted, and so on. They also provide an opportunity for the team to get to know each other.

The basic idea behind structured walkthroughs is that potential problems can be identified as early as possible so that their effect can be minimized. The benefits of this approach are seen in Exhibit 4.5.

Structured walkthroughs have been identified as being of considerable value in the development of information systems, and they should be held on completion of certain phases of the development. It is impractical to hold formal walkthroughs too often, as it causes unnecessary administrative overheads. The best approach is to maintain the spirit of the concept by team members, discussing all decisions with others without necessarily calling formal meetings. It is intended that the approach will normally promote discussion and exchange of ideas within the team.

For maximum benefit to be derived from the walkthrough, it is important that appropriate documentation is circulated well in advance of the walkthrough and that the following is ensured:

- Everyone attending is familiar with the subject to be reviewed.
- Each attendee should have studied it carefully.
- Minor points of detail are discussed before the walkthrough, so that valuable time is not wasted on trivial points.

Further, the following is important during the walkthrough:

- All errors, discrepancies, inconsistencies, omissions, and points for further action are recorded so that this can form an action list.
- One person should be allocated the responsibility of ensuring that all points from the action list are dealt with.

Formal walkthroughs should be attended by a number of team members because responsibility for the system is then placed on the whole team. All members of the team should be given the opportunity to contribute, from the most junior to the most senior. Walkthroughs are a very powerful technique and are most successful when they are carried out in an "ego-less" environment—that is, one in which the individual concerned with the particular activity does not feel solely responsible for it. The idea is not to criticize any individuals but to identify any potential problems and resolve them as early as possible in the information systems development process. It is important that all team members have responsibility for the overall information system, and the use of structured walkthroughs supports this.

## 4.8. Programs and Projects

The project is frequently part of a much larger program that consists of a number of integrated projects. The UK NHS NPfIT initiative discussed in Exhibit 2.1 is such a program, with projects related to pharmaceutical supplies, patient records, call centers, hospital bookings, a public Web site, and many more. This is obviously more complex than a single project because each project has to fit with related projects like pieces of a jigsaw puzzle (Figure 4.4). But advantages include the single collection of data and the ability to relate information from different applications.

In many senses, a program is a project, but it will tend to be much more long term (a project might be only of a few months' duration, whereas the whole of a program may take 5 years or more to implement) and is large (consisting of the scale of a number of projects) and very complex (because the projects need to integrate).

This suggests that there will be an extra layer of project management activities, that ensuring the overall program is coordinated, and that the overall program manager has an overview of each project and their project managers. We might call this overall view the *master plan*. Sometimes the projects are developed sequentially, but more often some of the projects are developed simultaneously, and therefore the task of the program manager is difficult. It is important that once a project is finished, it is tested not only as a "standalone" application but is also tested for compatibility with related applications, for the developers may be working on another project or may even have left the organization by the time the program is tested as a whole. However, the basic material for the project manager described in this book also applies to the program manager.

❖ **Figure 4.4**    A Program Consisting of Many Integrated Projects

**National Program for IT in Health**

Medical practictioner records

Call center

Patient records

Prescription medicines

Hospital records

Operating theater bookings

Consultant records

## 4.9. Interview With a Project Manager

Of these (developing budgets, customer support, staffing, policies, and procedures) what would you consider to be the most important?

"Defining the project is the most important, because no matter what you are doing, if you do not define it correctly, you will end up with garbage. If you do not spend time designing something and developing it, you will not end up with the quality that you have hoped to."

You said earlier that communication is necessary, and to what degree in IT project management?

"It is very important. In some ways it might be more important than defining the project. You have to be able to define a project or a problem, but what good are you if you are not able to communicate to the user or your team? Regardless of who is involved, you must have communication skills."

What type of qualities does an IT project manager have to have to be successful?

"Communication skills, adaptability, personable, intelligent, common sense, fiscally responsible and budget conscience . . . organizational skills are definitely a bonus, and you must be team oriented."

What is your favorite part of your job?

"When someone brings you an issue and they want it to be done differently and actually being able to change it and make it to their liking. Project completion is my favorite part of my job because I know that I have accomplished something."

What is the least favorite part of your job?

"Being asked repetitive questions of the same subject matter. Like when you have two passwords to log on to the network and then into the system. Explaining to users the same answer to the same question in different ways for them to understand gets very monotonous."

Why do you feel IT project management is a necessary function?

"If you do not manage the project, your team will be going in all different directions. If you do not manage the project, you will get the cart before the horse and it will wind up costing you more money in the long run."

Do you feel project phases are necessary in planning a project?

"Yes, only to the extent of the size of the project. You must reevaluate where you are from time to time. It cuts the project up into manageable pieces."

What advice would you give to someone who is interested in becoming an IT project manager?

"The most important thing would be to find a mentor and learn the dos and don'ts of their career and see how they work for you."

## 4.10. Chapter Summary

The project scope definition is an important activity in the system development life cycle. A well-developed project scope will help to achieve several important objectives: project planning, communication, resource allocation, time and cost estimates, monitoring progress, controlling quality, and evaluating outcome. A good project scope defines project *objectives, deliverables, milestones*, and *resources*. The project scope becomes the basis for the development of the work breakdown structure (WBS). The WBS breaks the whole project into manageable pieces or work units to be assigned to individuals with specified cost and time allocation. The WBS represents a work map that guides project activities. It specifically describes *what needs to be done, who will do it, how much it costs*, and *when it is due.* Based on the WBS, a project schedule or network of activity is developed to ensure timely completion of work units. We will look further into aspects of this chapter when we discuss Project Evaluation and Review Technique (PERT) in Chapter 6.

## DISCUSSION QUESTIONS

1. What are the challenges associated with expectation change, and how can the project scope help shape user expectations?

2. Discuss the difference between the project charter and the project scope statement. Can you replace the project scope statement with a project charter?

3. What would you do in cases where deliverables are difficult to define? Can you use milestones as deliverables?

4. Discuss the role of work units in a work breakdown structure for quality control. How would you use work units to control for quality?

5. This chapter suggests that "expectation gap" can be addressed and improved through *timely, relevant*, and *accurate* information. Discuss how information overload or redundant information might affect the expectation gap.

## EXERCISES

1. Describe a WBS and list its characteristics. How does a WBS differ from the project network? How are the two linked?

2. Describe an information systems project: Define its scope, list major activities involved in that project, and develop a WBS for it.

3. A good example of an event project concerns the organization of a conference where you would need to coordinate many activities and be mindful of deadlines and commitments. Assume an international conference is to be held in your city in 26 weeks' time. Describe objectives, scope, work breakdown structure, deliverables, milestones, and criteria for success.

4. If available to you, use MS Project to develop a WBS using the information provided in Figure 4.2.

# APPENDIX TO CHAPTER 4: HENDRICH ELECTRONICS INCORPORATED

## Background

Hendrich Electronics is a 5-year-old electronics retail company based in Las Vegas, Nevada. Their annual sales are $4.9 million. The company has dealt solely with retailing. However, recently the owner and founder, Anthony Hendrich Sr., felt that it was time for him to retire. He turned the company over to his sons Anthony Jr. (Tony has a degree in business from Harvard) and Michael (who has a degree in civil engineering from MIT). From the very beginning, Michael has had a strong intuition that his father's company could grow rapidly and efficiently if it extended its activity.

## The Staff

Currently Hendrich Electronics employs 39 people. All employees, including the cashiers, must have a college degree in MIS, CIS, or engineering to be considered for a position at Hendrich Electronics. This HR policy had been initially designed by Anthony Hendrich Sr. Thanks to this high-level recruitment policy, amongst other factors, the company has built a solid reputation of capability, reactivity, and efficiency.

## The Product

The initial activity of Hendrich Electronics was dedicated to the retail of computers (desktops and laptops) in Nevada and California. Now, on behalf of Hendrich, we must consider a product designed by Michael that could potentially change Hendrich's business dramatically.

Michael has been working with two others (also graduates from MIT) named Jeff Swanks and Kyle Bolton to build a junior enterprise called CPUPARTS4U. The purpose of CPUPARTS4U was to create a small electronic parts company (producing switchboards, circuits, and silicon chips). Their project received a positive reaction from investors, retailers, and manufacturers. Then after 1 year of unexpectedly good results, the three young partners decided to further develop this adventure together.

Motivated by this initial success, Michael and his two partners have worked hard to design a new "kind" of laptop. The current prototype of this new laptop has a lot of specificities and features that might represent a revolutionary product!

What makes this laptop unique is the fact that when completely folded down, it fits in the palm of your hand (approximately the size of a 2.5" HD drive). And when fully expanded, it is the size of a small-screen laptop (12"). It is so compact that it can be placed into a suit or a jacket pocket.

The new technology concerns the way this laptop is built. The screen, keyboard, etc. have patented mechanisms so that when the keyboard and screen are fully expanded, they automatically lock in place (and for the user it appears as a solid conventional computer). However, when you want to close the unit you press a lever that releases a lock and it quickly folds it into a 2.5" block.

*(Continued)*

(Continued)

In addition, underneath the laptop there is a new battery pack that when fully charged will run for 10 hours. There is also a built-in battery charger that automatically begins to charge the battery when the laptop is turned off, using solar or regular light energy (it will take only 2 hours for the battery to get fully recharged). It has also a DVD/RW drive, a built-in WiFi/DSL modem, 2 GB of RAM, 500 GB hard disk (2.5"), and a satellite navigation system. The last feature is the touch-screen system that enables you to use it as a PDA whenever you want.

The prototype has been hand built by the three partners and used for some months for testing. After several technical adjustments, it seems robust and stable enough to launch it in mass-production, as a first proprietary Hendrich product.

## The Competition

Considering here only the retail aspect of the company, Hendrich has three electronics retail competitors: Radio Shack, Best Buy, and Circuit City. All three companies sell higher brand well-known laptops (IBM, HP, Dell, and Sony, to name a few).

## The Problem

Currently the prototype described is still not available to the public (Michael hoped to debut it at the HITEC convention last year but ran into some technical glitches). Following research of manufacturers and a large survey conducted among the targeted audience (upper-middle-class, trendy people) they decided to set up the retailing price of the laptop at $1,200.

Even though the laptop has such great potential, Michael is having a hard time trying to convince both Anthony Sr. and Tony, his brother, that this is a good investment.

While both feel that the company needs to grow, the elder Hendrich feels that the company should stick strictly with retailing (after all, that is where their reputation lies). Tony, on the other hand, doesn't have enough confidence in his brother to let him go into uncharted territories with the company's reputation. To make things easier, the two other partners of CPUPARTS4U agreed to work in collaboration with Hendrich Electronics for the production and retail of the laptop. They would then stay on full-time to continue to create these laptops as well as help come up with bigger and better ideas. In order to argue that the laptop project can be profitable for Hendrich Electronics, Michael needs to present a complete proposal to Tony and Anthony Sr.

Anthony Sr. has told Michael that if he can't get the project off the ground in 7 months he won't be able to go through with it. If he can get it off the ground and there is a good showing at the HITEC convention, they will get the contract to sell the laptops exclusively through Hendrich Electronics stores.

## Task

A project management team has to work with Anthony Sr. to figure out how long it would need before the product will be ready (the expected time they are shooting for is this year's HITEC convention at the end of November). The team, along with Michael, has 2 weeks to come up with the information and create a presentation to convince the rest of the company why they should allow Michael to pursue this project. In addition he must also work with the finance and marketing departments to try to figure out if it would be in the company's best interest to go ahead with this new venture.

## APPENDIX TO CHAPTER 4: DISCUSSION QUESTIONS

1. Construct a mind map of the situation described.

2. Do you feel that Anthony Sr. is doing the right thing by making Michael prove his product's worth?

3. Do you think that Hendrich 5000 has what it takes to compete with other laptops?

4. If you were Michael what would be your strategy at the presentation to convince others that they should invest in your idea?

5. At the time of reading, what do you think are the "exciting new IT developments"? Make a case for and against your business or university investing in this new technology.

6. The case was put together through interviews at Hendrich late in 2007. What aspects would need to be changed if the product were being proposed today?

7. Prepare a PowerPoint presentation to market either the original product or your new one to potential investors. Highlight the project management issues. Follow the presentation guidelines shown in Appendix 4a.

## APPENDIX 4A: GUIDELINES ON GIVING AN EFFECTIVE PRESENTATION

In this appendix we suggest principles and guidelines to help you present your work. ***Presentation matters!*** You have done the work and now it is time to tell everyone what you have done. So you owe yourself and your audience a good presentation. If you don't properly prepare your presentation, you are doing yourself and your audience a disservice. Good work and a good report do not make up for a bad presentation. Prepare for it.

Our first guideline concerns the general preparation that we call ***positioning the presentation***. Here we suggest that you ask yourself what kind of presentation you would expect if you were in the audience. You need to make your talk applicable to their work. It is necessary to establish a frame of reference for your audience and explain some of the peculiarities of your work. You should treat your subject broadly enough to cover the range of interests of attendees. The title of the presentation will be of key importance to this. Your title should engage the audience.

We suggest that you ***use active titles*** for each of your slides. The title should give the reason for a given slide, and a good title provides reinforcement for what you say. Use words that both relate to your topic and are familiar for most attendees. Avoid ambiguity, as you are not trying (or should not be trying) to confuse your audience.

***Focus your presentation***. Only the most important points need to be stressed, and do not provide great detail unless essential. You may have spent a long time doing the work and writing

*(Continued)*

(Continued)

your report, but you should not expect your audience to absorb and understand every detail of your work. This does not mean you should not be proud of your work or underestimate your work. It means don't get carried away. Too many details in a short period of time will bore your audience. Stay close to the core of your topic. You will have to summarize your main points.

The next point relates to structure. You should *use a suitable structure*. A well-structured presentation is pleasing to the average listener. Ask yourself how difficult it would be if someone with little to no knowledge about your topic were to describe your presentation and its value. Again, think about your audience. If an average attendee were to summarize your presentation, what would he or she say? What would be the key statements or headlines?

Next, *determine proper timing.* List the major points you intend to cover. Allocate time spent on each topic relative to its importance. One approach would be to break down your presentation into several sections and divide the entire time accordingly. Space your slides evenly over time, let ideas "sink in," and don't rush through. Don't strain the attention span of your audience by lingering on one slide; consider making multiple slides.

*Give insights*. Qualitative insights are usually more important than quantitative results. However, give summary results backed up by graphs and illustrative details. Comparative analyses are easier to relate to: "Based on these data, we found that approach A was twice as effective as approach B for distance learning." Again, avoid jargon.

*Think of audience attention*. Audience interest level is highest at the beginning and the end of a presentation. A good introduction and good summary of conclusions are very important. A good introduction persuades your audience to continue listening. That is when your audience will size you up. A good conclusion will leave your audience with something to remember. There is a well-tested formula for giving a good presentation: *Tell them what you're going to tell them. Tell them. Tell them what you told them.* No matter how good your presentation is, your audience attention will diminish somewhat during the body of your talk. As soon as you mention "in conclusion . . . ," you get their attention, so use it.

*Use visual aids*. Sight and sound are the two senses that your audience will have to absorb your presentation. Other senses won't come into play. Give equal importance to visual aids. Here is a test: Go through your slides and see whether they are meaningful without words and your words are meaningful without visual aids. If the answer to both is yes, then make sure they are properly coordinated.

*Make it relevant*. Have a good reason for showing each and every slide you use. Ask yourself, "Why am I showing this slide?" Ask yourself whether the slide accomplishes what you want. Don't combine results of little or no value with those that have key values. It will diminish the significance of your key findings. If in doubt, use some sort of priority scale.

Similarly, *make it useful*. Make sure your slides are readable. Make sure your slides are easy to understand. Enlarging some prints, such as a computer printout, may not solve the problem. Avoid including too much information on a single slide. Use similarities with, and differences from, ideas to which the audience can relate. Relate your work and results to findings of others.

Finally, ***don't read your slides, and don't memorize.*** Rehearse for presentation length and spacing of slides. However, rehearsing too much may take away spontaneity, making your talk boring. Memorizing does the same. There is a difference between presentation and speech or oration. Presentation is like a talk with your audience. It is normal to be a little nervous; practice in order to improve the situation. Don't give excuses: "I know that you probably cannot read all the data on this slide, but . . ." You are telling them that fixing that problem was not important for you and that you do not care. Excuses will turn off your audience (rightfully). Take time to prepare an "excuse-free" presentation. Finally, don't forget: Some rules are meant to be broken, but have good reason!

## BIBLIOGRAPHY

Avison, D., & Fitzgerald, G. (2006). *Information systems development: Methodologies, techniques and tools* (4th ed.). Maidenhead, UK: McGraw-Hill.

Buzan, A. (2003). *The mind map book: Radiant thinking—Major evolution in human thought.* London: BBC Active.

Clark, K. B. (1989). Project scope and project performance: The effect of parts strategy and supplier involvement on product development. *Management Science, 35*(10).

Fowler, M., & Scott, K. (1997). *UML distilled: Applying the standard object modeling language.* Harlow, UK: Addison-Wesley.

Gary, C. F., & Larson, E. W. (2000). *Project management: The managerial process.* New York: Irwin/McGraw-Hill.

Hofstede, G., & Hofstede, G. J. (2005). *Cultures and organizations: Software of the mind* (2nd ed.). New York: McGraw-Hill.

Leffingwell, D. (1997). Calculating the return on investment from more effective requirements management. *American Programmer, 10*(4), 13–16.

Schneiderman, A. M. (1999, January). Why balanced scorecards fail. *Journal of Strategic Performance Management,* 6–12.

Turner, J. R., & Cochrane, R. A. (1993). Goals-and-methods matrix: Coping with projects with ill-defined goals and/or methods of achieving them. *International Journal of Project Management, 11.*

# 5

# Estimating Project Costs and Benefits

The triple constraints of time, cost, and scope set boundaries for information systems projects. The effective management of information systems projects depends, to a large extent, on how well these constraints are defined, documented, and managed. Each of these constraints is a yardstick for monitoring progress and ultimately for measuring project success. Cost estimates provide a fiscal boundary within which a project is designed, developed, and implemented. Accurate estimates are critical to the decision-making process. Management and project sponsors pay close attention to cost estimates in their decision to support a project and when evaluating its success. Experienced information systems project managers take cost estimating seriously and plan for it carefully. This chapter first describes ways of assessing project value. It then describes several techniques and sources to help estimate cost. It describes important considerations that help project managers in their efforts to develop reliable cost estimates. Last, it looks at group decision support whereby computer software is used to support decision making based on qualitative rather than quantitative analysis. But first we look at the UK record in estimating costs.

---

**Exhibit 5.1  Spiraling Costs in Public Projects—And It Is Not Just Information Systems! . . . and Some More Positive Examples**

## Spiraling Costs and . . .

"A new computer system to allocate benefit payments has suffered a 'massive breakdown' that could cost millions of pounds in excess and fraudulent payments. The failure of NIRS II, which cost £170 million [US $340m], could affect more than 80,000 benefit applicants." (Modified from the BBC News Web site [http://news.bbc.co.uk/1/hi/uk/168277.stm], September 10, 1998.)

"The UK's public sector IT projects in 2003 and 2004 are expected to cost more than £14 billion [US $28 bn], but UK government IT projects have often been accused of being over-ambitious and prone to disastrous delays and cost overruns." (Modified from *ComputerWorld*, November 26, 2004.)

"A new computer system used to process benefits payments has been scrapped at a cost to the taxpayer of £141m [US $282m]. The IT project, key to streamlining payments by the Department for Work and Pensions (DWP), was quietly axed at an internal meeting last month. The project had been central to delivering savings of more than £60m [US $120m] for the DWP by 2008. It is the latest in a long series of computer problems for the government. DWP pays out around £100bn [US $200bn] a year in benefits through a variety of computer systems." (Modified from the BBC News Web site [http://news.bbc.co.uk/1/hi/uk_politics/5315280.stm], September 5, 2006.) BBC, 5 September 2006)

"MPs are concerned that the cost of running the IT system used by HM Revenue & Customs has run out of control after the payments the Government department pays its technology suppliers ballooned to £8bn [US $16bn] from £4.5bn." (Modified from the *Independent*, March 14, 2007.)

"How much will the London 2012 Olympics really cost? The simple answer is, no one knows. So take your pick, anywhere from the official figure of £3.3bn [US $6.6bn] to the wilder shores of journalistic inflation, currently around the £10bn [US $20bn] mark." (Modified from the *Guardian*, January 25, 2007) . . . and two month's later . . . "The budget for the 2012 London Olympics has risen to £9.35bn [US $18.7bn], Culture Secretary Tessa Jowell has told MPs (Modified from the BBC News Web site, March 15, 2007.)

## . . . the Other Side of the Story

In their report "Delivering Successful IT-Enabled Business Change," the UK National Audit Office provided and discussed many examples of "success stories"—for example:

The payment modernization program for the Department for Work and Pensions has transformed the payment of benefits and pensions by paying entitlements directly into recipients' bank accounts.

The Small Business Service within the Department of Trade and Industry has created a Web site (businesslink.gov.uk) providing support, advice, and services to businesses in the UK.

The Department for Environment, Food and Rural Affairs, with the Eaga Partnership, has provided the Warm Front Scheme for citizens at risk of fuel poverty, which is a package of energy efficiency and heating measures to install or upgrade insulation and heating systems in their homes.

The Vehicle and Operator Services Agency's Operator Self Service has modernized the approach to issuing Heavy Goods Vehicle Licenses by redesigning the business process and IT support for the vehicle licensing business, enabling operators to carry out most license transactions online at any time.

eSourcing provided by OGCbuying.solutions enables secure collaborative tools used by procurement professionals and suppliers to conduct strategic procurement activities online, including tendering, negotiation, contract award, and management, to deliver value for money procurement solutions to the public sector.

The NHS UK Transplant service has created the National Transplant Database, which provides a fast and accurate matching system to enable organs to reach patients as soon as organs become available for transplant.

United States Department of Defense Identity Management Program provides military personnel with a Common Access Card to improve identity assurance and reduce fraud.

The New York City Mayor's Office's New York City 311 Citizen Service Center provides access to all government information and non-emergency services in the New York City area through a single telephone number. NYC 311 is available 24 hours a day, with operators providing services in over 170 languages.

The Enterprise Virtual Operations Center brings together real-time data from the City of Anaheim's (California) emergency services and makes the data securely accessible via the Internet, enabling city officials to see what is happening on all the city's critical response fronts.

## 5.1. Estimating Costs and Benefits

The overall cost of a project is a key determinant for management in deciding whether to support a project. This overall cost is based on the aggregate cost of work units described in the work breakdown structure (Section 4.3). The accuracy of a work unit estimate is a function of how well that work unit is defined and the knowledge and experience of the estimator. The work-unit approach makes the process of cost estimating more manageable. It is easier to estimate and assign cost for a work unit than a large section of a project. However, there might be situations in which the overall cost of the project is required for the initial decision and before the WBS and work unit analysis is done. In such cases, the project manager needs to provide estimates of the overall costs as best as possible and describe conditions that will influence the accuracy of those estimates. In other situations, some leeway regarding costs is accepted in the organization, and in others renegotiation might be possible, but very often the first estimate is the one that the project manager has to "live with."

Some costs are considered tangible, while others are described as intangible. Further, costs are classified as direct or indirect. These are all described below.

## Tangible Costs and Benefits

Tangible costs and benefits are easier to define and thus to measure. Consider, for example, setting up a computer network lab. This network will need monitors, microprocessors, routers, switches, connectors, cables, servers, and the like. It will also need an operating system and various applications software. First, we need to determine the type of hardware and software that will support the goals and objectives of the lab best (as described in the project scope discussed in Chapter 4). Next, we need to determine the vendors that we want to purchase from. Some organizations use a list of authorized vendors that they usually purchase from. This list is based on service, price, reliability, past experience, and the like. These vendors are then surveyed for estimates of hardware and software costs. Multiple vendors may be surveyed, and the average price may be used for cost estimates. Tangible benefits are also more straightforward to measure. For example, if a new information system saves 5 hours per week per person for 100 employees, then the total benefit for the year is 6,000 hours ($5 * 100 * 12 = 6,000$). The benefit in monetary terms can be calculated by multiplying the 6,000 hours by the average cost of workers per hour.

## Intangible Costs and Benefits

Intangible costs and benefits are more difficult to define and to measure. Consider, for example, a proposal to outsource the information system services of an organization. While this might be advantageous in terms of cost saving and efficiency, it can also have disadvantages associated with it. It is easier in this case to estimate the tangible costs and benefits of this decision. For example, it is easier to compare what it costs to provide the services internally compared with the outsourcing option. However, outsourcing the information systems function will diminish organizational expertise and know-how over time. Replacing such expertise is much more expensive if the organization decides in the future to reverse this decision and once again insource the information systems function. However, it is difficult to estimate the replacement cost of such expertise and know-how. Other examples of intangible costs in this case are the loss of control and the security risk. Again, it will be very difficult to allocate dollar amounts for the diminished control or information security. Examples of intangible benefits of insourcing include employee learning in the information systems development process that adds to the know-how of the department and organization or the increased satisfaction and use due to employee involvement in information systems development. While it is obvious that increased use of a system is beneficial, it is difficult to assign dollar amounts to the incremental increase.

## Direct Cost

Costs that are easily associated with a work unit are classified as direct costs. For example, if two individuals need to spend 10 hours each to accomplish a work unit, then these 20 hours are directly accounted for in the budget for that work unit. The project manager who is in charge of the entire project spends some of his or her time overseeing the progress of this work unit. Therefore, that portion of the project manager's time is also directly associated with this work unit and must be charged to the account for this work unit. There are other such costs that are usually prorated using percentages. These include management costs, facility expenses, rental arrangement costs, and the like. These costs are called ***direct overhead costs*** and usually occur for the entire project rather than a work unit. There are different ways of allocating these direct overhead costs to individual work units. One approach is to consider units of time spent on a work unit relative to the total time for the entire project. For example, if a project takes 120 hours to complete and a work unit in that project takes 18 hours to complete, then direct overhead costs for that work unit are 15%.

### Indirect Cost

Indirect costs are not easily associated with a work unit or a project. These include overall organizational costs that are incurred by all activities of the organization. For example, if an organization spends $1 million to enhance its image and credibility within the industry, the outcome of such expenditure is expected to benefit all units and functions of the organization. It is difficult to charge a portion of $1 million to a project in one department that has a life cycle of 5 years. Nevertheless, those dollars must be recovered by all activities of the organization. These indirect costs are often prorated. One approach to arrive at a cost percentage for a project is to consider the cost of the project relative to the overall administrative cost of the organization. Sometimes the number of employees in a functional area as a portion of the total number of employees in the organization is used for allocating these costs. To arrive at a relative cost of a project, the number of people working on the project is divided by the total number of people in the information systems function. In any case, these cost allocations are subjective relative to direct overhead costs.

## 5.2. Project Value

In this section we look at three techniques to estimate the value of a project—that is, the balance of benefits over costs (which can, of course, be negative).

### Payback Analysis

Payback analysis is a frequently used financial approach for deciding whether a project should be selected for development. Most organizations would like to know how long it takes before their technology investment results in a positive cash flow. *The payback period is therefore the length of time that it takes a company to recover the amount of money invested in the technology.* This will be the time after which the company starts earning from their investment. For short-term investors in technology the payback time will be 1 or 2 years, whereas organizations with a longer strategic plan may be looking into the future and are prepared to invest in technology and only expect returns in the long-term (usually seen as 5 or more years).

The payback occurs when the cumulative benefits are greater than cumulative costs. Consider two information systems proposals submitted by two departments for consideration and approval by top management. The first proposal is for an information system to track sales and advertising data and to produce reports and charts for the incremental sales increases that result from spending on advertising. This system will help management determine the relative impact on sales of print media, radio, and TV in the long term. The second proposal is for an information system that controls online communications between employees and customers and that reports frequency, duration, and outcome of such communication in terms of customer satisfaction and sales.

The projected cost and revenue for the next 6 years for Projects A and B are presented in Table 5.1. For example, cost and revenue for Project A during the first year of development is $20,000 and $0, respectively, resulting in net cost of $20,000. The first year numbers for Project B are $25,000 cost and $10,000 revenue, resulting in net cost of $15,000. The total cost over the 6-year period is $70,000 for Project A and $85,000 for Project B. The total revenue over the same period is $120,000 for Project A and $130,000 for Project B. The net benefit over the 6-year period is therefore $50,000 for Project A and $45,000 for Project B.

Payback analysis suggests that Project A, having recovered its costs, generates benefit in Year 4, whereas Project B recovers cost and generates benefit in Year 3. Therefore, Project B is seen as a better investment given these results using this technique. Notice that Project A generates more benefit in 6 years than Project B would. This analysis stresses *how quickly* costs of a project are recovered and how soon a project starts generating benefit; it does not take into account benefits over the life of the information system, in this case a 6-year period. Some organizations have a fixed payback time beyond which they would not support any project development plan. In our example, if the organization requires a payback time of only 2 years, neither of these two

❖ Table 5.1   Payback Analysis for Two Projects

| Project A | Yr 1 | Yr 2 | Yr 3 | Yr 4 | Yr 5 | Yr 6 | Total |
|---|---|---|---|---|---|---|---|
| Cost | 20,000 | 20,000 | 10,000 | 10,000 | 5,000 | 5,000 | 70,000 |
| Revenue | 0 | 0 | 30,000 | 40,000 | 30,000 | 20,000 | 120,000 |
| Difference | (20,000) | (20,000) | 20,000 | 30,000 | 25,000 | 15,000 | 50,000 |
| Cumulative | (20,000) | (40,000) | (20,000) | 10,000 | 35,000 | 50,000 | |
| Project B | Yr 1 | Yr 2 | Yr 3 | Yr 4 | Yr 5 | Yr 6 | Total |
| Cost | 25,000 | 25,000 | 15,000 | 10,000 | 5,000 | 5,000 | 85,000 |
| Revenue | 10,000 | 15,000 | 45,000 | 30,000 | 20,000 | 10,000 | 130,000 |
| Difference | (15,000) | (10,000) | 30,000 | 20,000 | 15,000 | 5,000 | 45,000 |
| Cumulative | (15,000) | (25,000) | 5,000 | 25,000 | 40,000 | 45,000 | |

projects would be approved. Some organizations use a payback period of only 1 year for IT projects, and projects that do not pass this severe test are not pursued!

The length of payback is influenced by organizational culture, strategic plan, top management decision pattern, or simply economic data. The payback for information technology investment is relatively shorter than other technologies where the rate of change is not as great. With rapid changes in information technology innovation and development, organizations are concerned that the technology they are investing in may be obsolete before long. This results in expectations of quick results. However, large and complex information systems development projects require long-term commitment, and expectations of quick results may not be in the long-term interests of the organization. Many projects seen as *strategic* rather than *operational* may be of this type and, as shown in Chapter 2, omitting them because they do not provide payback within a year or two may be to the detriment of the firm.

This poses challenges for project managers to convince top management that in some cases the long-term projection of results is necessary. They need to explain why a "quick return" policy may not always be in the company's best interest for long-term viability. The well-known cases of the frequent-flyer program by American Airlines and the direct ordering system by American Hospital Supply are good examples of long-term strategic decisions that involved significant cost and time commitment but resulted in important long-term competitive advantage. This does not mean that organizations should not expect a speedy payback in some cases. In fact, specific systems designed to respond to well-defined problems should normally recoup expenses quickly.

## Net Present Value

Net present value (NPV) is another approach that is often used to evaluate the expected monetary gain or loss of a project. It is based on the calculation of expected cash flow. Projects should reflect positive cash flow to be considered for development and the higher this positive cash flow, as calculated by NPV analysis, the more likelihood of support for its development. *This approach uses a rate of interest to calculate the present value of the future cost and benefit for a project.* The rate of interest used is based on the cost of capital. In other words, how much would the company earn from its capital if the company were to invest that capital elsewhere.

The formula for calculating NPV is:

$$\text{NPV} = \sum_{t=1 \ldots n} A/(1 + r)^t$$

where $t$ represents the year of the cash flows, $A$ represents the amount of cash flow each year, and $r$ represents the discount rate. Using a specified rate of interest, this formula sums up the present value for the number of years that estimates have been made. For example, at 15%, the present value of $3,000 cost projected for the third year of a project is $1972.50, calculated as:

$$\$3,000 * 1/(1 + 0.15)^3 \text{ or}$$
$$\$3,000 * 0.6575 = \$1972.50$$

Let us consider another example. The present value for $2,000 projected value in the third year for the same project and with the same interest rate is $1,512.20, calculated as:

$$\$2,000 * 1/(1 + 0.15)^3 \text{ or}$$

$$\$2,000 * 0.7561 = \$1512.30$$

The net present value for the third year cost and benefit for this project is a negative amount of $460.30 ($1,512.20 − $1,972.50 = −$460.30).

The sum of this calculation for estimated cost and benefit for all years represents the present value for the project and is used to make a decision. Most spreadsheet packages (such as Microsoft Excel) have a function to calculate NPV. However, it is useful to see the process and understand the discounted amount of one dollar for a given interest rate. To calculate the NPV for the two projects presented in Table 5.1, we can first calculate the *discount factor*, the present value of one dollar, for each year and use that to calculate the present value for the projected cost and revenue amounts given in Table 5.1. The discount factors for this example are shown in Table 5.2.

Using the discount factor and the cash flow information (difference between revenue and cost), we can calculate NPV for Project A as shown in Exhibit 5.2.

Following this process, we obtain an NPV of $20,176 for Project B. Therefore, Project B gives a better present value for the company based on these calculations. All else being equal, the NPV analysis suggests that Project B is a better option for development, even though Project A generates more cash inflow ($5,000) by the end of Year 6.

## Return on Investment

Return on investment (ROI) is another financial measure that is used to decide the relative worth of a project. ROI is calculated as discounted benefits minus discounted costs divided by discounted costs multiplied by 100. For example a 20% ROI means that if you spend $1 this year, it is worth $1.20 next year. To calculate the ROI for this

❖ Table 5.2   Discount Factors for 6 Years at 15%

| Year | Formula | Discount Factor |
|:---:|:---:|:---:|
| 1 | $1/(1+0.15)^1$ | 0.8696 |
| 2 | $1/(1+0.15)^2$ | 0.7561 |
| 3 | $1/(1+0.15)^3$ | 0.6575 |
| 4 | $1/(1+0.15)^4$ | 0.5718 |
| 5 | $1/(1+0.15)^5$ | 0.4972 |
| 6 | $1/(1+0.15)^6$ | 0.4323 |

**Exhibit 5.2   Estimating the Net Present Value**

Year 1 = .8696 * ($20,000) = ($17,392)

Year 2 = .7561 * ($20,000) = ($15,122)

Year 3 = .6575 * $20,000 = $13,150

Year 4 = .5718 * $30,000 = $17,154

Year 5 = .4972 * $25,000 = $12,430

Year 6 = .4323 * $15,000 = $6,485

NPV (Project A) = $\Sigma_{t=1\ldots n} A/(1 + r)^t$ = **$16,705**

❖ Table 5.3   ROI Analysis for Project A

| Year | Factor | Revenue | Disc. Rev. | Cost | Disc. Cost |
|------|--------|---------|-----------|------|-----------|
| 1 | 0.8696 | $0 | $0 | ($20,000) | ($17,392) |
| 2 | 0.7561 | $0 | $0 | ($20,000) | ($15,122) |
| 3 | 0.6575 | $30,000 | $19,725 | ($10,000) | ($6,575) |
| 4 | 0.5718 | $40,000 | $22,872 | ($10,000) | ($5,718) |
| 5 | 0.4972 | $30,000 | $14,916 | ($5,000) | ($2,486) |
| 6 | 0.4323 | $20,000 | $8,646 | ($5,000) | ($2,162) |
| Total | | $120,000 | $66,159 | ($70,000) | ($49,455) |

example, you need to divide the net income by investment that is $(120 - 100)/100 = 0.2$ or 20%. The higher the ROI, the better is the choice.

Tables 5.3 and 5.4 show the ROI calculations for Project A and Project B, respectively. These analyses suggest that Project A and Project B provide similar ROI (33.8% versus 33.1%). It might be necessary to consider other factors about these two projects since it is difficult in this case to make a decision solely on the basis of ROI.

ROI for Project A = $(66{,}159 - 49{,}455)/49{,}455 * 100 =$ **33.8%**

ROI for Project B = $(81{,}047 - 60{,}872)/60{,}872 * 100 =$ **33.1%**

A word of caution is appropriate here. There is a risk in using a single measure to evaluate the potential contribution of a project. While many organizations want information systems projects to have a fairly short payback period and as a result put more weight on the payback analysis for their decisions, they should still consider net

❖ Table 5.4   ROI Analysis for Project B

| Year | Factor | Revenue | Disc. Rev. | Cost | Disc. Cost |
|------|--------|---------|-----------|------|-----------|
| 1 | 0.8696 | $10,000 | $8,696 | ($25,000) | ($21,740) |
| 2 | 0.7561 | $15,000 | $11,342 | ($25,000) | ($18,903) |
| 3 | 0.6575 | $45,000 | $29,588 | ($15,000) | ($9,863) |
| 4 | 0.5718 | $30,000 | $17,154 | ($10,000) | ($5,718) |
| 5 | 0.4972 | $20,000 | $9,944 | ($5,000) | ($2,486) |
| 6 | 0.4323 | $10,000 | $4,323 | ($5,000) | ($2,162) |
| Total | | $130,000 | $81,047 | ($85,000) | ($60,872) |

present value and return on investment. However, many organizations put a limit on the payback period and would not consider projects that do not meet that criterion. Similarly, many organizations use a minimum rate of return on investment as a criterion for selecting projects. There are advantages and disadvantages to having rigid standards. Advantages include consistency in approval process, ease of communicating selection criteria, rapid evaluation process, less politics, and so on. Disadvantages include lack of flexibility for professional judgment, fewer innovative proposals by employees who are not sure whether their ideas will satisfy criteria, and the like.

## 5.3. Resource Estimates

All three methods described earlier rely on the estimates presented in Table 5.1. Cost and benefit estimates for any project are always subject to variations and adjustments. Therefore, some discretion is prudent, especially for close results such as the ROI results presented above for Projects A and B. Estimates are critical for allocating resources, monitoring progress, controlling quality, maintaining team moral, awarding merit, and ultimately ensuring project success. There are several ways of obtaining estimates, and most estimates are based on experience, documentation, expert opinion, or a combination of these sources. Each of these methods has advantages and disadvantages.

*Experience* is a valuable source for obtaining estimates. It incorporates different dimensions, such as the culture of the workplace, the pool of talent, the history of interorganizational cooperation, and human resource policies. It can also be affected by organizational culture and the top management decision-making style. In some cases, individuals giving estimates tend to overestimate cost, time, and other required resources. This is partly due to the fact that most information systems projects have tended to be behind schedule and over budget. Individuals react to this reality and tend to give "safe" estimates. Further, a study of human nature would suggest that individuals who expect to be involved with the information systems development process might pad their estimates, since it will appear to lighten their work and deadline. If only those individuals who are expected to work on the project provided estimates, then the overall cost and time estimates could turn out to be much higher than the actual figures.

*Documentation* is frequently used as a source for obtaining estimates, especially in environments in which information systems development activities are more formalized and projects are administratively closed. Documentation is considered a very useful source when it is relatively current and when it describes similar cases. To the extent that it deals with actual events of a project, documentation is free from bias and offers an advantage over estimates obtained from individuals. However, with the rapid growth of technology and developmental tools, documentation can quickly become dated, although information on relative cost and time for activities within a project is still useful. When using documentation for estimates it is important to consider events and situations that may have changed. This might include new laws, new equipment, changes in working hours, and the number of holidays and vacations.

*Expert opinion* is also a widely used source for obtaining cost, time, and other estimates. Internal expert opinion has similar pluses and minuses discussed under experience. Outside expertise can potentially benefit from broader experience and reduced game-playing. This source is often also used for new and innovative systems where little internal expertise is available. However, it might be limited, since outside experts may not have a good understanding of the organizational culture. Obtaining estimates through outside expertise is more formalized and costly compared with the two approaches described above. Outside experts and consultants often require internal visits and ask for more information as part of their work. Confidentiality is an important issue that management must consider when outside experts are sought, especially for the development of strategic information systems.

*Scenario planning* is also widely used in projects in which there is a greater element of risk (discussed more fully in Chapter 10 along with other techniques to deal with risk). Scenario planning looks at the different views about what the future might turn out to be and therefore enables the factoring in of many potential outcomes and estimates.

Again, it is prudent to use a combination of these approaches for situations in which highly innovative projects are considered or in which significant resources are involved. For example, using a combination of internal and external expertise has the advantage of knowledge and information about organizational culture (internal expertise) and a broad experience (external expertise). As described earlier, overestimation can happen, especially when individuals giving estimates expect to be involved with the project development. Underestimation can also occur. It happens where the same people who propose a project are involved with providing estimates and in their eagerness to obtain approval for their project they underestimate time and cost. Obtaining accurate time and cost estimates is an important skill set for successful project managers. The deliberate falsification of estimates is not only unethical (Section 1.8) but unwise, as the project manager will be seen as either unethical or incompetent. However, accurate estimation is not easy.

Issues of overestimation and underestimation pose challenges to the process of project selection. It is important to establish guidelines not only for proposal development in general but also for obtaining time and cost estimates. Guidelines could suggest that supporting material should be provided that details estimates and how they are arrived at. Track records for project activities and individual performance provide a historical backdrop for managers to adjust their expectations and provide a firm basis from which to make decisions accordingly. For example, managers may regularly ask project initiators or proposal developers to adjust their estimates by a certain percentage. Of course this prompts those initiating an idea or developing a project proposal to overestimate or underestimate cost and time accordingly. This cycle creates game play and a nonproductive environment.

But even the apparently simplest of estimates can in reality be difficult to make. To take one example, the contributions of colleagues will of course not be the same. A person-hour contribution from one worker will almost certainly be different from another. But most calculations are based on the assumption that the contributions from equivalent-status workers will be the same. Further, although we discuss the question of team selection in Chapter 9, in many circumstances the composition of the team will be determined by others and imposed on the project manager, and team members will differ in their effectiveness and individual efficiencies.

Organizational politics and game play are counter-effective and often result in poor estimates and wrong decisions. It is important to establish clear and realistic guidelines and communicate them to all employees. A project selection committee or individuals should follow these guidelines and be consistent in their analysis and in granting awards. It might be necessary to reward project teams and project managers who provide accurate estimates and complete their projects within time and within budget. While game play has two sides to it as described earlier, it is the responsibility of management to discourage it. Game play and politics are associated with organizational culture and that is closely associated with management decision-making style.

## 5.4. Estimating Software Development Costs

Project managers have found that poor estimating surrounding software production has been a major cause of problems. In the past, estimating the time and cost for software development seems to have been largely made on the basis of guesswork. However, this should no longer be the case. There are now many techniques to aid good estimation that can be used. Two of these techniques are CoCoMo and function point analysis.

*CoCoMo* is an acronym derived from *Constructive Cost Model*. The model is an approximation of the cost, effort, and time needed to complete a software project. The original CoCoMo model was published in 1981, based on a study of hundreds of software projects. In the 1990s and with the rise of new software development practices, such as the use of off-the-shelf components, the model was adapted to the needs of the day by the original authors. The name of the model was consequently changed to CoCoMo II (see http://sunset.usc.edu/research/COCOMOII).

CoCoMo comes in three forms—Basic, Intermediate, and Detailed—each one offering greater detail and accuracy. Basic CoCoMo identifies three classes of software projects and tries to give an estimation of the people-months needed to wrap up the project. The software project may consist of developing a simple, detached, and relatively small piece of code called Organic, a relatively complex software with some rigidity in requirements called Semidetached, or a completely integrated software with multiple hardware, software, and operational constraints referred to as Embedded.

CoCoMo, in its basic form, consists of the following formulas:

$$E = a_b(KLOC)^b{}_b$$

$$D = c_b(E)^d{}_b$$

$$P = E/D$$

Where E stands for effort, D for development time, P for people required, and KLOC for 1,000 lines of code. The coefficients $a_b$, $b_b$, $c_b$, and $d_b$ are determined by the class of the project and are given in the model documentation. So if Organic software of 9,600 instructions is to be developed, then:

$$E = 2.4(9.6)^{1.05}$$

or

25.799 (nearly 25.8 people-months)

and

$$D = 2.5(25.8)^{0.38}$$

or

8.596 (nearly 8 months and 18 days)

and finally

$$P = 25.8/8.6$$

or

3 developers are required

Basic DoCoMo gives a quick estimation of the time and human resources needed to accomplish a project, but it ignores some important factors such as personnel quality and experience, required reliability and complexity, and hardware constraints. Intermediate and Detailed CoCoMo take into account more factors in order to increase the reliability of the estimation. Obviously this increased level of accuracy comes at a price. It complicates the calculation and, more important, requires heavier data collection. CoCoMo II supports the use of either lines of source code or number of function points as input.

*Function point analysis,* is a method that measures the size of an information system in terms of functions. It tries to estimate the functionality of the system being delivered to the end-user, in a way understandable by both users and developers. It does this by analyzing the system in terms of function points. Basic function points are usually categorized into five groups: outputs, inquiries, inputs, files, and interfaces. A function point is one end-user business function, such as a query for a printed or an onscreen output.

The method has been used to estimate a software project's size, establish productivity rates, evaluate support requirements, estimate system change costs, and normalize the comparison of software modules. The criteria used are easier for analysts to estimate than simply the number of lines of program code. Even so, the complexity ratios and other adjustment factors require an experienced analyst to estimate. Tables have been created to help determine the effort and elapsed time required to complete the project.

An estimate of the technical complexity, along with such considerations as staff experience and deadline pressure, can also be calibrated in the formula to make allowance for these differences. The weight for each criterion is based on measurements from previously developed systems. At its most sophisticated, this approach will take into consideration supervision levels, documentation, quality levels required, training required, familiarization required, data conversion, reviewing required, technical support required, staff experience, and user involvement among other factors.

Function points have rather a large user community, with 1,200 members who can assist you in establishing an FPA program (see www.ifpug.org).

Our experience suggests that the Basic CoCoMo device usually provides a workable estimation for the project manager. Experienced software developers can provide further sophistication in estimating if required.

## 5.5. Multiple Estimates

Obtaining good estimates is challenging and difficult. It is easier to obtain estimates of work units and individual activities. Therefore, estimates should be gathered using a *bottom-up* approach and should start after individual work units are determined and defined. The exception to this is when a quick and rough estimate of the overall resources for a proposed project is sufficient for an initial decision. These are situations in which time is a real constraint or the project idea is so tentative that it does not warrant spending a great deal of time to obtain estimates at the moment. In such exceptional cases, the management gives some idea as to how rough an estimate is necessary for their initial go or no-go decision at the conceptual stage.

It is easier for experts to provide estimates for well-defined and specific tasks. It is easier to define work units if the project scope is clearly developed. Estimates that do not involve memory recollection are more accurate. If it is difficult to estimate time and cost for a work unit, it might be useful to revisit the definition and the expected outcome for that work unit. The involvement of team members and individuals who will be working on project activities for obtaining estimates is important. Their involvement normally leads to an increased accuracy of estimates as well as commitment to the project. This also encourages estimates from people who are the most knowledgeable about a task.

In many cases, *multiple estimates* of activity cost and time is strongly recommended. The same expert can be asked to provide a range of estimates for a project activity that includes *the best-case scenario, the worst-case scenario*, and *the most probable scenario.*

Weights can be assigned to each of these scenarios to obtain a more realistic average. For example, the best and the worst scenarios may be assigned 1 point, whereas several points (frequently 4) may be assigned to the most likely scenario. Alternatively, different experts can be asked to provide estimates for the same activity. Again, weights can be assigned to these estimates depending on what we know about the experts, their past estimates, and their knowledge and experience. In any case, efforts must be made to match the tasks and skills of those giving estimates.

In cases in which multiple estimates are obtained, average scores as well as the variance are used for decision making. The smaller the variance for a set of estimates, the more specific the results. Where there is a large divergence between estimates, it is prudent to provide for **contingency resources**, especially in cases where there is little or no flexibility in deadlines. We can calculate "upper limit" and "lower limit" measures of a project's duration using the average score and the variance. Let us assume that you have collected three estimates for each of the 27 activities of a project to develop a group decision support system for strategic decision making in your organization. Your calculations suggest an overall estimate of 165 hours for the entire project and a standard deviation of 29 hours. Assuming plus and minus 3 standard deviations, you can obtain the results shown in Exhibit 5.3.

| Exhibit 5.3 | Taking Account of Contingency Factors |
|---|---|
| The project upper limit | $(3 * 29 + 165) = 252$ hours |
| The project lower limit | $(-3 * 29 + 165) = 78$ hours |
| Upper limit as % of estimate | $(252/165)100 = 152.73\%$ |
| Lower limit as % of estimate | $(78/165)100 = 47.27\%$ |

This suggests that there is a very high probability that the entire project will be complete within 78 to 252 hours. This range suggests that the project completion time may be overextended or underextended by about 53%. Section 5.8 provides an overview of a DSS software package. More discussion on probability of completing a project on time is given in Chapter 6 on time management.

## 5.6. Phase Estimating

In some cases, estimates are possible only for the initial phase of the project, and projection of cost and time for the subsequent phases depends on the outcome of the earlier phases. It is unrealistic to obtain estimates for the entire project when there is a great deal of uncertainty associated with the design of the system or with the outcome or the final product. In such cases, detailed estimates are only made as the project progresses. This process is called **phase estimating**. Phase estimating can be based on the project development life cycle: initiation, planning, development, implementation, and closure.

In other words, detailed estimates of cost and time are made for one or two cycles at a given time, and rough estimates are generated for subsequent cycles. An example of phase estimating may be a three-stage projection of resources: The first one covers initiation and planning, the second one covers development, and the third and final one covers implementation and closure. After completion of one phase, detailed estimates are provided for the next phase and the process continues until the entire project is complete. Any approach to estimating cost and time, including the multiple-estimate approach, can be applied at each stage when detailed projections are necessary.

Phase estimating suggests that project owners and sponsors must commit to a project with incomplete information about how much it might cost and how long it might take, and that is rarely an easy situation. Information on project resources is important to project sponsors as they decide whether or not to support a project. It is a challenging job to convince sponsors, especially conservative-minded ones, to support a project without any certainty about its final cost. Incomplete information also makes project managers uncomfortable as they provide incomplete or inaccurate estimates for projects that involve a great deal of uncertainty. Inaccurate or incomplete estimates create credibility issues affecting support for future projects.

Phase estimating is an appropriate response to such situations. The project manager must convince the sponsors and other stakeholders that this approach is necessary. It is important to point out that the project sponsors have the option of terminating support after each phase if they are not satisfied with progress. In other words, their support for subsequent phases is conditional upon satisfactory progress of the ongoing phase. The sponsor does not have to make commitments to parts that they do not have estimates for, and the project manager does not have to provide estimates that may be unreliable. Both parties potentially benefit from this "compromise" approach.

## 5.7. Practical Considerations

Estimates are used to make decisions, to prepare schedules, to negotiate contracts, to set goals, to evaluate performance, to request funding, and so on. Expectations are based on estimates. Project stakeholders including the project manager would like to have and work with accurate estimates. While they can be based on realistic means and methods, estimates do not replace actual numbers. Events happen, technology advances, biases creep in, and priorities, goals, and objectives change. The project manager and team members should make every effort to obtain and report accurate estimates. They should be consistent in applying their methods to obtain estimates and should report to the stakeholders their methods of preparing estimates as clearly as possible. Any hint of secrecy in describing why a certain methodology is used will erode the *credibility of the estimates* and *of those preparing the estimates*, in the mind of the customer.

The strengths and weaknesses of the methodology should be clearly explained. It is not as important to apply a method that is prominent as it is to apply a method that is appropriate. The project manager must be able to articulate the reasons for using a certain method of estimating cost and time. It is also important to specify the time horizon for estimates. Cost estimates for equipment, software, expertise, and the like may change quickly, and if the estimating process takes too long the project manager may need to review and adjust estimates that were obtained early in the process. Further, a *learning curve* may become a factor when estimating time and cost for repetitive activities. The assumption here is that repeating the same activity over and over results in less and less time and cost for that activity. However, the learning curve results depend on the learning ability of the individual and the nature of the task. Of course there is a limit to how far one can improve the process or learn to do an activity faster. Based on experience, estimates for repeated activity are adjusted.

Estimates should be free of extreme projections. In other words, estimates must be based on *normal conditions* and free from extreme-case assumptions. For example, a normal shift includes 8 hours, and there are holidays and vacations that team members are entitled to. When you estimate that a project may take up to 8 weeks to complete, it is understood that you have considered a 40-hour-week schedule and thus a total of 320 hours, assuming no federal or state holidays fall within those 8 weeks. Any deviation from the norm must be described and justified. Exceptions to normal conditions are critical as you develop a network of schedules for project activities (see related discussion in Chapter 6 on time management and PERT). Consistency is also very important in the use of time units. Once the unit of time (hour, day, week, year) is specified for the project, it must be used throughout. Smaller information system projects often use hours or days as the units of time, while larger projects use weeks or months.

## Contingency Planning

It is not unusual in information systems development to expect out-of-the-ordinary situations. In fact, it is prudent to consider and plan for extreme or extraordinary situations. An appropriate way to prepare for extreme situations is through a *contingency plan* and *contingency funds.* When necessary, contingency situations are described and funds are appropriated for them at the planning phase of the project development life cycle. This involves a careful analysis of the situation. It is necessary to document and communicate to the sponsors what is meant by a contingency situation, how it is identified, how it is assessed, and how it is mitigated. Simply put, adding a margin to estimates of cost and time to cover contingencies is not convincing. In fact, such an approach can be counter-effective and indicative of poor planning. It may be interpreted as add-on "slush money" by watchful sponsors.

Contingency funds are not normally directly accessible to the project manager. The authorization to spend contingency funds is normally placed with management. This could be looked at as an additional layer of protection for the project manager as someone else or a committee will have to assess the needs for releasing these funds. The project manager can request a release of funds for extraordinary situations as specified in the contingency plan.

## Risk Analysis

In reality, events rarely happen as planned or as expected. Costs may be over what was budgeted for, and, as described earlier, contingency funds are appropriated in response to unexpected cost hikes. Similarly, time estimates can be seriously over- or under-projected. Any significant over or under in time estimation raises the question of whether the method was appropriate. A *risk analysis* of estimated times is appropriate when there is uncertainty regarding activity duration. It is necessary to identify and point out the level of risk associated with each activity. Risk analysis is part of a careful process for obtaining estimates. It is a useful way to communicate possible delays to the stakeholders, especially the project sponsors, to help them form realistic expectations.

A logical consequence of risk analysis is that it leads to developing alternative responses should potential risks realize themselves. While it may not be necessary to spend a great deal of time and effort in preparing a full-blown alternative schedule for risks that have some likelihood of happening, it is very useful to think about such possibilities and be prepared. The fact that the project manager and team members consider risks, analyze them, and try to determine the likelihood that they may happen prepares them for alternative responses. As seen in Exhibit 5.4, risk analysis serves multiple purposes. We look at risk in more detail in Chapter 10.

---

### Exhibit 5.4 The Purposes of Risk Analysis

- To identify possible risks
- To predict the likelihood of risks happening
- To estimate the potential impact of risks
- To communicate risks to stakeholders
- To prepare alternative responses.

---

Depending on the nature and size of a project, these outcomes may be more or less formalized, more or less extensive, and more or less detailed. Risk analysis may actually result in a change in the schedule if the likelihood of events happening and their impact are great. Sometimes a risk may become more evident as the project progresses. If that happens, and the risk is considerable, change may become necessary. A process for dealing with changes to requirements should be in place to evaluate change proposals and determine whether any changes should be made and how they should be implemented.

## Managing Changes to Requirements

Information system projects undergo several changes before they are complete. One of the main reasons for change is the fact that projects are proposed and approved based on estimates. Modern project management is a process of *constant negotiation, communication,* and *adjustment.* Change is often beneficial; innovative ideas or suggestions are often made by team members and individuals who are directly involved with the project. Change may also become necessary for external reasons, such as change related to the competition, vendors, and the law. All this suggests the need for an approach to manage changes in requirements. A *requirements change committee* or group can facilitate and encourage these proposals. This committee usually includes stakeholders from the entire organization, and its responsibilities are shown in Exhibit 5.5.

---

**Exhibit 5.5    Responsibilities of the Requirements Change Committee**

- Establish guidelines for submitting proposals for changes in requirements.
- Develop and communicate criteria for the evaluation of proposed change.
- Evaluate and approve change.
- Ensure compliance.

---

This committee should ensure that proposals for change are consistent with the overall goals and objectives of the organization and the broad scope of the project. This committee must also ensure that the change is doable. It is important to respond to change requests in a timely manner, especially for time-sensitive changes. The change management committee should provide in their processing guidelines a time limit for responding to time-sensitive changes. It may also provide a provision to process and decide on smaller changes more quickly. A proposal to change a project drastically, to the extent that the original scope is altered, might lead to cancellation of the current project and the start of a new one. Some changes may be significant and require additional resources. With the approval of management, these additional resources can be provided for through contingency funds. However, not all organizations are so enlightened, and in some the project manager may have to live with the original estimates. In all organizations, much work needs to be put into making these estimates as accurate as possible.

## 5.8. Software and Group Decision Support Systems

In this section we introduce ways in which computer software can support the project manager. The most important software in our context is for supporting *project management*, and we introduce that in Chapter 6 along with Program Evaluation Review Technique (PERT) and Critical Path Method (CPM), the most widely used techniques for scheduling, monitoring, and communicating time aspects of projects. The appendix to Chapter 6 shows the use of *MS Project* in this regard. Such packages are often sold independently, although MS Project is an option for the *MS Office* suite of programs and has the same look and feel as these other Office programs.

Earlier in this chapter (Section 5.2) we showed how *MS Excel* might be used to support the financial calculations to assess project investment, such as net present value techniques. *Spreadsheets*, such as those created using Excel, are often used for financial metrics and analysis of financial models and so may well be incorporated for simpler cost-justification procedures. In Section 10.2 we also show how Excel can be used to compare investments through scenario planning. Information systems are tools for decision makers, and decision makers of all types and all levels in one way or another use information system tools to analyze, rationalize, formalize, and make decisions. A spreadsheet is one of the most popular decision tools as it enables the decision maker to ask "what if" questions and be able to change and modify variables in a decision model to evaluate relative impact of each variable on the resultant outcome. They are easy to use and readily available, often included in a suite of software such as MS Office.

*Simulation* programs are also decision tools that enable decision makers to formulate and build a decision model and be able to analyze results and outcome. More complex computer simulations include probability estimates for variables that are included in the model. Monte Carlo simulation, for example, is a mathematical method that predicts the probability of possible outcomes for a given situation. Software such as *Simulink* (and *MathWorks* as a whole) and *Solver* will perform computer simulation in situations in which practical testing and experimentation will be too costly or too risky.

Newer decision tools—or as they are often called, **business intelligence software**—integrate functions of earlier tools and are intended to analyze current situations as well as forecast future trends. An example of these newer decision analysis tools is *Crystal Ball*, a suite of Microsoft Excel–based applications. Other decision-analysis tools include *iDashboards* and *Profit Metrics*. These newer decision tools are particularly useful in situations in which there is uncertainty and the need for forecast. They use predictive models and consider uncertainties and constraints in their solution. Although it is possible to use spreadsheets to simulate a situation or to build a forecast model, it is more difficult and less flexible to do so. These newer decision tools have easy-to-use interfaces and provide graphical output, and it is comparatively easy to combine and integrate outputs from other tools such as spreadsheets and databases.

Another new tool is *SimProject*, which is a Web-based project-management simulation tool that enables a project manager to break down a task into several milestones, just as MS Project would, and allow the user to monitor project progress and make adjustments based on what is learned about the project at any point. It also enables the user to provide qualitative and quantitative feedback at each milestone. The system provides simulated reports at each milestone that are useful for communication, interaction, and learning purposes. These reports are used by the team to make adjustments for the remaining activities of the project. In that respect, the system provides a dynamic environment conducive for learning as well as improving decisions.

As with any decision tool, it is important for the decision maker to (a) understand the tool and its functions, (b) be familiar with the data used by the tool, and (c) understand the industry and the business environment in which the decision is being analyzed and made for. *Crystal Ball*, for example, uses Monte Carlo simulation techniques with probability assumptions to forecast possible future outcome. These probability assumptions are also used to calculate Six Sigma figures to eliminate defects and variance levels of an activity within a set of events. These probability assumptions relate to revenue, costs, profits, and the like and will require intimate knowledge of the business as well as the industry. While decision-analysis tools vary in their power of analytical technique, user-friendliness, functions, and so on, they are equally affected by the quality of data they use.

Most of our discussion in this chapter has focused on estimating aspects of the project that are measurable, although we have discussed some intangibles and estimates using expert opinion and experience. We now turn to methods of gaining this advice using software to support the human interaction. Very often it is advisable in using expert opinion to have more than one person provide estimates, as it is not an exact science and experiences and experts will differ. Obtaining a consensus might be a better basis on which to judge these qualitative decisions than relying on the views and experience of only one person. There are computer packages available that support such group or team decision making. Of course, they can be appropriate for any group decision making that is the concern of many topics in this book and not just estimating project costs and benefits. Later in this section, we look at one such package—*ThinkTank*—in some detail. It is at the sophisticated end of the spectrum of software that supports group decision making.

Much, indeed most, information systems development work is carried out by a project team—that is, a group of individuals working in collaboration. Software tools are now available to support group work. They take many different forms. Some people might include email in this category, for example, because it can be used for information dissemination, although email systems have very limited groupware facilities. As we saw in Section 1.5, email might form the main medium for communications and decision making in groups.

*Lotus Notes* is a well-used group support system that places emphasis on communications between group members. It enables the documentation, sharing, storage, and access of information. It can be used to display the historical conversation over time between team members that led to a particular decision. One example of its use might be to communicate "notes" on viruses that can be displayed on a bulletin board for all the project team. The calendar can be used to coordinate schedules of physical and virtual meetings. In general, Lotus Notes can be used to help inform members of the project team about progress in real time as well as stimulate that progress.

While there are sophisticated collaboration suites and groupware available on the market, a combination of some basic Web or software applications may fulfill the same role as well. As mentioned above, some people may consider email as a group support application. If we add such electronic media as electronic mailing lists, newsgroups, instant messaging, Internet forums, and wikis to the list, we will not be far from attaining a complete collaboration suite. Indeed, open-source movements have been using these successfully as their only means of collaboration for a long time. Many low-budget project teams, especially those with geographically dispersed members, have been pursuing the same practice, since most of these tools are freely available on the Internet.

The collective discussions about design, specification, and development issues are held on a members-only forum or a newsgroup, where each subject takes the form of a discussion thread and everyone can contribute to the threads by responding to one of the posted messages. At the end of the day a copy of discussions are sent to all the members, through a mailing list, to keep them posted on progress. *Wikis* are very simple but flexible *content management systems* whose usage has gained momentum recently as a result of voluntary content-generation projects such as *Wikipedia.*

More critical or complicated situations may be dealt with using chat or instant-messaging software, which enable real-time communication. Chat systems have been around for two decades, although the instant-messaging services are adding new dimensions to online communication nowadays. File and photo sharing, voice and video conferencing, and graffiti boards are among the new enriching facilities integrated into *instant messengers.* With fast broadband Internet connections, instant-messaging software is competing with official telephony and videoconferencing services, as we know through the success of *Skype,* to give one example. The ever-rising quality of these services has convinced many workgroups to choose them as their primary means of communication.

The use of such systems may change the nature of group work from being largely face-to-face to largely online. Trust becomes a major factor as online work lacks the usual signals gained from face-to-face contact. Videoconferencing can have an obvious role here (and Skype now has video facilities). Web cameras used with email and Internet conversations can provide support, as can voicemail. Such systems also change roles, responsibilities, interactions, and the way work is carried out. Indeed, they may be introduced to achieve this result as well as encourage and support teamwork in general. Of course, there are also privacy and security implications as well as individuals' concerns about sharing their knowledge with others and perhaps losing their individual competitive advantage. The way such systems are introduced will therefore be a key factor in its potential for goodwill and better teamwork.

Angelo Failla provides a useful case study relating to how software is developed at IBM's international network of laboratories. Teams of work groups and managers can exist virtually in many different locations. Developers write code usually in small groups while managers divide the work between group members and groups. Electronic mail, forums (shared files), conference-call systems, faxes, and videoconferencing are all cited as tools supporting group work in the case study.

One of the most sophisticated group decision support tools available is *ThinkTank,* a product of GroupSystems (www.groupsystems.com). It supports innovative team spaces for sharing knowledge, discussing problems, coordinating effort, and collective decision making. It can be effective in situations where the group is working together in one room as well as where the team is dispersed geographically. It is sometimes used in special meeting rooms, called "pods," where each user has a workstation with the software installed. It supports brainstorming (see Section 10.2), categorization, electronic whiteboards, surveying, and voting in particular, and strategic planning, vendor evaluation, risk assessment, priority setting, and other aspects of project management in general. It can also be used with other software so that databases, spreadsheets, Web sites, and so on can inform the decision-making process.

❖ **Figure 5.1**   Agenda and Participants List for the Meeting

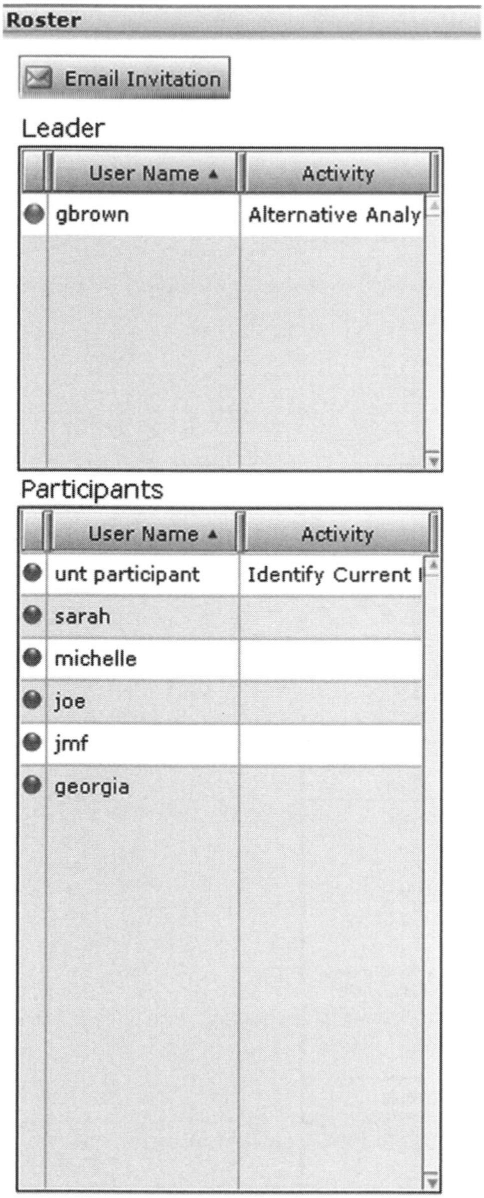

**Roster**

📧 Email Invitation

**Leader**

| User Name ▲ | Activity |
|---|---|
| ⬤ gbrown | Alternative Analy |

**Participants**

| User Name ▲ | Activity |
|---|---|
| ⬤ unt participant | Identify Current I |
| ⬤ sarah | |
| ⬤ michelle | |
| ⬤ joe | |
| ⬤ jmf | |
| ⬤ georgia | |

It can be used for remote decision making and not necessarily concurrently. This may be particularly useful in projects in which software is developed in different locations 24 hours a day. Video conferencing facilities offer people the opportunity to see as well as talk to others in another site or sites.

The brainstorming feature enables each member of the team to create ideas and comment on them. These are usually expressed anonymously so that it is the ideas that have force (or not) and not who is expressing those ideas. Brainstorming should encourage unusual thinking and ideas and innovation, and the option of anonymity when expressing these ideas reduces the inhibiting factors. Some ideas will be rejected but others will be kept and organized into separate categories for further evaluation. At the end of the meeting there is a complete record available, and this can be particularly useful to help organizational learning take place.

In the following figures we look at some of the potential of GDSS through *ThinkTank*. In Figure 5.1 the agenda and the list of participants is being formed for the meeting, and in Figure 5.2 we see the email list being formed so that the participants can be informed automatically of the meeting details. In Figure 5.3 we see important GDSS features: generating lists of ideas, brainstorming comments that elaborate on/or support the ideas, and organizing the ideas into categories. Figure 5.4 shows four categories (with a fifth one being generated) and the brainstorming discussion on the first of these consisting of 10 comments so far. Figure 5.5 shows the voting process where the team can rate a list of alternatives against as many criteria as desired, then view the degree of group consensus on an item. Finally in Figure 5.6, we see one report from the meeting giving a record of the voting. Other reports can be in graphical form.

❖ **Figure 5.2**   Setting Up the Session and Emailing Participants

| Sessions | Users | Admin |
|---|---|---|

| New | Delete | Start | Save to Disk | Load from Disk |
|---|---|---|---|---|

| Name | Description | Session Type | Status | Create Date | Created By | Last Accessed On | Last Accessed By |
|---|---|---|---|---|---|---|---|
| Expediting Innovation | We will brainstorm and rank ideas | Demo | Scheduled | September 22, 2006 2:04:22 | Brown, Georgia | September 26, 2006 9:51:08 | Brown, Georgia |
| Software Requirements Dem: | Identify and Prioritize Requiremer | Technology | Scheduled | September 25, 2006 7:25:18 | Brown, Georgia | September 27, 2006 10:19:3 | Brown, Georgia |

| Details | Settings | Roster | Agenda |
|---|---|---|---|

| *Session Name: | Software Requirements Demo | Start Date: | Wednesday | Time: | 9:00am | Conference Number: | 888 272 7337 |
|---|---|---|---|---|---|---|---|
| *Passkey: | 3013 | End Date: | Wednesday | Time: | 11:00 | Conference Code: | 8643259 |
| Description: | Identify and Prioritize Requirements for a New Project | Location: | Vista Conference Room and Online | | | Status: | Scheduled |
| Session Type: | Technology | | | | | | |

Direct URL:   http://thinktank.groupsystems.com/gsiii/index.html?sessionID=521

| Save | Cancel |
|---|---|

❖ **Figure 5.3**   Generating Ideas, Brainstorming, and Categorizing

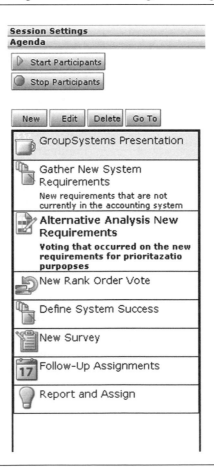

❖ **Figure 5.4**   Categories and Related Discussion

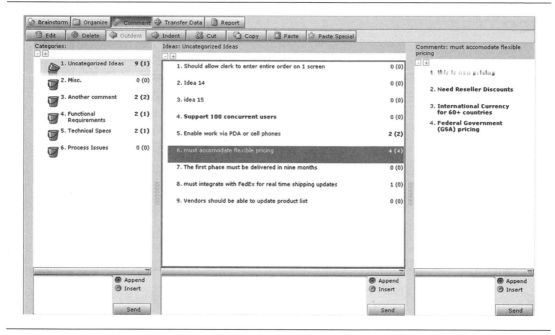

❖ **Figure 5.5**   Multi-Criteria Voting

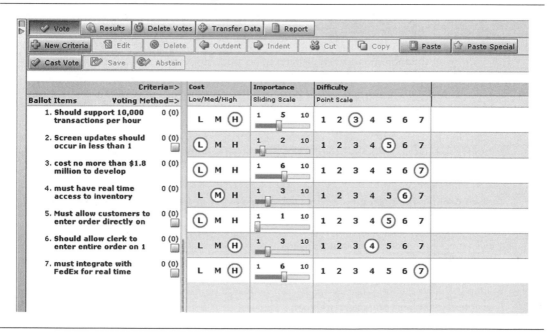

❖ **Figure 5.6**    Meeting Reports

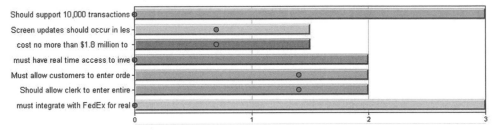

Average vote score

## 5.9. Interview With a Project Manager

**What skills should project managers possess?**

"Soft skills should include patience, and a penchant for organization, and meticulousness. These are paramount for the success of any project, but especially for someone entrusted with the successful completion of a usually expensive project."

**Does a project manager need to know everything that is going on in the company?**

"This depends on the scope of the project and what the outcome is expected to provide for the company. Any manager in any field should understand the fundamental aspects of his or her business, even if it is not related to the manager's particular area of education. For example, my entire career has been spent in IT, yet I work for a pharmaceutical company. As a result, I take a mild interest in the goings-on in this industry and, in particular, all aspects of the company's business. After all, I am but one cog in the larger machine."

**What kind of control does a project manager hold (human resource, funds, etc.)?**

"By and large, a project manager is entrusted with the responsibility and resources chartered to get a given project completed. This includes human resources, a budget (for overtime, material), etc. Project managers receive as much autonomy over the execution of the project as management deems appropriate, and they in turn delegate small amounts of their authority to lead personnel and other individuals. Ultimately, the project manager will be held responsible for the outcome of the project, whether over budget, on time, or whatever."

Do project managers usually get their way? What are some obstacles?

"If the project manager is seasoned, and has a solid track record of success, he or she is usually afforded the privilege of having almost total autonomy over a project, to a certain predefined limit. For example, a vice president, under whose auspices a project is being run, may authorize the project manager to exceed the budget by 2%."

Did you get coaching on your first project assignment?

"Yes, but not much, unfortunately. I was given the project, simple instructions on what was expected as the outcome, and I winged it from there. I took project management courses afterward because I knew there had to be a better way. There was."

Do you find project management challenging or overwhelming? How?

"Project management is definitely challenging. It is often difficult to wrangle the various human resources, material resources, contractors, calendar, and other factors together to create a successful outcome. However, it is this challenge that makes it exciting and worthwhile. If a project ever becomes overwhelming or seems out of control, it's time for a pause and redirection."

Do you find your estimates of scope, time, and cost in your past projects to be accurate? If not, how off were you?

"In virtually every project there are some indefinable elements, things that are difficult on which to put a time frame or dollar value. It is these areas that usually end up busting the budget. Not enough time allocated to research and development on some element, or not enough money allocated to budget, or not enough resources allocated to balance either one. However, experience lends itself to getting closer to the mark each time at making better 'guesstimates.'"

Why do you think so many projects wind up finishing late?

"Not using software on big projects, not thinking through the lead times and costs. Different scenarios should be played out and costs attached and the lead times should be figured out. This is difficult, but you have to look at who you are competing with for resources, what has priority, and if you will have to work around other projects. The planning has to be done right, the timeline, dependencies, lead times, timing, and fiscal aspects all have to be thought out."

How do you control/avoid scope creep?

"Easy: Design the Scope and Requirements document in such a way that it clearly defines what you are setting out to accomplish. Make sure this document is circulated among all the principals and have their full and complete buy-in. After the project begins, if there is any request to expand or enhance the scope, refer the requestor to your S&R document."

*(Continued)*

(Continued)

Finally, what advice would you give to a candidate on becoming a project manager?

"Learn all you can about project management in school. Take on a real-life project for your school, church, or other organization, and treat it as if it were for IBM or General Motors. Utilize these practice projects to develop empirical understanding of what works, what doesn't, and above all, how you react under pressure, and how to manage that behavior. This will give you insight into project management in general, and how to succeed with yourself and your delegates."

## 5.10. Chapter Summary

Estimates of cost and time provide a boundary for the entire project. Sponsors need reliable information on cost and time before they can decide whether to support a project. Estimates are critical to plan resources, monitor progress, and evaluate performance and ultimately for measuring success. It is useful to distinguish between tangible and intangible costs as well as between direct and indirect costs. Tangible and direct costs are more easily determined, whereas intangible and indirect costs are more difficult to determine.

There are several ways to analyze project value. One approach is called payback analysis, where it is determined how long it will take an organization to recover the project costs. Another approach is called net present value (NPV), where cash flow analysis of a project costs and benefits is performed. The third financial analysis is called return on investment (ROI), where discounted benefits and costs are used to assess investment value. These financial analyses are used to compare information system project proposals and to determine which project to fund. Estimates of cost and time based on experience, documentation, or expert opinion can be obtained. A combination of these sources can also be used to obtain estimates. In some situations it might be necessary to obtain more than one estimate to improve reliability.

In some situations it is difficult to obtain up-front estimates for the entire project. In such cases, phase estimating is used where detailed estimates are provided for the early phase of the project and rough estimates are projected for the later phases. Detailed estimates are then generated for the subsequent phases as the project progresses. Phase estimating is necessary for innovative projects or when the final outcome is dependent on results from the design phase. In reality things change and it is not always easy to obtain accurate and reliable estimates. It is prudent to plan for change and analyze potential risks. Contingency plans should be prepared to address unexpected events and respond to change. Modern project management involves constant negotiation and communication, and effective project managers prepare for what can be expected as well as events that are usual or unlikely.

# DISCUSSION QUESTIONS

1.  Assume you are working for an organization that is keen to invest in information technology to improve employee innovation, productivity, customer satisfaction, and management control. However, top management in your organization has a short-term payback expectation for their technology investment. Explain to the leadership of your organization why such a policy may be dysfunctional in the long term.

2.  Three methods are described in this chapter for obtaining cost and time estimates. Advantages and disadvantages for these methods are also described. Provide additional discussion on the pros and cons of each approach (experience, documentation, expertise opinion). What has been your experience?

3.  This chapter argues that organizational game play and politics are a function of management decision-making style. Do you agree with this statement? Why? Is it possible to totally eliminate organizational politics? How should a project manager deal with these?

4.  As an information systems project manager, how would you address issues of politics and game play that affect time and cost estimates for your projects? Would your reaction to cost and time overestimation be the same as your reaction to cost and time underestimation?

5.  How would you convince a conservative management that effectiveness criteria are as important as efficiency criteria in decisions concerning new information systems projects?

6.  Describe and distinguish between a contingency plan and risk analysis.

7.  Project sponsors are often reluctant to set up project contingency funds that seem to imply poor project planning. Some perceive contingency funding as an add-on slush fund. Others say they will face the risk when it materializes. Often such reluctance to establish contingency reserves can be overcome with documented risk identification, assessment, contingency plans, and planning for when and how funds will be disbursed. What else would you do to convince your sponsors?

8.  Risk should be monitored and based on defined milestones and decisions made regarding risks and mitigation strategies. Some project managers keep a list of frequently occurring risks and use it in the review and control process (see the table below). How would you track risks in order to maintain awareness and prepare mitigation strategies?

| Risk Item | # of Occurrences in 3 Months | Possible Mitigating Response |
|---|---|---|
| Inadequate planning | 4 | Revising the entire project plan |
| Poor scope description | 3 | Meeting with sponsors to clarify scope |
| Leadership problem | 2 | Assigning a new project manager |
| Poor cost estimates | 2 | Revising cost estimates |

# EXERCISES

1. Read the report of the National Audit Office discussed in Exhibit 5.1 (www.nao.org.uk) and prepare a presentation to top management entitled "Recommendations for Organizations Embarking on Major IT-Enabled Business Change."

2. Use a spreadsheet to calculate NPV for Projects A and B in Table 5.1.

3. Calculate the ROI for information provided in Table 5.1 using different interest rates.

4. The following table gives projected revenues and costs as well as the interest rate for two proposed projects. Use payback analysis, net present value (NPV), and return on investment (ROI) to recommend one of these projects for development (show your work). Suggest other factors that would influence your decision.

| Interest Rate: 12% | | | | | |
|---|---|---|---|---|---|
| **Project 1** | **Year 1** | **Year 2** | **Year 3** | **Year 4** | **Year 5** |
| Revenues | $3,000 | $3,000 | $3,000 | $3,000 | $3,000.00 |
| Costs | $5,000 | $1,000 | $1,000 | $1,000 | $1,000.00 |
| Cash Flow | (−$2,000) | $2,000 | $2,000 | $2,000 | $2,000.00 |
| **Project 2** | **Year 1** | **Year 2** | **Year 3** | **Year 4** | **Year 5** |
| Revenues | $5,000 | $4,000 | $3,000 | $2,000 | $1,000.00 |
| Costs | $2,000 | $2,000 | $2,000 | $2,000 | $2,000.00 |
| Cash Flow | $3,000 | $2,000 | $1,000 | $0 | (−$1,000.00) |

5. Search the Web and find out more about newer decision analysis tools such as *Crystal Ball, iDashboards,* and *Profit Metrics.* Write a one-page report and describe the similarities between these tools and the more traditional decision-analysis tools. In what ways do these tools differ from the earlier ones?

6. Search to find information that will enable you to compare and contrast MS Project with *Crystal Ball* and MS Project with SimProject. List the pros and cons of each from the perspective of a project manager.

# APPENDIX TO CHAPTER 5: CUSTOMER RELATIONSHIP MANAGEMENT AT MEDICALCO

To manage prescription drug benefit for 60 million customers, MedicalCo has made a significant investment in its Customer Relationship Management (CRM) over recent years. Computer applications and system procedures are developed and used to schedule customer service representatives and balance call traffic to ensure the speed and service quality. A network of six call centers in five states within the United States handles over 40 million customer calls per year. Frequently, customer service representatives have service penalties associated with the speed of answer and thus the service is painstakingly managed to avoid penalty. Yet, the call centers and customer service representatives are not always able to resolve all issues online. The unresolved cases are queued for follow-up by a team of customer service representatives within each dispensing pharmacy. The majority of customer and client complaints have been traced to this queuing process.

## Customer Relationship Management

CRM systems incorporate information acquisition, information storage, and decision support functions to provide one-to-one customer service. CRM helps organizations to interact with their customers through a variety of means, including phone, Web, email, and salespeople. CRM enables customer representatives to access data on customer profile, product, logistics, and the like to analyze problems and to provide online and rapid response to customer queries. Companies use CRM to not only create customer profiles but also to anticipate customer needs, conduct market research, and prompt customer purchase. It is suggested that it costs up to 12 times more to gain a new customer than to retain an existing one. A problem needs to be resolved on the first contact, or the chances are the customer with an option will never call back.

In the pharmaceutical industry, CRM has become a great investment and plays a significant part in managing customer requests. Accurate data, effective processing, and cross-functional integration are critical success factors in improving customer satisfaction. Product information (e.g., specification, inventory, price, delivery method) are readily available to customer representatives to facilitate immediate and accurate response to customers in their first contact. Callbacks are minimized as they involve cost (in employee time) and the risk of losing the customer. Processes are streamlined and quality control is imbedded within the system to ensure continuous and consistent monitoring of customer service.

## CRM at MedicalCo

MedicalCo specializes in the prescription benefit management industry. It dispenses medications produced by over 60 manufacturers on behalf of its clients. MedicalCo clients include major employers, government agencies, HMOs, and Blue Cross/Blue Shield and other insurance providers. The employees or members of these organizations are provided with a prescription drug benefit that MedicalCo manages on behalf of its clients. Currently, MedicalCo represents over 60 million Americans through its various clients and fills over 500 million prescriptions per year.

*(Continued)*

(Continued)

This benefit is utilized in two ways. First, MedicalCo negotiates contracts with retail pharmacy chains to provide its clients prescription coverage at discounted costs. Members are provided with a prescription drug card that they present to the retail pharmacist along with their prescription. The retail pharmacist uses this card to access member-specific coverage information through a proprietary MedicalCo online system. This system provides the pharmacist with information about the member's drug history, co-pay and eligibility. After filling the medication for the member, the pharmacist uses the same system to process a claim to be reimbursed for the negotiated drug cost and administrative fee for dispensing the medication.

Members also have the option of using a home-delivery pharmacy. MedicalCo operates 12 home-delivery pharmacies across the country. These pharmacies are divided into prescription processing centers and prescription dispensing centers. A member can submit a prescription through five different means: mail, fax, phone voice response system, Internet, or by speaking with a customer service representative. Each client submits all of his or her prescriptions to the same prescription processing center. Depending on the type of medication, the actual prescription could be dispensed through a different prescription dispensing center.

Once a prescription processing center receives a prescription, it is responsible for entering all information necessary to prepare for dispensing. The process for accomplishing this varies based on whether the order is for a new prescription or a refill of an existing prescription. In the case of the refills, members are issued a bar-coded sticker that can be scanned to access all of the necessary information from the original prescription. A new prescription is more complex.

All documents received through the mail are scanned into images that can be retrieved later for any purpose. In the case of new prescriptions, once the images are available, a pharmacist enters the information into the system on the right side of the screen while looking at the images on the left side of the screen. The order is then subjected to a series of administrative and professional edits. The administrative edits look for current eligibility, drug coverage information, account balance, and address or personal profile information. The professional edits include a drug utilization review that ensures they are not taking multiple drugs that interact with each other or an allergy that would be impacted by the drug. If there were any questions about what the doctor prescribed then a call would be made by a pharmacist. There are also edits that target specific medications that have lower cost, therapeutically equivalent alternatives. Pharmacists then call doctors to discuss switching the medication to the alternative. This is primarily focused on saving the plan and customer money while maintaining the same therapeutic outcomes. There are also some disease-management edits that concentrate on prescribing behaviors relative to specific disease states. These would also prompt a call to a doctor to discuss the appropriateness of the medication prescribed by the doctor.

Once all of these edits are identified and appropriately resolved, the prescription is then ready to be dispensed. As mentioned earlier, the type of prescription dictates where it will actually be dispensed. There are two automated pharmacies that dispense primarily pills, tablets, and capsules. Therefore, a prescription that is capable of being dispensed through automation would be electronically transferred to one of these two pharmacies. If the prescription were a prepackaged item, refrigerated medication, a narcotic, a controlled substance, or a compounded medication, it would be dispensed in any one of seven pharmacies across the country. The remaining three pharmacies are strictly prescription-processing centers and do not dispense any medications.

Integrated throughout the prescription-processing and -dispensing process are extensive customer service capabilities. All information relative to past prescriptions and prescriptions currently in process is accessible by a customer service representative (CSR) via another proprietary system. In addition, client plan design and personal profile information is also available within this system. With 60 million customers to support, customer service handles over 40 million calls per year through its network of six call centers. A complex set of systems and applications are used to schedule CSRs and balance call traffic to ensure the speed with which calls are answered meets the expectations of clients. These six call centers have the ability to route telephone calls transparently to a customer. Any question can be answered by any CSR in any call center via the system. This allows customer service to balance call traffic based on staffing and demand in real time.

Although the call centers and CSRs have integrated systems, they are not always capable of resolving a member's issue via the system. In these cases, there is a follow-up system to address the member's question or concern. A common example is when a member calls about the status of his or her order that is currently in process. If the member needs the medication earlier than when the system projects it will be dispensed, then a message is sent electronically to the dispensing pharmacy. Within each dispensing pharmacy is a team of CSRs who are staffed exclusively to follow up on member issues that the call center CSRs are unable to resolve. This team would work these electronic messages, called queues. Each queue is defined based on its pharmacy location and the nature of the request. There are 26 different queues that are used by each dispensing pharmacy. If the specific nature of the request does not fit into one of the first 25 queues then the CSR would use the 26th queue, which is a general queue.

## Barriers to Success

There are great expectations for what CRM can accomplish in terms of customer profile, product information, rapid response, predicting customer needs, retaining customers, conducting market research, promoting sales, and reducing cost. However, despite considerable organizational and executive commitments, these expectations have not always been materialized.

The company, MedicalCo, greatly depends on CRM to interact with their customers. Doctors and patients in the company member plans send their prescriptions by mail, fax, phone, or through a Web site. At automated pharmacies, 99% of the prescriptions are filled within 24 hours of receipt. Some of these pharmacies may fill more than 800,000 prescriptions per week. Before a prescription is filled, potential drug interactions are automatically checked and issues are flagged and forwarded to a registered pharmacist for investigation and resolution. There are numerous other issues that customer service representatives use the system to address. For example, a member patient may request drugs to be sent to a different address while on holiday or may request a speedy delivery before travel. These messages are received at call centers and queued for action at pharmacies or packaging centers responsible for that particular package.

A close analysis of CRM system at MedicalCo suggests several processes that are either not followed or not clearly understood by customer service representatives. These issues relate to standard operating procedure, accountability and ownership, callback information content, customer contact process, billing issues, and dispensing and replacement processes. Below, factors identified as barriers to CRM success in the company are described and possible remedies are suggested.

*(Continued)*

(Continued)

*Standard operating procedure.* Compliance with standard operating procedure results in current complaints more than any other factor. It includes wrongly sequenced queues, closing of incomplete files, forwarding incomplete electronic forms, and the like. This issue relates to employee behavior and may be addressed through training as well as improved description of procedures. However, training alone or improved description of procedure may not be adequate if noncompliance is widely spread and has become routine or if the system's information product does not readily support compliance with standard operating procedure. The CRM system can be redesigned so that it will enforce much of standard operating procedure and make compliance a part of interaction with the system.

*Accountability and ownership.* The issue of accountability is another readily identified factor that has created discontent among CRM users and customer service representatives. Under the current system, it is difficult to determine who is accountable for events such as filing customer contact forms without action, violating queue sequence for customer contact forms, keeping commitments made to customers, and not verifying address prior to refill and shipping. This has created role ambiguity and role conflict with adverse effects on information product intended outcome. The interaction between task needs and technology application has created a problem that cannot be addressed through defining responsibilities alone. Levels of responsibility and accountability need to be established and communicated, and violations are then easily identified.

*Callback information content.* The third factor influencing CRM outcome at the company relates to the quality of information generated through the use of customer contact forms. This information is often unclear or even wrong and is used to generate customer queries and determine queues. This in turn influences queue procedure that is identified as another factor affecting customer representatives. Information technology is expected to empower the individual employee to provide an accurate and timely response to customers. Lack of employee confidence in information content has an adverse influence on system use. The system needs to more effectively and more easily control for information quality at data entry, data integration, and data manipulation level.

*Customer contact process.* Information technology and CRM are expected to provide the mechanism through which long-term, individualized relationships with customers can be created and maintained. To accomplish this, the company must ask what makes a specific customer unique and then tailor services in response to that uniqueness. The current system does not create an environment that helps sustain a steady business from customers. The customer contact form was designed to collect information on a single issue rather than multiple ones. As currently practiced, this form generates multiple issues and that in turn complicates routing of issues to appropriate pharmacies or packaging centers. The system should facilitate generation of separate forms for multiple issues and avoid providing the option of multiple issues on a single form.

*Billing questions.* This issue suggests ineffective integration of accounting function (e.g., accounts receivable) with CRM in the company. Customer service representatives are not familiar with how to respond to customer queries for billing, and the system does help them explain expenses to customers. Customer service representatives have difficulty interpreting accounting codes on the billing screen. The system needs to more fully integrate accounting functions as well as to help customer representatives respond accurately to billing questions.

*Dispensing and replacement process.* Since a number of pharmacies and packaging centers are involved in dispensing medicines to customers, it is important to link back recurring customer requests or changes to the specific center or pharmacy designated to fill that prescription. Customer service representatives find it difficult to queue a replacement request. The system does not automatically identify where a replacement request should be queued. The dispensing and replacement process is unclear to many customer representatives, and the existence of "front end" and "back end" pharmacies makes it more difficult to know where to queue issues. These issues may not have existed at the time the system was developed. Rapid growth and packaging and dispensing automation have further complicated the process.

*Queuing procedure.* There seems to be a significant confusion over the queue system and how and where customer contact forms should be queued. In the current system, queuing occurs because a customer service representative in a call center cannot systemically resolve the customers concerns online. There is a need for an environment that integrates all systems at the company and that will enable customer service representatives in call centers to resolve the vast majority of member needs without the need to queue anything. The system must eliminate the need for customer service representatives to memorize procedures for each pharmacy and generate a standard form that is easily understood by all representatives and pharmacy people alike.

## People and Technology

These issues can be viewed under two broad categories of "people" and "system." This grouping facilitates generalization of the issues and determination of remedial actions. Summary analysis of these issues relative to "people" or "technology" is presented in the following table. The technical subsystem relates to processes, tasks, and technologies while the social subsystem involves people attributes such as skills and attitudes as well as organizational attributes such as reward systems and authority structure. This model provides a useful framework that helps identify the interaction between two sets of influential variables. The interaction between system and people issues is evident in a majority of the factors identified as causing discontent with CRM in the company. Further, these factors interact among themselves and sometimes exasperate the situation.

It is important to realize that while some of these issues are linked to employee and user behavior, many of them are inherent attributes of the system and existing processes. Over the course of the last few years, extensive training efforts have been aimed at addressing these issues at MedicalCo with minimal effectiveness, suggesting that systems-related issues are as problematic. In any redesign of the system, one of the key objectives must be to eliminate or minimize the number of issues that need to be queued. To accomplish this, the multiple systems that are not currently integrated need to be able to directly communicate with each other. An integrated system will enable a customer service representative in a call center to resolve member needs online without the need to queue.

*(Continued)*

(Continued)

## Summary Analysis of Barriers to CRM Success at MedicalCo

| Factor | Organizational | | Technological | |
|---|---|---|---|---|
| | Cause | Solution | Cause | Solution |
| Compliance with standard operating procedure | Lack of understanding and enforcement | System usage, training, policy and procedure | Lack of system checks | Incorporate automatic SOP enforcement |
| Accountability and ownership | Lack of policy and procedure for tracking responsibilities | Enacting policy and procedure | Lack of system tracking or monitoring | Incorporate system tracking or monitoring |
| Callback information content | Lack of understanding with proper system usage | System usage training | System error, lack of assistance from system | Correct system error, improve system help features |
| Customer contact process | Lack of understanding with proper system usage | System usage training | Lack of system checks | Incorporate automated system checking |
| Billing issues | Lack of understanding with internal processes in other functional areas | Cross-functional training | Lack of system integration from other areas | Improve system integration |
| Dispensing and replacement process | Lack of understanding with internal processes in other areas and system usage | Cross-functional training, system usage training | Lack of assistance from system | Incorporate system help features |
| Queuing procedure | Lack of understanding with proper system usage and standards | System usage training | Lack of assistance from system, lack of standards | Incorporate system help features and standards |

## APPENDIX TO CHAPTER 5: DISCUSSION QUESTIONS

1. Present the MedicalCo case to its management, providing a balance of positive as well as negative aspects, and suggest a program to improve the present situation. In preparing for this, use some form of software (perhaps as unsophisticated as email or as sophisticated as *ThinkTank*) to prepare your group presentation without face-to-face contact. Discuss the advantages and disadvantages of this form of communication in your presentation.

2. Compare the CRM application at MedicalCo with similar systems in the pharmaceutical industry and elsewhere that you can find out about, for example, on the Web.

3. Prepare a presentation for a competitor of MedicalCo suggesting how it could gain competitive advantage by developing a system that improved on MedicalCo's CRM. Prepare a project plan for developing this application.

## BIBLIOGRAPHY

Chen, M. T. (1997). The modern project manager, *Cost Engineering, 39*(3).

Failla, A. (1996). Technologies for coordination in a software factory. In C. U. Ciborra (Ed.), *Groupware and teamwork: Invisible aid or technical hindrance?* Maidenhead, UK: Wiley.

Kinsella, S. M. (2002). Activity-based costing: Does it warrant inclusion in a guide to the project management body of knowledge? *Project Management Journal, 33*(2), 49–55.

National Audit Office. (2006). *Delivering successful IT-enabled business change.* London: The Stationery Office (www.nao.org.uk).

Rad, P. F. (2002). *Project estimating and cost management.* Vienna: Management Concepts.

# Managing Information Systems Project Time and Resources

**Themes of Chapter 6**

- ❖ What is project time management?
- ❖ What characteristics define an effective project manager?
- ❖ What principles are important in project management?
- ❖ What tools are useful?
- ❖ What skill sets are important?
- ❖ What is the life cycle of an information systems development project?
- ❖ What are the stages in the information systems development life cycle?
- ❖ Why is there a need for good information systems project managers?
- ❖ How is the balance between sociocultural and technical factors achieved?

This chapter describes project time management and its importance to the success of information systems projects. A vital characteristic of successful project managers is the way they manage time and the way they help team members manage time.

A critical success factor for effective time management is timely communication of standards and expectations. Setting milestones provides appropriate reference points for the project manager and team members. This chapter describes the *Program Evaluation Review Technique (PERT)* and *Critical Path Method (CPM)*, the most widely used tools for scheduling, monitoring, and communicating time aspects of projects. Using this network approach, this chapter also describes how to analyze project schedules and modify them to meet deadlines. Finally we provide suggestions that will help you keep to deadlines.

This chapter discusses techniques, but it is important to understand that although such techniques can be helpful to the project manager, the use of such techniques does not guarantee success. Indeed, as our discussion with Terry Young, an experienced leader of research projects shows, a combination of experience, a willingness to negotiate, and the commitment of people can be even more important (Exhibit 6.1).

---

### Exhibit 6.1    The Case Against the Use of Techniques (A Discussion With Terry Young)

Although I learned about PERT charts at university, I have never really used them at work, and I have not used many software-based tools either. My first experiences of project management were in a commercial research center. The central drive was to keep to schedule and budget through monthly reviews. The company had a strong financial drive, and I would get the project returns monthly.

The first largish project that I worked on was a European collaboration to develop a combination of circuit elements for optical communication. We built lasers, electronic drivers, waveguides, switches, photo-detectors, and preamplifiers. Planning was done by a group and again was financially constrained. Partners would tend to negotiate a share of the program and then work out what they believed they could do against their own internal strategies within the constraints of the program. The process produced a plan with a granularity of around one to three person-months. Once finalized, this became the project plan against which progress would be reported.

Success or failure depended largely on being able to deliver meaningful outputs from that plan—to satisfy the partners (who might want to reduce your funding at the next round if they were unhappy) and the company (which had to find the matching funds).

One way or another, this was the basic model for all the work I did—plan using experience, cost up, and then monitor monthly against hard financial figures. On the whole this worked well. We were optimistic about how long things would take, but only mildly so, and generally within the safety zones set up through contingency budgets. Project plans would generally consist of a description, followed by milestone achievements and the dates by which each was expected.

As I became more senior in the organization, I took more interest in the bidding and in the monitoring of projects—especially those projects that fell within my own financial codes. Overall my role required skills in recruitment, staff development, contracts, negotiation, bid management, and review. Costing was generally done through discussion and involved an analysis of what our best guesses were and what we thought the constraints were. Risk was explicitly addressed but again was constrained by not wanting to frighten the customer with the level of risk.

Monitoring involved reviewing projects. I was expected to review small projects (less than US $150,000, typically) each month with my staff. Larger projects were reviewed monthly with a team that included my boss, the financial director, and the site director. I was typically responsible for somewhere between $US 5–8 million per annum worth of projects and might have 20 to 30 small projects and 4 to 5 large ones for review. This gave a very clear idea of how much progress could be made in a month and how much it would typically cost.

I also would make up my own consolidated spreadsheet, which reviewed how the division as a whole was doing. Ironically, in view of the amount of data we were given, the process became very internalized and intuitive. We used the project-management terminology and understood what it meant, but we did not often apply it formally.

The other element of the process was the ancillary systems—risk registers, health and safety, export licenses, quality, and so on. People management was also my responsibility—annual reviews, target setting, personal development, and pay reviews. These things tended to go on a biannual cycle.

My take was that experience and consensus were more important than the use of specific techniques, and we tended to apply the latter in only a general way or when the project was big. However, it is true that people working on big projects ($US 20 million to over $100 million) were much more formal and rigorous in their approach.

When I entered the university sector recently, I obtained a grant portfolio of around US $10 million. My research focus lies in the value of healthcare technology and services. However, I discovered it was time to learn a whole new set of skills. I recruited a project manager with commercial experience. But the academic teams hated it. They found it too bureaucratic and, I suspect, too restricting. We had to back off, and what worked best was to set academic targets. Along with my academic colleagues, I reasoned and cajoled the team members through to their deliverables.

The thing I have learned from both experiences is the importance of working with people and getting people on our side. The most optimistic estimate can come in on time and to budget with a really committed team. The most generous contingency (and more) will always be spent by a team conditioned to fail, and the use of techniques will hardly affect the result either way.

## 6.1. Time as a Resource

Time is a resource if it is managed effectively; otherwise it will be a constraint. Timely delivery of information systems projects has been one of the biggest challenges for information systems project managers. Managing time effectively is therefore a critical component for project success. Time management relates not only to the anticipated planned activities but also to unexpected events—last-minute changes, personnel issues, conflict resolution, and so on. A successful project is the one that is on time, within budget, and delivers what is expected. Project managers should set the standard for a timely outcome by example. If project managers cannot control their time, then they will have difficulties controlling team members, and consequently the entire project is likely to be late. Project managers often work on tight deadlines and feel they have no time to think about time and its effective use. To be effective, a project manager must be organized and *prioritize* work. Depending on work habits, this could be done in different ways and may or may not be very formal.

A good way of understanding project time management issues is to consider personal time management. Organizing your own time might seem to be a fairly simple requirement, yet we all know how difficult it is in practice to use our time effectively. *To find out whether you have a time management problem, ask yourself the questions shown in Exhibit 6.2.*

---

### Exhibit 6.2    Questions to Ask When Assessing Your Time Management

- Do you spend a lot of time responding to email messages?
- Do you spend a lot of time returning calls?
- How often do you work overtime?
- How often do you miss social events?
- How often do you reschedule your appointments?
- How often do you feel you need a large block of time to finish a task?
- Do you have a gatekeeper for unexpected visitors who take up your time?
- Do you prioritize your work? Based on what?
- Do you plan your vacation?

---

You may or may not be able to do something about all of these, but you will get a feel for whether you need to think about your own time management. In any case, whether you are able to address all these questions successfully or not is less important than the realization that time management is important. Information technology is like a double-edged sword, and it can cut both ways. Effective use of information technology can be a significant advantage to time management, but sometimes it can use your time ineffectively.

We will use email as an exemplar of potential time management issues. Email can have a significant positive impact on communications in terms of timeliness, convenience, accuracy, cost, storage, retrieval, and so on. But it can be a problem if not handled efficiently. You may send or receive a message at any time, but it is not a good use of your time if you check whether you have new mail every few minutes. It is not very difficult to surmise a rough distribution pattern for your incoming messages after a while. For example, you may notice that early in the week you get a lot of messages and it slows down toward the end of the week. You also know that when you get into your office on Monday morning there is a long list of email waiting for you, and it is worse when you return from a vacation.

*Organize your own time management to accommodate your own email patterns.*

With the ease of connectivity at hotels, conventions, airports, and elsewhere, many people tend to check their email messages when they travel out of town. While this may be useful when traveling on business, it does not help your overall productivity if you are on vacation. You must plan your vacation to *disconnect* with daily and routine work. Project managers often work under pressure for time, resource, and high expectation reasons, and that can cause work stress and burnout. Your vacation must provide a relief from all that. You must plan your communications, including email and voice messages, to give yourself flexibility. If you attend to your email continually and voicemail messages throughout the day you are an ineffective time manager. You may want to have a simple routine for checking your messages such as once in the morning and once in the afternoon. If you are preparing to leave for a meeting you should not check your email unless you expect a message about that meeting. A last-minute and unexpected email message can cause you to enter a meeting distracted, disorganized, and sometimes late.

This simple example relating to personal time management can be used to consider the time management of people in the organization generally. Activities need to be monitored, patterns detected, and appropriate plans organized so that time is used both efficiently and effectively.

## 6.2. Monitoring Time

Project managers who end up with a great deal of overtime or repeated delays should evaluate their time management principles carefully. An effective and experienced project manager should be able to evaluate with reasonable accuracy how long the project will take and how many staff hours are available for the project (leaving some margin of error for unexpected interruptions). Repeated delays and prolonged overtime may be the results of inaccurate evaluation of these two important components of time management.

It is possible to keep track of a small number of activities in your mind. But for multi-activity projects you will need a more systematic approach to control or keep track of time. In picking a method, try to select one that you feel comfortable with and can easily create and revise. For example, a simple status form such as the one shown as Figure 6.1 can help your time management.

A similar form with minor changes, like the one shown as Figure 6.2, can be used for daily activities.

❖ **Figure 6.1**   Status Form

| Activity tracking for project .........n a m e............ | | | | |
|---|---|---|---|---|
| **Activity** | **Date Required** | **Duration** | **Start Date** | **Status** |
|  |  |  |  |  |
|  |  |  |  |  |
|  |  |  |  |  |

❖ **Figure 6.2**   Activity Form

| Activities to be completed today .........d a t e......... | | | | |
|---|---|---|---|---|
| **Activity** | **Time Required** | **Duration** | **Start Time** | **Status** |
| | | | | |
| | | | | |
| | | | | |

An effective project manager has a priority list. The lack of prioritization has an adverse effect on time management and decision making. People procrastinate either habitually or because they do not know how to finish the job. In either case, indecisiveness impacts negatively on time management. You may have worked with people who take too long to make a decision, not because they are not sure what to decide but because they hesitate to decide, fearing the consequences. Decision making is a part of a project manager's responsibilities, and often project managers must make decisive decisions within a short time. Indecisiveness can affect project organization, progress, personnel, and ultimately the outcome. Decisions have consequences, and that comes with the job. This does not mean that you should not consider all facts or should not solicit input from others or should not think about consequences. All this is essential to good management. However, consider the laws of diminishing returns, where, beyond a certain point, additional time and energy is unnecessary and if continued can be counterproductive.

Managers, including project managers, are said to spend most of their time in meetings. Many managers would argue that they attend too many meetings and most meetings are too time-consuming. What is important is not so much the number of meetings one attends or the amount of time spent in meetings but what is accomplished in relation to time spent. Frequent meetings lose significance and may become an end to themselves rather than a means to achieving goals. Sometimes people "fill in the space" with unnecessary and even irrelevant remarks, leaving everyone else frustrated at this "waste of time." Attending meetings can be tiring and is amongst the least favored activities that managers do, together with report writing and documentation. An effective project manager conducts a meeting with a few principles in mind (see Exhibit 6.3).

---

**Exhibit 6.3   Principles About Meeting Management**

- Longer meetings do not necessarily produce better results
- The need for an agenda that is communicated to all
- The need for continued focus and control
- Opportunity for participation by all
- Summation of outcome and closure

## 6.3. Project Activity Network

A typical information systems project management job involves planning, scheduling, and controlling all activities necessary to design, develop, implement, or maintain a computer application on time and within budget and meet user expectations. Information systems projects involve activities relative to hardware, software, networks, database, procedure, and people. Large and complex projects involve the participation of groups and individuals other than team members. These might include user departments, outside consultants, vendors, and government agencies. Projects will include a variety of interdependent tasks and expertise that require systematic record keeping and good communication channels.

It is very important for the project manager to be able to monitor progress for each activity at all times. To help information systems project managers plan, schedule, and control projects, a variety of methodologies currently exist, many of them in the form of software tools that are easy to use and modify. This section will describe the techniques of *Program Evaluation Review Technique (PERT)* and *Critical Path Method (CPM)* for planning, scheduling, and controlling information systems project activities. Although PERT and CPM were developed separately and for different reasons, there are similarities between them. In recent years features of both methods have been combined in project management software tools, such as Microsoft Project (see appendix). As shown in Exhibit 6.4, PERT/CPM helps project managers in their role in a number of ways.

---

### Exhibit 6.4 Potential of PERT/CPM

- Estimate minimum time required for completing the entire project.
- Identify critical activities that must be completed in time for the entire project to be completed as scheduled.
- Show progress status for critical activities.
- Show progress status for noncritical activities.
- Estimate the length of time that these noncritical activities can be delayed.
- Estimate the likelihood of completing the entire project on schedule.

---

PERT/CPM shows the *sequence* and *duration* for each activity and enables the information systems project manager to determine which task may become a bottleneck and thus delay the entire project. It illustrates the interrelationship of events and activities involved in a project. PERT is described in terms of a network that consists of activities connected by arrows. Each activity is labeled by a number or a character and has a beginning, duration, and ending. You should be able to refer to each activity on this network in terms of when it starts, when it ends, and how long it takes to complete. Where each activity is depicted on the network suggests its position relative to other activities; activities that it follows and activities that it precedes.

Consider, for example, activities involved for a Web page development project. We will use a simplified version just to demonstrate the principles of a typical PERT/CPM network. This project involves the nine activities that were identified when producing the work breakdown structure discussed in Chapter 4. We can also estimate the duration for each activity and establish a sequence. The information can be organized as follows in Figure 6.3.

❖ **Figure 6.3**   Development of a Personal Web Page

| Activity | Activity Description | Duration (Days) | Preceding Activities |
|----------|---------------------|-----------------|----------------------|
| A | Determine user needs | 2 | – |
| B | Review software and languages | 2 | – |
| C | Purchase software | 1 | B |
| D | Design format and style | 3 | A, C |
| E | Write programs | 5 | D |
| F | Review outcome product with user | 1 | E |
| G | Make revisions | 2 | F |
| H | Select server site | 1 | – |
| I | Install on server and test | 2 | G |

Note that the total time required to complete the project is 19 days, but the project can be completed within 16 days because activities A, B, and H can start at the same time and they do not have preceding activities, making them independent of other activities. The PERT/CPM network diagram, shown in Figure 6.4, depicts these nine activities together with the estimated duration for each. An arrow presents each activity. Activity duration is shown below the arrow. The network depicts the interdependence of all activities needed to complete this project. It correctly identifies activity B as the predecessor for activity C, activities A and B as the predecessors for activity D, and activities G and H as the predecessors for activity I, the final activity. An activity can start only after the preceding activity is complete.

Using this network we can determine the total project completion time by identifying what is called the **critical path.** A **path** is a sequence of connected activities that extends from the starting node (1) to the completion node (8). The critical path in a network represents the longest path activities. Analyzing our nine-activity network, we can identify three paths. One path includes activities B, C, D, E, F, G, and I, which are connected by nodes 1–2–3–4–5–6–7–8. Another path includes activities A, D, E, F, G, and I, which are connected by nodes 1–3–4–5–6–7–8. And the third path includes activities H and I, which are connected by nodes 1–7–8. The total path duration for the first path is 16 days (2 + 1 + 3 + 5 + 1 + 2 + 2), for the second path is 15 days (2 + 3

❖ **Figure 6.4**   Network of Nine Activities

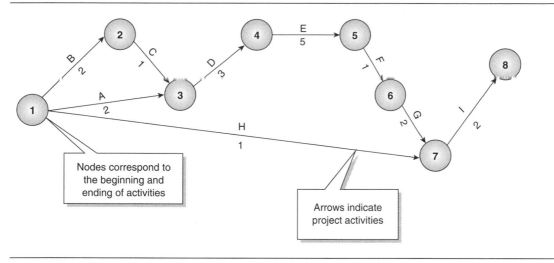

Nodes correspond to the beginning and ending of activities

Arrows indicate project activities

+ 5 + 1 + 2 + 2), and for the third path is 3 days (1 + 2). Thus the first path with the *longest* path activities is the critical path in this network.

To reduce the total duration of the project, we will need to examine activities on the critical path and try to see if we can shorten the duration of any of those activities. However, as we reduce duration for some activities on the critical path another path may become the longest, making it the new critical path. This process can get complicated as the network gets larger and more complex. A more systematic approach is required that helps identify properties of each activity within the network. It starts by determining the earliest start and the earliest finish as well as the latest start and the latest finish times for each activity as part of what is called *critical path analysis.*

## 6.4. Critical Path Analysis

To analyze the critical path, we must first compute *earliest start (ES)* and *earliest finish (EF)* time for each activity in the network. Starting at the origin of the network that is node 1 in our diagram, we assign 0 to the start of all activities that begin at node 1. The earliest finish time for an activity is calculated by adding the duration for that activity to the earliest start time for that activity. For example, activity A starts at time 0 and has a duration of 2 days to complete. Thus the earliest finish time for activity A is 0 + 2 = 2. Using the abbreviations ES and EF to represent earliest start and earliest finish and *t* to represent time duration, the relationship can be expressed as:

$$EF = ES + t$$

The earliest start time for activities with multiple predecessors is the largest finish time among all preceding activities because all activities leading to any specific activity must be complete before that activity can start. For example, activity D on our network can start only after activities A, B, and C are complete. Even though activity A is estimated to take 2 days, activity D cannot start until activity C is complete—that is, on Day 3 because activity C cannot start until its preceding activity, B, is complete. Thus, *the rule for setting the earliest start time for any activity is to consider the latest of the earliest finish times for all preceding activities.* To make our network more informative, we present ES and EF information above the arrow next to the letter representing each activity as shown in the revised network diagram (Figure 6.5).

❖ **Figure 6.5**   Network of Activities With ES and EF

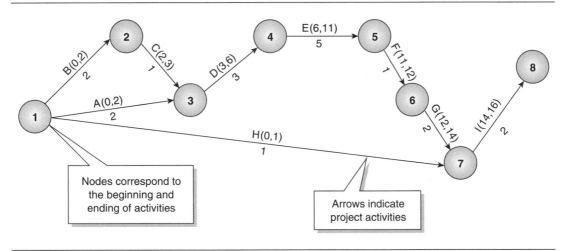

Once the earliest start and earliest finish times are worked out, we need to calculate the *latest start (LS)* and *latest finish (LF)* times. To do this, we must start from the last node and work backward, calculating LS and LF for each activity. In our network, we start from node 8 and activity I first. For activity I to complete on time, the latest finish time must be 16 (the same as EF time), and since it takes 2 days to complete this activity we can calculate the latest start time by subtracting 2 from 16. Using the abbreviations LS and LF to represent latest start and latest finish and *t* to represent duration, the relationship can be expressed as:

$$LF = LS + t$$

or

$$LS = LF - t$$

Using this expression we work backward and calculate the latest start time and the latest finish time for each activity on the network. If there is more than one activity leaving a node, *the rule for calculating the latest finish time for that activity is to use the smallest value of the latest start time for all activities leaving that activity.* This simply means that LF for any activity must be the same as the *smallest* LS for all activities following it. Otherwise it will cause delay in one or more of those activities that follow it. Using the relationship expressed as LF = LS + *t* (or LS = LF − *t*), we work backward to calculate LS and LF for activity G:

$$LF = 14$$

$$LS = 14 - 2 = 12$$

We need to continue this calculation for all activities. To reflect this information on our network diagram, we present LS and LF values below the arrow next to the duration for each activity as shown in Figure 6.6. The start and finish times shown on the diagram give detailed information for all activities. For example, Figure 6.7 depicts the information about activity H as part of the entire project network diagram.

❖ **Figure 6.6**   Network of Activities With ES, EF, LS, and LF

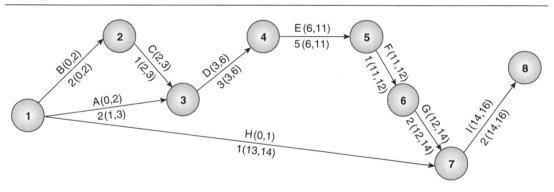

Note that activities with values of ES = LS and EF = LF form the critical path (Figure 6.6). Thus values in brackets above the arrow are identical to values in brackets below the arrow. Other activities are said to have *slack,* or free time. For example, activity A has 1-day slack time, calculated by LF − EF (3 − 2 = 1) or LS − ES (1 − 0 = 1). Similarly, activity H has 13 days slack time, calculated by LF − EF (14 − 1 = 13) or LS − ES (13 − 0 = 13). This means that activity A can start 1 day late and activity H can be delayed 13 days without any effect on the completion time for the entire project. Thus, ***activities with zero slack time form the critical path.*** This information can be presented in a tabular form in Table 6.1. Activities B, C, D, E, F, G, and I have zero slack and thus form the critical path.

To summarize, PERT/CPM provides answers to the important questions listed in Exhibit 6.5.

❖ **Figure 6.7**   ES, EF, LS, and LF for Activity H

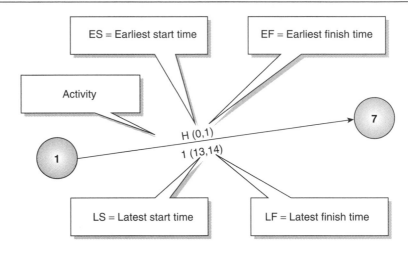

❖ **Table 6.1**   Activity Schedule for Web Page Development

| Activity | Duration | ES | LS | EF | LF | Slack |
|----------|----------|----|----|----|----|-------|
| A | 2 | 0 | 1 | 2 | 3 | 1 |
| B | 2 | 0 | 0 | 2 | 2 | 0 |
| C | 1 | 2 | 2 | 3 | 3 | 0 |
| D | 3 | 3 | 3 | 6 | 6 | 0 |
| E | 5 | 6 | 6 | 11 | 11 | 0 |
| F | 1 | 11 | 11 | 12 | 12 | 0 |
| G | 2 | 12 | 12 | 14 | 14 | 0 |
| H | 1 | 0 | 13 | 1 | 14 | 13 |
| I | 2 | 14 | 14 | 16 | 16 | 0 |

The outcome of any PERT/CPM application depends on:

- A complete list of activities necessary to complete the project
- A proper sequence of activities and identification of preceding activities
- Reliable activity estimates

Once this information is established, a few steps are required to complete the procedure as shown in Exhibit 6.6.

---

**Exhibit 6.5    Potential of PERT/CPM**

- What is the total time to complete the project?
- What are the scheduled start and completion times for each activity?
- What activities are critical and must be completed as scheduled in order to complete the entire project on time?
- What are noncritical activities, and how long can they be delayed before affecting the completion time for the entire project?

---

**Exhibit 6.6    PERT/CPM—The Final Steps**

- Draw the network diagram showing all activities and their preceding activities.
- Calculate the completion time for the entire project, determining the earliest start time and the earliest finish time for each activity on the network. The earliest finish time for the last activity gives the project completion time.
- Calculate slack times by determining the latest start time and the latest finish time for each activity, working backward through the network. For each activity, the difference between the latest start time and the earliest start time or the difference between the latest finish time and the earliest finish time is the slack time.
- Determine the critical path by identifying activities with zero slack time.

## 6.5. Estimating Activity Duration

It is important to estimate activity duration as accurately as possible. To do this, information systems project managers rely on experience, documentation, and input from experts. Experienced information systems project managers tend to use past projects as a basis for estimating activities. They may modify such estimates upward or downward depending on changes in technology, the skill level of team members, vendor reliability, resource availability, and so on. For example, a new technology may speed up certain activities but at the same time may call for a higher skill set that requires training of project team members. Often a new technology is learned through self-training, and that too requires additional resources. Documentation such as reports, time sheets, and work plans also provide project managers with details about previous projects. In many cases reference to historical data is a better option than relying on memory. Experience and historical data are useful for repeat projects. Estimating activity time for unique projects is likely to prove more difficult.

In estimating activity duration for unique projects or when experience is lacking or historical data do not exist, information systems project managers can get input from experts to estimate activity duration. In fact, when uncertain, information systems project managers may obtain multiple estimates for each activity and take the weighted average rather than relying on a single estimate. A popular approach for estimating activity duration involves obtaining three estimates. One estimate is referred to as *optimistic*, and it is based on the assumption that everything is under control and the activity will progress according to an "ideal" plan. Another estimate is referred to as *pessimistic*, and it is based on the assumption that whatever can go wrong will go wrong. The third estimate is referred to as the *most likely*, and it is based on a reasonable assumption of normality, somewhere between the other two.

These three estimates provide a range of values from the best possible situation to the worst possible one. To avoid putting undue emphasis on the extreme estimates, the most likely value is counted four times compared with optimistic and pessimistic values. For example, if we have optimistic, most likely, and pessimistic estimates of 3.5 weeks, 5.5 weeks, and 9 weeks for a given activity, we can calculate the *t* value for that activity using the following formula:

$$t = (o + 4m + p)/6$$

where $o$ is for the optimistic estimate, $m$ is for the most likely estimate, and $p$ is for the pessimistic estimate. Thus, the expected duration for the activity in our example is:

$$t = (3.5 + 4(5.5) + 9)/6 = 5.75 \text{ weeks}$$

Given the distribution among the range of values for this activity, we can calculate the variance in these values using commonly used standard deviation formula. The variance is the square of the standard deviation and is calculated using the following formula.

$$\sigma^2 = ((p - o)/6)^2$$

This formula assumes that standard deviation is approximately 1/6 of the difference between the extreme values of the distribution. Using this formula, the variance for our example will be:

$$\sigma^2 = ((9 - 3.5)/6)^2 = 0.84$$

The variance reflects the degree of uncertainty in the estimated value for any activity duration. The greater the range between the optimistic estimates ($o$) and the pessimistic estimates ($p$) the greater the variance and uncertainty.

We will review what we have covered for PERT/CPM through an example. Consider an information system project with seven activities listed in Table 6.2. The systems analyst has obtained three estimates that represent *optimistic*, the *most likely*, and *pessimistic* times (in days) for each activity. The activity sequence is also determined, and preceding events for each activity are shown. Given this information we want to:

1. Draw the network diagram.

2. Determine duration for each activity.

❖ **Table 6.2**  Uncertain Duration Estimates for Seven Activities

| Activity | Preceding Activities | Optimistic (o) | Most Likely (m) | Pessimistic (p) |
|----------|----------------------|----------------|-----------------|-----------------|
| A | - | 6 | 7 | 8 |
| B | - | 6 | 9 | 14 |
| C | A | 7 | 9 | 11 |
| D | A | 5 | 10 | 12 |
| E | C,B | 7 | 10 | 12 |
| F | D | 8 | 8 | 11 |
| G | E,F | 5 | 8 | 10 |

3. Determine the critical path.

4. Compute slack times for noncritical activities.

5. Compute the expected project completion time and the variance.

6. Use the variance information and compute the probability that the entire project will be complete in 35 days.

The PERT/CPM network for the information system project is shown in Figure 6.8. The network depicts the preceding activities as described in Table 6.2.

Next, we need to compute the duration for each activity using optimistic, the most likely, and pessimistic estimates given in Table 6.2. For example using the formula provided above, the expected duration *t* for activity A will be:

$$t = (o + 4m + p)/6$$

$$t_A = (6 + 4(7) + 8)/6 = 42/6 = 7 \text{ days}$$

Using the above formula for variance and the distribution between values of 6 (optimistic), 7 (most likely), and 8 (pessimistic), the variance for activity A will be:

$$\sigma^2 = ((p - o)/6)^2$$

$$\sigma^2_A = [8 - 6)/6]^2 = 0.11$$

Note that for the variance formula we only use extreme values of optimistic and pessimistic. Using the data in Table 6.2 and the above formulas, we continue and calculate expected duration and variance for all activities. Table 6.3 provides the expected

❖ **Figure 6.8**    Network of Seven Activities

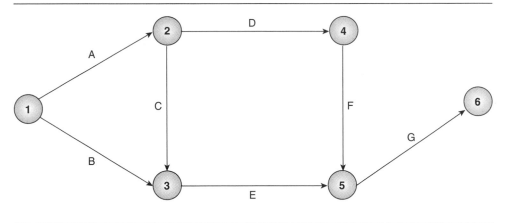

❖ **Table 6.3**    Expected Duration and Variance for Seven Activities

| Activity | Optimistic (*o*) | Most Likely (*m*) | Pessimistic (*p*) | Expected *t* (days) | Variance $\sigma^2$ |
|----------|------------------|-------------------|-------------------|---------------------|---------------------|
| A | 6 | 7 | 8 | 7.0 | 0.11 |
| B | 6 | 9 | 14 | 9.3 | 1.78 |
| C | 7 | 9 | 11 | 9.0 | 0.44 |
| D | 5 | 10 | 12 | 9.5 | 1.36 |
| E | 7 | 10 | 12 | 9.8 | 0.69 |
| F | 8 | 8 | 11 | 8.5 | 0.25 |
| G | 5 | 8 | 10 | 7.8 | 0.69 |

duration and variance for each of the seven activities. In this example, activity duration is estimated in terms of days. For larger projects, weeks and months may be used to estimate activity duration. Whatever is the unit of estimates, it should be used consistently throughout the estimating process, in progress reports, and other documents.

Based on the information given in Table 6.3 for activity duration, we now proceed to establish the earliest start (ES) and the earliest finish (EF) times for each activity going forward through the network. Figure 6.9 shows the network of seven activities together with activity duration as well as ES and EF information. On this network, the earliest finish time for the last activity, G, is 33.6 days. That means the expected duration for the entire project is 33.6 days.

❖ **Figure 6.9** Network of Seven Activities With ES and EF

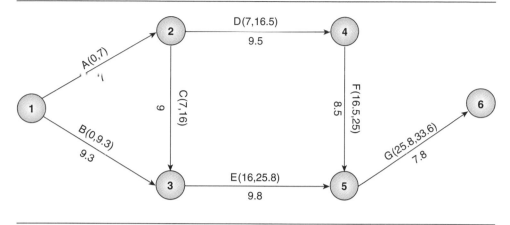

❖ **Figure 6.10** Network of Seven Activities With ES, EF, LS, and LF

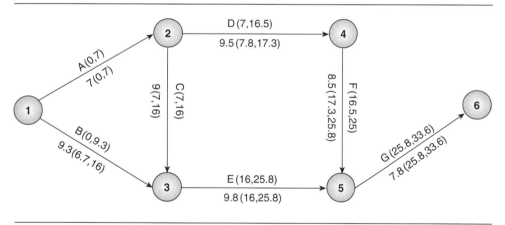

Next, to find the critical path we need to calculate the latest start (LS) and the latest finish (LF) times by working backward through the network. The information computed through this procedure is given in Figure 6.10, showing the network schedule. The information about the earliest start (ES) and the earliest finish (EF) times as well as the latest start (LS) and the latest finish (LF) times are summarized in Table 6.4. This information suggests that activities A, C, E, and G form the critical path for this project. These are the activities with zero slack time. The slack times for noncritical activities are shown in the last column of Table 6.4. Note that activity B can start anytime between zero and 9.3 days without affecting the overall project duration.

❖ Table 6.4   Activity Schedule for the Project With Seven Activities

| Activity | Earliest Start ES | Earliest Finish EF | Latest Start LS | Latest Finish LF | Slack (LS – ES) |
|----------|-------------------|--------------------|-----------------|------------------|-----------------|
| A | 0 | 7 | 0 | 7 | 0 |
| B | 0 | 9.3 | 6.7 | 16 | 9.3 |
| C | 7 | 16 | 7 | 16 | 0 |
| D | 7 | 16.5 | 7.8 | 17.3 | .8 |
| E | 16 | 25.8 | 16 | 25.8 | 0 |
| F | 16.5 | 25 | 17.3 | 25.8 | .8 |
| G | 25.8 | 33.6 | 25.8 | 33.6 | 0 |

Information system project managers are often asked whether a project will be complete by a certain date and the probability of that happening, similar to the last question on the list of questions we posed for the seven-activity project. To compute a response to our final question, we need to use the calculated variance for activities on the critical path and a commonly used table of standard normal distribution. This table gives the information for any value between the mean and a given value of standard deviation from the mean. This value is expressed by the letter $z$ and is calculated by dividing the difference between the mean and the desired completion time (35 days in our example) by standard deviation($\sigma$). As you will recall, the standard deviation is the variance squared. To calculate the variance for the entire project we simply add variance for activities on the critical path. If we represent the duration for the entire project by the letter $T$, we will have:

$$\text{Variance (T)} = \sigma^2_A + \sigma^2_C + \sigma^2_E + \sigma^2_G$$

$$= .11 + .44 + .69 + .69 = 1.93$$

We then compute the standard deviation for the project's completion time as:

$$\sigma = \sqrt{\sigma^2} = \sqrt{1.93} = 1.39$$

The $z$ value for the normal distribution at day 35 is computed as:

$$z = (35 - 33.6)/1.39 = 1$$

For $z = 1$, the normal distribution table suggests the probability value of 0.3413. The chapter on quality includes a normal distribution table (Figure 12.3). This value is a portion in one-half of the area under the normal distribution curve. Thus the probability of completing the project in 35 days is 0.3413 + 0.5000 = 0.8413. Thus there is an 84% chance that the project will be completed in 35 days. We summarize responses to our six questions in Exhibit 6.7.

---

**Exhibit 6.7    Responses to Our Six Questions**

1. The network diagram is shown in Figure 6.8.

2. The durations are shown in Figure 6.9.

3. The critical path includes A - C - E - G (see Table 6.4).

4. Slack times for noncritical activities are shown in the last column of Table 6.4. Three activities have slack time.

5. The expected project duration is 33.6 days (see Figure 6.9) and the project variance is 1.93.

6. There is an 84% chance that the entire project will be completed in 35 days.

---

## 6.6. Resource Implications

The allocation of resources to a project is a task that can make or break a project, and we look in Chapter 9 at the process of forming a project team. However, in this section we consider the more mechanistic aspects. In Table 6.5 we show a simple form using Microsoft Project to support the resource allocation task. Here we are allocating time of people (Joe, Bill, and Ted) to activities (Tasks 1, 2, and 3).

By including the hourly rates of people in the resource details we can calculate the costs of our resource usage for each task as shown in Table 6.6.

This information can be used to generate a resource allocation graph using a computer software package such as Microsoft Project (see the appendix to this chapter). As you will see when using this software or another planning tool, although it may take

---

❖ **Table 6.5    Allocating People Hours to Activities**

| Resource Name | Work | Details | T | W | T | F | S | S | M (14 May '07) | T | W | T | F | S |
|---|---|---|---|---|---|---|---|---|---|---|---|---|---|---|
| Joe | 36.8 hrs | Work | | 6.4h | 6.4h | 6.4h | | | 6.4h | 6.4h | | | 1.8h | |
| Task 3 | 4.8 hrs | Work | | | | | | | | | | | 1.8h | |
| Task 1 | 32 hrs | Work | | 6.4h | 6.4h | 6.4h | | | 6.4h | 6.4h | | | | |
| ⊟ Bill | 28.8 hrs | Work | | 4.8h | 4.8h | 4.8h | | | 4.8h | 4.8h | | | 1.8h | |
| Task 3 | 4.8 hrs | Work | | | | | | | | | | | 1.8h | |
| Task 1 | 24 hrs | Work | | 4.8h | 4.8h | 4.8h | | | 4.8h | 4.8h | | | | |
| ⊟ Ted | 46.4 hrs | Work | | 5.6h | 5.6h | 5.6h | | | 5.6h | 5.6h | 5.6h | 5.6h | 2.4h | |
| Task 3 | 7.2 hrs | Work | | | | | | | | | | | 2.4h | |
| Task 2 | 39.2 hrs | Work | | 5.6h | 5.6h | 5.6h | | | 5.6h | 5.6h | 5.6h | 5.6h | | |
| ⊟ Bill (half time) | 11.2 hrs | Work | | 1.6h | 1.6h | 1.6h | | | 1.6h | 1.6h | 1.6h | 1.6h | | |
| Task 2 | 11.2 hrs | Work | | 1.6h | 1.6h | 1.6h | | | 1.6h | 1.6h | 1.6h | 1.6h | | |
| Ted (half time) | 0 hrs | Work | | | | | | | | | | | | |
| David | 0 hrs | Work | | | | | | | | | | | | |
| Printing | 0 | Work | | | | | | | | | | | | |

❖ **Table 6.6**  Costs of Tasks

| | Task Name | Total Cost | Baseline | Variance | Actual | Remaining |
|---|---|---|---|---|---|---|
| 1 | Task 3 | £348.00 | £348.00 | £0.00 | £0.00 | £348.00 |
| 2 | Task 1 | £1,400.00 | £1,400.00 | £0.00 | £0.00 | £1,400.00 |
| 3 | Task 2 | £756.00 | £756.00 | £0.00 | £0.00 | £756.00 |
| | | | | | | |

time to learn, it does support much of the work of the project manager and eases progress tracking, re-planning, and what-if analysis. Further, the quality of presentation is much better than attempting the same by hand.

Software packages can also aggregate the various resources, such as the number of people working on the activity, and attempt to smooth their use throughout the project. This *resource smoothing* process can be particularly useful as management reviews and approves of plans. It is usually better to use resources as smoothly as possible in the lifetime of the project, otherwise staff will be used efficiently for only part of the project. Although the examples presented here and in the appendix would not be too difficult to replicate by hand, software is required for a project that has hundreds of activities and tens of people working on it. Such numbers are by no means unrealistic. Resource smoothing in such circumstances can have a dramatic effect in reducing overall costs.

Normally, although not necessarily, as Fred Brooks has observed (see Section 3.3), there is a tradeoff between time and cost (assuming the same quality); in other words, the more resources allocated (and the more costly the project), the quicker it can be finished. Conversely, resource smoothing may well delay the project as fewer resources may lead to critical activities being delayed. However, by taking resources out of noncritical activities, the reduction in cost may not be associated with an equivalent increase in project time. It might also be possible to exchange certain resources if talents are duplicated. The project manager may also like to input various estimates of resource availability, basing them on past experience in terms of minimum, most likely, and maximum figures. This will give three different results for time/cost comparisons.

Many project control packages will report on inconsistencies within the network, such as the same resource being used at the same time on more than one activity. Although the plan should allow for minor deviations, the package may permit the project manager to ask "what if?" questions so that the consequences of more major deviations can be seen—for example, the implications of reallocating staff, unexpected staff leave, or machine breakdown. Useful reports from a package might also include a list of activities presented in order of latest starting date and earliest starting date and information by department or by resource or by responsibility.

Packages can simulate the effects of prolonging an activity—reducing resources applied to it or adding new activities. Similarly, they can be used to show the effects of changing these parameters on project costs. The project manager may be faced with two alternatives: a resource-limited schedule, where the project end date is put back to reflect resource constraints, or a time-limited schedule, where a fixed project end date leads to an increase in other resources used, such as people and equipment. As Exhibit 6.8 shows, a package can also monitor progress to reveal the present situation and look at alternative plans to get a failing project back on track.

---

**Exhibit 6.8    Progress Monitoring**

- Compare the time schedule with the actual progress made.
- Compare the cost schedule with the actual costs.
- Maintain the involvement of users and clients.
- Detect problem areas and re-plan and reschedule as a result.
- Inform management of the new plan and get their agreement.
- Provide a historical record, both for projects meeting goals and those that do not, as they can both be useful for future project planning.

---

## 6.7. Avoiding Project Delay

Information systems projects are often not completed on time. Timely delivery remains a difficult task for information systems project managers. Every project manager has reasons for justifying delays. Here are a few suggestions to help more timely delivery.

*Communications.* Time estimates for each activity as well as progress toward completing each activity must be clearly communicated to team members and be readily available to them at all times. Project managers need to decide what method of communication will best serve their situation. Information systems technology and project management tools such as MS Project and spreadsheets are readily available and easily applicable for preparing timetables and controlling schedules. Yet, many projects are late even when a software tool is used to keep track of time. Many project managers use software to keep themselves informed of project activity time and progress. However, they often keep that information to themselves. It needs to be communicated to team members.

*Methods.* Activity times are as good as the methods used to estimate them. Complex and sophisticated methods do not automatically produce reliable estimates. It takes time and needs careful preparation. Rushing through that task will result in project delay later on. Estimates are as good as their source. Experience is, by and large, the best source of estimating time requirements, and that requires good documentation and archiving. For new activities for which we have no records, the judgments of many experts provide a useful source. Team members must understand those methods and believe that estimates are realistic; people will more readily accept and comply if they understand how estimates are prepared.

*Separation.* Team members are responsible for work units that they are specifically assigned to and they are accountable for. Project managers are responsible for separating team members' work and responsibilities from those of stakeholders such as users and functional managers who may want to influence the project timetable or process. Team members might be bogged down by stakeholder interference or unexpected demands. Project managers should prepare and communicate clear policies in order to help team members with their time management.

*Support.* Team members must feel confident of project manager support in order to stick to their schedule. Often when functional managers get involved with the project planning they tend to continue that involvement into the development phase, and that could create confusion for team members and their responsibilities. Project managers must act as a buffer between team members and the management in order to provide necessary breathing space to the project team for timely completion of their tasks. Project managers must use their political influence to support and protect their team members.

*Analysis.* Often project delay is due to poor up-front needs analysis. By and large the temptation by system developers is to get to the development phase of a system too quickly and as a result they rush through the analysis phase. To avoid delay later on, project managers must provide leadership to ensure careful needs analysis is carried out before allowing the project to go on. Poor up-front needs analysis may ultimately cause significant project delay, especially in terms of project rework.

*Closure.* Many people do good work but they just don't know when to stop, and that is not unique to information systems professionals. The laws of diminishing returns suggest that marginal benefit relative to time and effort spent on a task will eventually reach a point where benefits turn into costs. Team members need to be reminded that similar to the project itself, each task requires closure and members need to move on to the next tasks. A similar problem exists when people kill a lot of time searching for some information on the Web that may not exist or may be easier to get elsewhere, such as by asking colleagues. Project managers are responsible to move resources, including human resources, on to the next phase and next project.

## 6.8. Interview With a Project Manager

This interview took place with a project manager at one of the largest contractors in the United States.

What would you consider to be the most challenging aspect to being a project manager?

"My company currently has many projects. In fact, they have more projects than project managers. This requires that all of us manage multiple projects concurrently. I am managing three of the top ten projects currently assigned to the IT department. I would say that both proper prioritization and time management are the most challenging. You must ensure you spend the right amount of time on the right project to ensure all your goals are met."

What project management tools and computer software do you find the most useful?

"We are using Project 2002 and Project 2002 Server as our project management software tools. These allow us to track all of our projects and provide pretty accurate time estimates. It's best to estimate the project up front and then provide a work breakdown structure once the estimate is provided. This is a pretty accurate method, provided you have the expertise at your disposal to input accurate time estimates on the project."

What skills are essential to becoming a "successful" project manager? How many projects have you been involved in, and how many have actually been a "success"?

"People skill has to be the most important for both internal and external communications. Many times you run into people who are very contentious, and keeping the peace can be both extremely important and paramount to the continued success of your project. Next to that would be organization, especially when you're controlling multiple projects such as we do. Without the ability to stay organized and on track, your project will most assuredly fail! For instance, as a project manager, recording information is everything. Maintaining your paperwork and relaying information to people helps keep your infrastructure [resources] on time, on schedule, and under budget. Most projects fail because everything wasn't recorded and something was omitted during the processing of requirements. Without defining the proper user requirements up front, you can bet your bottom dollar that the project has a good chance of failing.

A good case in point would be a colleague of mine who was in charge of a file expense recording system. He failed to ensure the data he was given was both accurate and complete. The project began suffering immensely from scope creep, and the project ended up over time, and over budget, as well as incomplete."

How do you forecast the necessary time to complete a step in the work breakdown structure?

"We use two methods for forecasting time. Both are software driven and were good when we first purchased them. The way they work is that you plug in input transactions, output transactions, and other deliverables and then the program will provide you an estimated time. We are currently preparing to evaluate some different software, as it is more exact than what we currently employ."

*(Continued)*

(Continued)

When calculating project costs, do you budget in slack time or do you provide a full assessment and a separate contingency assessment? If you do use the contingency assessment, how do you determine what constitutes an appropriate amount?

"Estimates are sometimes, if not most often, overstated by experts. One project we had, not too long ago, estimated a particular timeframe for completion. We provided this estimate to our experts who had actually been involved with a project very similar to this one. They gave us an estimate that cut the original one in half, and we still ended up under time. Estimating is a science that is very difficult to master. One of the estimate tools we own is called QFM. It utilizes historic industry data as a factor where it takes knowledge obtained across the industry and factors that into the calculations for budgeting time. It always seems to provide us a poor time estimate, as they always seem out of whack by our experts.

Contingency time isn't something that is well accepted by our upper management. They feel that putting down something called 'contingency' on paper leaves open too many questions. They feel it makes us look unprepared and that we are looking for a way to factor in extra costs. We're always expected to factor the contingency time across the entire project."

How do you successfully manage customer expectations without overwhelming them with too much information about the project?

"People skills! Know your customer! By knowing the technical expertise of your customer, you have a pretty good idea of what or how much information to provide. Remember that scope creep is always a huge danger, so you should know how much to tell your customer, but you should always know where the 'borders' of the project are. Failure to clarify requirements can cause major problems as the project progresses. We call this the 'Bring Me a Rock' syndrome. Basically, the customer asks you to bring them a rock. When you provide it, they say it's too big. The next rock you bring is too small. The next one is too round. This goes on and on and on! You should always negotiate with the user up front for the scope of the project. If something is brought to you later, you must draw the line or negotiate different project phases. You close out the requirements list and then start a second one for the 'second generation' of the project."

How do you ensure project team members are spending adequate time on their project-specific tasks when these people are not under your direct supervision?

"I use time sheets and weekly reports and weekly meetings to keep track of specific project tasks. Project Server is great for this, as everyone must put in their own time into the program. I can download this weekly to obtain a results synopsis and know where to direct more of my attention."

What was the last project under your management? Was the project a success? What hurdles prevented you from successfully completing the project, or what main factors contributed to the successful completion?

"The last project I managed was an Automated Customer Price List Tracking program. The project was originally built by the customer in Microsoft Access, which sat on one person's desktop and allowed no one else to access. We changed this into an enterprise application and brought it to a successful completion. The problems we encountered were the fact that the person who had built and maintained it no longer worked at the company. We had to figure out what the logic behind the application was before we could prepare any type of estimation of the project, and this was extremely difficult.

I haven't had a project that failed, but another colleague of mine did. This was a tracking application that just finished 3 weeks ago. It finished 3 weeks late in fact! This was due to scope creep caused by the customer, and we had already received, in writing, the customer confirmation that they knew this would happen due to the additional functionality requested."

Have you had to cancel a project after significant resources (time, money, and personnel) were already spent? If so, were there repercussions that affected your management of future projects?

"Yes!! In fact, I had just finished the project the day before and it was being deployed as I was on my way to work. I received a call from our management screaming at me to stop its deployment immediately! We stopped it right away and later found out that this project was pretty much dead. I had inherited this project from the desk of someone who had been laid off months prior to its scheduled completion. It had been overlooked until the customer had called on a status update. The original estimate provided by the, now departed, project manager had been way off. Additionally, he had not recorded the entire project scope, and much of what the project was expected to do was not available. We lost a lot of money on that project."

Of the projects you have managed, which one was the most challenging? Please explain.

"The Oracle 11-5-8 update has to be the most challenging yet. This project started back in the summer of 2000 and went into production in 2002. It was a huge effort that cost $3 million in the first year, had three project managers, and consisted of implementing both new hardware and software. The software being used was Oracle, and we had to have it upgraded twice before we could get it to work. This required a huge collaborative effort with the people at Oracle (the customer had a contact there and insisted on us utilizing it as the back end). Budgeting the resources was most challenging, as there was a lot of overtime involved and it was costing a lot to keep the project going. We managed to pull it off, though!"

How were you able to control a project effectively if there were three project managers?

"The size of the project pretty much required that many. One project manager was a functional manager, another was in charge of documentation, and I was in charge of coordinating the efforts. This is where documentation and devotion to constant communication becomes necessary. What helped out a lot was co-locating the functional managers for both us and the customer. By working together [side by side], they were able to get instant answers and feedback when it was required."

*(Continued)*

(Continued)

Tell me about the most difficult client contact you have made in the last 6 months. What obstacles did you face? How did you overcome them?

"I was put in charge of the Work Smart Standards project, which was managed by the Department of Energy (DOE). The DOE asked me to take over for them, and that's when I found out about the problems! No formal requirements had been developed. This caused me to stop the entire project and develop those requirements and time estimates before going anywhere. Several hands have a stake in this, including the DOE, my company, and the federal government. The bureaucracy is unbelievable! I finished the estimates several months ago, and I'm still waiting for an okay to proceed."

As a project manager, what are some tips you would give to aspiring project managers?

"Stock up on aspirin and antacids! Seriously, I would say that a project manager should always stay upbeat and take things with a grain of salt. What I mean is that if you get too caught up in the pressures of the job, you're just waiting for something to happen, and it probably will. Always learn from your mistakes and take it all in stride. Most of all have fun doing it!"

Do you feel organizations consider formal project management processes and training a waste of resources?

"My company most definitely does not! We are always getting the training we need, and there is an open-door policy anytime something doesn't seem to be going right.

Of course, we're not without problems. A good case in point is the title of project manager. Since my company is a project management company, we actually have a department of people who have the title of project manager. Since we are a small part of the overall company, politics decided we shouldn't be called project managers."

Do you think employees are adequately evaluated/compensated for their participation in projects, especially when this participation is above and beyond their day-to-day responsibilities?

"I'm not sure how others do this, but when I feel someone has really worked hard, I write letters to their immediate supervisors and department managers recognizing them for their efforts. I have no more control after that point, and so I can't tell you if they receive anything more than a pat on the back."

How many of your projects have involved the participation of a third-party company? What unique challenges did you encounter with this type of project team configuration?

"Most of our projects involve a third party. We are a contractor, and therefore we contract to different companies all the time. Oracle and Northrop-Grumman are a couple of examples. It's really hard to narrow down what unique challenges there are because they vary from company to company. Coordination is probably one of the factors I would say is challenging. Another is aligning our ideas and strategies with theirs."

## 6.9. Chapter Summary

Timely delivery of any information systems project is a critical success factor. Together with cost and project scope, time is considered a constraint in the triple-constraints concept. A large project with many activities requires careful scheduling that allocates time for each individual activity. Communicating and monitoring these activity times is an important task for the information systems project manager. One of the most widely used tools for managing time and schedule is PERT-CPM. This helps the management of the overall project duration as well as the individual activities. This time management tool *helps to set time, identify activity sequence, communicate time constraints, and monitor progress.*

A critical part of developing a PERT-CPM network is obtaining reliable estimates. Sources for estimating activity time include the experience of project managers themselves, input by others involved in similar project activities, and documentation. This chapter highlights the importance of time management and suggests ways to schedule activities better and monitor their progress. It also suggests ways of estimating the likelihood of project completion within a specified time and how time improvement can be made through the critical path analysis. Finally, it discusses resource implications and discusses ways in which resource use can affect project time.

## DISCUSSION QUESTIONS

1. Discuss the idea that time is a resource but also a constraint. Is this a contradiction?

2. Describe signs that tell you if an information system project manager is managing time effectively or not. What specific suggestions do you have for a project manager who is deficient in time management skills?

3. Discuss ways of obtaining good estimates for a project activity. What are good sources of getting estimates? What is prudent to do when you need to estimate an activity for the first time? Is it prudent to overestimate time for new activities or underestimate them?

4. How does information on variance help you assess uncertainty? What would you do when you have higher confidence in one of the estimators?

5. In Exhibit 6.1 we had the views of Terry Young, who argued that experience, the willingness to negotiate, and the commitment of people were far more important than the use of techniques such as PERT to achieve a successful project. Yet others argue that the correct use of techniques will more likely lead to a positive result. Argue each case and also suggest a "middle ground."

# EXERCISES

1. Consider the IS project with seven activities (Table 6.2) described in this chapter. Use the variance given in Table 6.3 and compute the number of days that gives the project manager a 95% chance of completing the entire project.

2. Again, consider the IS project with seven activities (Table 6.2) described in this chapter. What will happen if activity F took 1 day longer than it is estimated to complete?

3. It is often suggested that project managers obtain three time estimates for work units that have significant uncertainty associated with their time estimates. Assume you have collected three time estimates for each activity for a performance monitoring system at an international airport baggage handling systems. Your "cost estimate worksheet" suggests the following:

   Project estimate:                     250 hours

   Project standard deviation:           18 hours

   Based on this information and assuming three standard deviations from the mean to include approximately 99.75% of the area under the normal distribution curve, calculate:

   - Project highest credible hours
   - Project lowest credible hours
   - Upper confidence limit
   - Lower confidence limit

   Explain to the airport executives, your project sponsors, what these numbers mean.

## APPENDIX TO CHAPTER 6:
## AN INTRODUCTION TO MICROSOFT PROJECT

MS Project is a project management tool that allows the tasks involved in a project to be structured in an informative way. We provide two tutorial exercises to using MS Project in this appendix. With software, the best way of getting to know it is through practice. We have used the 2007 version of Microsoft Project.

# PART 1. ENTERING TASK DETAILS AND START DATE

1. Start MS Project. **Project1** will appear on the screen, as shown below:

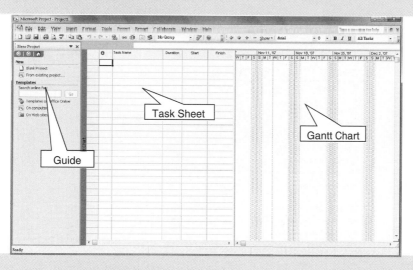

Common to all of Microsoft's 2002, XP, and Vista applications, there is a guide displayed along with the main task sheet and Gantt chart. The guide is shown on the left. The task sheet is a spreadsheet-like table on the middle of the screen, while the (currently empty) Gantt chart is on the right-hand side. You will see the Gantt chart being created as you enter information into the task sheet.

2. To give us more room to see what we are doing, close the guide by clicking on the ⌧ to the right of **New Project** ( New Project ▼ ✕ ).

3. Save the project with the file name Project1. Now we will create the project plan.

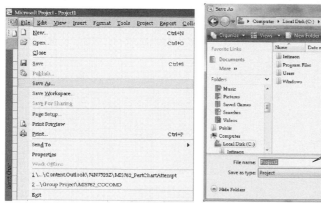
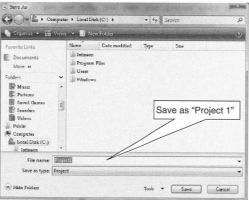

*(Continued)*

(Continued)

4. Using the WBS contained at the end of this first tutorial example, type in the task names in the column that says **Task Name**.

| | ❶ | Task Name | Duration | Start | Finish | Predecessors | Resource |
|---|---|---|---|---|---|---|---|
| 1 | | DEFINITION | 1 day? | Tue 11/13/07 | Tue 11/13/07 | | |
| 2 | | Write requirements document | 1 day? | Tue 11/13/07 | Tue 11/13/07 | | |
| 3 | | Done | | Tue 11/13/07 | Tue 11/13/07 | | |
| 4 | | ANALYSIS | | | | | |
| 5 | | Interview users | | Enter tasks in this column | | | |
| 6 | | Prepare functional specification (FS) | 1 day? | Tue 11/13/07 | Tue 11/13/07 | | |
| 7 | | Negotiate FS with users | 1 day? | Tue 11/13/07 | Tue 11/13/07 | | |
| 8 | | Revise FS (1 time only) | 1 day? | Tue 11/13/07 | Tue 11/13/07 | | |
| 9 | | Renegotiate FS (1 time only) | 1 day? | Tue 11/13/07 | Tue 11/13/07 | | |
| 10 | | Approval obtained | 1 day? | Tue 11/13/07 | Tue 11/13/07 | | |
| 11 | | DESIGN | 1 day? | Tue 11/13/07 | Tue 11/13/07 | | |
| 12 | | High level software design | 1 day? | Tue 11/13/07 | Tue 11/13/07 | | |
| 13 | | Mid level software design | 1 day? | Tue 11/13/07 | Tue 11/13/07 | | |
| 14 | | User acceptance of design | 1 day? | Tue 11/13/07 | Tue 11/13/07 | | |
| 15 | | PROGRAMMING | 1 day? | Tue 11/13/07 | Tue 11/13/07 | | |
| 16 | | System A | 1 day? | Tue 11/13/07 | Tue 11/13/07 | | |
| 17 | | Module 1 | 1 day? | Tue 11/13/07 | Tue 11/13/07 | | |
| 18 | | Module 2 | 1 day? | Tue 11/13/07 | Tue 11/13/07 | | |
| 19 | | Module 3 | 1 day? | Tue 11/13/07 | Tue 11/13/07 | | |
| 20 | | System B | 1 day? | Tue 11/13/07 | Tue 11/13/07 | | |
| 21 | | Module 1 | 1 day? | Tue 11/13/07 | Tue 11/13/07 | | |
| 22 | | Module 2 | 1 day? | Tue 11/13/07 | Tue 11/13/07 | | |
| 23 | | Module 3 | 1 day? | Tue 11/13/07 | Tue 11/13/07 | | |
| 24 | | Module 4 | 1 day? | Tue 11/13/07 | Tue 11/13/07 | | |
| 25 | | Programming complete | 1 day? | Tue 11/13/07 | Tue 11/13/07 | | |
| 26 | | SYSTEM TEST | 1 day? | Tue 11/13/07 | Tue 11/13/07 | | |
| 27 | | System integration and test | 1 day? | Tue 11/13/07 | Tue 11/13/07 | | |

As you type, MS Project will query the length of each task. Don't worry about that for the moment. We will put in names first, then indent, then type in durations, and then define predecessors.

5. Once you have typed in all the names, indent the sub-tasks as shown in the WBS. Note, for instance, that **DEFINITION** is a top-level task name, while **Write requirements document** is a sub-level task and must be indented in MS Project using the indent ( ➔ ) button located middle-right of the toolbar ( ⬅ ➔ ✛ ━ Show ▾ ). All inden-
tations must be as

they appear in the work breakdown structure. You will notice that all major task names are now shown in bold. **NOTE:** A number of tasks can be indented at the same time by selecting the rows and clicking on the indent button.

| | 🛈 | Task Name | Duration | Start | Finish | Predecessors | Resource |
|---|---|---|---|---|---|---|---|
| 1 | | − **DEFINITION** | **1 day?** | **Tue 11/13/07** | **Tue 11/13/07** | | |
| 2 | | Write requirements document | 1 day? | Tue 11/13/07 | Tue 11/13/07 | | |
| 3 | | Done | 1 day? | Tue 11/13/07 | Tue 11/13/07 | | |
| 4 | | − **ANALYSIS** | **1 day?** | **Tue 11/13/07** | **Tue 11/13/07** | | |
| 5 | | Interview users | 1 day? | Tue 11/13/07 | Tue 11/13/07 | | |
| 6 | | Prepare functional specification (F | 1 day? | Tue 11/13/07 | Tue 11/13/07 | | |
| 7 | | Negotiate FS with users | 1 day? | 13/07 | Tue 11/13/07 | | |
| 8 | | Revise FS (1 time only) | 1 day? | Tue 11 | Tue 11/13/07 | | |
| 9 | | Renegotiate FS (1 time only) | 1 day? | Tue | | | |
| 10 | | Approval obtained | 1 day? | Tue | | | |
| 11 | | − **DESIGN** | **1 day?** | **Tue 11/13/07** | **Tue 11/13/07** | | |
| 12 | | High level software design | 1 day? | Tue 11/13/07 | Tue 11/13/07 | | |
| 13 | | Mid level software design | 1 day? | Tue 11/13/07 | Tue 11/13/07 | | |
| 14 | | User acceptance of design | 1 day? | Tue 11/13/07 | Tue 11/13/07 | | |
| 15 | | − **PROGRAMMING** | **1 day?** | **Tue 11/13/07** | **Tue 11/13/07** | | |
| 16 | | − **System A** | **1 day?** | **Tue 11/13/07** | **Tue 11/13/07** | | |
| 17 | | Module 1 | 1 day? | Tue 11/13/07 | Tue 11/13/07 | | |
| 18 | | Module 2 | 1 day? | Tue 11/13/07 | Tue 11/13/07 | | |
| 19 | | Module 3 | 1 day? | Tue 11/13/07 | Tue 11/13/07 | | |
| 20 | | − **System B** | **1 day?** | **Tue 11/13/07** | **Tue 11/13/07** | | |
| 21 | | Module 1 | 1 day? | Tue 11/13/07 | Tue 11/13/07 | | |
| 22 | | Module 2 | 1 day? | Tue 11/13/07 | Tue 11/13/07 | | |
| 23 | | Module 3 | 1 day? | Tue 11/13/07 | Tue 11/13/07 | | |
| 24 | | Module 4 | 1 day? | Tue 11/13/07 | Tue 11/13/07 | | |
| 25 | | Programming complete | 1 day? | Tue 11/13/07 | Tue 11/13/07 | | |
| 26 | | − **SYSTEM TEST** | **1 day?** | **Tue 11/13/07** | **Tue 11/13/07** | | |
| 27 | | System integration and test | 1 day? | Tue 11/13/07 | Tue 11/13/07 | | |

Indent sub-tasks

*(Continued)*

(Continued)

6. Starting from the top again, type in the durations in the **Duration** column. For instance, the 30-day duration for **Write requirements document** is entered by typing **30** in the **Duration** column. Make sure that all **0** durations are also entered, otherwise the default 1 day is left (and that's wrong). **BEWARE:** You only enter durations for sub-tasks, not for main tasks (the names in bold). It's Project's job to work out the duration of main tasks based on the information you enter for the sub-tasks. Probably now is a good time to save the project file ( 🖫 ). So do it!

| | ❶ | Task Name | Duration | Start | Finish | Predecessors | Resource Names |
|---|---|---|---|---|---|---|---|
| 1 | | − **DEFINITION** | **30 days** | **Tue 11/13/07** | **Mon 12/24/07** | | |
| 2 | | Write requirements document | 30 days | Tue 11/13/07 | Mon 12/24/07 | | |
| 3 | | Done | 0 days | Tue 11/13/07 | Tue 11/13/07 | | |
| 4 | | − **ANALYSIS** | **10 days** | **Tue 11/13/07** | **Mon 11/26/07** | | |
| 5 | | Interview users | 10 days | Tue 11/13/07 | Mon 11/26/07 | | |
| 6 | | Prepare functional specification (F | 8 days | Tue 11/13/07 | Thu 11/22/07 | | |
| 7 | | Negotiate FS with users | 8 days | Tue 11/13/07 | Thu 11/22/07 | | |
| 8 | | Revise FS (1 time only) | 4 days | Tue 11/13/07 | Fri 11/16/07 | | |
| 9 | | Renegotiate FS (1 time only) | 5 days | Tue 11/13/07 | Mon 11/19/07 | | |
| 10 | | Approval obtained | 0 days | Tue 11/13/07 | Tue 11/13/07 | | |
| 11 | | − **DESIGN** | **18 days** | **Tue 11/13/07** | **Thu 12/6/07** | | |
| 12 | | High level software design | 17 days | Tue 11/13/07 | Wed 12/5/07 | | |
| 13 | | Mid level software design | 18 days | Tue 11/13/07 | Thu 12/6/07 | | |
| 14 | | User acceptance of design | 0 days | Tue 11/13/07 | Tue 11/13/07 | | |
| 15 | | − **PROGRAMMING** | **37 days** | **Tue 11/13/07** | **Wed 1/2/08** | | |
| 16 | | − **System A** | **37 days** | **Tue 11/13/07** | **Wed 1/2/08** | | |
| 17 | | Module 1 | 37 days | Tue 11/13/07 | Wed 1/2/08 | | |
| 18 | | Module 2 | 26 days | Tue 11/13/07 | Tue 12/18/07 | | |
| 19 | | Module 3 | 17 days | Tue 11/13/07 | Wed 12/5/07 | | |
| 20 | | − **System B** | **33 days** | **Tue 11/13/07** | **Thu 12/27/07** | | |
| 21 | | Module 1 | 33 days | Tue 11/13/07 | Thu 12/27/07 | | |
| 22 | | Module 2 | 25 days | Tue 11/13/07 | Mon 12/17/07 | | |
| 23 | | Module 3 | 14 days | Tue 11/13/07 | Fri 11/30/07 | | |
| 24 | | Module 4 | 19 days | Tue 11/13/07 | Fri 12/7/07 | | |
| 25 | | Programming complete | 0 days | Tue 11/13/07 | Tue 11/13/07 | | |
| 26 | | − **SYSTEM TEST** | **25 days** | **Tue 11/13/07** | **Mon 12/17/07** | | |
| 27 | | System integration and test | 25 days | Tue 11/13/07 | Mon 12/17/07 | | |

Enter durations in this column

7. Next, we need to tell MS Project how one task is related to another. If Task 2 depends on the completion of Task 1, we say 1 is the predecessor of 2 (it has to be done first). The WBS gives us that information. So, let's define the predecessors.

8. To make the predecessor column easier to see, use your mouse to drag the right-hand frame bar of the task sheet out, making the Gantt chart smaller as a result. Then find the predecessor column and enter a 2 for Task 4, ANALYSIS, as shown below:

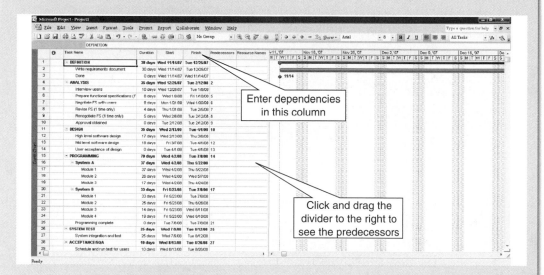

*(Continued)*

(Continued)

9.  Double-check that you have entered the right predecessors; if it looks OK, save the file ( 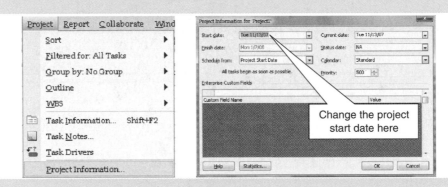 ).


9.  Double-check that you have entered the right predecessors; if it looks OK, save the file ( 💾 ).

10. So far, so good. One problem, though: The project doesn't begin today; it starts on March 31, 2010! We had better change the start date. To change the scheduled start, click on **Project>Project Information**. The **Project Information** dialog box will appear.

11. Pull down the **Start Date** field and advance the calendar to 2010 and then March, then click on the 31st, as shown:

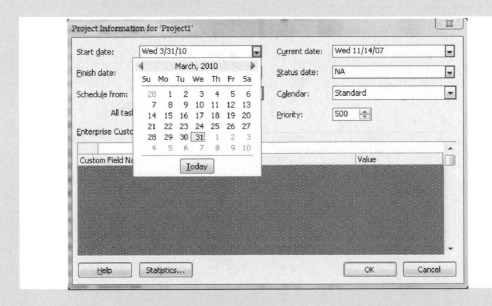

12. Click on **OK**. MS Project will now recalculate calendar start and end dates for all the project activities based on this start date. Scroll down to Task 34 (Project end), if you have done everything right, the end date for the project should read 2/1/11.

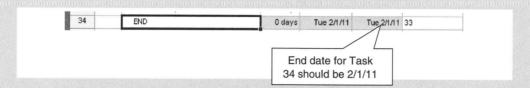

End date for Task 34 should be 2/1/11

## PART 2. DEFINING TASKS AS MILESTONES, AND VIEWING THE PROJECT

1. Tasks 3, 10, 14, 25, and 34 are milestones in the project—that is, points at which significant progress in the project should have been made and is open to review. To identify Task 3 as a milestone, double-click on Row 3. The **Task Information** dialog box will appear.

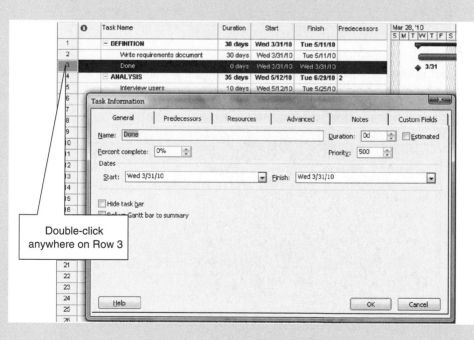

Double-click anywhere on Row 3

*(Continued)*

(Continued)

2. Click on the **Advanced** tab. This dialog box allows us to more precisely define the task, including name, duration, start times, and constraint types. If you have important constraints to apply to a task, this is the box to use.

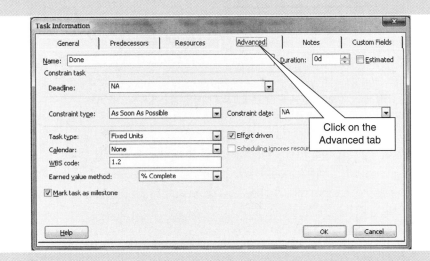

3. For our milestone, since we have already assigned a **0** duration to the task, MS Project automatically identifies task 3 as a milestone. Otherwise, it would be necessary to click on the Mark Task as Milestone box.

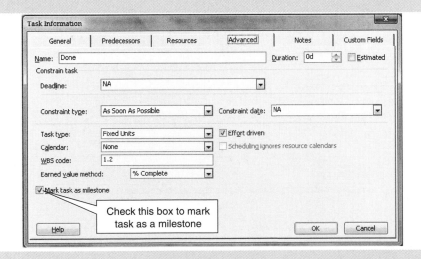

In the Gantt chart, a diamond will denote the milestone. Check that Tasks 10, 14, 25, and 34 are all defined as milestones.

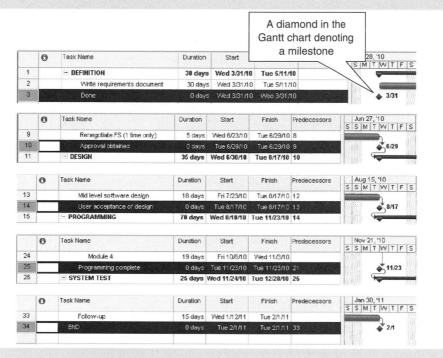

A diamond in the Gantt chart denoting a milestone

(Continued)

(Continued)

4. I know you're dying to see the complete Gantt chart, so we'll do that one last task. First, reduce the size of the task sheet so as much of the Gantt chart can be seen.

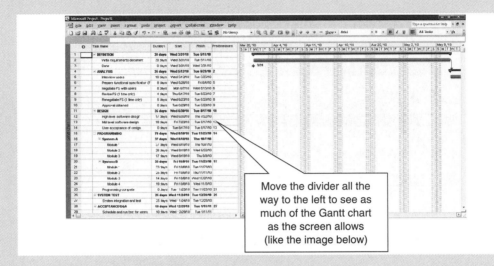

Move the divider all the way to the left to see as much of the Gantt chart as the screen allows (like the image below)

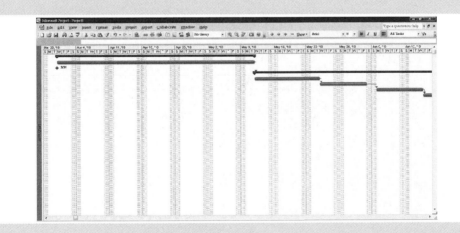

5. Now click on **View>Zoom . . .** and when the **Zoom** dialog box appears, click on **Entire project**.

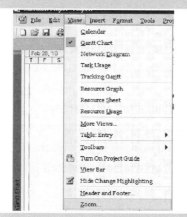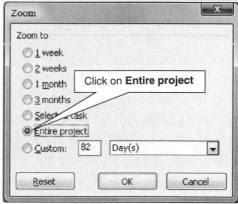

6. Click on **OK**. Now click on **File>Print Preview** and a condensed version of the Gantt will be shown, ready for printing.

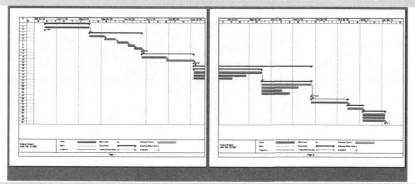

*(Continued)*

(Continued)

## PART 3. CREATING AND ASSIGNING A CUSTOM CALENDAR

1.  The calendar that MS Project uses to calculate dates does make allowances for lunch breaks, weekends, etc, but the defaults do not necessarily fit those we would like to use. To make a more realistic calendar, we must create, save, and then assign a custom calendar to the project. A custom calendar allows certain hours and/or days to be defined as nonworking. When assigned to a project, the Gantt chart is adjusted automatically and a new end date is likely to appear. To create a custom calendar, click on the Tools>Change Working Time . . . The calendar currently shown is MS Project's Standard (default) project calendar, as shown below:

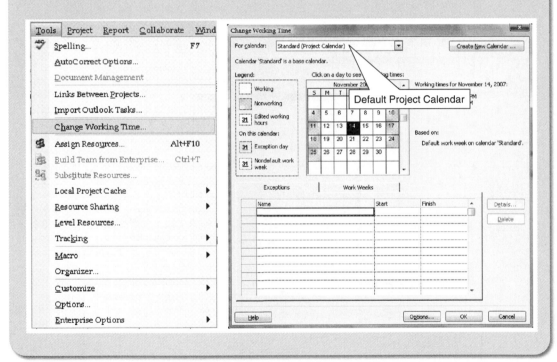

2. To create a customized version, click on the **Create New Calendar** . . . button.

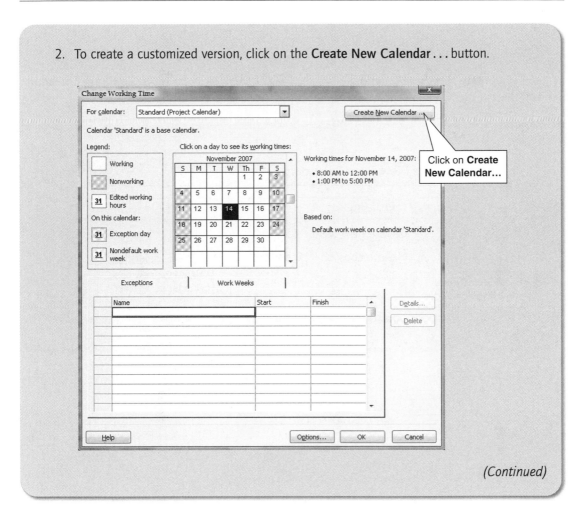

*(Continued)*

(Continued)

The **Create New Base Calendar** dialog box will appear. Click on **Create New Base Calendar**, and then in the **Name** field, type:

**Project1.**

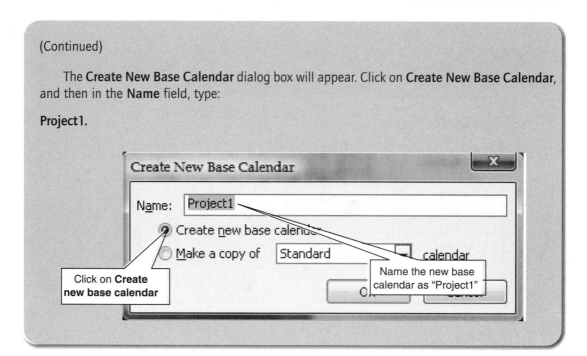

3. Click **OK**. The **Change Working Time** dialog box will reappear, with Project1 shown in the **For** field.

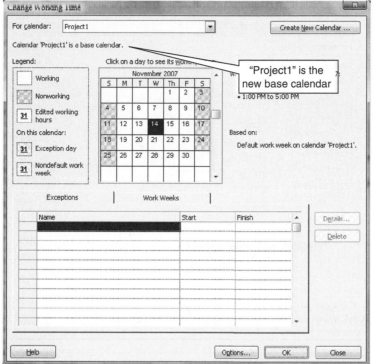

*(Continued)*

(Continued)

4. Click on the **Work Weeks** tab on the bottom half of the **Change Working Time** dialog box. Then, click on the **Details . . .** button on the right.

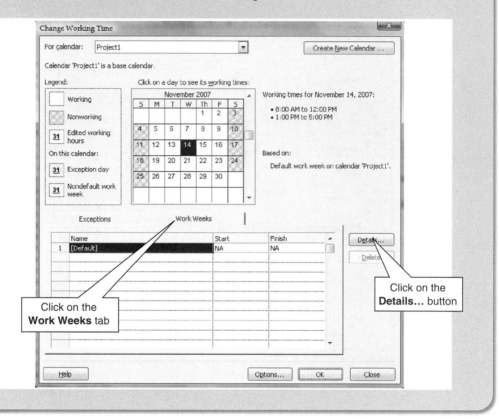

A **Details for "[Default]"** dialog box will appear.

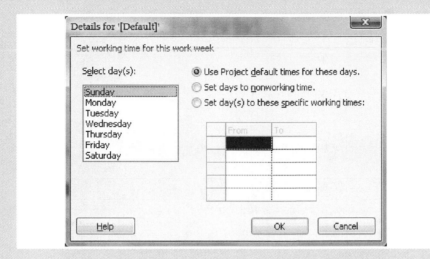

Select the days Monday, Tuesday, Wednesday, Thursday, and Friday by clicking on Monday and dragging down to Friday or by holding down **Ctrl** or **Shift** to select all five days. Also click on **Set day(s)** to these specific working times.

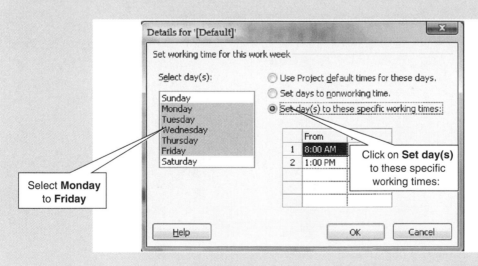

Select **Monday**
to **Friday**

Click on **Set day(s)**
to these specific
working times:

*(Continued)*

(Continued)

5.  In the **From:** time field, change the 8 to a 9 (to read 9:00 am).

6.  In the **To** field, type:

    12:30

7.  In the second row **From** field, type:

    1:30 pm

We will leave the end-of-the-day time at 5:00 pm. So, click **OK**.

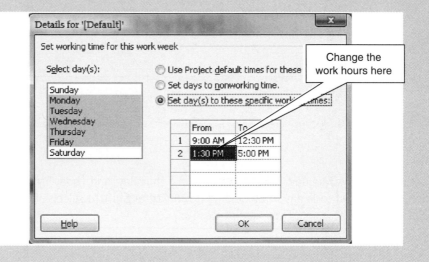

8. Now scroll down the calendar to May 2010 (using the scroll bars to the right of the calendar), and click on the 24th (Memorial Day).

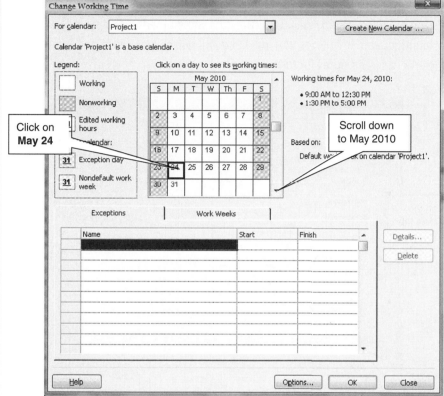

(Continued)

9. To make this day a holiday, click on the **Exceptions** tab. In the **Name** field, type Memorial Day to name the holiday, and press **Tab**. Project will automatically populate both **Start** and **Finish** fields with 05/24/2010 (the date highlighted in the calendar). This day is now highlighted in blue (exception day) and will not be counted by MS Project in calculating start and end dates for tasks.

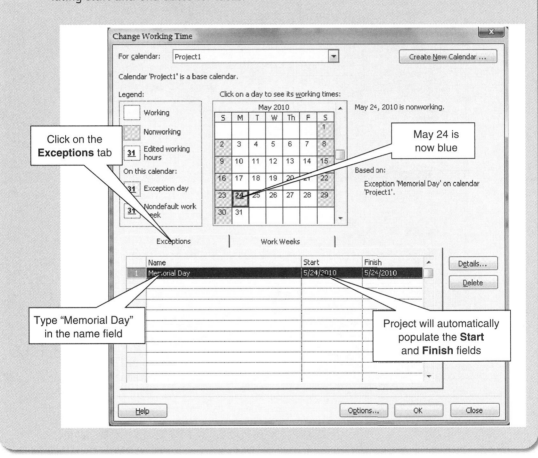

10. Using the same method, define the following days as holidays:

September 6, 2010 (Labor Day)

November 11, 2010 (Veterans Day)

January 17, 2011 (Martin Luther King Jr. Day)

February 21, 2011 (Presidents Day)

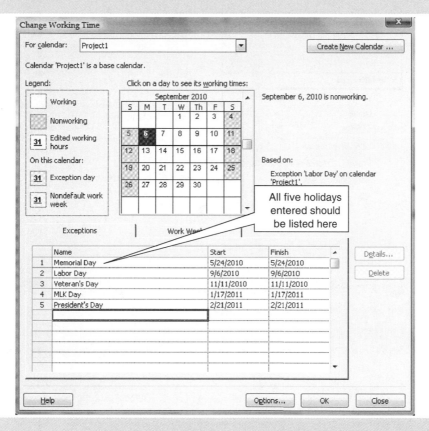

*(Continued)*

(Continued)

11. After entering the last holiday, save the calendar by clicking on the **OK** button.

12. To assign this customized calendar to Project1, click on **Project>Project Information**.

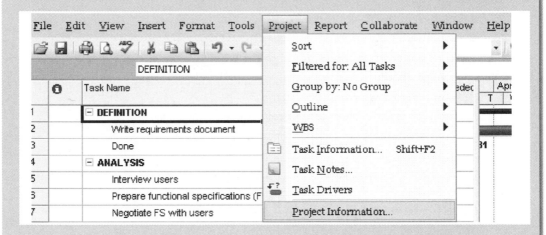

13. Using the combo box in the **Calendar** field, select Project1.

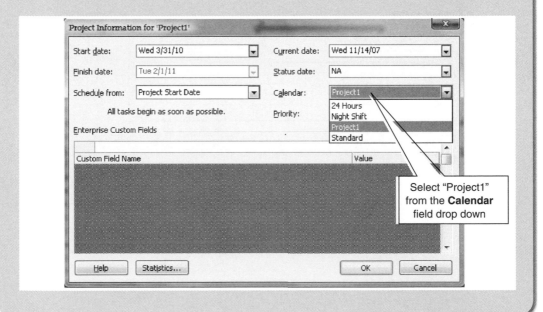

Select "Project1" from the **Calendar** field drop down

14. Click on the **OK** button. The Gantt chart will have the customized calendar assigned. By looking at the finish date, you will notice that the completion date for the project has moved forward from February 1 to March 24. It's a good thing we remembered all those nonworking days!

| | 🔒 | Task Name | Duration | Start | Finish | Predec |
|---|---|---|---|---|---|---|
| 33 | | Follow-up | 15 days | Tue 3/1/11 | Thu 3/24/11 | |
| 34 | | END | 0 days | Thu 3/24/11 | Thu 3/24/11 | 33 |

The final Gantt chart will look something like that shown below:

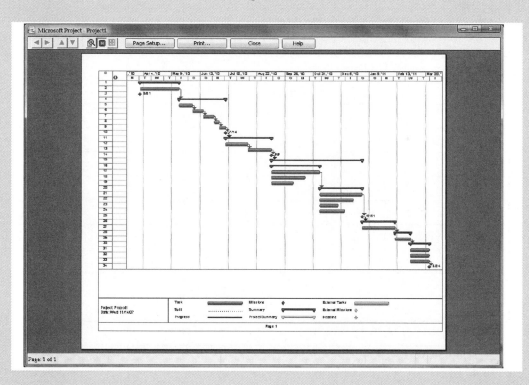

*(Continued)*

(Continued)

## Work Breakdown Structure (WBS)

### Status Form

|  | Task Name | Duration | Predecessor |
|---|---|---|---|
| 1 | DEFINITION | | |
| 2 | Write requirements document | 30 | |
| 3 | Done | 0 | |
| 4 | ANALYSIS | | 2 |
| 5 | Interview users | 10 | |
| 6 | Prepare functional specification (FS) | 8 | 5 |
| 7 | Negotiate FS with users | 8 | 6 |
| 8 | Revise FS (1 time only) | 4 | 7 |
| 9 | Renegotiate FS (1 time only) | 5 | 8 |
| 10 | Approval obtained | 0 | 9 |
| 11 | DESIGN | | 10 |
| 12 | High-level software design | 17 | |
| 13 | Mid-level software design | 18 | 12 |
| 14 | User acceptance of design | 0 | 13 |
| 15 | PROGRAMMING | | 14 |
| 16 | System A | | |
| 17 | Module 1 | 37 | |
| 18 | Module 2 | 26 | |
| 19 | Module 3 | 17 | |
| 20 | System B | | 17 |
| 21 | Module 1 | 33 | |
| 22 | Module 2 | 25 | |
| 23 | Module 3 | 14 | |
| 24 | Module 4 | 19 | |
| 25 | Programming complete | 0 | 21 |
| 26 | SYSTEM TEST | | 25 |

| | Task Name | Duration | Predecessor |
|---|---|---|---|
| 27 | System integration and test | 25 | |
| 28 | ACCEPTANCE/SQA | | 27 |
| 29 | Schedule and run test for users | 10 | |
| 30 | OPERATION | | 29 |
| 31 | Training | 15 | |
| 32 | Technical support | 15 | |
| 33 | Follow-up | 15 | |
| 34 | END | 0 | 33 |

## Second Example: Creating a New Project

1. Select **File > New** and click on **Blank Project** in the **New Project** task pane that appears:

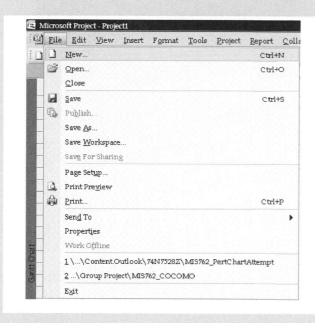

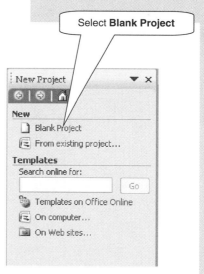

Select **Blank Project**

*(Continued)*

(Continued)

2. We will begin the new project by determining the basic project information. Since the start *or* finish date is usually the anchor of a project—the steps of a project are built around either the start date or the finish date—we will enter this information first in the **Project Information** dialog box.

   Select **Project > Project Information**. The **Project Information** dialog box will appear:

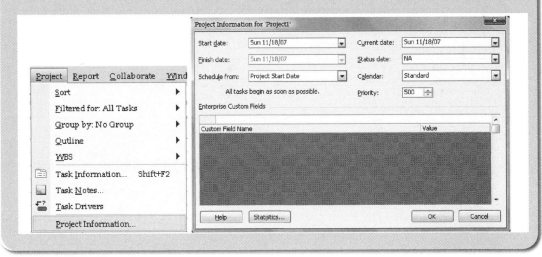

3. Select **Project Finish Date** from the **Schedule from:** drop down menu and select **Fri 5/8/09** in the **Finish date:** field and click **OK**. These entries indicate that the project deadline is Friday, May 8, 2009, and MS Project will automatically schedule tasks backwards from the deadline.

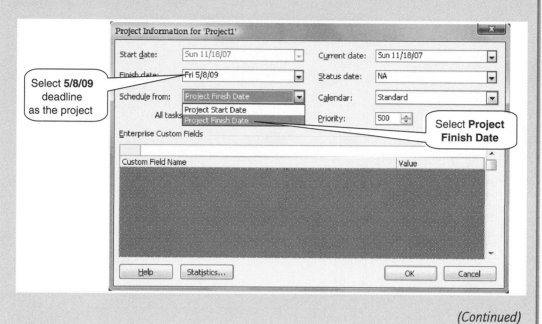

*(Continued)*

(Continued)

4. Next, we will define the work week. Select **Tools > Change Working Time . . .** and the **Project Information for 'Project1'** dialog box will appear. Click on the **Work Weeks** tab:

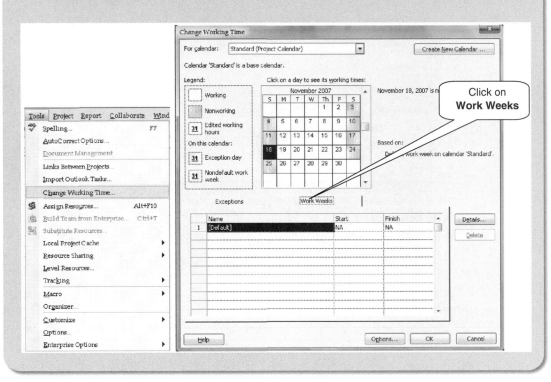

Then, click on the **Details . . .** button:

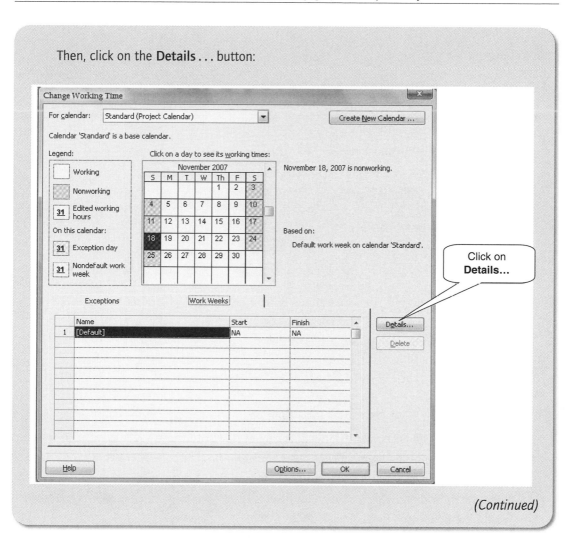

*(Continued)*

(Continued)

The **Details for '[Default]'** dialog box will appear:

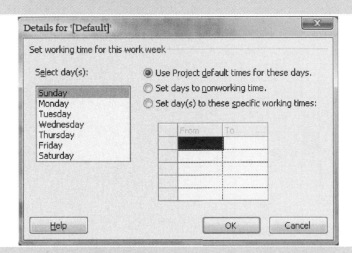

5. We will now define the work week and the work hours. Select **Monday, Tuesday, Wednesday, Thursday**, and **Friday**. Click on **Set day(s) to these specific working times:**. In Row 1, change the **From** time to **9:00AM** and the **To** time to **1:00PM**. In Row 2, change the **From** time to **2:00PM** and the **To** time to **6:00PM** and click **OK**. These entries let MS Project know that the project team only works from 9 am to 6 pm on Mondays to Fridays, with a 1-hour lunch break from 1 pm to 2 pm.

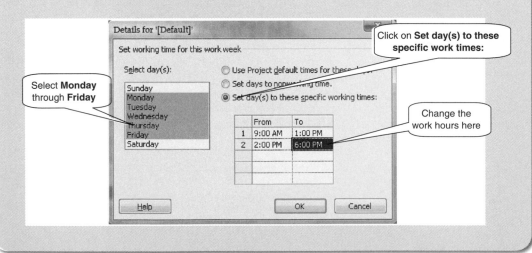

6. Back at the **Project Information for 'Project1'** dialog box, click on the **Exceptions** tab. We will now enter exceptions to the work week we just defined—we will enter holidays as nonworking days.

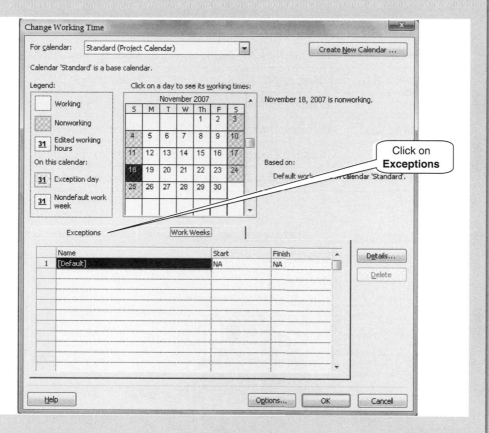

*(Continued)*

(Continued)

We will enter the holiday name in the **Name** column and the date in both the **Start** and **Finish** column. Click **OK** when you are done.

| Name | Start | Finish |
|------|-------|--------|
| Memorial day | Monday, May 26, 2008 | Monday, May 26, 2008 |
| Independence day | Friday, July 4, 2008 | Friday, July 4, 2008 |
| Labor day | Monday, September 1, 2008 | Monday, September 1, 2008 |
| Thanksgiving day | Thursday, November 27, 2008 | Thursday, November 27, 2008 |
| Christmas day | Thursday, December 25, 2008 | Thursday, December 25, 2008 |
| New Year's day | Thursday, January 1, 2009 | Thursday, January 1, 2009 |

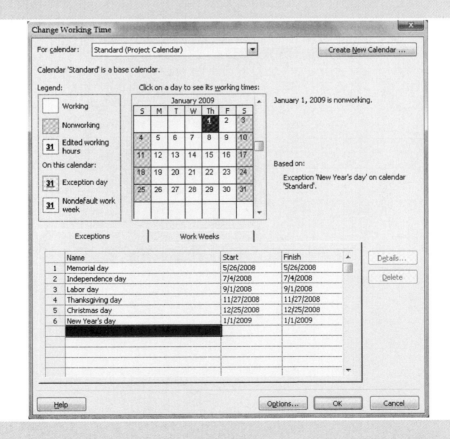

7. Next, let's enter the financial estimates to time usage. Click on **Tools > Options** and the **Options** dialog box will appear. Click on the **General** tab. Under **General Options for 'Project1,'** set the **Default standard rate** to **$35.00/h** and the **Default overtime rate** to **$52.50/h** and click **OK**.

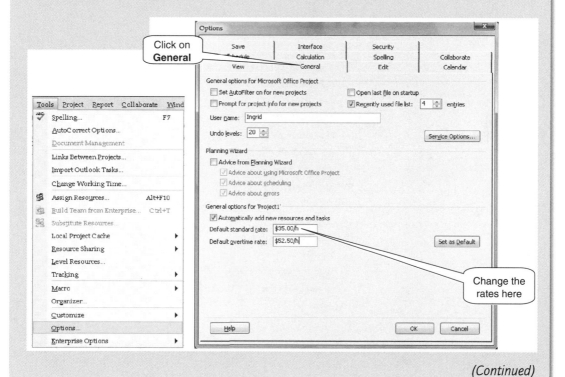

*(Continued)*

(Continued)

8. Now that we've set the basic project parameters, we will enter personnel resource information. Select **View > Resource Sheet**. The main project screen will change from the Gantt chart view to the resource sheet view.

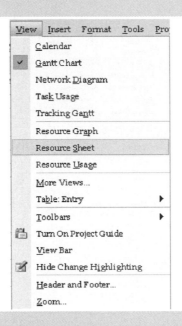

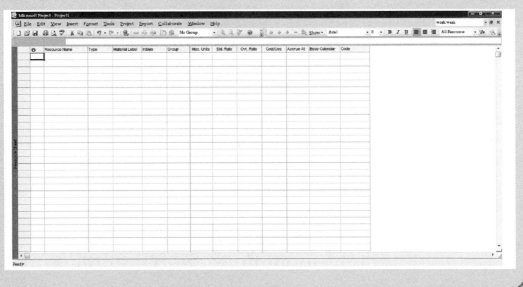

In the first row of the **Resource Name** column, type *Susan Johnson.* Under **Type**, select **Work** from the combo box list. Under **Initials** enter *SJ.* MS Project will automatically fill in the remaining fields using the rates we entered previously. In the following rows, enter the information for the rest of the project team.

| Resource Name | Type | Initials |
|---|---|---|
| Richard Smith | Work | RS |
| James Williams | Work | JW |
| John Brown | Work | JB |
| Mary Miller | Work | MM |

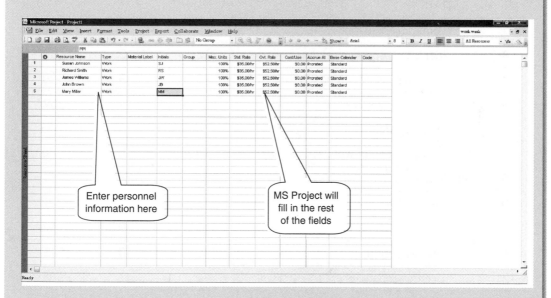

Now, return to the Gantt chart view by selecting **View > Gantt Chart.**

*(Continued)*

(Continued)

## Entering Project Tasks

Once the basic project information has been entered in MS Project, we are ready to add the project tasks. Enter the tasks and task information below. Type in the **Task Name**, **Duration**, and **Predecessors**. Select the **Resource Name** from the drop-down list.

The Gantt chart will be created as you enter the tasks. Notice that MS Project creates the Gantt chart *backwards* from the May 8, 2009, deadline we defined earlier.

| Task # | Task Name | Duration (Days) | Predecessors | Resource |
|---|---|---|---|---|
| 1 | INITIATION | | | |
| 2 | Form project team | 5 | | SJ |
| 3 | Identify prospective vendors | 12 | 2 | JW |
| 4 | Issue Request for Proposals (RFP) | 20 | 3 | SJ |
| 5 | Review proposals | 25 | 4 | MM |
| 6 | Select vendor | 5 | 5 | RS |
| 7 | Finalize scope of work with vendor | 10 | 6 | SJ |
| 8 | PLANNING | | | |
| 9 | Preliminary design | 15 | 7 | JB |
| 10 | Review & approval | 10 | 9 | MM |
| 11 | Finalize design | 10 | 10 | JB |
| 12 | Licenses & permits | 40 | 11 | RS |
| 13 | Develop execution plan | 10 | 6 | SJ |
| 14 | EXECUTION | | | |
| 15 | Prepare site for construction | 15 | 12 | RS |
| 16 | Prepare to begin construction | 5 | 12 | JW |
| 17 | HAND OFF TO CONSTRUCTION TEAM | 0 | | |

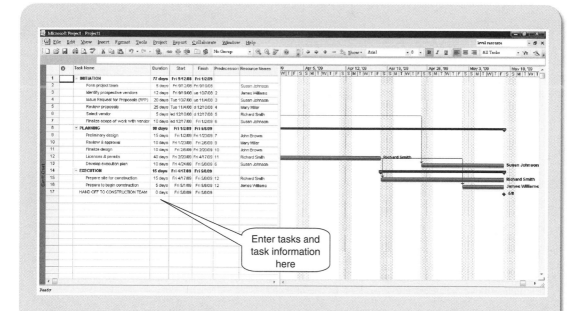

## Entering Material Resource Information

1. **Select View > Resource Sheet.**

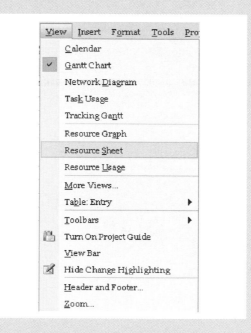

*(Continued)*

(Continued)

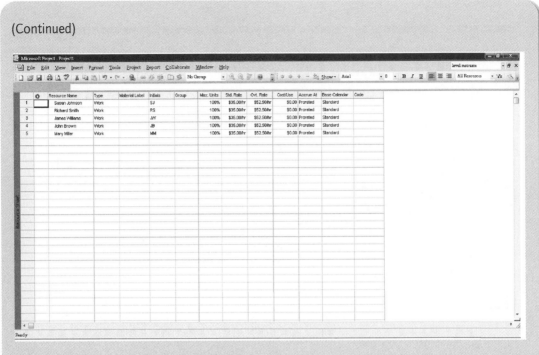

2. In the empty cell below row 5, type *Product A* for **Resource Name**. Select *Material* for **Type** and type *box* for **Material Label**. Enter *$100* for **Std Rate**.

3. In the next empty row, type *Product B* for **Resource Name**. Select *Material* for **Type** and type *lbs* for **Material Label**. Enter *$200* for **Std Rate**.

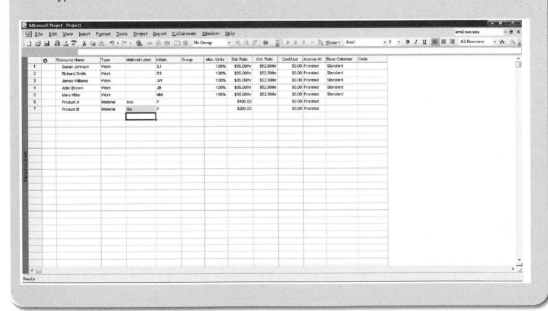

4. Return to the Gantt chart view by selecting **View > Gantt Chart**.

5. Double-click anywhere on Row 9 (Preliminary design). The **Task Information** dialog box will appear.

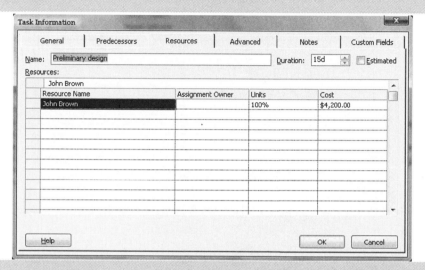

Click on the **Resources** tab. In the empty field below John Brown in the **Resource Name** column, select *Product B* from the drop-down list. Type in *5* (5 lbs) in the **Units** column and click **OK**.

*(Continued)*

(Continued)

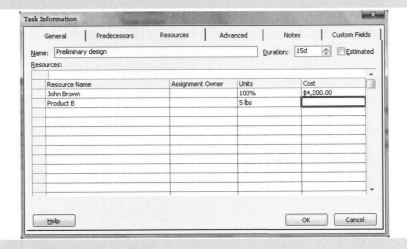

6. Double-click anywhere on Row 12 (Licenses & Permits). The **Task Information** dialog box will appear.

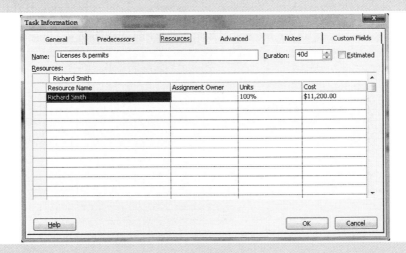

Add *3.5 boxes* of Product A to the task and click **OK**.

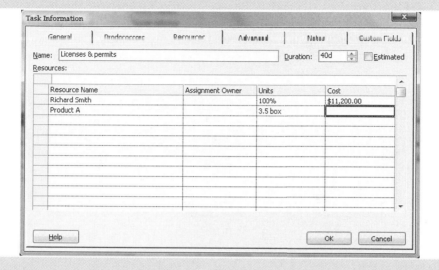

7. To view summary information for the project, select **Project > Project Information**. The **Project Information for 'Project1'** dialog box will appear.

*(Continued)*

(Continued)

Click on the **Statistics . . .** button. The **Project Statistics for 'Project1'** dialog box will appear. The dialog box contains various key statistics pertaining to our project—i.e., estimated project start and finish dates, estimated duration, estimated number of work hours, and estimated total cost. All of these statistics are calculated by MS Project based on the parameters we have entered so far.

**Project Statistics for 'Project1'**

|  | Start | Finish |
|---|---|---|
| Current | Fri 9/12/08 | Fri 5/8/09 |
| Baseline | NA | NA |
| Actual | NA | NA |
| Variance | 0d | 0d |

|  | Duration | Work | Cost |
|---|---|---|---|
| Current | 167d | 1,456h | $52,310.00 |
| Baseline | 0d? | 0h | $0.00 |
| Actual | 0d | 0h | $0.00 |
| Remaining | 167d | 1,456h | $52,310.00 |

Percent complete:

Duration: 0%    Work: 0%

Close

Click on the **Close** button when you are done reviewing the project statistics.
To a more detailed breakdown of the estimated cost, select **View > Table: Entry > Cost**.

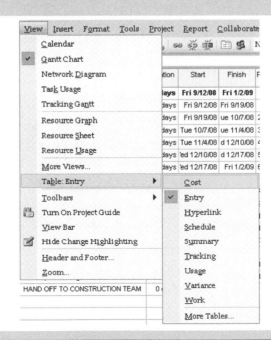

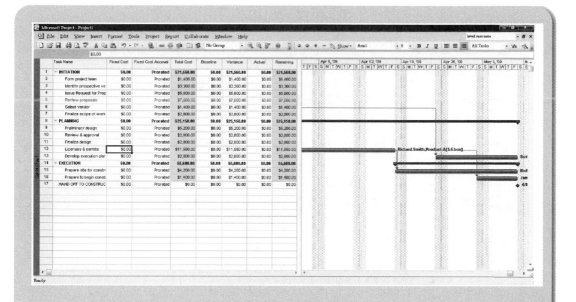

9. For a summary view of the project tasks, select **View > Table: Cost > Summary**.

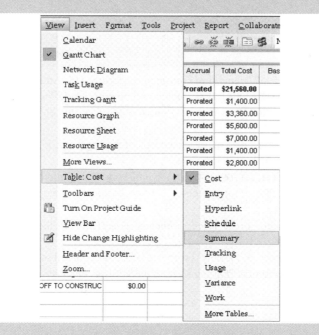

*(Continued)*

(Continued)

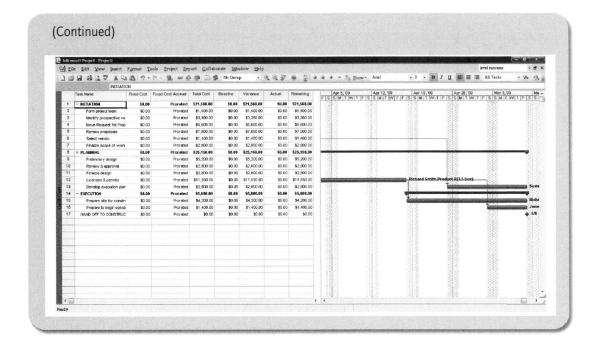

# BIBLIOGRAPHY

Brooks, F. P. (1995). *The mythical man-month.* Harlow, UK: Addison Wesley.

Cadle, J., & Yeates, D. (2004). *Project management for information systems.* Harlow, UK: Pearson.

Chatfield, C. S. (2003). *Microsoft Project 2003 Step by Step.* Redmond, WA: Microsoft Corporation.

Kerzner, H. (2003). *Project management: A systems approach to planning, scheduling, and controlling.* New York: Wiley & Sons.

Lowery, G., & Stover, T. (2001). *Managing projects with Microsoft Project 2000.* New York: Wiley.

Nicholas, J. M. (2004). *Project management for business and engineering* (2nd ed.). Burlington, MA: Elsevier.

Schwalbe, K. (2006). *Information technology project management.* Boston: Thomson Course Technology.

Van Genuchten, M. (1991). Why is software late? An empirical study of reasons for delay in software development. *IEEE Transactions on Software Engineering, 17*(6).

# 7

# Leading Information Systems Projects and Being a Team Member

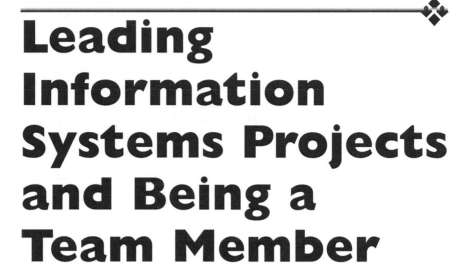

**Themes of Chapter 7**

- ❖ How can a project manager gain and keep the trust of colleagues?
- ❖ What are the communication skills required of the project manager?
- ❖ How is it possible to reduce stress?
- ❖ How can conflict between team members best be resolved?
- ❖ What are the basic skills of the project manager?
- ❖ What is required of the team member?
- ❖ What jobs are available in project management?
- ❖ How can people qualify for these jobs?

**T**he way in which a project team is led obviously greatly affects how well the team performs and therefore the success of the project. This in turn will affect the reputation of the team members, but most of all the project manager, as he or she is responsible for the success of the project as a whole. As the book is about project management, in some respects the whole book is about leading information systems projects. Indeed, there are many cross-references in this chapter to sections elsewhere in the book where particular issues are dealt with in more detail in different contexts. However, in this chapter we explore mainly personal questions about leadership and its impact on team motivation and team spirit, such as those related to values and trust. These will be influenced by the corporate culture as well as the personalities of the individuals concerned. Some of these issues relate to communication skills or how to deal with stress and conflict, but many are to do with personal and organizational values. Even so, there are other skills required, including those relating to technical and business competence. The latter are usually gained through training and experience and are discussed elsewhere in the book. However, we concentrate here on people issues. A later section turns the topic around: how to be a good member of a project team. Readers are likely to be team members before team leaders, so it will also be pertinent, and we can learn how to be a team leader from our experiences of being a team member. This is followed by a final section looking at job opportunities in project management and qualifications. We also present the first of our substantial case studies, which help to bring all the material of the book together and enable students to get the real feel of what it is like to be involved in a large project management task. But we are unlikely to work at our best for a project manager whom we do not trust, so we will look at that first.

However, we start (unusually) with two exhibits. Exhibit 7.1 looks very briefly at Stephen Covey's very influential "seven habits" (see bibliography for more details). Covey emphasizes how we should move from dependence to independence and eventually to interdependence in order to benefit from our interaction with others. It is a holistic approach to working in an environment that enables us to benefit from the support of everyone in our work place and produce results that will benefit everyone in our environment. Exhibit 7.2, based on the practice of Enid Mumford, suggests that leadership may be more about "setting an example," "values," "delegating," and "participation for all."

---

### Exhibit 7.1   Covey's Seven Habits

1. *Be proactive.* Be responsible for our actions and conducts. Commit ourselves to tasks that we undertake and carefully examine results and outcome of our actions as they influence others.

2. *Begin with end in mind.* Use the end as a frame of reference to be effective in your proactive approach.

3. *Put first thing first.* Develop the principle of personal management and be able to prioritize and organize by relying on personal integrity.

4. *Think win/win.* Seek solutions for problems that are mutually beneficial.

5. *Seek first to understand, then to be understood.* To be effective in communication you must first try to understand others' point of view by paying attention to all forms of communication, including words, sounds, and body language.

6. *Synergize principles of creative communication.* Develop tolerance and understand that the whole is greater than the sum of its parts. Avoid being defensive in your communication.

7. *Sharpen the saw: principles of balanced self-renewal.* Work and develop the four dimensions of renewal: physical, spiritual, mental, and social.

SOURCE: See Covey, S. R., 1989 and 2004, in bibliography.

In a more recent book, Covey proposes an eighth habit, about personal fulfillment and helping others to achieve their own fulfillment.

---

**Exhibit 7.2   Enid Mumford: Another View of Leadership**

Enid Mumford practiced a humanistic set of principles associated with technology and change. She was a leader, though her leadership was expressed by example rather than through being called a manager. She regarded the social aspects at least as important as the technical aspects. In any change situation, she argued that attention must be paid to providing a high-quality and satisfying work environment for employees and that this would be more likely if they played a major role in the change, perhaps making the decisions themselves rather than have decisions made for them by the change agents.

One of her largest sociotechnical projects was with the Digital Equipment Corporation in Boston. She argued successfully that the object of good design of a system is an improvement in the quality of working life and job satisfaction of those who had to work with the new system. At British chemical company ICI, she had to study the situation firsthand in the office not only to understand the management's objectives in installing technology but also to note how the technology would affect the individual members of the workforce and how that workforce could and would respond.

She had a profound belief that the understanding and knowledge of each stakeholder at any level in the organization could contribute to the design, implementation, and operation of systems, even if the new system was based on a technology that itself was evolving. Indeed, she argued that without the contribution of all stakeholders, new or changed systems had a high risk of failure.

Through her intervention, she demonstrated that the contribution and even the leadership of members of the workforce led to the implementation of effective systems that combined an improvement in the quality of working life with the outcome of meeting the managerial objectives of improving the effectiveness of the business.

Hard-bitten managers of the authoritarian school were persuaded to try her participative methods, provided she was there to coach the team and guide the team leaders. Participation—that is to say, active and legitimized involvement in and influence on, systems design—could be seen as a breach of managerial prerogative by the "old school," and thus Enid had some interesting political moments with senior executives. However, her achievements often spoke louder than rhetoric.

SOURCE: Inspired by the Enid Mumford special edition (2006) of the Information Systems Journal, 16(4).

---

## 7.1. Trust

It is important that team members trust you. Some of that may come automatically with the job (at least in the short term). Team members may well assume that you have the experience to do the job and that you will exercise good judgment, but if they think this is not borne out in practice, then trust can easily be lost and it will be much more difficult to achieve your objectives. On the other hand, trust may only come following a long spell of consistent and fair behavior. It has to be earned through you yourself working hard and making an effective contribution to the goals of the project. Consistency is one of the key criteria to first obtaining and then keeping the trust of colleagues. As a project manager, if you agree face-to-face and then go in another direction at a meeting, then trust will be lost and will be difficult to retrieve.

High ethical standards are important, and this issue was discussed in Section 1.8 (the appendix to Chapter 1 contains professional codes of ethics). Team members are unlikely to give full commitment to the project and the project manager if they think the latter is behaving unethically. Again, it will be difficult to persuade a senior manager to *champion* the project, if there is an inconsistency of ethical values between top management and the project manager.

The project manager needs to be committed to the project and all members of the project team. Trust is a two-way process, and if you do not listen and value what your team members say, it is unlikely that they will listen to you and show you respect. This respect to others can be gained through asking advice and delegating appropriately and you yourself trusting colleagues to do a good job. This is sometimes referred to as *empowerment*. Such encouragement may be at least as important as the more obvious financial or status incentives for people to do their best.

Empowerment here involves giving the responsibility of doing a good job to individual team members. This is likely to be more successful, *at least in the long run*, than coercing people to work hard and achieving objectives through threats. Respect and trust are much less likely to be earned through disciplinary measures.

However, the trust of everybody is difficult to maintain if there is conflict between team members. In these circumstances, as you are the project manager you must take responsibility and make decisions. Sometimes it is necessary, therefore, to resolve the situation by coming to a clear decision. The team is more likely to understand your resolving a situation if the overall decision-making process has been fair. Team members need to know the decision-making process—that is, who is involved in the decision and what the criteria are. There needs to have been full opportunity to discuss the issue. You may also need to ease the situation before announcing a decision formally, by discussing the issue with colleagues on a one-to-one basis, so that colleagues are at least aware of what might be an undesirable outcome to them and feel their views were not ignored. If you have the trust and respect of your colleagues, they are more likely to go with the decision positively, rather than reluctantly.

It is important to **lead by example**, delivering work of the highest quality yourself, neither making excuses nor blaming others for your own mistakes. Nobody is perfect, and when you make mistakes it is important to be honest about it. If you have the respect of colleagues, mistakes will be forgiven. Likewise, you must be prepared for mistakes of colleagues and support them to put things right. Discussing the matter with colleagues informally on a one-to-one basis can help. Performance appraisals enable these concerns to be discussed more formally, but it is important that such discussions are not totally negative. The team member should end the meeting motivated to do well or better, not dispirited.

# 7.2. Communication Skills

The best project team member is often seen as the person that should be promoted to project manager. In some respects this is surprising because the skills required to be a good team member are not the same as those for a good project manager, at least the emphasis is not the same. In short, the team member is a doer while the project manager needs to manage, inspire, and support others and is much less of a doer.

In the project manager's role, communication skills are particularly important. In this section we look at some of these skills:

## Presenting

A skill that will be particularly important concerns presentation—in particular, presenting the project proposal and progress report to management. Normally this will involve preparing a series of PowerPoint (or similar) slides. There is no substitute for good *preparation*, and this can also reduce the likelihood of nerves interfering with the quality of the presentation. One aspect of preparation concerns *knowing your audience*, and this should ensure that you know what to include and what not to include and the presentation is at the right level. In other words, the content must be appropriate to that audience. The content needs to be fair in presenting different arguments, particularly if a decision needs to be made. Otherwise you might be accused of being manipulative.

Once the general content has been worked out, it needs to be well structured so that your audience can follow your arguments. The "story" can be told in a hierarchical fashion, although there are other possibilities, such as following the structure of a good detective novel. Probably the best advice is to encourage you to do a "*dry run*," a practice run through the content with some or all of your team. It can be a great boost to confidence as you will get to know your material and time the presentation better and get some feedback before the big event. This can ensure that the content is balanced as well as accurate. Colleagues might also comment on whether there are areas that can be made more interesting—you do not want to bore your audience—and on your use of color, photographs, and graphs on your slides. Some guidelines on giving an effective presentation were given at the end of the appendix to Chapter 4 (Appendix 4A).

## Interviewing

A project manager may be part of an interviewing panel if the candidate is applying for a post working in that manager's project team. Even before the interview, time needs to be spent studying the candidate's CV, looking for gaps as well as strengths. Many project managers may well concentrate on experience and technical skills when interviewing, and it is important to dig deep at times to ensure the candidate's knowledge and experience are not superficial, but the ability to be a good team member also relates to things like attitudes, friendliness, and so on. An important question is therefore this: *Can you work with that person as a colleague?* You will want to appoint the best person, so it is also important for you to impress the candidate as well as the candidate impressing you. However you should not oversell the job, as this will lead to disappointment afterward and a potentially less effective team member than expected. Along with the formal interview, time needs to be spent informally discussing the job, and this can be done when showing the candidate around. Discussion should not be rushed, so a whole day may be allocated to interviewing two or three people. This may seem a very large investment in time, but it is worth it, as a mistake will be very costly.

## Discussing

At the outset, we have argued that successful project managers need to be good communicators. We have discussed formal procedures such as interviewing and presenting, but time spent informally discussing the project on an equal and often one-to-one basis can be invaluable. Informal face-to-face discussions can help resolve present difficulties and expose potential difficulties in the future. Without such sessions the project manager can seem distant and inapproachable and as a consequence out of touch. Symptoms of poor relationships might reveal themselves as conversations in which one person is talking (or dictating) with the other one not listening or the atmosphere is one in which there is sarcasm and ridicule between the participants or the discussion is entirely negative and there seems to be a "blame culture" in the team.

Some writers argue that the best form of management can be best described as *management through conversation*. Relationships in which serious issues can be worked through in a friendly conversational way enable good advice to be given (and taken). The project manager needs to spend time setting up such a relationship and that requires time getting to know people informally, perhaps away from the work setting. Conversations about sports, cinema, music, or the newspapers are not necessarily a waste of time. They help to establish trust in the relationship as well as friendliness and openness. Time spent earlier in the project on this pursuit can pay huge dividends later when the pressure is on and decisions need to be made and work done quickly. It is then that you need cooperative colleagues.

## Motivating

One important skill of the project manager is to motivate others—in particular, members of your project team. This has two aspects: motivating the individual and motivating the team. Some leaders are naturally inspiring and charismatic, but all project leaders can be helpful, challenging, and hardworking. We have also discussed above the potential value of delegation on the individual, empowering them. But motivating the team as a whole is also very important as the contribution of the team as a whole should be greater than the sum of the individual contributions.

A first meeting is important in setting standards, means of communication, and, in general, getting to know your colleagues. One approach is to try to encourage a sense of fun and camaraderie in the team at the beginning, and this in turn should help to instill trust and a willingness to help each other—in other words, develop a good *team spirit*. Celebrating the reaching of intermediary objectives can help this process along as can encouraging participation more generally. Many program managers start their project with a team-building course, perhaps using external specialists to run the course. Sometimes this might reveal gaps in the team. These might be in particular skills or personality traits. Meredith Belbin's research has suggested that a diverse group is one of the most important factors in forming teams that will lead to a successful outcome.

### Marketing

To some extent, many of the activities that we have listed under communication skills concern marketing. The project manager needs to market the information system from the beginning when looking for funding and commitment of team members and other stakeholders to the end when the system becomes operational. Unlike in the early days of IT, top management is no longer willing to "give the nod" to any request for funds for information technology projects. *People need persuading and convincing.* The view that "IT doesn't matter" is not uncommon, and the information systems project manager needs marketing skills. We suggest some arguments to counter this view in the appendix to Chapter 3. Some company managers wish to reduce expenditure on IT, which many see more of a cost than an investment. As discussed in Chapter 2, the potential "buyers" need to see information systems as a help to achieving their goals, and stakeholders need to be educated about the potential of information systems. In this way the full potential of information systems is much more likely to be realized and thereby the IT/IS function gains a much improved reputation within the organization.

All this requires good communication skills. However, "good words" need to be backed up by competence, credibility, ethical behavior, and commitment so that the trust described in the previous section is deserved. Emphasis on these aspects is likely to be rewarded in both the short and the long term, as "success breeds further success." Then a reputation for delivering on its promises may become ingrained and the information systems function and their project managers become trusted partners in the business. Although there is some cynicism about information technology and information systems, this is not the case everywhere, but every opportunity needs to be taken to market the information systems function, evidencing this with a history of good practice.

## 7.3. Planning

We look elsewhere in the book into the content of project plans. Here we are looking more at the principle of planning. Planning helps you and your colleagues by providing a structure or framework for your thinking about a project. It focuses your thinking into those areas that are relevant. It also helps you make decisions at the appropriate time and justify them once they are made. The process of planning might reveal a shortage of resources, and the plan can provide the explanation to management as to why these resources are needed and to explain the risks associated with not complying with the plan.

A plan can be used as a defense against a management wish to cut costs or to change delivery times inappropriately. Thus a plan is also a communication tool. It might be illustrated by a PERT chart (Chapter 6), which can help contrast the plan with actual progress. As with all plans, the PERT diagram needs to be kept up-to-date.

The plan may reveal a need for further resources, including staffing, training, and hardware and software.

However, these plans should not be distorted for political gain—for example, suggesting an inappropriately long deadline (and "impress" people when it is delivered early) or inappropriately short deadline (to impress early on but only to deliver late and disappoint). Neither of these tactics will work in the long term as game-playing, dishonesty, and malpractice will be identified.

It will take time, but constructing a good plan will help to ensure resources are not wasted in inappropriate pursuits. *Thinking must precede action.* Another important guideline is that *the person who executes a plan is the best person to do the plan.* This means that the project manager will do the overall plan but needs to delegate the planning of activities to those doing them, though of course the project manager needs to comment on and agree with these individual plans and construct the overall plan.

## 7.4. Stress Management

Stress is often confused with pressure. The latter is normal. Deadlines exert pressure, loyalty to others exerts pressure, and pride in your work exerts pressure. These are potentially positive pressures. Sometimes pressure on the information systems project manager will seem a large burden. Yet consider the jobs of air-traffic controller, policemen and -women, emergency hospital staff, and restaurant chefs. The pressure on them is at least as great, and probably more intense. Some people enjoy pressure and are bored without it.

However, when the pressure turns to stress it becomes negative and constraining. People differ with regards to the point when pressure turns to stress. But this may occur when, for example, your "to do" list becomes so large that you feel helpless and finish up doing nothing, or your personal relationships become very unpleasant because you are so frustrated at your limited achievements or your partner complains that you do not give him or her adequate attention and time or says that you are moody.

Poor project management can cause stress for your team members. They may see you, for example, dithering on decisions, not involving them in any way, being unreasonable in your requirements, or display an aggressive style in your relationships with them. *Delegation* is important and even though you could do a job, it may not be appropriate use of a manager's time. Delegation can help in two ways. First it can relieve some of the pressure from you, and second it can be seen positively by your colleagues as they may feel more in control of "their" task and they may enjoy the added responsibility. But they must be clear about what is expected of them, and you need to give appropriate feedback so that they are aware of progress. On the other hand, it is not good delegation if a manager always seems to be checking up.

Targets and "to do" lists can be useful but should be realistic (indeed, they can suggest that delegation is essential). Again, doing overtime can relieve pressure, but it will be negative if overtime periods become prolonged. Sometimes stress is caused because colleagues lack the skills needed. In this case it is important to identify these needs early and make suitable training programs available. In other cases stress can be relieved by doing another activity (including taking a break). This might put the problem in perspective and enable you to look at it afresh.

One particular symptom of stress where this approach can often help is "*paralysis by analysis*," where you have spent too much time looking at the issue. Looking at it afresh, after a short period, may well enable you to make a reasonable decision or take positive action. However, don't put off the decision forever, as making no decision is unlikely to solve a problem.

## 7.5. Conflict Management

Conflict is often the result of stress, but it is sometimes simply part of the job. After all, no one is the same: We have different experiences, expectations, cultures, education, and the rest. So it is natural for people to see things differently. Indeed, where everyone sees things together in one way, usually referred to as *groupthink*, it is usually the result of a lack of motivation or interest or fear of reprisal. Groupthink occurs when the group seems to overestimate the potential of the group and underestimate the potential of the world outside that group. This is usually not helpful in leading to the best decision.

However, though disagreements are normal, the project manager needs to try to keep things calm through allowing different views to be aired and mediating in a fair and egalitarian way. Conflicts are likely to occur relating to scheduling, staffing, money, technology, procedures, and personalities. This is normal, but conflict should not get out of hand, so, if possible, it should be dealt with early. There may be a problem-solving mode to deal with this particular type of conflict, a way of finding a compromise where none of the players "lose face," or a way of smoothing the disagreement by looking for aspects where there may be agreement. Project managers should not withdraw from the conflict but confront it and deal with it.

Sometimes it is necessary for the project manager to impose a decision. Certainly, the project manager must be aware of those scenarios that may be acceptable (even if some are not ideal) and those that are definitely not acceptable. You are the project manager, it is your responsibility. But imposing a decision should be seen as "reasonable," and this requires that you fully understand the issues and the alternatives. The best principle in steering the decision making is to concentrate on the issues and the arguments made, not the personalities making them. So you need to understand the issues well. Any decision that you make should be made on this basis, and you need to state your reasoning to all parties. Sometimes it will be necessary to follow up on this with one-to-one discussions, trying to persuade and encourage others to conform to the decision.

## 7.6. Essential Skills and Qualities of Effective Project Managers

In this section we look at particular skills that are required for the project manager. Of course no one is perfect, but it is useful to bear in mind the types of skill that will be useful. There are many training programs that might support some of these. For example, they may be featured in a course entitled Organizational Skills.

*Prioritize.* Without prioritizing, tasks will be done in "any old" fashion, and the project is unlikely to finish up on time and on budget. The important ability to make sure the urgent tasks with the highest payoff are tackled first helps team members to stay focused, might make decision making easier, and should ensure that there is some early payoff. This does not imply, of course, that only one task is done at any one time, just that tasks are done according to need, assuming that the dependencies on the network permit multitasking (see Section 6.3). There may be groups of priority, those tasks in priority 1, 2, and so on.

A related difficulty concerns the issue of how well tasks need to be carried out. Many tasks do not require the perfectionist's touch; others do. Experience and know-how are helpful in determining this, although advice from team members as well as customers and managers may be called upon usefully. The various approaches used in the information systems development approach DSDM (Section 3.3) might help in determining a good strategy for prioritizing.

*Be proactive.* Many project managers tend to react to events. This may be reasonable when dealing with a management instruction about resources or a customer request for a change in requirements, but it is not always appropriate. Where possible, a good project manager will predict change in the environment (for example, be aware of a likely increase in hardware prices) or would like some change to happen (for example, motivate colleagues by instilling a better reward system for team members). In these cases it is beneficial if the project manager is proactive, trying to steer things in the direction that is good for the project and make things happen. Thus buying hardware early might be a positive proactive decision to counteract a potential increase in hardware prices and discussing a bonus system with management a proactive strategy to effect a change in reward systems. Similarly, if the project manager identifies missing skills in the project team early, it will be easier and less costly to deal with it at the beginning of the project life cycle than if it is identified later through failure in a deliverable. The worst thing that project managers can do is to ignore problems and hope they will go away. They will not go away and will only become greater problems afterward.

*Be thorough.* It is important to know the requirements thoroughly: Be aware of any legal requirements, know the formal (and informal) company procedures to be followed, and verify that techniques (such as the work breakdown structure, PERT diagrams, and payback period costing) have been used correctly. The project manager is responsible and therefore will get the blame if, for example, an important requirement is missing or the date of delivery has been miscalculated. This applies whether you performed the task or delegated it. It does not help by you blaming a colleague on the team—you are the person responsible.

*Be strong.* It is vital that you do not accept a reduction in resources or a reduction in estimated time to completion if your calculations suggest that these are not feasible. The project plan should be thorough (and kept up-to-date) and therefore will be defendable and should be defended. Of course it is difficult and stressful to argue with management, but you and your project (and therefore management themselves) will all suffer if management demands are unrealistic and you agree to an unfeasible timetable.

*Be willing to share.* Good project managers will be willing to involve others and take advice, even though the responsibility finally rests with them. Sometimes outside expertise from consultants will be required and should be sought when you are unsure about a major issue. Sharing can lead to better decisions, but it also enables colleagues on the team with expertise to feel valued. A decision reached by consensus is also more likely to be supported than one arrived at through coercion. Where a project manager is sure of the abilities of members of their team, many decisions and work can be delegated. Of course the project manager may well have proven experience in work that will now be delegated and done by others. But this means advising team members, helping where needed, and having good review systems in place. It does not mean doing the job yourself.

*Negotiate.* When negotiating, we are looking for an agreement where both parties feel satisfied with the outcome. We see this every day when we negotiate to purchase a product. At the end of the negotiation, the salesperson knows that there is still a good profit and the customer knows the price agreed is less than the original ticket price. Both sides have moved from the original situation, but the outcome is satisfactory to both. Preparation is important for successful negotiation (indeed, it is vital for most of the issues discussed in this chapter). Without it, then the project manager may "give away" an important tenet of the project. A loss of one feature of the application may have negative implications that pervade the whole of the project.

*Be positive.* Good project managers will champion their project and praise the work of the project team. If the project manager is negative or cynical when talking about the project, then everyone else will be negative about the information system and the team working on its development. But good words need to be backed up by good deeds. However, unless people know about these good deeds, success is unlikely to be rewarded. The project manager is the person to market the achievements. Of course problems will occur and need to be discussed and resolved, but, within reason, opportunities to be positive about the project should not be missed. It also makes people aware of the project, which will also be important for its ultimate success.

*Support your colleagues.* Being positive about the project is also a good way to support your team colleagues, but it is also appropriate to mentor junior colleagues, praise colleagues for work well done, delegate some responsibility where appropriate, and recommend training programs to fill gaps in background. Just-in-time training is often best as it is only when people realize there is a gap in their background to carry out the job successfully that they commit themselves fully to the training program.

*Question everything.* Carefully asked and tactful questioning in the early stages of a project can save a great deal of work later. An error in the detail will be more difficult and time-consuming to identify and correct toward the end of the schedule.

Questioning does not imply criticism, although it is often taken as such in situations where communications are not good. It reflects a wish to support colleagues and ensure that the final product will be as specified. General questions are useful at the beginning of a discussion, but it is also necessary to focus in on particular aspects. If the detail is not right, then the overall information system will not be right.

It is often difficult for people to explain something well even if it is correct. But very often the inability to explain well is due to poor thinking, analysis, or design. Of course some colleagues might be so steeped in the technology that they find it difficult to communicate in terms that others might understand. In such cases it can be useful for the questioner to state his or her understanding in simpler language so that this can be confirmed or otherwise. This can also reveal misunderstandings such as assumptions that are not commonly shared. Creative questions can help here, such as, "are there other ways to achieve that?" On the other hand, some people find the generation of ideas easy but focusing on solutions much more difficult. Take advantage of people's positive attributes. Again, much will depend on the people concerned, personal relationships, experience, and company culture in finding the best way to approach questioning.

*Be organized.* Good time management can enable the best use of your own contribution and also help to avoid stress. If you do not meet your deadlines, then you cannot expect your colleagues to meet theirs. This also implies good diary management. If you do not turn up for a meeting, are double-booked, or late, then it obviously sets a bad example for everyone else. Good meeting management is also important. Meetings are necessary on some occasions, but ensure that they are only as long as required, that there is an agenda known to participants beforehand even if it is just a list of bullet points (people know what the topics are and have time to think about them before the meeting), and that only those people to whom the meeting is relevant are invited. At the meeting take notes (or have a colleague do so) so that minutes can be completed afterward and stick to the agenda (let others speak, but only to this agenda). Sometimes it is necessary for project managers to state and argue their views, but it is often best for a project manager to act as facilitator, enabling different views to be expressed in a reasonable fashion, allowing time for reflection and discussion, and coming to an agreed decision. Often the latter requires the project manager to *sum up the "feeling" of the meeting* (which should not simply be his or her view unaffected by the discussion!) and suggest a way to resolve the issue.

*Implement a good review process.* A supportive review process will ensure work is checked but also help to prevent team members being offended. Having your own work reviewed will also instill that atmosphere of support, not incrimination, as does asking for advice. Make clear that the objective of the process is to improve quality, not to criticize people. Another advantage of a good review process is that it also spreads knowledge to others. Such a process can also provide an opportunity to give positive feedback. Praising someone's work, if it is good, is as important as pointing out areas that need looking at. Where appropriate, it is useful to go outside the team for reviewing. For example, asking the customer and other stakeholders to do review work will encourage stakeholder involvement and commitment as well as get some valuable feedback.

In our own research, during interviews with project managers, we asked them to assess the importance of 12 project management skills. To gauge the importance of these skills, a 5-point Likert scale was used in the study. A clear definition of each skill was provided. Respondents were asked to rate the importance of each skill as follows:

1 – Not at all

2 – A little

3 – Moderate

4 – Much

5 – A great deal.

Forty-two project managers responded to this survey of skills and the results presented in Figure 7.1 are based on that sample. It is clearly seen through Figure 7.1 that in our study, communication and leadership skills ranked highest.

❖ **Figure 7.1**   Ranking Project Manager Skills

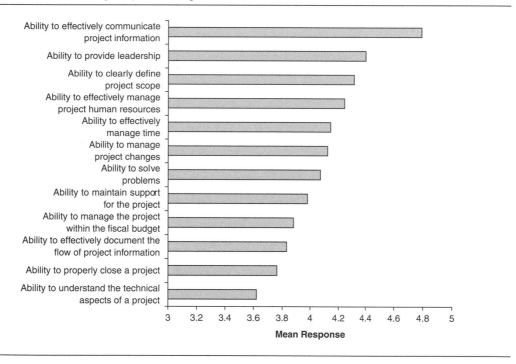

## 7.7. Being a Good Team Member

We now turn the topic around: how to be a good member of a project team. We focus in this book on leadership, yet readers are likely to be team members before team leaders (for example, in groups when working on the case studies or as team members in the early stages of your career). Further, we can learn much about how to be a good team leader from our experiences of being a team member. Conversely it is also important in being a good team member to consider what the team leader might require of their team members. Being a good team member can be just as demanding as being a good team leader. Here are some important requirements for the team member:

- Develop communication skills.
- Support others in your team.
- Project management training is for everyone!

The first requirement is to **develop communication skills**. For example, it is important that the team leader and members know of any problems that you have. Problems are unlikely to go away by themselves, and discussing them with the project manager and other team members may lead to solutions. Good communication skills require good listening as well as good talking so that all participate. They also include competence and good behavior when using media such as email, group decision support systems, and teleconferencing. Good team members reflect on what has been said, trying to clear any points of potential confusion, but when they hear of good ideas, they are enthusiastic and positive.

Some people can be selfish, but a good team member will **support others in your team**. This means being ready to listen to alternative ideas, not blaming others for problems nor bragging about your own successes, and getting involved by sharing ideas, proposals, and solutions. This will encourage ideas and, in general, a sense of mutual trust. Conflicts might occur, but good communications and an otherwise supportive atmosphere should resolve them more easily so that consensus is achieved. Remember the team should be working together toward a common goal, and this requires the commitment of all the members toward this goal. Supporting others also implies a fair contribution when carrying out the work, in writing up, and so on. "Free riders," who contribute little, don't deliver on their commitments, yet expect to gain from the contributions of others in the team, will be revealed as such in the long term, if not the short. In general, teams rely on the ethical behavior of all.

From the above, it should be evident that **project management training is for everyone!** It should also be apparent that many of the requirements for being a good team member—for example, communication and training—are similar to the requirements related to being a good team leader.

We will discuss aspects of these requirements in more detail in Chapter 9, where we discuss issues about forming the project team.

## 7.8. Careers in Project Management

Information and communication technologies continue to play critical roles in today's global economy. Although there are troughs and peaks on the way, the general trend for employment in these fields is a continually upward one. The U.S. Bureau of Labor Statistics continues to predict significant growth in employment for computer professionals. Yet there is a misconception about the IT job market, that outsourcing and offshoring (see Chapter 11) are reducing that demand. But it is apparent that the supply side is not keeping up with demand. Offshoring and other trends mean that information system jobs and opportunities are evolving and new skill sets that can respond to new business and market reality are in demand. A 2007 survey of IT leaders with hiring authority suggests a growing need for IT professionals with project management, security, and architecture skills, as well as strong interpersonal abilities. A recent study by Forrester Research also reports that many organizations train existing personnel in response to current skills shortages. The following table summarizes top skill sets that are in demand.

❖ **Figure 7.2**  Top Skills for Which Organizations Will Hire (% of Organizations)

| | |
|---|---|
| Security | 31% |
| Project management | 26% |
| Network management | 26% |
| Infrastructure architecture | 25% |
| Enterprise architecture and design skills | 24% |
| Business process skills | 19% |
| Risk management | 14% |

SOURCE: Forrester Research

Companies are concerned about skilled personnel in several areas, especially in areas of security and project management. Both these areas have been affected by the information system offshoring phenomenon. The increased level of offshoring activities has understandably increased the need for more skilled information system project managers and security personnel. Important activities of information system projects that are discussed in this book—such as project planning, team management, time management, cost estimate, quality assurance, risk assessment, and communication—have assumed new and more important dimensions. Indeed, these new skill needs have created new opportunities for well-trained information system professionals. Recent salary survey reports by payscale.com, computerjobs.com, and others suggest $50,000 for starting project manager positions and over $100,000 for experienced project managers.

The experience of outsourcing manufacturing jobs suggests that IT professionals in developed countries must learn new skills and update their capabilities to meet the challenges and demands of new and more advanced job requirements. Information system professionals must prepare for jobs that cannot easily go offshore and that combine IT skills with less narrowly focused disciplines. Information systems professionals who can work closely with business units and add value to their employers continue to be in great demand. Effective project management requires more cross-functional capabilities and continues to be influenced by the ability to deliver projects and meeting business needs on time and on budget.

The demand is particularly strong for IT professionals who understand how to combine their computer skills with business know-how. Senior IT managers surveyed for a recent study at the Johns Hopkins University ranked "access to the host country's skilled workforce and talents" as the most important reason (equal to "reduced labor cost") for IT offshoring. IT managers in this study believe offshoring can create more jobs. They ranked the followings as most likely jobs to grow: mission-critical systems security, architecture, and design; core products, requirements specifications, strategic planning; products' key performance and functional specifications; proprietary hardware and software design; systems integration; products' ergonomics, appearance, and aesthetics specification; project management; and direct human interaction with the customer.

Even the lost jobs, which are the focus of most political debate, have a modest impact when viewed at the national level. A study by the Association for Computing Machinery found that while 2% to 3% of U.S. technology jobs are moved overseas each year, the ongoing computing boom results in the creation of more jobs than are lost. Moreover, the number of "replacement" jobs that can be calculated is clearly an underestimate, since IT continues to creep into every business and every job, defying the usual classifications of what is a "computer-based job." Columbia University economist Jagdish Bhagwati suggests that for highly skilled fields such as IS, "If we do a real balance sheet, I have no doubt we're creating far more jobs than we're losing." He continues:

> It may be argued that the offshoring phenomenon will change the traditional perception about IS as a primarily back-office support function that was readily delegated to, and managed by, "specialists." New information system professionals in general and information system project managers in particular must learn to deal with a more integrated, more business-centric, more mature, and more visible discipline. (As quoted in the *Wall Street Journal,* March 28, 2007)

Having seen the figures of hiring opportunities (also see the exercises at the end of this chapter) we turn to qualifications. Studying project management through a book such as this one will give you a very good introduction to the field. But once hired you may also be required to study toward a particular certificate, such as that of the Project Management Institute (PMI). Such qualification is not a replacement for the study of this book (and vice versa). Indeed PMI qualification requires such education along with agreement to accept their code of ethics (see appendix to Chapter 1) and considerable experience as well as passing their Project Management Professional examination. The latter is based on the contents of the PMI Project Management Body of Knowledge. Project management is clearly a crucial skill in information systems work, and understanding the contents of this book, followed by experience and certification, can lead to a very profitable as well as enjoyable career.

## 7.9 Interview With a Project Manager

The tables were turned somewhat in the following extract from an interview with a project manager. Before he was promoted to project manager 2 years ago to manage this project, he was a highly respected and very experienced team member. The project had recently been completed following 20 months work. In fact, the project is seen largely as a success by the company management, but the project manager felt that one aspect was a great disappointment and that was his deteriorating personal relationships with his team. He wanted to know "**what went wrong?**" so that he would not repeat the same mistakes in his next project, and it is this part of the interview that we report on here.

Can we now turn to discussing the aspects of the project that did not work well?

"I would like to focus on personal relationships in the project team, particularly the fact that I became alienated from some colleagues. Indeed a few members of the team have made it clear to management that they do not wish to work on another project with me as project manager. I work hard and know my job, and in any case, this project was largely a success. Although I say it myself, I am basically a nice man, and I do not really understand why personal relationships deteriorated so badly."

How did that alienation show itself?

"It showed itself in a number of ways! First, halfway through the project, one key member (very experienced) stopped talking to me socially (although he did his job and answered work questions), but he did not respond to my 'good mornings.' It soured the atmosphere of the whole team. Second, I had advised management to shortlist four people for a post to replace someone who had left. I put a lot of time and effort putting this shortlist together. Three of my colleagues, all senior people, then came to me as a group and said that we should only interview two of these people as they felt that the other two would not fit in well. After an argument (it was not a discussion), I gave way and told management that we had changed our mind. It was a bad decision, as we finished up appointing someone that was nowhere near ideal. Third, one of these senior people in my team told me that I manipulated the group and he didn't trust me."

Of course the first example you gave could be the result of a difficult colleague (not you), but there does seem to be a pattern here.

"Yes, and I don't understand it. I have done a few of the "how to be a good manager" courses. I did most of the recommended things. I am not autocratic, I don't order people around. My project was seen by management as a key project, and to be fair, they were very supportive. I did my job well—the proof is in the success of the project (and I got a pay rise at the end of the project). And you are correct: This man is a well-known awkward case; in fact, he is an obnoxious so-and-so (and the personnel manager agreed with me on this). He seemed to come to meetings just to put me down and try to get anything I wanted stopped. But it upset me personally, as his behavior tainted me as well as him."

*(Continued)*

(Continued)

Why did you add this guy to your team?

"My strategy was to get the best talent available for my project team. And to be fair he is very competent and experienced. I did not put the team together to have fun; we had a job to do that was important to me and the business. But I should have got him sacked from the project. If I had to choose, I would prefer a successful project from the business point of view with a poor atmosphere within the project team, than the other way around, but this guy was too much."

Having both is not impossible! Tell me about the process that led to the shortlist of four candidates.

"I am very open and fair, and all the project team could look at all the applications. People made written comments on each candidate. I looked at these as well as the CVs and thought four were 'appointable' in principle. It is true that two of these did get some negative comments from my colleagues in the team, but they were very experienced people, which made up for the deficiencies expressed. In any case, we could always decide not to appoint on the day if these weaknesses showed themselves as being too much. Then I was accused of ignoring team members' comments, which just was not true, and that I had been manipulative. If it is manipulative to want to look at the four best people, then I plead guilty. I felt very stressed to face this accusation after I had been so fair, and I lost my temper and finally shouted 'Okay, you can have your way.' Unfortunately this happened in the work's canteen, so it wasn't kept private. We lost two potentially good people, especially as the person we offered the job to first decided she did not want to come and the other one was appointed but no one felt very enthusiastic, and he has indeed been a disappointment, to say the least. What a disaster—this affair risked the project as a whole. "

Did you discuss the matter with your colleagues afterward?

"No. I was so annoyed with them and so stressed out most of the time that I thought it best not to raise the subject again with them. Maybe I was 'too democratic' in letting them get their own way. They acted as a separate clique operating within the project team, forcing their own agenda and not the best agenda for the project. I should have said that I was the project manager and my decision was final on this; after all, I had top management support in this."

What about the trust issue?

"To be honest, this hurt me greatly. What did he mean? I never truly lied to anyone in the team, neither him nor anyone else. Obviously at times you need to be a bit evasive to maintain discipline and team spirit, but I never deserved this. You can surely see that this was not my fault; I was just unlucky with my team members. I will be more careful next time.

I am still angry about all this, even though the project finished a few months ago. I did everything for the project and my team. Do you realize I haven't had a holiday for 2 years and hardly a weekend without going to work for some of that time? And this is the thanks I get."

## 7.10. Chapter Summary

In this chapter we have looked at the personal skills and qualities required of the project manager. One of the most important requirements is that team members trust their project manager. The latter must be seen as being ethical, consistent, and fair. Delegation is a good skill to use as this empowers and motivates colleagues, although it does not mean that project managers are then "rid of it." They need to support colleagues in doing their tasks. The project manager needs to set a good example in their own work, time keeping, and organization. Good communication skills are vital to a project manager, and that means formally, such as presenting and interviewing, and informally, such as discussing and motivating. The project manager also needs to market the project and the team positively. There will be times when the project is stressful—for example, when there are conflicts or tasks that are not being realized according to plan. There are a number of skills that may help, such as the ability to prioritize, to share decision making, and to negotiate, along with the general category of organizational skills.

## DISCUSSION QUESTIONS

1. Read Exhibit 7.1 again. Break up into seven teams. Each team should search and find more about one of the habits described by Covey. Prepare a short presentation for class with your own comments added.

2. On reading Exhibit 7.2, do you think that leadership by example is feasible? Do you think Enid Mumford's ideas were too optimistic and unrealistic?

3. "The way to deal with teenagers is to decide if a principle is really important or not. If it is important, you must argue with your kid and ensure that your rules apply. If it is not important, really important, then don't bother. You will find that you argue much less and the household atmosphere is a lot better." Do you think this advice applies to project managers?

4. Consider the interview with the project manager in this chapter, and in discussing the following questions make any assumptions that you make known:

   - Do you think that the interviewer should have been more directive in offering advice? If so, what advice would you have given?
   - Do you think that the project manager was correct in saying that the project was a success?
   - Do you think he was "too democratic"?
   - Do you think he will ever become a good project manager? If so, how might you speed his development?

5. Read some of the cases in this book or on the Web and identify personal skills being used by the project manager. Did these skills (or the lack of them) contribute to the project's overall success and failure?

## EXERCISES

1. Make a table listing the skills required of a good project manager on the left-hand side and your team members on the top. In the cells use a scale from 1 to 5, where 1 = lacking a skill and 5 = excellent skill. Identify skills that are not covered in the course. Suggest that your lecturer covers these skills.

2. Search CIO job descriptions and list major component of their job description. See if you can find from the literature how the CIO job description has changed over time.

3. Search the U.S. Bureau of Labor Statistics site and write a one-page summary report on the status of the information systems job market. Search similar sites for the European job market and compare with results from the U.S. market.

4. Search the Web and find out more information about Forrester Research surveys, including how they relate to the information systems job market. Prepare a short report to share your findings with the class.

5. Search the Web for salary survey report by organizations such as payscale.com and others and prepare reports of median salary for IT professionals by "years of experience," "job title," "industry type," "job location," "gender," and "company size." Compare median salary for IT professionals in public vs. private organizations. Which company pays highest to IT professionals: IBM, Accenture, EDS, or HP?

## APPENDIX TO CHAPTER 7: NGC NATURAL GAS COMPANY

### Supply Chain Management:
### ConsultCo Statement of Work for New IS

NGC Natural Gas Company is undergoing an unprecedented amount of change. Since 1997, the marketing, sales, and distribution of natural gas have been deregulated in some areas of the United States. Natural gas is now sold by an approved group of natural gas distribution companies. As such, the company will no longer be in the business of purchasing and selling natural gas to residential and commercial customers. However, the delivery of natural gas through the existing (and future) pipeline infrastructure will continue to be operated by NGC as a regulated utility governed by the area public utility service commission. NGC will continue to upgrade and perform maintenance on the existing pipeline infrastructure. The efficient execution of the activities is critical to the future success of this organization.

NGC recognizes that business benefits can be achieved by enhancing its existing supply chain processes and supporting them with upgraded information technology systems. The current supply-chain information systems are based on mainframe-based technology with applications that do not adequately support current and future business processes and needs. Therefore, NGC will replace these information systems with the supply-chain modules provided by an ERP supplier. This project proposal document explains the project management approach to implementing ERP information technology software systems. It includes project scope, deliverables, goals, objectives, cost estimates, and benefits. A detailed work plan outlining the activities, responsibilities, and duration for this project implementation is also included.

## Background

NGC is a leading regional energy services holding company and provides distribution service to approximately 2 million customers. NGC interfaces with 18 different marketers that provide customers with customer care and billing services. Although natural gas distribution is NGC's core business, it is also engaged in other energy-related businesses, including retail energy marketing, customer care services for energy marketers, and wholesale and retail propane sales.

## Current Situation

Currently, the Materials Management Organization at NGC Natural Gas Company uses a mainframe-based information technology system to meet its material management business needs. The existing application, which supports all aspects of the supply-chain process, is an integrated suite of modules implemented in 1983. Specifically, this software package provides application support for the Purchasing, Inventory, and Accounts Payable functions. Although NGC has continuously upgraded this system with new software releases, it still does not provide the functionality needed to meet future supply-chain processes and business needs.

Based on a recent software needs assessment, company executives have decided to purchase and implement an ERP solution. Specifically, the company has decided to purchase and install several ERP software modules, including Purchasing, Inventory Management, Accounts Payable, and Employee Expense Reporting. NGC also plans to prepare for the future implementation of the Inventory Planning and Demand Planning modules. This state-of-the-art tightly integrated and automated ERP system will replace the existing mainframe materials management computer system.

## Enterprise Resource Planning

As part of this statement of work, we include a brief section on the principles of ERP. What are ERP systems? Enterprise Resource Planning can be defined as a set of applications such as manufacturing, human resources, financial, and distribution software that facilitates the "balancing and synchronization" of a large enterprise. Balancing and synchronization occurs through proactive optimization of the business functions (e.g., global queries for goods and services among divisional entities and viewing the enterprise supply chain). Enterprise planners, through the proper configuration and use of the ERP system, should be able to conduct "what if" exercises at the enterprise level in a matter of hours. Although still in development, ERP has quickly gained acceptance, particularly among larger multinational organizations. Real-time data processing and enterprise-wide synchronization and integration are underway and are expected to ramp up quickly as technology improvements continue in line with increases in software package functionality. ERP is the natural progression of integrated computer information systems.

ERP is not the cure-all solution for inefficient process structures. ERP will not correct ineffective organizational structures. Last, ERP is not easily achieved. Successful deployment of ERP principles requires fundamental changes in people, processes, and technology.

*(Continued)*

(Continued)

## Company Goals and Objectives

The strategic goals and specific objectives set forth below represent NGC Natural Gas Company's key priorities for action for the next 3 to 5 years. These action areas have been selected after careful consideration of external trends in the information technology marketplace as outlined in a recent competitive research study conducted by our consulting company. Additionally, it was recognized from the outset that resource constraints including time, capital funds, and human resources require diligent priority setting if NGC is to continue unwaveringly in its quest for even higher levels of quality and service.

- To be the leading provider on natural gas service in the region
- To implement projects that maximize profits and minimum operating cost
- To improve supply chain operations and efficiencies
- To design, develop, and install an information technology infrastructure which can leverage current and future technologies such as e-commerce
- Formalize processes and control systems that will enhance managements ability to manage the new additions, replacements, and maintenance of the natural gas pipeline infrastructure

## Project Goals and Objectives

The overall goal of this project is to design, develop, and implement a state-of-the-art information technology computer system that will enable substantial increases in the efficiencies and effectiveness (e.g., capacity, cycle time, flexibility, predictability, productivity) of the company's materials management supply chain. Other goals and objectives include the following:

- Manage the organizational change issues required to support future state business and information system processes.
- Manage the design and development of an information technology infrastructure required to support the installation of four ERP applications.
- Manage and streamline business processing reengineering activities for the procurement to payment and expense reimbursement business processes

## Project Organization

Because ERP software system implementation projects cross the traditional functional boundaries of an organization, our projects are structured and organized such that company stakeholders are involved early and frequently. We accomplish this by simply organizing the roles and responsibilities of the core project team around the ERP software modules being implemented and the organizational structure. The project team structure for this project is shown below in Figure A7.1.

❖ **Figure A7.1**  Project Organization Structure

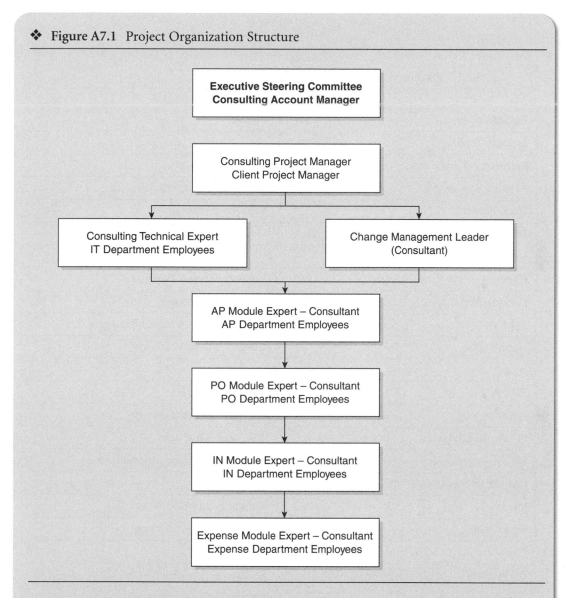

## Roles and Responsibilities

As the organizational chart (Figure A7.1) indicates, two individuals will be performing the role of project manager. One individual, assigned by NGC, will be responsible for managing company resources, and the other individual, assigned by ConsultCo Consulting, will be responsible for managing consulting resources. To eliminate duplicate effort or gaps, separation of duties are listed in Table A7.1. Additionally, roles and responsibilities were defined for project team members, which are listed in Table A7.2.

*(Continued)*

(Continued)

❖ Table A7.1    Project Manager Responsibilities

| Responsibility | Person |
|---|---|
| Budgets/Funding | |
| Authorize Funding/Budget | NGC CEO |
| Adherence to Budget | NGC project manager |
| Track/Report NGC Costs | NGC project manager |
| Track/Report Costs | ConsultCo project manager |
| Schedules | |
| Planning | ConsultCo project manager |
| Planning Support | NGC project manager |
| Adherence | NGC & ConsultCo project managers |
| Track/Report | ConsultCo project manager |
| Issues | |
| Identify | Entire Project Team |
| Track/Report | ConsultCo project manager |
| Resolve NGC Issues | NGC project manager |
| Resolve Project Issues | NGC and ConsultCo project managers |
| Changes of Scope | |
| Identify | ConsultCo project manager |
| Track/Report | ConsultCo project manager |
| Approve | NGC CEO |
| Deliverables | |
| Track Status | ConsultCo project manager |
| Review for Quality | NGC project manager |
| Present for Acceptance | ConsultCo project manager |
| Approval and Sign-off | NGC project manager |
| Team Management | |
| Team Structure | ConsultCo project manager |
| Acquiring Resources | NGC project manager |
| Management of Third Parties | NGC project manager |

| Responsibility | Person |
|---|---|
| Allocation of Resources | ConsultCo project manager |
| Overall Direction | ConsultCo project manager |
| Specific Direction to NGC Team | NGC project manager |
| Specific Direction to Team | ConsultCo project manager |
| Methodology & Management Procedures | |
| Development | ConsultCo project manager |
| Approval | NGC project manager |
| Monitoring | ConsultCo project manager |
| Adherence | NGC & ConsultCo project managers |
| Status Reports | |
| Collect Information | ConsultCo project manager |
| Write – Draft | ConsultCo project manager |
| Review | NGC project manager |
| Present | ConsultCo project manager |

❖ **Table A7.2**  Team Member Responsibilities

| Resource/Role | Time Required | Description | Firm |
|---|---|---|---|
| Sponsor CEO | One meeting per month | • Provides executive oversight of the project while strategically targeting NGC overall project objectives <br> • Provides timely guidance to the project managers on an as-needed and immediate basis <br> • Oversees overall project objectives with relation to NGC budget objectives <br> • Provides first point of contact for strategic level issue resolution <br> • Authorizes project change orders <br> • Attends and presides over monthly steering committee meetings | NGC |

*(Continued)*

❖ **Table A7.2** (Continued)

| Resource/Role | Time Required | Description | Firm |
|---|---|---|---|
| Executive Steering Committee | One meeting per month | • Provides an ongoing assessment of the balance between project priorities and other resource priorities<br>• Provides advisory level project support and strategic direction<br>• Communicates with the rest of the company about the project | NGC & ConsultCo |
| Project Manager ConsultCo | Full-time | • Analyzes alignment of program mission and desired results with scope of work and approach<br>• Develops the overall implementation plan<br>• Puts an integration process and plan in place<br>• Manages the integrated program plan<br>• Drives resolution of project issues<br>• Drives implementation of risk management strategies<br>• Shares in the management of project scope, bringing all potential changes of scope, with implications to cost and timeframe to the project sponsor for approval | ConsultCo |
| Application Analysts (4) | Full-time | • Responsible for the design and configuration of the ERP modules with regard to the To-Be models of the Procure to Pay and Expense Reimbursement processes within ERP | ConsultCo |
| Process Analyst ConsultCo | Full-time | • Responsible for the process analysis and the conceptual design of the Procure to Pay and Expense Reimbursement business processes | ConsultCo |
| Org Change Analyst ConsultCo | Full-time | • Is responsible for stakeholder assessment and the conceptual organization design | ConsultCo |

| Resource/Role | Time Required | Description | Firm |
|---|---|---|---|
| Technical Advisor ConsultCo | Full-time | • Provides technical guidance in the design, development and testing of the required modifications, data conversion, interfaces and reports | ConsultCo |
| Project Manager NGC | Full-time | • Analyzes alignment of project mission and desired results with scope of work and approach<br>• Manages the project against NGC budget<br>• Supports the development of project plans<br>• Provides initial review of all project deliverables<br>• Works within NGC to provide required project resources and manages the work effort of NGC project personnel<br>• Shares in the management of project scope, bringing all potential changes of scope, with implications to cost and timeframe to the project sponsor for approval | NGC |
| Application Analysts (3 from Business, 3 from Core Services) ConsultCo | Full-time | • Perform as a business process experts for NGC in the Procure to Pay and Expense Reimbursement processes<br>• Responsible for the design and configuration of the ERP modules which correspond to the Procure to Pay and Expense Reimbursement processes | NGC |
| Change/ Communication Analyst ConsultCo | Part-time | • Responsible for identifying stakeholders<br>• Assessing stakeholders<br>• Determining communication channels and methods | NGC |
| Technical Staff NGC & ConsultCo | Full-time | • Builds, extracts, maps, and tests interfaces and conversions<br>• Builds and tests reports as defined by the specifications<br>• Builds and tests modifications as defined by the specifications<br>• Supports development lab operations and systems integration testing | NGC & ConsultCo |

*(Continued)*

(Continued)

## Overall Approach

ConsultCo Consulting will partner with NGC Natural Gas Company and approach this ERP implementation using the firm's methodology. This is a process-based software implementation methodology consisting of three main activities: (a) Solution Assessment, (b) Solution Design, and (c) Implementation which combined together seek to:

Understand the business environment and current business process

Create a cross-functional understanding and ownership of business issues and problems

Recommend process and organizational improvements

Integrate the supply-chain solution within the holistic organizational view

Now that the Solution Assessment phase is complete, we are ready to proceed with the next two phases: the Solution Design phase and the Implementation phase, which are both discussed below. The Solution Design and Implementation phases are accomplished by executing predefined work activities and deliverables as outlined in our methodology. A high-level flowchart showing the sequence of the three phases is shown in Figure A7.2.

❖ **Figure A7.2** Flow Chart of Methodology

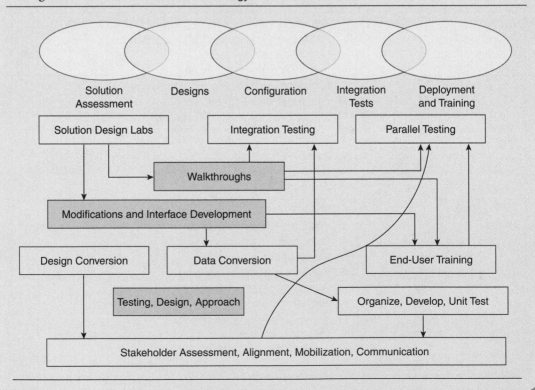

Following the Solution Assessment, ConsultCo Consulting will partner with NGC Natural Gas Company to *design and implement* the ERP business solution. As is depicted in the diagram above, the tight integration of these project activities lends itself to the following combined discussion of the Design and Implement steps.

The *Solution Design approach* is the technique of choice for affecting the system design, build, and test in a concurrent fashion. Solution designs are the key component in the successful implementation of new ERP software and related business processes. They are collaborative, cross-functional workshops used to validate and define the following:

- NGC's future ERP enabled business processes and organization
- The structure and configuration of ERP tables, panels, and business data elements
- Solution design workshops offer several important business design advantages:
- Business risk associated with the implementation is reduced by using a process- not functional-based approach.
- This method allows for a holistic view of the enterprise, thus reducing risks of incompatible, nonintegrated designs.
- Work products are deliverables generated from these work activities and are discussed in more detail in future sections of this document.

## Integrated Project Plan

We have learned that one of the best ways to meet the needs and expectations of our clients and major stakeholders is to manage and control a project using an integrated project plan. We believe that a well-defined project plan ensures that all tasks are identified and that participates and stakeholders have a clear understanding of the work required. Once the project plan is developed, we take the information and break it down into work packages, which will be discussed later. The Integrated Project Plan developed for this project is shown in Figure A7.3.

## Work Breakdown Structure

In order to better control and manage the quality of the project scope, deliverables, and work activities defined in the Integrated Project Plan discussed above, we have broken the project work down into smaller manageable, logical work units, called work packages. This method of breaking down the work is known as the work breakdown structure (WBS). This WBS identifies all project-related work, activities, and deliverables required to provide the hardware, software, organizational change, facilities, and related services that make up this information technology–based implementation project. Individual and group assignments and responsibilities against these work activities are shown at the functional and project team level as shown in Table A7.3.

*(Continued)*

(Continued)

❖ **Figure A7.3** High-Level Integrated Project Plan

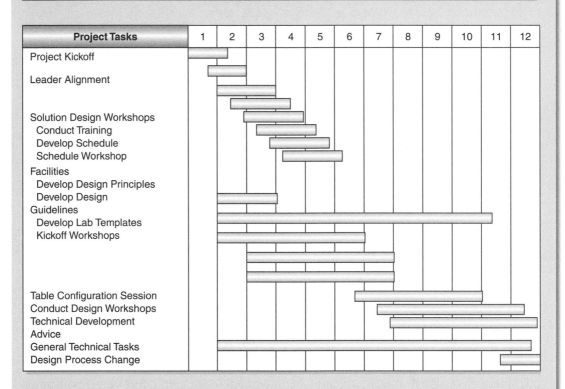

❖ **Table A7.3** Work Breakdown Structure

| Activity | Purpose/Description | Work Products & Deliverables | Responsibility |
|---|---|---|---|
| Solution Design Planning | Develop design workshop Schedule meetings and facilities Customize documentation templates | Design workshop schedule Customized design templates | Change management leader & project manager |
| Solution Design Execution | Design table values and configuration as well as process and organization designs Prepare, execute, review & summarize | Design document Prototypical system | AP module expert PO module expert IN module expert Expense module expert |

| Activity | Purpose/Description | Work Products & Deliverables | Responsibility |
|---|---|---|---|
| Application Table Set Up and Configuration | Define specific values to represent client's configuration needs<br>Load application tables with values | Loaded & configured table values | AP Module expert<br>PO Module expert<br>IN Module expert<br>Expense Module expert |
| Conversion and Interface Approach | Determine overall data conversion approach and approach to each individual conversion program<br>Determine overall interface approach and approach to each individual interface program | Interface/conversion approaches | Technical design expert |
| Interface Design | Map legacy data to/from ERP data structures | Interface specifications | Technical design expert |
| Interface Program Development | Develop and unit test of Interface programs | Interface programs built and tested | Technical design expert |
| Report Design | Map ERP data structures to fields on the report and create the report layouts | Report specifications | Technical design expert |
| Report Program Development | Develop and unit test report programs | Report programs built and tested | Module experts |
| Conversion Design | Map legacy data to be converted to ERP data structures with the use of the appropriate conversion tools | Conversion specifications | Module expert |
| Conversion Program Development | Develop appropriate electronic conversion tools | Conversion programs built and tested | Module experts |
| Modification Design | Identify and design specifications | Modification specifications | Module experts |

*(Continued)*

❖ Table A7.3 (Continued)

| Activity | Purpose/Description | Work Products & Deliverables | Responsibility |
|---|---|---|---|
| Modification Development | Develop and unit test modifications approved | Modifications built and tested | Module experts |
| Process Measurement & Management | Identify key performance indicators<br>Baseline current process performance<br>Set To Be KPI goals<br>Ongoing measurement & root cause analysis<br>Process modification | KPIs | Project manager |
| Stakeholder Mobilization & Alignment | Assess stakeholders commitment to changes<br>Determine interventions<br>Facilitate issue resolution | Ongoing alignment and commitment to project success | Change management leader |
| Organization Design | Prepare knowledge skills and abilities Matrix for To Be roles | To be KSA matrix | Change management leader |
| Organization Development | Detail job design<br>Determine staffing requirements<br>Develop staff realization plan (staff acquisition, reduction and reassignment) | Job descriptions<br>FTE staffing<br>Staff realization plan | Change management leader |
| Communication Design | Develop communication strategy<br>Determine messages and methods | Communication strategy<br>Communication messages | Change management leader |
| Communication Development & Delivery | Develop communication content<br>Develop feedback mechanisms<br>Deliver communication | Communication (newsletters, presentations, luncheons, etc.) | Change management leader |
| Education Design, Development & Delivery | Training needs assessment<br>Determine course approach and modules<br>Design & develop module content<br>Conduct training<br>Design & develop online help, job aids | Needs assessment<br>Training curriculum<br>Training modules<br>Help/job aids | Change management leader |

| Activity | Purpose/Description | Work Products & Deliverables | Responsibility |
|---|---|---|---|
| Reward and Recognition Design & Development | Define behavioral measurement Determine evaluation procedures Develop R&R components | New rewards and recognition | Change management leader |
| Develop Test Scenarios and Test Plans | Descriptions and scripts of business scenarios used to test the system | Integration test plan Test scenarios/scripts | Change management leader |
| System Integration Testing | Testing of business processes using sample converted data in a production simulated environment during integration testing | Test results Integration tested system | Module experts |
| Technical Infrastructure | Maintenance, support, and verification of the Wide Area and Local Area networks in support of this implementation Acquire and install necessary H/W and S/W in support of implementation project phase needs Management, configuration, and backing up of the ERP databases in support of implementation phase requirements Management and performance of the migration of modifications from one database to another design and management of the ERP system security | Reliable networks Stable operating H/W and S/W environment Stable and available databases Appropriate user access profiles | Technical design expert |
| Production Cut-Over Planning | Plan for full conversion from legacy systems to ERP applications | Final data conversion plan | Project manager |
| Deployment Planning | Plan for Phase 3 of this project, "Cut-over to Production" | Deployment plan Cut-over and system evolution SOW Cut-over & system evolution activity level project plan | Project manager |

*(Continued)*

(Continued)

Listed below is a more detailed description of the project deliverables mentioned above.

❖ Table A7.4   Description of Key Deliverables

| Deliverable | Description | Responsibility |
|---|---|---|
| Design Document | Contains configuration data and process designs | Project manager |
| Interface/Conversion Approaches | Overall and specific approaches to techniques to be followed in coding interfaces and conversions generally and specifically | Module leader |
| To Be KSA Matrix | To Be knowledge, skills, and abilities required for new or changing roles | Change management leader |
| Communication Messages | Case For Action Content tailored by stakeholder group | Change management leader |
| Interface and Conversion specifications | Design and document the interface and conversion requirements | Module leaders |
| Reports and Modifications specifications | The design specification integrated code as required for the mitigation of the gaps identified in the project plan | Module leaders |
| Integration Test Plan | Overall approach and calendar for integration testing | Project manager |
| Integration Tested System | The end-to-end testing of the systems including data conversion, interfaces, modifications, configured ERP software, reports, and business processes as defined in the implementation phase SOW | Module leaders |
| Cut-Over & System Evolution SOW | Cut-over and production strategy and timing plan to be prepared, support defined in subsequent SOW | Project manager |
| Cut-Over & System Evolution Activity Level Project Plan | High-level project planning for initial production period and subsequent project activities | Project manager |

## Constraint Prioritization

Our company recognizes that the ultimate success of this project is meeting or exceeding the expectations of senior management, stakeholders, and the project steering committee. We also recognize that these expectations are based on our project manager's ability to balance and manage tradeoffs among three primary constraints—namely, scope (performance), cost (budget), and schedule (time). A simple but effective project management tool, the flexibility matrix, will be used to focus decision making, guide tradeoff discussions, and manage limited resources. Based on previous discussions with your senior management team the following rating system was developed for these three project constraints.

## Project Scope

We have learned that ERP system implementations are often complex and difficult to achieve. In order to achieve maximum benefits from this implementation, we believe the scope of this project can be defined most clearly by breaking it down into six categories. Our consulting methodology describes these categories as the "domains of change," which look at the work to be performed in different perspectives and represent a complete and exhaustive statement of the total work effort.

There are three domains of change that relate to the functional aspects of the business:

1. Business Process scope: Describes the work activities within the organization

2. Organization scope: Describes the people, culture, skills, teams, departments

3. Location scope: Describes the geographical location and physical facilities

There are three domains of change that relate to the technical aspects of the business:

1. Application scope: Describes the specific business software applications

2. Data scope: Describes the content, structure, relationships, and business rules

3. Technology scope: Describes the hardware, system software, development tools

The following scope definitions define the areas of the project that are both in and out of scope. Any areas not specifically identified as "in scope" are assumed to be "out of scope." In some cases, specific areas listed as "out of scope" are presented below for clarity.

*(Continued)*

(Continued)

❖ **Figure A7.4**   Project Priorities and Tradeoffs Matrix

| Tradeoff Factors | Inflexible – Most Critical | Adaptable – Negotiable | Accepting – Will Concede |
|---|---|---|---|
| Scope (Performance) | | | Low |
| Resources (Budget) | High | | |
| Schedule (Time) | | Medium | |

Additional discussion on how the above prioritization ratings will be used on this project can be found in the management approach section of this document.

## Business Process Scope

The business process domain addresses what the enterprise does, how it does it, in what sequence it does it, what business rules it follows, and what type of results it obtains. Change in the business process domain drives change in all other domains. The primary "core" business process involved in this project is the procurement-to-payment process, which touches all aspects of the supply chain. In Table A7.5, shown below, is an outline of the areas of the NGC business that we have identified as being both in scope and out of scope. We believe that clarity in scope definition minimizes scope creep and increases the likelihood of project success.

## Organization Scope

Organization domain deals with the people in the enterprise: their culture, their capabilities, their roles, their team structure, and their organization units. It also addresses the support systems that make organizational change possible. In Table A7.6, shown below, is an outline of the areas of the organization that will be included as part of this system implementation.

## Location Scope

The location domain addresses the place where the enterprise conducts business operations, both in terms of location type and specific physical facilities at a location. Table A7.7, shown below, outlines the locations that are both in and out of scope for this project.

❖ Figure A7.5   Domains of Change

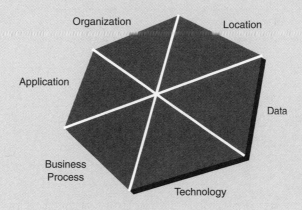

❖ **Table A7.5**   Business Process Scope

| In Scope |
|---|
| ❖ Recognize requirements |
| • Identify materials and services |
| • Requisition process |
| ❖ Source and award |
| • Request for quote process |
| • Contract management process |
| • Purchase requisition process |
| ❖ Receiving process |
| • Receive materials and services |
| • Inspect materials and services |
| • Process receipts |
| • Receive, stage, and store inventory |
| • Process material returns |
| ❖ Manage payments requests |
| • Manage AP request |
| • Manage procurement card activity |
| • Manage vendor payments |

*(Continued)*

❖ **Table A7.5** (Continued)

| |
|---|
| ❖ General management |
| • Manage inventory and non-inventory items |
| • Manage suppliers |
| ❖ Inventory management |
| • Manage inventory accounting |
| • Manage inventory storage locations |
| • Manage inventory carts |
| • Maintain inventory replenishment |
| • Perform physical inventory |
| • Manage material transfers |
| • Manage inventory adjustments |
| **Out of Scope** |
| ❖ Construction management |
| • Bills of materials |
| • Supervision of inventory usage |
| • Contract negotiation |
| • All other processes, not listed in the in-scope section |

❖ **Table A7.6** Organization Scope

| |
|---|
| **In Scope** |
| Purchasing, warehouse, & distribution (approximately 30 system users) |
| Facilities engineering (fewer than 10 system users) |
| Accounts payable (approximately 10 system users) |
| Employee expense reimbursement (approximately 20 system users) |
| **Out of Scope** |
| Gas marketers |
| Pipeline building contractors |
| Operations and maintenance |
| Asset management |
| Technical operations and services |
| End user training services |
| Construction, planning, management, & contractors |

❖ **Table A7.7**   Location Scope

| In Scope |
| --- |
| Corporate headquarters, corporate warehouse, central accounts payable |
| Remote distribution centers (approximately 21 locations) |
| **Out of Scope** |
| All gas marketers & facilities |
| All third party construction company sites & facilities |
| All vendor locations |
| All other locations, not listed in the in scope section |

## Application Scope

The application domain deals with the capabilities, structure, and user interfaces of the software provided for the business users. Table A7.8, shown below, provides a list of the software components included as part of this implementation.

❖ **Table A7.8**   Application Scope

| ❖ In Scope |
| --- |
| • ERP modules |
| • Inventory |
| • Purchasing |
| • Accounts payable |
| • Expense tracking |
| ❖ Design, development, unit test the following data conversions |
|     • Vendors |
|     • Inventory items and non-inventory items |
|     • Vouchers |
|     • Purchase orders |
|     • Purchase requisitions |
|     • Control tables |

*(Continued)*

❖ **Table A7.8** (Continued)

| ❖ Design, development, unit test the following interfaces |
| :--- |
| • Purchase order fax |
| • Web invoicing |
| • Electronic data interchange (EDI) |
| ❖ **Out of Scope** |
| • Electronic commerce procurement |
| • Handheld inventory tracking devices |
| • All other applications, not listed in the in scope section |

## Data Scope

The data scope domain addresses the content and structure, relationships, and business data rules surrounding the information that the enterprise retains permanently. Table A7.9, shown below, outlines the data that will be included in work activities of this project.

❖ **Table A7.9**   Data Scope

| **In Scope** |
| :--- |
| Item master |
| Vendor master |
| Requisition details |
| Purchase order details |
| Expense report details |
| Voucher details |
| **Out of Scope** |
| Purchase order acknowledgement history |
| Inventory transaction history |
| Receipt transaction history |
| All other data items, not listed in the in scope section |

## Technology Scope

The technology domain addresses the hardware, system software, and communication components used to support the enterprise. Table A7.10, shown below, contains the technology information that is both in and out of scope for this project.

❖ **Table A7.10**   Technology Scope

| In Scope |
| --- |
| Database server |
| Application server |
| Windows configuration for ERP modules, SQL, crystal reports |
| Fax server (PO dispatch) |
| Electronic data interchange (EDI) transaction processing |
| **Out of Scope** |
| Internet, Web-enabling technology |
| Electronic commerce procurement |
| Database administration, server performance tuning |
| Other operating systems; Windows NT, MS Sequel Server, etc. |
| All other technology components, not included in the in scope section |

## Project Management

We define project management as the process of identifying, monitoring, controlling, and balancing the project's three primary constraints: scope (performance), cost (budget), and schedule (time). In order to achieve these objectives, we must establish an agreement and written procedures for the following items:

A performance baseline

A process to monitor progress

A clear means of communication

An open approach to dealing with issues

An objective change control procedure

A process to recognize and manage risk

A document management process

A procedure for accepting deliverables

A definition of what represents project completion

*(Continued)*

(Continued)

## Performance Baseline

This is the foundation or baseline for all the key project management activities related to this project. It is also called the Statement of Work, and it identifies the work activities that will be tracked, defines the boundaries for scope control, identifies responsibilities, and clarifies many of the areas where issues may arise that need to be controlled and managed.

## Process to Monitor Progress

A detailed integrated project plan is the key vehicle for monitoring and measuring progress. We believe that the specific activities that each team member works on and progress made against completing those activities are the only objective measure of where the project stands against the budget and schedule. To capture this information, each team member will record his or her time spent on project activities against the budgeted time as outlined in the integrated project plan. Each team member will be required to enter this information weekly in the time and budget software tool developed for this project. In addition, each team member will be required to provide estimates of the effort remaining for each project activity in weekly status reports.

Weekly status reports will include critical information such as work accomplished, issues, problems, and planned work. This information will be analyzed by the project manager to determine where the project stands versus budget and schedule. A project management summary report will be submitted to the project steering committee each week with this information.

## Means of Communication

Because the success of this project is critical to the organization, it is imperative that a formal process be used to encourage timely and accurate information reporting. The two key vehicles that will be used to provide this communication include a weekly status report and a weekly status meeting.

As mentioned earlier, all core team members will provide weekly progress reports. This information, and the analysis of it, will be summarized into an overall project management progress report for the project steering committee, which will be presented at the weekly status meeting held each Thursday afternoon in the main conference room. This project summary report will contain the following information: significant problems, progress summary, accomplishments, planned activities, schedule status, budget status, team morale, and other important issues critical to the success of this project.

In order to make this weekly status meeting effective, the project steering committee must be committed to attendance and participation. The critical success factors in making the meeting worthwhile include executive sponsor participation, intervention when management action is required, management support in time of crisis, and recognition of and rewarding hard work and dedication.

The main purpose of these status meetings is to allow the steering committee the opportunity to review project progress and status, consider impacts at a strategic level on the organization, review high-level issues and make recommendations on their resolutions, and provide advisory level guidance to the project manager.

## Issues Management

Every project has issues that hinder progress. It is important that these issues are identified and resolved quickly by the right person. The first step in effectively dealing with these issues is to make the entire project team aware of the importance of identifying issues and getting proper resolution. We will then use the following procedure to encourage that the issues are visibly tracked:

*Identify issues:* When the project begins, we will start identifying any issues that could hinder our ability to meet the objectives of the project. Issues can be identified by anyone involved with the project.

*Document issues:* The person who identifies an issue must document it.

*Assign responsibility:* The project manager will determine the appropriate individual who will be responsible for resolving each issue. The responsible person must be an individual who has the knowledge and authority to make decisions regarding the issue. The executive steering committee and project manager will assign a priority to each issue.

*Monitor and control:* All issues will be tracked on an issues log that will be maintained to formally track the status and resolution of each issue.

*Progress reports:* As mentioned earlier, the issues log will be a part of the weekly status report and discussed in the weekly project status meetings.

*Communicate issues:* The issues log and documented resolutions of issues will be made available to the steering committee members and all other project team members.

## Change Control

The Change Control Procedure is a crucial mechanism that can affect the success or failure of this project. This process is the primary vehicle for containing scope and ensuring that the executive steering committee and project manager has the opportunity to make timely tradeoffs between the three key project variables of cost, time, and scope. It is imperative that potential changes are identified early, documented carefully, and resolved at the appropriate levels of responsibility.

Changes are broadly defined as work activities or work products not originally defined by this statement of work. More specifically, changes will include the following:

- Any scope item not listed in this statement of work
- Variances of actual work effort from estimated effort
- Delays caused by schedule slippage
- Risks that actually occurred
- Assumptions not remaining valid
- Investigative work to determine the impact of major changes
- Any rework of completed activities or acceptance deliverables

*(Continued)*

(Continued)

## Risk Management

Project risk management is the art and science of identifying, analyzing, and responding to risk throughout the life of a project. It is our belief that proper risk management can often result in significant improvements in the ultimate success of an information systems project. We believe that identifying and effectively managing risk helps to keep the project on schedule and within budget.

We view risk management as a continuous process comprising six activities, grouped into two major categories: risk assessment and risk mitigation. The major activities of risk assessment include identifying risks, analyzing risks, and planning mitigation strategies. Moreover, the major activities of risk mitigation include mitigate risks, access mitigation effectiveness, and reassess exposure.

After identifying potential project risk at the project kickoff meeting held earlier this month, the project team used four common information-gathering techniques, including brainstorming, the Delphi technique, interviewing, and a SWOT (strengths, weaknesses, opportunities, and threats) analysis to identify some additional risks that could jeopardize this project. All of the risks and the associated mitigation strategies identified are listed in Table A7.11 shown below.

❖ **Table A7.11**   Potential Risk Management Conditions

| Risk | Impact Description | Mitigation Strategy |
|------|--------------------|---------------------|
| Business users assigned full-time to this project are pulled away to work on other business issues outside the scope of this project. | This potential risk could cause delays to the project. Replacing or increasing project staff may cause learning curve as new members come up to speed. | Staff planning process needs to be effective in order to relieve core team members of current activities. |
| The executive management team may not be available to provide the necessary support to achieve the project objectives. | Slow response to open issues affects the project schedule, causing delays due to slow decision making or reopening or changing of decisions made earlier. | ConsultCo Consulting resources and NGC Natural Gas executive managers must access the degree of impact and develop a strategy for executive alignment with the goals of the project. Attendance at all scheduled meetings is imperative. Delegate these responsibilities to others, if necessary. |

| Risk | Impact Description | Mitigation Strategy |
|---|---|---|
| The project scope cannot be maintained as defined in this Statement of Work. | This potential risk could cause delays and costs overruns for this project. The impact for changing the scope in midstream could be significant. | Apply rigorous change control procedures to any deviation from the project scope baseline as described in this Statement of Work. |
| Deliverables are not reviewed and approved promptly by executive steering committee. | If deliverables are not reviewed and approved in a timely fashion, expectations of work quality may not be met. | Specify terms of the deliverable acceptance process. Monitor review/acceptance process in status meetings. |
| Technical infrastructure inadequate or not deployed. | Inadequate technical infrastructure system to support ERP module deployment. | Ensure that the technical infrastructure analysis is part of the early analysis and strategy investigation. |

## Document Management

Throughout the project, documents will be produced that need to be kept through the life of the project. These documents will be organized, labeled, and maintained in project notebook binders in the company's project library. As documents are produced they will be given to the project administrator to be logged and filed in a central place inside the company's project library. Examples of these documents include change control documents, issues-resolution documents, deliverable acceptance and procurement documents, contract and legal documents, project reference materials, work papers, work products, and other important project-related documents.

## Financial Justification

We worked diligently with your management team to evaluate the potential benefits of funding this project. Because the initial estimates of the payback period are considered long by your management group and the cost of capital is higher than normal for companies competing in your industry, we decided to use the net present value (NPV) method to evaluate cost–benefits and the financial aspects of this investment. The graph shown below provides a graphical display of the results of our NPV estimates. Two estimates were generated: one showing the high-range benefits and the other showing low-range benefits, with payback periods ranging from 49 to 69 months, respectively. The results of these calculations clearly prove that the benefits outweigh the costs and that we should proceed with this system implementation.

*(Continued)*

(Continued)

❖ **Figure A7.6** Business Case Calculations

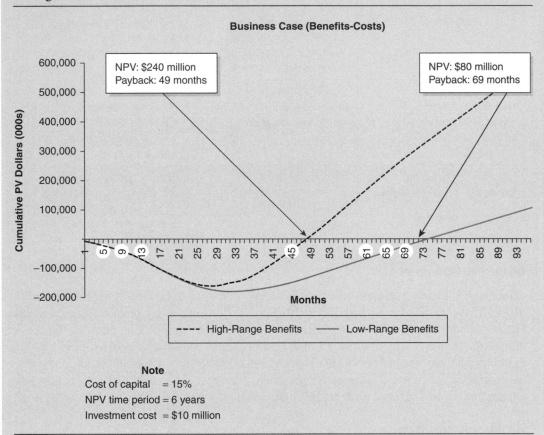

Our financial analysis reveals cost savings in several different areas of the supply chain, including labor, material, IT expense, freight, storage, accounts payable. See Figure A7.6.

## Project Audits

To ensure the highest quality service from our consulting firm, our quality assurance department will conduct periodic project audits. It is our philosophy that project audits are one way to validate whether the project manager and team are utilizing the appropriate project management tools, concepts, and techniques to support our methodology. We also believe that ongoing project audits are an excellent way to learn and improve the professional skills of our consultants while keeping the project on track.

❖ **Figure A7.7** Potential Cost Savings

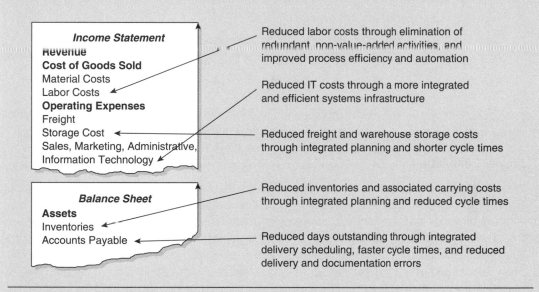

*Income Statement*
**Revenue**
**Cost of Goods Sold**
Material Costs
Labor Costs
**Operating Expenses**
Freight
Storage Cost
Sales, Marketing, Administrative,
Information Technology

Reduced labor costs through elimination of redundant, non-value-added activities, and improved process efficiency and automation

Reduced IT costs through a more integrated and efficient systems infrastructure

Reduced freight and warehouse storage costs through integrated planning and shorter cycle times

*Balance Sheet*
**Assets**
Inventories
Accounts Payable

Reduced inventories and associated carrying costs through integrated planning and reduced cycle times

Reduced days outstanding through integrated delivery scheduling, faster cycle times, and reduced delivery and documentation errors

Our audits are well-structured and are performed jointly by the project manager and the quality assurance director. Both individuals review and critique the progress of the project in an honest and factual way so that senior management will have a realistic view of the condition and performance of the project. Our project audit report template (see the reports at the end) provides the foundation on the issues, problems, and opportunities that need to be addressed. One particular area that will receive special attention is the status area. This section of the report provides a quick view of the status of the project for each key area. The information reported here requires the auditor to designate the issue one of three "traffic light" colors using the following guidelines:

Green: No open issues. The risks to the project from this area are minimal.

Yellow: There are open issues and problems either awaiting resolution or under corrective action. The risks to the project from this area are moderate.

Red: There are significant problems and issues either awaiting resolution or under corrective action that will jeopardize the overall success of the project. Serious corrective action must be taken immediately.

## Acceptance of Deliverables

All of the completed deliverables identified earlier will be formally submitted, reviewed, and approved by the project steering committee. This section outlines the key components to this acceptance process:

*(Continued)*

(Continued)

Only one person identified as the acceptor of the deliverable

Each deliverable will include an acceptance form for signature

Each deliverable will include a clear definition for acceptance criteria

Comments for each deliverable must be documented (in writing)

Each deliverable will be reviewed and accepted within a specified timeframe

To avoid delays in the project schedule and the associated increased cost due to slow deliverable review, deliverables not reviewed and approved within 5 business days will be considered accepted.

## Project Completion

We will consider the project complete when all of the deliverables identified earlier are accepted by NGC Natural Gas Company. In addition, a post-project review report will be created and distributed to senior management and core project team. This report will highlight lessons learned from the project, concentrating primarily on what went right, what went wrong, and the reasons why. It will also include project performance measurements and statistics so that the project can be evaluated against similar completed projects within the organization. This information will be placed in the company's project library and kept in archives so that it can be used to support more accurate time and cost estimations for future projects of similar size and scope.

## CRITICAL SUCCESS FACTORS

We would like to conclude this Statement of Work by discussing the fundamental concepts that we believe to be critical factors to the success of any information systems technology project. These critical success factors will be used extensively on this project.

### Involve the End-User

We recognize that end-users are an integral part of the system development process. In turn, we will involve end users in design workshops, in the development of screens and reports, in the creation and test of prototypes, and in the development of models and interfaces. Therefore, the project manager will be prepared to involve individuals and groups within the entire organization, including both system and non-system users.

### Expect Change

Changes are a normal part of any systems project, but when changes are not recognized and managed well, the project results become endangered. Our project management approach emphasizes the importance of recognizing changes, assessing their impact on the overall design, goals, schedule, and budget, then making conscious, informed decisions about whether and when to make change. The key to managing change effectively is to weigh the need for change against the cost and delay it will cause. Change will be handled in a nonadversarial and efficient manner. We believe the only way to effectively manage change is to be open and honest.

## Understand Business Goals

To be successful, we believe that the project manager and team must clearly understand the business goals of the organization and how they relate to the project. Ultimately, project success will be determined not only by how well the system solution meets the targeted business requirements but also by whether the overall business goals and objectives are achieved.

## FEES & EXPENSES

Based on the scope and approach, estimated duration, resources requirements, and level of participation articulated in this Statement of Work, ConsultCo Consulting estimates the costs of its professional services to be $10 million, exclusive of expenses.

ConsultCo will invoice NGC Natural Gas Company for all direct expenses: travel, lodging, meals, and other project—related expenses. It is estimated that direct expenses for this project will be approximately 15% to 20% of professional consulting fees. Invoices will be submitted monthly, outlining the total professional fees due and break out expenses incurred to date by category—e.g., air travel, lodging, auto rental, meals. Invoices are due and payable upon receipt.

## Example of Project Audit Report

| Project Audit Report | | | Date: |
|---|---|---|---|
| Client: | Project Name: | | Project #: |
| Project Manager: | | Account Manager: | |
| **Project Summary** | | | |
| Start Date:<br>Planned End Date:<br>Project Type (T&M, FFP, T&M Cap): | | Detailed Project Plan in Place (Y/N):<br>Tracking Weekly Actual to Tasks (Y/N): | |

| Project Status Areas:<br>(one check per row) | Green<br>No Impact | Yellow<br>Moderate Impact | Red<br>Major Impact |
|---|---|---|---|
| Major Issues | | | |
| Schedule Status | | | |
| Technical Status | | | |
| Budget/Cost | | | |

*(Continued)*

(Continued)

| Project Status Areas: (one check per row) | Green No Impact | Yellow Moderate Impact | Red Major Impact |
|---|---|---|---|
| Staffing | | | |
| Client Perception/ Responsibilities | | | |
| Invoice/Receivables | | | |
| Contract Status | | | |
| Project Expectations | | | |
| Project Appraisals | | | |

## Project Status Area Detail

### MAJOR ISSUES, SIGNIFICANT PROBLEMS, and the ACTIONS to be taken

**A few items to consider:**

1. List issues in priority sequence, with the top priority listed first

2. Include actions taken or to be taken

### SCHEDULE STATUS (Attach Exhibit I Project Schedule/High-level Gantt chart, or Phase Dates):

**A few items to consider:**

1. Note status of major deliverables and milestones

2. Provide explanation on changes to the schedule

### Project Status Area Detail

### TECHNICAL STATUS (e.g., architecture, database, batch design)

**A few items to consider:**

1. IT strategy issues

2. Performance issues with software or hardware?

3. Any issues related to new technology?

4. Any issues regarding support from product vendors?

5. Status of setting up facilities

6. Deliverable issues

7. Are the selected tools meeting expectations?

8. Status of hardware deployment

## BUDGET/COST STATUS (Attach Exhibit II Budget/Cost Summary)

**A few items to consider:**

1. Provide narrative explanation on budget/cost summary model. Do not calculate "Estimates To Complete" by simply subtracting Actual (i.e., billable) from Original Budget. The ETC number should be calculated from task/activity estimates. A zero variance is usually an indication that the ETC is not based on detailed estimates. Do not simply refer to Exhibit II.

## STAFFING STATUS (Attach Exhibit III Staffing Plan)

**A few items to consider:**

1. Do you have the resources needed to complete the project on time and within the budget?

2. List changes in staffing

3. Outline full-time versus part-time resources

4. Current status of project expectations and appraisals

5. Staffing conflicts

## CLIENT PERCEPTION/RESPONSIBILITIES

**A few items to consider:**

1. How does the client perceive the CSC Pinnacle team?

2. Discuss client meetings (meetings with steering committee, etc.)
   Is the client fulfilling their responsibilities?

## INVOICE/RECEIVABLES

**A few items to consider:**

1. Status of invoicing and receivable days outstanding

2. Note any changes in client invoice approval procedures

## CONTRACT STATUS (Attach Exhibit IV Contractual Documents Status)

**A few items to consider:**

1. Provide status (i.e., plan to meet with client on xx/xx/xx) for contracts pending approval

*(Continued)*

(Continued)

---

ACCOUNT STRATEGY ISSUES/ACTIONS

**A few items to consider:**
Provide information on strategy for leveraging additional resources on project, obtaining next phase, or additional work in other business areas

---

## APPENDIX TO CHAPTER 7: DISCUSSION QUESTIONS

1. Each class group should present the NGC case with different perspectives, for example:

- An outline of the case from a general management perspective
- A presentation showing how the case fits in with the company strategy
- A presentation from the project manager of NGC to team members at the beginning of the project
- A presentation from the project manager of ConsultCo to team members at the beginning of the project, pointing out potential synergies and conflicts with NGC project manager
- A presentation of the work breakdown structure, network and critical path
- A presentation of the risk management and change management processes
- A presentation on enterprise resource planning (ERP) systems and their potential impact on the firm

## BIBLIOGRAPHY

Aspray, W., Mayadas, F., & Vardi, M.Y. (Eds.). (2006). *Globalization and offshoring of software: A report of the ACM Job Migration Task Force.* New York: Association for Computing Machinery. Retrieved from www.acm.org/ globalizationreport.

Belbin, M. (1999). *Team roles at work.* London: Butterworth-Heinemann.

Berkun, S. (2005). *The art of project management.* Sebastopol, CA: O'Reilly.

Career Resources (2007). http://career-resources.dice.com/job-technology/hot_skills_shift_to_project_management_ security_architecture.shtml

Covey, S. R. (1989). *The seven habits of highly effective people.* London: Simon & Schuster.

Covey, S. R. (2004). *The 8th habit: From effectiveness to greatness.* London: Simon & Schuster.

Djavanshir, G. R. (2005, November–December). Surveying the risks and benefits of IT outsourcing. *IT Pro* (a publication of IEEE Computer Society), 32–37.

Kotter, J. P. (1990, May). What leaders really do. *Harvard Business Review, 68*(3).

Loo, R. (2002). Working toward best practices in project management: A Canadian study. *International Journal of Project Management, (20),* pp. 93–98.

Posner, B. Z. (1987). What it takes to be a good project manager. *Project Management Journal, 28*(1).

Whitehead, R. (2001). *Leading a software development team: A developer's guide to successfully leading people & projects.* Harlow, UK: Addison-Wesley.

# Developing the Project Plan

**Themes of Chapter 8**

- ❖ Why do we plan the project?
- ❖ Why is it not always appreciated?
- ❖ What is technical competency?
- ❖ What is management competency?
- ❖ What are the major steps in a project plan?
- ❖ What are the detailed activities in a project plan?

**M**ost people consider information systems project management competency from the two perspectives of *technical competency* and *managerial competency*. Technical competencies include hardware and software issues as well as detailed activities such as scheduling, estimating, quality control, and the like. Managerial competencies on the other hand relate to broader issues of planning, leadership, personnel, resource management, and so on. To be successful, a project manager needs to be competent in both of these areas. This chapter describes the importance of planning for the successful development and implementation of information systems projects. It describes steps involved in project planning as well as steps for the execution of a project plan. We then look at PRINCE, which is an approach to project planning that is the preferred approach of the UK government that has been influential internationally. Finally, this chapter describes a case that illustrates the importance of planning for information systems projects. But first our exhibit concerns a debate that will be fairly familiar to all students and their teachers: Whose side are you on?

---

### Exhibit 8.1    A Conversation With a Student: Whose Side Are You On?

**Student:**  Good morning, Professor Jones.

**Professor:**  Good morning, Mr. Hmmmmm.

**Student:**  I'm sorry, but I can't make the coursework deadline.

**Professor:**  But we agreed that the deadline was today and that there will be a fail grade of 0 for anyone who missed the deadline.

**Student:**  But that's not fair, as the Internet was down for 2 days.

**Professor:**  But we allowed for contingencies such as this when the coursework was set 5 weeks ago.

**Student:**  But I was also ill for a few days.

**Professor:**  If you have an official sick note from the doctor, this will be accepted, and you can hand in work late. Have you a sick note?

**Student:**  No. I was too ill to go to the doctor, and my phone was not working.

**Professor:**  Pity.

**Student:**  Also I want extra time to perfect the coursework. I don't want to give you material that is not up to the high standards I require of myself.

**Professor:**  What is your average coursework grade?

**Student:**  Around 55%. But I think I can really do some excellent work here.

**Professor:**  Even so, today is the deadline.

**Student:**  I have trouble with people like you who say, "there are deadlines." My main concern is toward you bureaucrats who impose timelines on things. I admit that there are deadlines at which point a specific thing will need to happen—for example, a system needs to be ready for the new tax year on January 1; an ambulance routing system responding to an emergency call must be immediately put right if it goes wrong, etc.—but everything else is not a deadline but a convenience. Now, even in education, where we should be aiming to achieve our best work, we all appear to accept bureaucrats who impose timelines on things. I feel that coursework as a piece of work has its own internal time-life-span. With the motivation right, the quality is better, and the focus is on the work not the timeline. What you are saying is aim to exert as little as possible for minimum achievement; just make the deadline. Control the process, and make it stupid. What about quality?

**Professor:**  Good point, and I take your question as rhetorical. But the deadline is today.

---

## 8.1. Purpose of a Project Plan

Information systems projects often involve significant resources, require diverse talents and skills, influence many individuals and groups in different departments, and require close collaboration with end-users. This means that for any project a great deal of coordination, communication, and negotiation is required to produce a successful outcome. Planning is an effective mechanism that helps information systems project managers accomplish these objectives. Planning is a mentally challenging task, and it is often avoided for reasons such as "it is time-consuming," "the project is not big enough to warrant a plan," "plans do not get implemented," and "we need action, not planning." These arguments are not convincing and should not be accepted. Planning can help save much time and inconvenience in the long run. To give you an idea of what planning can do for project management, consider the questions shown in Exhibit 8.2. These and other important questions can be answered where there is a proper project plan. A good plan should make it clear where you are going and how to get there.

---

**Exhibit 8.2    Questions Related to Establishing a Project Plan**

- Is it clear what the project is supposed to deliver?
- Is it clear who will be working on the project?
- Do you have a breakdown of activities?
- Is it clear when deliverables are due?
- Do you have established communication channels?
- Are you clear who the stakeholders are?
- Do you have milestones and due dates for them?
- Do you know what resources are available?
- Do you know what to do if you run into obstacles?
- Do you know what to do if functional areas do not cooperate?
- Are you aware of project risks and their impact?

---

Despite the clear advantages, planning is not often appreciated. There are two primary reasons for this. One is that planning is a challenging and mentally demanding task. Careful planning requires knowledge, experience, and commitment. Information systems project planning involves a clear understanding of the technology, resources, talents, culture, politics, and procedures. The second reason for the lack of appreciation for planning relates to its perceived disconnect with action. Project managers and team members who think of themselves as "doers," or those who would want to be considered as such, often jump into "action" without a clear understanding of the long-term goals. They tend to ignore the broad perspective of design, development, implementation, use, and impact of a project.

This kind of action-oriented information systems development approach generates short-term momentum at the cost of long-term benefits. Team members and stakeholders involved with information systems development activities such as primary users and sponsors of the project soon realize that any system is a subsystem of a larger system and to be useful the subsystems must fit together within the larger system. Organizational goals and objectives should invariably take priority over departmental and functional goals and objectives. Likewise, as we saw in Chapter 2, information systems project goals and objectives must be aligned with those of the organization. Projects with goals and objectives that are not aligned with organizational goals and objectives either do not get funding approval or run the risk of cancellation later on. It is critical to have the management onboard for support before the project starts. Top management support is especially important for large projects that require a significant resource commitment.

Planning places the project within a larger perspective and describes the project manager as the implementer of organizational goals and objectives. Remember, *projects are tools and mechanisms by which organizations realize and implement their goals and objectives*. A plan is implemented through actions. It must be seen as a road map for defining and executing activities. A good plan is *realistic, doable*, and *easy to understand*. It is an effective tool to monitor progress and evaluate success. More specifically, as shown in Exhibit 8.3, a plan helps in a number of areas.

---

### Exhibit 8.3    The Potential of Project Planning

- Define project scope.
- Develop an activity list and work breakdown structure.
- Define activity sequence and duration.
- Estimate resources.
- Develop support and commitment.
- Establish milestones.
- Establish communication channels.
- Define responsibilities.
- Define due dates.
- Identify risks.
- Set standards.
- Monitor progress.
- Integrate project outcome.

---

This list suggests the range of knowledge and abilities that are required to develop a useful plan. It further suggests that a useful plan must be comprehensive and at the same time it must guide execution. A plan is a living document that must be adhered to by all stakeholders, especially the project manager and team members. Project planning starts with the project scope (see Chapter 4) that defines the project outcome. In other words, the project plan guides activities that accomplish what is described in the project scope. The project manager plays a significant role in the development of a plan and is responsible for its implementation.

## 8.2. Project Planning Process

Information systems project planning outlines ways, means, and methods through which the project goals will be accomplished. Once a project is approved, the first decision should be to appoint a project manager. One of the first responsibilities of the project manager is to develop a project plan. Sometimes the core of a project team is also involved in assisting the project manager with the development of the project plan. The following steps and issues are important in developing a workable project plan.

*Project requirements.* Project managers must understand project requirements clearly before they can formulate a plan. The project requirements are closely linked and described through business needs. The project manager must analyze and understand business needs as well as project needs and make sure that they support each other.

*Project phases.* Project phases allow large projects to be divided into manageable components (see Section 1.6). The larger the project, the more critical this step is in the project plan development. Phases should be linked to deliverables, which are the products or services that the project will achieve—for example, a completed training program, a software module that has been fully tested, or successfully implemented hardware. To the extent possible, phases are determined to provide the customer with important functions of the new system as early as possible with minimum risk to the business unit.

*Work units within phases.* Each phase is divided into work units or activities with each work unit linked to a single deliverable. A work unit is defined through its duration (start date and time, completion date and time), the resources required, and the person responsible for it (see Chapter 6). A clear definition of a work unit leads to more accurate estimates for resources and ultimately to a more reliable assessment of outcome.

*Project milestones.* Milestones are clearly defined events with significant importance to the customer and the project development life cycle and can be used to measure progress. For example, a milestone in an information systems development life cycle is when a prototype of the information system is complete and ready for testing. A milestone should lead toward the successful completion of a project. Indeed, an important milestone is the one where the customer accepts delivery of the product and signs off. A milestone is typically associated with a deliverable that can be defined, measured, developed, and demonstrated.

*Management approval.* Executive approval is necessary for a project to start. This support is also necessary throughout the project, and its progress toward a successful outcome. The project manager must identify all sources of power and influence that could affect a project and make sure that the project is supported. To be effective, the project plan must be approved by the management and accepted by all stakeholders (Section 1.7).

*Project resources.* The critical resources for an information systems project include human resources and hardware and software. The talent and skills of the team members and their interaction is critical to the success of a project. Project team member selection and team building is an important task for project managers. Hardware and software need to be planned carefully and ordered from the supplier for timely delivery.

*Project constraints.* The critical constraints for an information systems project include time and budget. A project starts and ends on specific target dates. The project duration is usually divided into shorter times for phases and work units. Some projects may have more flexible timeframes than others. However, a prolonged project is likely to lose support and raise concern. As we saw in Chapter 6, PERT/CPM or MS Project are useful tools that help project time management. A budget is assigned to a project at the initial justification stage. It is usually divided into phases and then work units with some flexibility to transfer funds between phases and work units.

*Potential issues.* The project manager is ultimately responsible for the successful delivery of the project outcome. Important issues that influence all projects and that a project manager must carefully consider include *strategic* issues such as long-term viability of a project, *tactical* issues such as day-to-day operation, *resource* issues such as human resources and technology, and *success* measures such as customer satisfaction with deliverables. Reflecting on these issues enables the project manager to prepare for alternatives.

*Policy and procedures.* Policy provides a general guide for decision making and problem solving. Policies provide broad parameters for decision making. Procedures describe detailed approaches to implement policies. Procedures are particularly important for individuals working on a project for the first time or individuals who are not familiar with how things are done within the organization.

*Planning pitfalls.* The fact that every project is unique provides opportunities and challenges for the project manager. Following a generic recipe can be problematic. While lessons can be learned from each project, the limits of what can be learned from a past project must be understood. The uniqueness of a project provides opportunities to the project manager to fulfill organizational goals and objectives through the project.

*Planning techniques and tools.* There are a number of useful and effective project management techniques and tools, including Gantt charts, work breakdown structures (WBS), Critical Path Method (CPM), Program Evaluation and Review Technique (PERT), and MS Project. The project manager must decide which ones work best for a given situation. However, techniques and tools alone do not guarantee success, however well they have been used. The ability to relate business issues, think critically, and communicate effectively is probably the most important skill set for good planning. Techniques and tools are merely a support function to enable the project manager to carry out the tasks efficiently.

*Input from colleagues.* The WBS and the PERT network, including the critical path, are crucial parts of the project plan. Team members are asked to provide task inputs concerning the resources and time needed to complete a task (activity). They are expected to fill out forms detailing the specific of each task. These form a kind of mini contract with the project manager and therefore very important in forming an accurate project plan.

## 8.3. Planning and Project Success

Planning is a systematic approach to understanding the project from the beginning to the end with the phases involved in between. A project plan is the primary means of communication among all stakeholders. A project plan must be accepted and adhered to by all stakeholders, and that requires broad involvement. It must be the result of collective efforts. It must have a summary that describes the project scope, phases, methods, deliverables, milestones, limits, responsibilities, and due dates clearly. Exceptions and contingencies are described and possible risks identified. A project plan predetermines a set of actions to realize goals and objectives of an organization through the project scope. A project plan acts like a road map for the execution of project activities. Planning involves flexibility because of the unpredictable nature of some of the events and activities. As seen in Exhibit 8.4, good planning helps project success for a number of reasons.

---

### Exhibit 8.4    The Benefits of Good Planning

- It clarifies what needs to be done before the work starts.
- It makes work manageable by breaking down the project into phases.
- It defines the confines of each work unit in terms of time and budget.
- It clarifies who is responsible for a task.
- It gives perspective and links work units to the overall project.
- It links the project to organizational goals and objectives.
- It is a source of reference for clarifying issues.
- It provides the basis for performance evaluation.
- It provides the basis to monitor progress.
- It provides the basis for measuring success.
- It provides the basis for establishing communication channels.
- It helps the formation of realistic expectations.
- It helps generate support for the project.
- It provides boundaries for the triple constraints of cost, time, and requirements.
- It provides the project manager with the opportunity to demonstrate administrative and leadership skills.
- It provides the project manager with the opportunity to set standards and describe expectations.
- It reduces uncertainty.

While each project is different, these points apply to most information systems projects. They also provide a frame of reference for evaluating good project plans. If a project plan does not address these issues, or a majority of these issues, it may be necessary to go back and review that plan. Sometimes for small projects the project manager may decide to develop the system by ad hoc decisions and an informal process. While this might work in some cases where there is a highly dedicated workforce, it has the potential to create conflict, confusion, and crisis.

## 8.4. Practical Considerations

In the final analysis, a good plan helps management with decision making, monitoring, and execution. Although the content of a plan is not cast in stone and can be altered if necessary, it must provide a sense of stability, continuity, and focus. In other words, drastic change in the content of a plan may mean that the project focus is altered. Information systems project plans are more likely to go through change because of the following reasons:

*Early adopters.* In the information systems intensive environments, users tend to rely on self-training and self–learning, and as a result their expectations are continuously changing. Some users are motivated and learn rapidly about new and upcoming technology. This could lead to unrealistic expectations of information systems features that may not be practical or cost effective at the early stages of technology development.

*Reluctant users.* Because of their training and background, some users are hesitant to apply new technology in their work. These people often know their work and their business but are afraid of change or lack confidence in learning new tools. This also could provide problems due to inappropriate expectations.

*Expectation gap.* The rapid change in the technology availability, capability, and ease of use influences user expectations. There is an expectation gap between the technology potential and its benefits. Users often tend to expect the latest, the fastest, and the most flexible systems and may well believe the "hype" often associated with new technology at face value.

*Knowledge gap.* Some organizations have a rich pool of individuals with business knowledge developed over the years. These individuals are not necessarily technology savvy. Some organizations have a rich pool of individuals who have high expertise on technology application but are not necessarily experienced in business. These situations create a knowledge gap that can negatively influence an application or the innovative use of technology. Indeed, it may be expecting too much for the project manager to have knowledge of the business (for example, the supply chain, strategy and planning, organizational hierarchy, human resource management, and the rest) along with up-to-date technical expertise of specific technologies. It is therefore more realistic to expect that the team, of which the project manager is head, possesses this width and depth of expertise.

Because the above factors are very dependent on the particular people involved and the organizational culture, it is not possible to provide a specific and generic project plan for all occasions, but thinking fully about the above issues will likely achieve an appropriate plan for the particular situation. A good project plan will consider these organizational and human issues, and experienced project managers build flexibility into their plan in response. The technology may become mature in the future and be able to meet "current" expectations, but it is not fulfilling those expectations now. Sometimes users are not prepared to wait; they expect the best features now. Sometimes users develop false expectations because the internal developers or external vendors "oversell" the technology. It is important for the project plan to clarify the project outcome and prepare realistic user expectations.

## 8.5. Projects in Controlled Environments (PRINCE)

PRINCE is a structured and standard approach for project management originally designed for all IT projects of the UK government, although it is now used elsewhere and not just for IT projects. It is available from the UK Office of Government Commerce. The present version is actually PRINCE2, but we will shorten this simply to PRINCE here. A project is seen as having the criteria shown in Exhibit 8.5.

---

### Exhibit 8.5  The Criteria for a PRINCE Project

- A defined and unique set of deliverables
- A set of activities and their sequence to construct the products
- Appropriate resources to undertake the activities
- A finite life span
- An organizational structure with defined responsibilities

---

Here are the approach aims for projects to have: a controlled and organized start, middle, and end; regular reviews of progress against plan and against the business case; flexible decision points; automatic management control of any deviations from the plan; the involvement of management and stakeholders at the right time and place during the project; and good communication channels between the project, project management, and the rest of the organization. These stated aims coincide with the general approach that we have specified in this book.

The PRINCE approach aims to deliver the end products at a specified quality within budget and on time. Unlike many methodologies—for example, SSADM—the emphasis is placed on the delivery of these products, not the activities to achieve their production. All of the stakeholders should be involved during the project as appropriate, but the management structure of a PRINCE project is expected to consist of the following:

- Project board, with a senior executive as member along with a senior user
- Project manager who fulfills the day-to-day management

- Team leaders who report to the project manager
- Management champion for the project, who agrees to the business case and outlines the justification, commitment, and rationale for the project.

The project is driven by the business case, and this is reviewed frequently. This suggests why the project is being done, the likely benefits, and who is going to pay for it. The formation of detailed plans is a cornerstone of the approach. The highest level of plan is the project plan—that is, an overall plan for the project—and this is broken down into stages. A detailed plan gives a further breakdown of activities within each stage. Although the project plan is important in showing the overall scope of the project, major deliverables, and resources required, it is the stage plans that are used for day-to-day control.

Ken Bentley describes in detail the components of PRINCE, including business case, organization, plans, controls, risk, quality, configuration management, and change control, and these are as shown in Figure 8.6.

---

### Exhibit 8.6   The Components of PRINCE

1. **Business case:** This drives the whole project, capturing the reasoning for initiating the project in the first place

2. **Organization:** This is the project team structure

3. **Plans:** These are based on products

4. **Controls:** Information that reveals problems and ways to deal with them

5. **Risk:** Identify and manage risk factors

6. **Quality:** Standards and methods to assess quality

7. **Configuration management:** Components of the final product

8. **Change control:** Determines how change is handled

---

The technical aspects include the product breakdown structure as well as PERT charts, which link the activities, showing their interdependencies, to create the end date. Resource plans identify the resource type, amount, and cost of each resource at each stage. Gantt charts are used to help resource allocation and smoothing. However, the use of techniques and tools is optional.

Meeting quality expectations, like times and costs, is seen as an important aspect of the approach. There are quality controls, which are defined in the technical and management procedures, and the descriptions of the deliverables in terms of fitness for purpose also represent a statement about quality. The acceptance criteria need to be explicitly stated.

❖ **Figure 8.1**   Overall PRINCE Approach

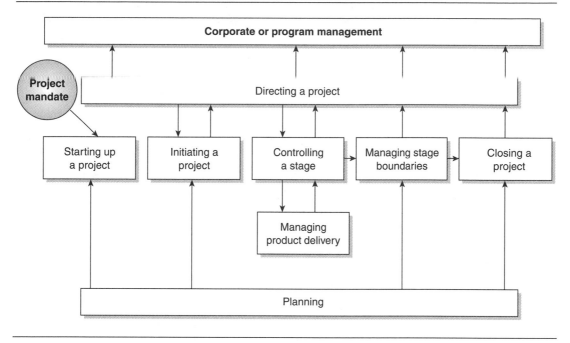

SOURCE: Modified From Bentley, 2002.

Within a PRINCE project there are eight processes (Figure 8.1), which are detailed in Exhibit 8.7.

PRINCE produces a set of reports that help control, in particular, the monitoring of actual progress against plan and against the business case. Some of these reports are expected to form the basis of discussions at meetings. These meetings are normally held at the initiation and at the end of each stage in the project (and sometimes mid-stage as well). The reports highlight such things as progress, exceptions, and requests for change.

However, the first document produced is the project initiation report, which outlines the business case, defines a high-level plan, formally initiates the project, lists overall objectives for the project, and defines personnel responsibilities. It may be more detailed—for example, identifying job descriptions for each person, providing a detailed cost–benefit analysis for the business case (sometimes referred to as a feasibility report), examining the risks associated with a project, and dividing the project into well-defined stages.

End-stage assessment is a control point that, if successful, signifies acceptance of the deliverables promised for that stage and provides authority to go on to the next stage. Mid-stage assessment may occur if the stage is of long duration, problems have been identified such as deviation from the plan, or there have been requests for change.

---

### Exhibit 8.7 The Eight Processes of a PRINCE Project

1. **Directing a project:** As we saw above, there needs to be overall direction to authorize the project, approve the go-ahead, and monitor progress and closure.

2. **Starting up a project:** This short stage includes the appointment of the project team, agreeing to the aims of the project, deciding on the project approach, defining quality expectations, and planning and drawing up the contract (whatever form that takes) between customer and supplier.

3. **Initiating a project:** This includes agreeing that the project is justified, establishing management procedures, and creating the detailed plan and the project initiation document.

4. **Controlling each stage:** This process describes the monitoring and control activities, authorizing work to be done, gathering progress information, reporting, and taking necessary action if there is deviation from the plans.

5. **Managing product delivery:** Work is allocated to the team, planned, and carried out. Quality criteria are checked and reports made to the project manager. Finished products are formally accepted.

6. **Managing stage boundaries:** This process ensures that the plan is adhered to or updated as necessary and the next stage approved.

7. **Closing a project:** The project manager gains the project board's approval to close the project at its natural end (or premature end if necessary). Customer satisfaction needs to be agreed upon in the former case. Maintenance procedures need to be in place. Lessons learned need to be assimilated as part of the organization's knowledge-management process.

8. **Planning:** This involves designing the plan, defining the project's products, identifying dependencies, scheduling resources, and allocating risks.

---

At the end of the project there is a project closure report, which lists the project's achievements in terms of deliverables achieved, performance in terms of comparisons of actual against forecast duration, cost and resource usage, and quality in terms of errors or exceptions. It also provides information to help organizational learning—for example, experience with the use of tools and development methodologies. The report also includes formal acceptance letters from senior technical staff, users, and operations staff. There is also expected to be a post-implementation review.

Ken Bentley provides a very detailed step-by-step guide to the approach and provides an excellent checklist and series of questions to address at each stage of the project. We also recommend the PRINCE Web site (www.ogc.gov.uk/prince2/), which also provides a set of 28 templates to document each aspect of PRINCE. Indeed, they might be useful for program managers following any project management approach. These templates include those for documenting acceptance criteria, the business case, communication plans, end project report, end stage report, exception report, issue report, lessons learned report, post-project review plan, project brief, project plan, project quality plan, quality log, and risk log. There is also an online demonstration package that shows how to manage successful projects with PRINCE2.

## 8.6. Interview With a Project Manager

How long have you been project manager?

"Actually for only 3 years, but I have learned so much about project management in that time that I feel very experienced!"

What would you say were the three most important lessons that you have learned?

"I think there are many more than three very important lessons, but the importance of a good project plan, good communications, and the contract would be on my list. They are all based on particular experiences, so I can give you an example each time."

OK, start with the project plan.

"Time needs to be spent on the detail. The tasks need to be understood fully to allocate time and people resources to the task. But it is not always so simple. An obvious example is that if a task takes 10 days for 6 people, you can't assume it will only take 5 days for 12 people. I made that mistake early on and forgot about fixed aspects and communication aspects. The inter-relationship between the tasks also needs to be fully understood. I understood it for my last project and got it right. However, there was a problem. My project was part of a much larger project and so there were a number of project teams. Aspects of my project were dependent on another project, and that was delayed, causing unexpected problems for me. On one occasion things got bad and we required a high-level mediator to suggest a compromise."

Tell me about the importance of communication skills.

"These are the most important of the expected skills of the project manager. I am fairly young for a project manager, and it is politically difficult for me to say no to a high-ranking manager. You cannot agree to an unrealistic end date, even if it is difficult not to say yes to a request from your boss. But you have to stick to your guns. I find team leadership easier and I am always willing to support my team members. For example, what is the point of saying no to a vacation request—as another project manager did—when the person does little and is not cooperative generally because of being forced to stay. Better say yes to the holiday and you have someone who is going to be loyal and pull every stop when the chips are down! I am not saying that you should be a 'buddy' to team members, but you should be supportive. However, I have found relationships with management difficult at times, and also, as illustrated in the discussion on the project plan, relationships with other project managers can be difficult. If there are team members more experienced (or, more likely, simply older) than you on the team, this can pose a management problem. You often have to be more gentle and flexible and aware of their pride so that 'it might be better if you try this' is more appropriate than 'do this.'"

Explain the importance of the contract and/or memorandum of understanding.

"These should be very strong from a legal point of view. There should be no loopholes. One contract was a particular problem. For example, we had agreed on a penalty clause for late provision. This is fair

*(Continued)*

(Continued)

enough. However, in order to progress we needed information from the client. Frequently they did not show up at agreed-upon meetings, so we could not progress and were late and we had to bear the cost!"

You suggested that there were other important lessons that you have learned.

"There are lots, in fact, from the seemingly trivial to the larger issues."

You interest me—what do you mean by a trivial issue?

"Well, something that occurred recently. We were not happy with some test results. It turned out that the people testing the system were colleagues of the developers and were reticent to point out some flaws and they 'signed off' on some modules that were not adequately tested. OK, we spotted that early, but there are lots of things like that which might appear trivial but could well damage the project."

... and a more important issue?

"Well, documentation is important as well. A 'trivial' issue concerning documentation relates to versioning. Make sure that each update has an associated date and/or version number, so that we know what the latest version is, and also make sure that the documentation is simultaneously kept up-to-date. Again, this 'lesson' has been based on an unfortunate experience, but documentation as a whole is important."

Finally, what training were you given? Did you look at PM books?

"I was given some support through working with project managers, doing a course, and we had access to books on IS project management. The latter were not of much help. Technical issues are probably less than a third of all the issues of an IS project manager. It may be surprising, but my experience suggests that it is the cultural and 'people' issues that are far more important. The books I saw gave the proportion as two-thirds technical. Also there is not enough 'real' material in books (indeed like this interview). It is as if learning bookwork 'do this and it will work' will make you a good project manager. Well, it won't. Truth is, project management is political, fuzzy, and complex. Also, no book tells you that a lot of project management is 'fire fighting,' thinking on your feet, arguing–compromising–making up cycles with colleagues, and just trying your best. You have to be both clever and reasonable at the same time. I describe real-life project management, not the theory, which hardly exists in my practice."

## 8.7. Chapter Summary

Planning is a time-consuming and mentally challenging task. It is one of the first activities that the project manager must undertake. Key team members must be involved with the development of the plan, but the primary responsibility rests with the project manager. Planning provides an opportunity for the project manager to demonstrate business knowledge and technical expertise. A good project plan provides a road map for the project development life cycle. It identifies responsibilities and provides boundaries of cost and time. It is a tool for establishing communication channels. A project plan puts the project in the perspective of organizational goals and objectives and puts work units in the perspective of the overall project. A good project plan is a tool for decisions, monitoring, and execution. It sets policies and procedures and is a source of reference for resolving differences. A project plan is a critical success factor. A manager who cannot plan a project cannot lead.

## DISCUSSION QUESTIONS

1. Following your reading of Exhibit 8.1, whose side are you on? Should lecturers be more flexible with respect to coursework deadlines (and customers with respect to suppliers' project plans)? Should plans be seen as inherently malleable? What might be the consequences of such flexibility (or leniency)?

2. This chapter argues that there are two broad perspectives for information systems project management skills. One is *technical competency*, which relates to hardware and software as well as other detailed activities. The other is *managerial competency*, which includes broad-based issues of a project. Discuss and list examples of each. Do you think it feasible for one person, the project manager, to have both sets of competencies?

3. It is suggested in this chapter that an "action-oriented" information systems development approach is often concerned with short-term objectives and sometimes at the expense of long-term goals. Does this mean that action is not necessary? What is your interpretation?

4. This chapter suggests that one of the reasons that planning is not appreciated is that it is perceived as an activity that does not support action. A good plan should provide a roadmap for activities, for monitoring progress, and for measuring success. Discuss how you would develop a plan that would support these objectives?

5. Do you think PRINCE would be appropriate for developing projects in an SME (small to medium-sized enterprise) or is it suitable only for large projects in larger organizations?

## EXERCISES

1. What makes an information systems project plan different from other plans, such as constructing a bridge, planning a conference, planning a holiday, or developing a new degree program?

2. List and describe skills necessary for developing a good information systems project plan. What kinds of skill are necessary for planning? Divide your answer into technical skills and organizational and business skills.

3. Search the Web or other sources for an information systems project plan. Describe that plan and its components and give your opinion about it.

4. Match the PRINCE templates (see www.ogc.gov.uk/prince2/) with particular deliverables discussed in the book as a whole. Are there any missing templates? Are there areas not discussed in the book?

## APPENDIX TO CHAPTER 8: LONDON AMBULANCE— FROM FAILURE TO SUCCESS

### Introduction

The computer system associated with the dispatch of London ambulances, known as the London Ambulance Service Computer Aided Dispatch (LASCAD) system, has had a mixed history. The 1992 system became widely known as a major information systems failure. In this appendix we describe aspects of the 1992 failure and the successful system that came afterward.

The 1992 LASCAD system failed following a significant slowdown and failure to reliably dispatch ambulances, and the system was replaced with manual procedures for taking and recording calls and dispatching emergency vehicles. This failure hit the national headlines with suggestions that 20 to 30 people died as a result (*Guardian* newspaper, October 29, 1992). Some Londoners recall phoning the emergency ambulance service to be greeted with only a recorded message. In fact, the reported death toll was greatly exaggerated by the press, but the failure was clearly a disaster for the London Ambulance Service with the service in very poor repute.

Historically, the first full-time ambulance service was established in London in 1897, and with the coming of the National Health Service (NHS) in 1948 it was made a duty for ambulances to be available for those who needed them, and this still applies today. Indeed, the current LAS is the largest ambulance service in the world, and its area of responsibility covers 7 million people in an area of 620 square miles. The LAS comprises 70 ambulance stations, 700 vehicles (around 400 ambulances, plus helicopter, motorcycles, and other patient transfer vehicles), and over 3,000 people (670 paramedics, 300 control staff). On average, the accident and emergency (A&E) service responds to 2,500 calls per day (1,500 of which are emergency calls). The demand for emergency services has increased steadily over the years, with an annual growth rate of 16% in some years.

### The Story of the 1992 Failure

On the night of Monday, October 26, 1992, there was an unusual number of emergency calls, which the system could not cope with. The operators were unable to deal with the messages that the system was producing and unable to clear the queues that developed. These queues slowed the system, and increasingly when ambulances completed a job they were not cleared. Thus the system had fewer resources to allocate, and eventually the system knew the correct location and status of fewer vehicles, resulting in duplicated and delayed allocations, a buildup of exception messages (which reveal circumstances that cannot be automated) and the awaiting attention list, and an increased number of callbacks and hence delays in telephone answering. Exception messages scrolled off the tops of the screens, and it was difficult for the operators to retrieve them. Any that were not dealt with generated more exception messages. At one point a decision was taken to wipe the exception report queue in an effort to clear the system, but unfortunately this probably had the effect of generating even more exception messages.

The result was chaos in the emergency service, as multiple vehicles appear to have been sent to some incidents and none to others. Sometimes the closest vehicle was not the one dispatched. Crews reported ambulances from far afield passing them on the way to a call for which they were better placed. Crews began querying allocations and requesting information, which led to an increase in radio traffic and radio bottlenecks, which further delayed things. The crews were very frustrated as they took the brunt of the usually angry reaction from the public when they did turn up.

Unsurprisingly, the problems of October 26 and 27 hit the newspaper headlines with a vengeance, and questions were also asked in Parliament. The following day the LAS chief executive, John Wilby, resigned, and Martin Gorham, deputy chief executive of South West Thames Regional Health Authority, was appointed in his place, on a temporary basis.

In operational terms, the London Ambulance Service was soon back to where it was prior to the 1992 system—that is, manual operation, using pen and paper. This continued essentially until the introduction of the new LASCAD system in 1996.

The British government set up a public inquiry, and their report suggested that the London Ambulance Service should continue to seek a computer solution for ambulance dispatch but that "it must be developed and introduced in a time scale which, whilst recognizing the need for earliest introduction, must allow fully for consultation, quality assurance, testing, and training." In relation to the management of LAS, a restructuring was recommended together with a range of new appointments, including a project manager and an IT director.

## The New Chief Executive

Gorham was a career NHS manager and had been in the NHS for about 25 years, mainly in hospital management. He had been director of corporate planning for a large health authority and had been introducing and managing change in hospitals and health services for most of his career.

He observed a difficult history of industrial relations in the LAS and thought it best to start by establishing a period of stability and was not going to be rushed into changing things. He spent some time in the central control room and also with the ambulance crews and went out with them on calls. He also talked to the union representatives and tried to establish some kind of dialogue, as he saw their role as particularly important. Gorham decided to keep in place the director of support services, who was also acting as director of operations. He was the project manager for the computer project in the control room and was disliked by the unions, but he had good experience.

## The New IT Director

A new computer-based system had been recommended by the government report and most of the subsequent investigations into the LAS also called for a computer system to be adopted, and the pressure was to do something quickly. However, Gorham and his team felt strongly that to introduce a new computer system quickly was likely to lead to at least some of the same problems that had afflicted the 1992 system. He felt that the risk was too high and so adopted a very cautious approach. As Ian Tighe, the new IT director, commented, "Most observers were certain that change should come far quicker than it was, and at times it was very hard to resist the pressure to dash into early change." However, resist it they did.

Tighe states that he spent "9 months really just listening to people, and only dealing with those things that were desperately urgent. The rest of the time I just learned about the service,

*(Continued)*

(Continued)

what it was and what it did, how people did things, what gave them concerns. So that when you sit down with people and talk about bringing in change, you're doing so from a position of some knowledge, not definitive knowledge, but some knowledge, and you understand what they do and how they do it. At the end of this period I produced a strategy document specifying what I felt we should do next, given what we know, given the past, this is what we should do, and this is how we do it." In outline, the strategy for a new system advocated reducing the complexity of operation, concentrating on key deliverables, paying attention to staff and their needs, establishing a workable but acceptable pace for delivery and implementation, and, finally, it was to be built on a number of prior infrastructure changes.

Tighe observed that the LAS had been suffering from under-investment for some years: Problems with the electrical supply, the switchboard, the existing control room, and an aging ambulance fleet evidenced that the infrastructure needed updating. This was achieved as a first step before developing a new CAD system. All improved the actual situation as well as people's morale and their views about the potential of technological investment. For example, better radio systems helped ambulance crews feel more secure.

Meanwhile, in response to the inquiry, Gorham developed an action plan that included a new management structure with new appointments. It had become obvious to him that a substantial restructuring of the service was required. The management resources needed to be increased to deal with this high-profile and complex organization. Gorham made seven appointments of directors, and further restructuring led to the supporting structure required.

Gorham also came to the conclusion that the existing staff rostering system was not helping to deliver the kind of service that was needed. He argued that far too many crews were in the wrong place, and there wasn't nearly enough coverage on evenings and weekends. New rosters were devised based on research commissioned by LAS to identify patterns of demand and ways of matching resources to that demand. The outcomes were to keep ambulances within clearly defined local working zones, to match the deployment of ambulances with the established pattern of demand, to have some ambulances stand on the streets at critical locations, away from the stations, and to change the working patterns to reflect the demand at different times of the day and week. The staff voted against it, which indicated, despite some improvements, the continuing problems with management/staff relations. However, the majority voting against was too small to result in any real support for industrial action. So Gorham went ahead and pushed through the new rosters, and they started to show benefits quite rapidly.

So although no computer system had been introduced, many of the necessary infrastructure changes had been made, each providing a *degree* of benefit in their own right but not enough. So the final piece of the strategy was the new LASCAD system. With this it was hoped that the big productivity benefits would accrue and that the performance measures set by the government could be achieved.

## Developing a New CAD System

A new hardware platform was chosen for the system. The old system was essentially a PC architecture, which was not thought to be up to the job. The new system was to be UNIX based with

Informix as the database software, supporting 60 workstations. The dispatch software itself was written in the C programming language and developed in-house. A review of what was available in the dispatch marketplace had been undertaken, but the conclusion was that they were inadequate for the LAS. The strategy was to implement the system slowly in small simple chunks without having the full range of command and control facilities available—in essence, a prototype approach. The packages available in the marketplace all did much more than wanted initially, and the functionality could not be separated and presented in phases. Tighe wanted to control the pace of change. Beyond that they did not mirror closely enough the way that the LAS wanted to organize dispatch. They did not want to be forced into a particular way of working because a package demanded it. Given the history, the system had to be acceptable to the staff. There was also a worry about a package coping, with the large volumes required for the LAS.

Once the decision had been made to develop in-house, Quentin Armitage was appointed from West Midlands Police. Armitage did most of the actual programming with help from Tighe. This was a very small development operation.

One of the principles concerning the new system was that it should initially be as close as possible to the functioning of the manual system—it should not introduce new ways of working. This was felt to be necessary because the staff were closely wedded to, and believed in, the existing manual ways. Also, from their experience, they were not enamored with computers and felt that computers were not able to undertake dispatch tasks, or even aid in such tasks. The way forward was to duplicate the manual system as far as possible, with the opportunity to enhance this, once the system was in place and accepted. Thus the screen format was to follow as closely as possible what prints out on paper, and the printed version of the call should also be the same format.

Another difference was in terms of project management. The previous system had specified that PRINCE should be used, but the developers appointed did not know PRINCE, and therefore it was not really followed. PRINCE exception reports were never raised because of the fear of delivering bad news. This time it was different: PRINCE was used as the main project-driving method, but the culture had to be changed to make it work. The project management method was used throughout, so everyone understood it, the reports required, the project assurance team, the significance of it, etc. It began with the warm-up projects and thus people knew about it long before the computer system was implemented.

Clearly a highly participative approach to systems development was required to fit with the overall approach to the rebuilding of the LAS. One of the techniques employed was to have open forum sessions that anybody could attend where questions were answered honestly. People wanted to know what was happening. There were a good number of these forum-type sessions, but in the end they became quite poorly attended: Whereas initially the meetings would attract 30 to 40 people, in the end only 2 or 3 were turning up. This was interpreted as a success because it meant that people were happy, that they thought things were now being dealt with adequately and in the required depth. As well as these forums, a number of working groups or teams were established to discuss requirements, design procedures, forms, etc. All the stakeholders were represented. Thus people who wanted to be involved would participate in the working groups while those who didn't want to be directly involved could attend the forums to hear what was happening and why.

*(Continued)*

(Continued)

Essentially the approach adopted was that of prototyping, and it was decided that the first part to be tackled would be the management of the resources—i.e., the ambulances, their locations, and deployment. This seemed sensible as it would deliver important benefits and users could see designs and suggest changes. They saw that they could have considerable influence. "Competing prototypes" would be discussed and one version chosen and modified and therefore consensus was achieved. Clearly the system could have been developed much faster without this, but it was deemed to be the overriding consideration, and unless you go through that process there is no feeling of involvement.

The training of users was a very important issue and indeed one that had been highlighted in the report as an area of weakness in the previous system. Although some training had taken place, it was too early, and by the time the system had been implemented the skills had been lost. This time a great deal of effort was devoted to training, not just on the computer system but training on all the procedures, both computer and manual. Part of the testing process was about gradually gaining the confidence of the users. Indeed the need for full training was one reason why implementation was delayed but was seen as absolutely necessary.

## Introduction of the New CAD System

The first part of the new computerized system, the call-taking, went live on January 17, 1996, and had thus taken around 18 months to develop and implement. After about a week of successful running the whole operation moved into the new control room (known as CAC, Central Ambulance Control). Subsequently, various additional functionality was provided in February, July, and September 1996, and indeed still continues, indicating the staged approach that was adopted with a little more added at each stage.

The system was by no means a full CAD system but was essentially a system to register calls and pass them to the dispatchers. It enabled the operators to receive a call and enter the details of an incident directly into the system. The computerized Gazetteer, using a Postal Address File, looked up the location and provided a map reference within 1 second. Once a valid address was established the details were routed to a screen in the appropriate sector desk for the controller to allocate a vehicle. The system provided the controller with information on which of the 150 or so deployment points around London was the nearest to the incident, and the controller would then dispatch an appropriate ambulance. The system additionally provided the location of the nearest hospital for the controller to pass to the ambulance crew.

One of the most important enhancements of the basic system was that of September 1996, which provided for the first time an element of reengineering of the original manual process. This was the addition of "early call viewing" for the controllers. Once the call takers had established the address of the incident, that information was immediately available to the controllers to begin the dispatch process—i.e., before the call had finished.

## Success

The system was proving successful, but this was not just a one-off effort. The improvements were sustained, although it should be remembered that it was not just the computer system but also all the other management, organizational, and infrastructure changes that contributed. Emergency calls have been handled with success, and times have continued to improve, building on this initial success.

In other terms it was a success, too. People began to believe in the ability of IT to contribute to the LAS. The public was also impressed. The number of complaints dropped quickly. The politicians were also impressed. The House of Commons Health Committee Report of December 1996 stated that they

> were struck not only by the technological improvements but by the orderly and efficient atmosphere in the Central Ambulance Control. . . . We warmly welcome the improvements in response times that the management and staff of the LAS have achieved . . . and the effective way in which new technology appears to have been introduced. We wish to congratulate both management and staff for their efforts in turning around an organization which . . . was on "the brink of collapse" only four years ago.

## Lessons From LAS

Clearly each case is different and no two situations are really the same. Nevertheless, there are perhaps some general lessons that might prove useful to a wider audience.

Firstly, a clear lesson from the LAS is that no matter how bad things are, how many people are on your back, it is still possible to turn things around, though only with a great deal of hard work. The culture of an organization is critically important. LAS had a culture of mistrust, a history of very poor industrial relations, a very damaging pay dispute, an antipathy toward computers, and a fear of management intentions. The key to the change was the acceptance that the staff essentially wanted to be able to do a good job. A very open, participative style of management, involving people builds trust for all the stakeholders.

Further, the decision not to be rushed, despite the very strong political pressures, was a critical decision. No one agreed to a date that they believed could not be met, which shows that having the right people in place is also clearly very important. Gorham was willing to adopt a very open style of management. He led by example and he was a "role model" and encouraged others to adopt the same attitudes. He, of course, says that he had a good team, which is obviously correct, but he built that team. He spent a lot of time and effort recruiting the right people, with the right attitudes and experience. On the IT side, Tighe and Armitage were crucial. For those already on the job, he invested heavily in management development and training. So getting the right team is not accidental but is probably the most important element in a successful project. Adequate resources were also clearly key to the turnaround of the LAS. The "warm-up" projects involved the expenditure of large scale resources. The turnaround could probably not have been achieved without this investment. Successful projects cannot be done on the cheap.

In relation to systems development lessons, there are a number that can be highlighted. However, and it is a lesson in itself, the general managerial and development issues are closely intertwined. The IT function was highly integrated with the business, both in a physical and a conceptual sense. The approach to IT was integrated with the whole approach to people management in general. Also the IT department was seen as an essential and integrated part of the business.

*(Continued)*

A participative/prototyping approach to development was adopted that did not just address the computer part but included the whole business system, including the integration of the manual procedures. The participation of the users and stakeholders in the development was crucial, if, as has been seen, sometimes frustrating for the developers themselves.

Again, as for the rest of the business, the people were key. The appointment of the IT director, Ian Tighe, was very important. He was good on both sides, technology and management, including dealing with people. A very important aspect was the lack of experience of the previous system developers. A further lesson, and one that is often stressed but certainly well worth emphasizing, is the importance of testing. Both system testing and business testing—i.e., making sure it all works together. Testing helps to ensure it all works on a normal day but also that it will still work on exceptional days. More than that, testing is about understanding what happens when something does go wrong. What happens when the backup system is activated? Does it work? Does everyone know what they should be doing? Testing ensures not only that it works but that people are confident that it will work.

The LASCAD case has been adapted from *IT at the Heart of Business*, by G. Fitzgerald, 2000, London: BCS.

## APPENDIX TO CHAPTER 8: DISCUSSION QUESTIONS

1. Do you think the LASCAD success was more about "having the right team," "having the right project manager," or "having the right approach"?

2. What aspects of "organizational culture" were changed for the system to be successful?

3. Why do you think the British press discussed the first LASCAD failure greatly but virtually ignored the success story discussed in the appendix?

4. Do you think lessons need to be learned again (see, for example, Exhibit 2.1, in Chapter 2 and related articles on the Web)?

5. What aspects of "organizational culture" were changed for the system to be successful?

6. Devise criteria for comparing the LASCAD failure and success and devise a table to compare the two. What aspects do you regard as project management aspects (or do you regard all these aspects to do with project management)?

7. "In the final analysis, success of an information system is about people—and to some extent politics—and not about technology." Discuss in the light of the LASCAD case.

8. Discuss the attributes of Gorham and Tighe that make them good leaders and project managers.

9. Find out about how London Ambulance and other accident and emergency services have progressed in their use of ICT over the last year or two by accessing the Internet. What project management perspectives can you ascertain?

10. Each class group should present the LASCAD case (as the NGC case of Chapter 7) with different perspectives but comparing the success and the failure, for example:
    – An outline of the success and the failure from a general management perspective
    – A presentation showing how the success and the failure fit in with the government and organizational strategy
    – A presentation from the project manager to team members at the beginning of the projects.
    – A presentation of the risk-management and change-management processes.

11. Role-play a live television program in which each leading player in the failure is attempting to defend his/her position while being interviewed by a journalist.

# BIBLIOGRAPHY

Avison, D., & Fitzgerald, G. (2006). *Information systems development: Methodologies, techniques and tools* (4th ed.). Maidenhead, UK: McGraw-Hill.

Baccarini, D. (1996). The concept of project complexity: A review. *International Journal of Project Management, 14*(1).

Bentley, K. (2002). *PRINCE2: A practical handbook.* Oxford, UK: Butterworth-Heinemann.

Beynon-Davies, P. (1995). Information systems "failure": The case of the London ambulance service's computer aided dispatch project. *European Journal of Information Systems, 4,* 171–184.

Fitzgerald, G. (2000). *IT at the heart of business.* London: BCS.

Hopper, M. D. (1996). Complexity: The weed that could choke IS. *Computerworld.*

Page, D., Williams, P., & Boyd, D. (1993). *Report of the public inquiry into the London ambulance service.* London: Her Majesty's Stationary Office.

PRINCE2, Office of Government Commerce, http://www.ogc.gov.uk/methods_prince_2.asp

Torkzadeh, G., & Weidong, X. (1992, June). Managing telecommunications by steering committee. *MIS Quarterly, 16*(2), 187–199.

Torkzadeh, G., Chang, J. C. J., & Hansen, G.W. (2006). Identifying issues in customer relationship management at Merck-Medco. *Decision Support Systems, 42*(2).

Van Genuchten, M. (1991). Why is software late: An empirical study of reasons for delay in software development. *IEEE Transactions on Software Engineering, 17*(6).

# Forming the
# Project Team

## Themes of Chapter 9

❖ How can the project team be formed?

❖ How will the project team work together?

❖ How can we create the right synergy?

❖ How can we ensure collective responsibility and avoid a blame culture?

❖ How can we encourage open communications?

❖ What kind of attitudes can be expected from members of a team?

❖ What are the relationships between team characteristics and project success?

The successful development and implementation of any project depends to a large extent on the project team and how well team members work together. The project team members must not only be competent at their tasks but also must be able to complement each other to create the right synergy. The collective efforts of team members should be greater than the sum of individual efforts. An effective team takes collective responsibility for what is to be done rather than individual members trying to pass on the blame to others or earn the credit for themselves. The communication and interaction among team members should be open and effortless. Team members should be willing and eager to help each other and learn from one another. This leads to the understanding that *when the team wins, everyone wins, and if the team fails, everyone fails.* This chapter will describe the importance of forming the right team for a given project and what kind of attitudes the project manager should expect from members of a team. This chapter also describes the relationship between team characteristics and project success. It will describe the importance of teamwork and individual characteristics that the project manager should look for when forming a project team. This chapter ends with an interview with an information system project manager. The appendix includes a discussion on the *Sarbanes–Oxley Act* (usually shortened to **SOX**), which has had a huge impact on the business world, and not only in the United States. The act is not really about ICT or IS directly, but it has implications for ICT because of its data/information accuracy and security aspects. The appendix discusses these particular issues as well as associated ethical issues. But we start with Exhibit 9.1, which examines some aspects of good communications that are important in all project management activities, not just helping to ensure an effective project team.

---

### Exhibit 9.1    Get to the Point

Information is useful when it is *accurate, timely*, and *relevant*. You must have heard managers who ask for a "complete" explanation of some event. Alternatively, managers who, when asked how much information they need to make a decision, will respond "give me all that you have" or "give me what you can find on the subject." People ask for "complete information" or "all the information" when they do not really know what they are looking for or how to go about dealing with an issue. And that is counterproductive.

Experienced managers know exactly *what type of information they need, when they need it, and in what form*. Information overflow is a problem that is easily generated, given the power of computers and information systems. The principles of accuracy, timeliness, and relevancy are important when you give or receive information. When requesting information you need to be clear about what type, what form, and by when. When giving information you need to follow the same principles.

Project managers spend a great deal of time preparing proposals for new projects. Effective proposals clearly describe (a) that there is a need for a system, (b) what it will take to develop that system, and (c) how it will be developed. While the written proposal is always necessary and important, especially for reference, it is often the short presentation that will influence top management and the steering committee to whether they approve the proposal.

Often you are given as little as 20 minutes to present your idea and make your point. Your presentation must be accurate, timely, and relevant. Also, remember that many people including top management have a short span for concentration. Use your time effectively and avoid any discussions that do not directly relate to your case or may distract your audience. Give the abstract and get to the outcome as soon as you can; make your point short and sweet in a short few minutes, before you lose their attention.

Use the same principle when giving a status report of a project. Assume you need to send an email to give a progress report. Use a few short statements: (a) You could use one clear statement to describe the current status. For example, "we are 1 week behind with the third milestone of the project." (b) Then give a short statement that clarifies what that delay means to the bottom line. For example, "this will delay project delivery by at least 1 week." (c) Next, describe your specific response to the problem. For example, "we plan to have three people on overtime for 3 hours a day for 4 days to make up for lost time." (d) Then give a clear short explanation of how this happened. For example, "we fell behind because the vendor sent us the wrong routers for the network and we had to wait for replacement."

You do not need to be defensive with your explanation; you need to be factual and give your professional assessment when necessary. The first statement in your message will get the attention of your audience: missing the deadline for a milestone. The second statement describes the consequence: late delivery. The third statement tells your audience that you have thought about the problem and have an idea of what it will cost: using overtime in response. Finally, the fourth statement puts the problem in context: a clear explanation.

People want to know very quickly the status of the project. Next, if something is not right, they are interested in knowing whether anything can be done about it. Remember, project status is about where the project is at that point in time. You can provide the main line of your report in the subject line of your email message. That way, you are giving the bottom line even before your email is read. That also tells your audience whether they should open that email now or leave it for later.

## 9.1. Team as a Core of Activity

The project team is the unit that undertakes project activities that are defined and described in the project plan (Chapter 8) and the work breakdown structure (Section 4.3). While the project manager is responsible for the project development life cycle and its successful completion, team members carry out the actual work and make sure that individual work units are completed on time, within budget, and according to the specifications. We introduced the role of the individual team member in Section 7.7, and an effective team is more than the sum of its parts. It exhibits *synergy, excitement, cooperation, innovation, coordination,* and *drive.* The project manager must form a team that shares a common vision for the successful completion of the project. While individual members differ in values, skills, styles, and other traits they must function as a team and treat project objectives as common goals. A highly effective information systems project team has the following characteristics:

*Competency.* This describes the pool of talents that includes diverse knowledge and skills capable of performing the range of activities described in the project plan. The team competency can be broadly defined through technical skills and managerial skills. The first one includes an understanding and experience with hardware, software, communication channels, and the like. The second one relates to interpersonal skills, leadership, written and verbal communication, and so on. As we saw in Chapter 8, along with these technical and managerial skills, the team needs to have technical and managerial knowledge.

*Common purpose.* Team members relate, understand, and work toward achieving the same set of objectives as described in the project plan. This is an important characteristic that helps channel collective efforts toward the ultimate goal of the project.

*Sense of trust.* The team exhibits a sense of trust among themselves as well as among members and the project manager. Team members feel they can rely on each other for support. They feel comfortable discussing mistakes for everyone's benefit without concerns for being chastised. Lack of trust among team members creates secrecy, rumor, and ultimately a nonproductive environment.

*Positive attitude.* The team exhibits a proactive and a realistic "can-do" attitude, especially when it is faced with setbacks and difficulties. Most projects will face difficulty (resource issues, vendors' untimely response, unexpected turnover) at one time or another before they are complete. An effective team will show a problem-solving attitude toward unexpected problems and, to the extent possible, will try to resolve them within the allocated time and budget.

*Outcome oriented.* The team needs to know who the stakeholders are and understand and appreciate that project success is ultimately measured through customer satisfaction and that customers of a project include owners, managers, sponsors, and users. The team strives to produce results that meet the specified needs of the customer.

*Problem solving.* The team accepts task responsibility and seeks creative means to accomplish goals and objectives, especially when faced with unusual situations. The problem-solving skill includes the ability to see a problem before it arises and prepare for an appropriate response for it in a timely manner. Experienced project managers and competent teams are expected to be proactive toward such situations. While this higher expectation poses a challenge for the project manager and the team, it also suggests respect for and recognition of the team's competency.

*Synergy.* The team identifies itself as a unit that exhibits high levels of synergy and coordination. The communication among team members is frequent, open, and effective. Without synergy, the team's energy as well as the project's resources are dispersed and spent rather aimlessly. Everyone is going in their own direction rather than working together toward common goals. With synergy, the team will produce greater results than the sum of individual efforts. Experienced project managers are very mindful of team synergy as they select members to form a project team.

*Responsibility.* Team members consider their successes and failures as outcomes of the unit, not the individual. The individual member succeeds when the team succeeds and vice versa. This does not mean that individual responsibilities do not matter. On the contrary, when individual members do not accept or understand responsibilities for their tasks, the chances of project success are greatly diminished. Thus, team members must not only feel responsible for their specific tasks but also for the outcome of the entire project.

*Openness.* The team exhibits openness for exchanging ideas. Team members do not hesitate to get input from other team members or to seek help when they need it. Closed and rigid environments discourage innovation and critical thinking and as a result are prone to failure. In an environment that is open to the exchange of ideas, team members often propose changes that are necessary and if not dealt with in time they eventually evolve into bigger problems.

*Professionalism.* Team members hold high standards and have integrity. They treat each other with respect and behave professionally in their interaction with the customer and stakeholders. Project managers play a key role in this respect through their own behavior and treatment of others. They must establish, communicate, and adhere to a code of professional conduct. Established organizations such as the Project Management Institute (PMI), the Institute for Electrical and Electronic Engineers (IEEE), the British Computer Society (BCS), and the Association for Computing Machinery (ACM) have codes of professional conduct that are available on their Web sites, and they share common principles (see appendix to Chapter 1).

A highly effective team seeks to exceed customer expectations by completing the project ahead of schedule and below budget. An effective team that exhibits energy, synergy, and the willingness to go the extra mile, when needed, is the best resource that the project manager could ask for. Sometimes the project team has already been formed, but in other circumstances the project managers have the opportunity to form an effective team, and that will be one of their first responsibilities.

It is worth investing time and effort early in the project development life cycle to select individuals with clear potential to form an effective team. Sometimes projects fail primarily because the team does not function as an effective unit, despite the fact that there are sufficient resources, there is a good plan, and there is a clear scope statement.

## 9.2. Teamwork Attitudes

Teamwork is effective when team members demonstrate a willingness to work with each other, understand that the synergy among them results in a better outcome than the sum of individual efforts, and that successes and failures are shared by all. As seen in Exhibit 9.2, a highly effective team displays several characteristics.

---

### Exhibit 9.2    Characteristics of a Highly Effective Team

- Members want to be part of the project team.
- There is representation on the team from all functional areas.
- Members understand and accept individual responsibilities.
- Members clearly understand project objectives.
- Members understand that they share successes and failures.
- Members see the big picture as well as their own contribution to the entire project.
- Members communicate openly and frequently with the project manager and among themselves.
- Members have respect for and feel accountable to the project manager.
- Members trust and respect each other.
- Members are committed to the project full-time and for the entire duration.

Collectively, these team attributes lead to a positive attitude toward teamwork. These are difficult conditions to meet for every project. However, the project manager can facilitate most of these conditions through the following:

- Clear definition of the project goals and objectives
- Establishment of effective communication channels
- Careful selection of team members

Many information systems projects fail because members cannot work as a team. An important factor that influences a group to function as a team is a sense of common purpose. Goals and objectives of a project can be used to create that sense of purpose. Everyone on the team should clearly relate to the project goals and specifically to the needs of the customer and the project owner.

Information systems project teams have unique characteristics that pose opportunities and challenges for the leadership. Some of the characteristics stem from the fact that ICT changes so rapidly and team members often work under strict schedules. Some are because user needs and expectations change as new technologies are introduced. Some are because team members are highly focused in their specific areas of expertise and do not always relate to the bigger issues of project management such as interorganizational relationships or alignment with the organizational goals and objectives.

Sometimes customer needs are well understood by the project manager but are not communicated effectively to the project team. This could be due to inadequate or inappropriate means of communication. Some people tend to spend a lot of time in front of the computer. These people find email to be a very effective means of communication, while others may find it more effective to have face-to-face interactions. There is no hard-and-fast rule as to which means of communication will work best. Project managers must identify and establish communication means that work for a given situation carefully. For example, in situations when there is a need for immediate interaction and feedback, a meeting might be the most effective means of communicating the message and accomplishing the goal. Such meetings are often followed by an email message to confirm what was discussed or agreed.

Where feasible, selecting team members is another important responsibility for the project manager. The project manager must ensure that selected members exhibit, among other things, a teamwork attitude. As described later in this chapter, the project manager must follow a systematic process for selecting team members. Most experienced project managers realize characteristics of a highly effective team. However, in reality, organizational, environmental, budgetary, and other constraints sometimes limit what a project manager can do. The project manager must ensure broad representation from functional areas (across departments and divisions) on the team, even if such representation may result in a weak spot within the team. A mix of generalists and specialists might be appropriate, but most of all, it is important to ensure that all members want to be on the team and that the team functions as a unit.

In the process of team development, the project manager must assess the overall talent represented in the team and prepare the team for areas that need greater development. Sometimes teams are selected solely on the basis of technical competency.

Such selections have obvious shortfalls that are related to interpersonal skills, teamwork attitude, understanding the overall objective of the project, and the like. Teamwork attitude can go a long way in addressing some of the skill problems that may exist within the team. Significant learning and development occurs as team members interact to help and learn from each other. This is particularly true for new and innovative information systems projects that are proposed by team members. The project manager should facilitate the process of integration, ensure that everyone feels an equal member of the team, and encourage the teamwork attitude from the start.

Teamwork attitude is not necessarily an inherent individual trait. It can be developed through practice and experience. Some individuals have a good teamwork attitude depending on whom they work with; conditions must be right. These individuals may be very sensitive to issues such as punctuality, reliability, or even the way they are communicated with. These individuals find it difficult to work with others who do not have the same traits or the same work habits. Some individuals do not have team work experience but are willing and eager to learn from others. The key for the project manager is to develop and energize the team to work together despite differences in style, traits, and skills. Establishing hard rules for every process does not necessarily result in creating the right attitude. This task is more difficult and requires sensitivity toward individual characteristics. The project manager must learn about each team member to be able to lead the team to project success effectively.

## 9.3. Team and Project Success

The project manager should try to create a sense of camaraderie among team members by providing the team with a common vision. This is a challenging task, especially for large projects where hundreds of professionals representing different functional areas may work on different parts of the project. The establishment of effective communication channels among team members and among key members and the project manager goes a long way to help such situations. A large project is often broken down into several sub-projects, and the project manager acts as a "clearing house" for messages among these sub-projects.

In these situations, the project manager needs to use discretion in disseminating information among team members and stakeholders. Not every piece of information needs to be shared with everyone. It is easy to create information overload by copying everything to everyone. When people receive frequent irrelevant email messages that have little or no value to their work, they tend to ignore subsequent messages from that source and in doing so run the risk of losing valuable information. Therefore, one can argue that information overload could negatively affect productivity. Experienced information systems managers establish effective communication channels and use discretion in providing *timely, accurate*, and *relevant* information. What is timely, accurate, and relevant may vary from situation to situation and from case to case, making it necessary to use discretion.

Another challenging situation for creating a sense of camaraderie among team members is when individuals from different functional areas work part-time on the project. It is difficult to develop synergy and commitment in such situations. As stated earlier, it is important to involve individuals from different functional areas. However, such involvement should be full-time and for the entire duration of the project. The continuity of commitment to a project gives a sense of ownership to team members and helps them participate fully in the affairs of the project. Sometimes part-time involvement happens because functional managers are reluctant to let their key individuals leave and work on a project for a long period of time. In such cases, it is important to focus managers' attention on the organizational benefits of the project that will in turn benefit their functional area. By participating in information systems development activities, these functional areas are in effect contributing to the accomplishment of organizational goals and objectives.

*Organizational culture* is also an important factor in forming a project team. Some organizations have clear and established procedures for forming an interdisciplinary team to work on a project. Others may have a totally ad hoc approach toward forming a project team. In any case, assigning individuals to a project must be done in consultation with the project manager. In situations where a functional manager or the general manager appoints individuals to a project without input from the project manager, the teamwork will be less effective. Individuals who work on a project should report to the project manager, and their performance on the project should be evaluated by the project manager. In special situations when a team member works part-time on a project, the performance evaluation can be done by the functional area manager in consultation with the project manager. The project manager should work on developing interorganizational contact and communication continuously to facilitate collaborative tasks such as joint evaluations of team members who work partly for the project and partly for a functional area.

Sometimes, in the case of small projects, individuals from functional areas work on a project for a short period of time and as a result continue to report to their functional managers and are evaluated by them for the work they do on the project. The project manager, in such cases, may well have no input for selecting these team members or appraising their performance. This will result in a situation where some team members are selected and appraised by the project manager and some are appointed and appraised by functional managers. This raises the issue of consistency in evaluation as well as team morale, loyalty, commitment, and synergy. It is difficult, in such cases, to create a common vision for the project team and a sense of camaraderie among its members.

In summary, a highly interactive and communicative management style is necessary for the project manager to *inform and stimulate* team members on the one hand and *inform and collaborate* with functional managers on the other. There is a critical balance that needs to be established. The project manager must create an identity for the project team by establishing a common purpose that is understood and accepted by all members. Forming this identity helps the project team to stand out and be recognized as a unit. The project manager must also provide the necessary interface with the rest of the organization and ensure that the project is considered by all as a mechanism for accomplishing organizational goals and objectives. In part, this interface will identify the project team as an integral part of the organization. The project manager is the conduit for this two-pronged communication channel, forming an identity for the team while making sure it is an integral part of the organization.

## 9.4. Team Development

As described earlier, forming a project team at the early stage of the project development life cycle is an important responsibility of the project manager, although sometimes the team is already formed. Depending on the size of the project and the extent of talents, the project manager usually has options in selecting members. Experienced project managers take advantage of the broadest pool of talent available within the organization. If necessary, the project manager can look outside the organization for special talents that are not available from within. A systematic approach, such as the one that includes the following steps, will enable the project manager to form an effective team.

*Talent pool.* The initial step in forming a project team involves putting together a list of individuals with the potential to contribute to the project. This should be an interdisciplinary list that includes individuals from different departments and functions within the organization. In addition to skill competency and experience, it is important that the project manager gathers information about work experience, habits, strengths, and weaknesses of each individual on the list. The ultimate goal is to form a team of competent individuals that works—individuals on the team that will interact and collaborate to produce the required results effectively.

*Task pool.* Based on the scope and specification of the project, the project manager needs to develop a comprehensive list of possible activities and tasks required to achieve project goals and objectives. For example, if the proposed system is to help with organizational resource planning then the task pool should include skills relative to inventory, human resources, and planning. Alternatively, if the project specification suggests the need for special hardware, equipment, or facility, the list should include tasks and skills that directly relate to these activities. There are several other tasks that are required for almost all projects, and the project manager must make sure they are considered. These include communication, documentation, personality traits, teamwork, and the like.

*Task–skill match.* The project manager must not only identify individuals who are skilled and competent to do the job but also must make sure that they do the job to the best of their ability. One effective way to get people to perform to the best of their abilities is to assign them tasks that match their talent. When assigning responsibilities, the project manager must consider the level of difficulty in a task as well as the nature of the task. Underutilization of team potential is often due to an inappropriate skill–task fit. Assigning a highly experienced and skilled individual to a task that requires minimum expertise is not only poor use of resources but it may also lead to morale issues for the individual. Motivated and skilled individuals like challenging assignments that give them the opportunity to make meaningful contribution as well as to enhance their expertise.

*Appointment.* The final list of individuals must have the depth and breadth necessary to carry out all activities of the project and to satisfy objectives in a timely manner. That means appointing sufficient numbers of people with necessary expertise. Once this list is ready, the project manager needs to do two things: (a) obtain authorization from appropriate departments for selected individuals who will be working on the project for the estimated development life cycle, and (b) formally appoint these individuals to the project team. Individuals need to know that they are authorized to work on a new project, they need to know when their new assignment starts, and they expect to have an idea of the length of time that they will be working on their new assignment.

*Acquaintance.* It is important that the team members get to know each other as a team and appreciate different members' style, ability, and work habits before they actually start to work on the project. The project manager can facilitate this through a brainstorming session in which the project scope is discussed and ideas and input are solicited. It is important in this forum that team members develop a clear understanding of what the project is about and what the sponsors' expectations are. This participative process provides an opportunity for the project manager to assess each member's ability and potential for contribution as they discuss the project scope and suggest ideas for its development. In this forum, individual traits are likely to surface that give the project manager the opportunity to evaluate and determine ways of relating to each team member.

*Performance.* At this point, all members are assigned their responsibilities. They understand the triple constraints of time, budget, and specification for their respective tasks. This information about each work unit and its constraints is defined through the work breakdown structure. Team members must also understand that as part of their responsibilities they must communicate to the project manager their work progress as well as potential problems that may delay project activities. They must understand that their line of communication is through the project manager. In large information systems development projects, the project is often divided into several smaller segments and a key member is appointed to be responsible for each segment. In such cases, the line of communication may be confined to each segment. In any case, the project manager must determine what works best for the project and the team. Highly formal communication may put strains on team interaction and prove to be ineffective, especially when close and frequent collaboration between team members is necessary.

Most project managers may go through a similar or a more informal way of team development process. As shown in Exhibit 9.3, a systematic approach to forming the project team helps the project manager in several ways.

This model for team development also gives the project manager the opportunity to learn early in the process about team members: their style, their uniqueness, their way of interaction, and so on. It also gives team members a similar opportunity to develop the necessary understanding about their project leader and co-members of their project team. This is an effective approach toward eventually accomplishing all the project objectives.

> ### Exhibit 9.3   Advantages of Forming the Project Team Systematically
>
> - Review and list project activities.
> - Review and list needed talents.
> - Match individuals with appropriate tasks.
> - Observe and learn about team members as they interact with each other.
> - More formally assign tasks and appoint members.
> - Establish communication channels.
> - Link responsibilities to the project objectives.

## 9.5. Team and Project Execution

Sometimes project managers do not get much choice as to who their teams are composed of—it is a fait accompli. But whether the project manager has or has not a say, the job is to make the team work. The initial phase of project development is important in setting the tone and the trend for project activities. Project managers can save time and effort later in the project when they follow a systematic approach to team development and ensure that *priorities, responsibilities*, and *authorities* are clearly established and understood up front. It is often suggested that experienced individuals make good team members and contribute to the success of the project. This statement is true in its general sense. Sometimes team members have significant experience in projects that have narrow and similar focus. These individuals may find it difficult to adjust to a new and completely different situation. Project managers must recognize this and help these individuals adjust to new ideas and the new project.

Experienced individuals within the organization are often in high demand for different projects. This high demand for a person's time and expertise may be stretched to the extent that it makes that person unavailable or unsuitable for the project. Something will have to give for over-committed individuals; it is either the quality that will suffer or the deadline that will be pushed back. Thus, the fact that an individual is highly experienced or has relevant expertise *does not make that person necessarily most suitable for the project.* Highly motivated individuals with less expertise will be able to make significant contributions to the development of a project. All things considered, the project manager must be able to assess and determine the bottom-line contribution that a team member makes toward a project.

Sometimes team members develop strong loyalty and fondness for a specific tool or technology and become partial toward its use. This may hamper new technology transfer and acceptance. For example, consider computer simulation as a management tool for decision making and problem solving. This approach is quite appropriate and powerful for situations where repeated trials and experiments are either not possible or, if possible, too costly. Individuals with extensive experience in simulation modeling and its application may consider it as a panacea or a solution for all situations. This is obviously not always the case, as shown by the saying "I have a hammer, and all problems are nails." The project manager must determine which technology or method is appropriate for a given situation.

The project manager should interview key individuals before selecting them for the team, except in situations where this practice is not allowed by the organization. Some organizations do not allow direct interviews because of the negative effects of rejection on the individual, internal politics, and the like. However, when allowed, interviews provide an opportunity for the project manager to select key individuals and use them for recruiting other members of the team. To generate a list of candidates, the project manager should seek volunteers; the project focus should be described and all employees within the organization invited to apply. This will enable the project manager to generate a list of individuals who want to be involved and feel they can make a contribution. When interviews are not possible, the project manager may use organizational contacts to obtain needed information before making a decision. The interorganizational relationship in general and contacts with functional managers in particular, provide useful avenues to the project manager for obtaining information about team candidates.

Sometimes it is necessary to recruit individuals from outside the company because the required talent is not available internally. The company may use an outside agency or advertise itself. Either way, recruitment is both expensive and risky. It is essential to be able to specify your requirements clearly. This should avoid a lot of wasted time. The job specification should include specific duties, skills, knowledge, and experiences required. More difficult is to specify in writing the personal attributes required. But these also need to be specified and assessed at the interview. The person needs to be a good team player, work well under pressure, and so on.

As mentioned earlier, the first meeting of the team is important because it establishes the ground rules for project activities. The project manager should determine whether there are team members with narrow work experience in this meeting. By providing clear guidelines and purpose, the project manager can set an appropriate direction for project activities and the interaction among team members. Some of the ground rules described in this first meeting may change later as the project gets underway and team members interact with each other. The project manager must evaluate and consider changes that are proposed by team members and ensure that they benefit the ultimate goals of the project as described in the scope statement.

The first meeting of the project team should be well organized, prepared, and conducted to accomplish the required objectives. The project manager should prepare and communicate the agenda for all meetings, especially the first meeting. As mentioned earlier, in this meeting the ground rules are set and team members are given clear guidelines for their conduct within the team. The project manager must ensure that this meeting focuses on main issues and avoids getting bogged down with trivial issues. The team members must come away from this meeting feeling that:

- They are participating in an important project that makes clear contribution to the organizational goals and objectives; they feel good about being on the team.
- The project has a competent leader who knows what needs to be done and knows how to get things done; they feel confident about the direction and outcome.

- They are selected as team members because they can make the project accomplish its objectives; the project needs their expertise.

Long meetings are not necessarily more productive. A meeting must be just long enough to accomplish what is intended for that meeting. It is difficult to prescribe a time limit that will work for all meetings. It is the responsibility of the project manager to manage the meeting and make sure that it runs its required course. To be effective, a meeting must:

- Have a beginning that ensures a prompt and orderly start
- Have a focus through an agenda that describes what is to be covered
- Follow a logical sequence without going back and forth
- Have closure that gives a sense of accomplishment

The first meeting of the team could be organized as a retreat where members spend a day or more away from the work environment to review, discuss, and finalize issues of the project fully. In the case of a retreat or long meetings, the project manager may involve experienced individuals on the team to help with breakout sessions. Exhibit 9.4 suggests an agenda for the first meeting planned as a retreat.

---

**Exhibit 9.4    Agenda for the First Planning Meeting**

- Project scope
- Project stakeholders
- How the team was selected and its characteristics
- How the project plan will be developed and who will be involved with it
- Communications and feedback channels
- Principle deliverables
- Principle milestones
- Team conduct (interaction, communication)
- Progress, quality, success measures
- Subsequent meetings and format

---

Successful project execution is sometimes a function of how well team members respond to deadlines. Every project goes through a period of heightened attention or "busy" time, even when there has been no change in deadlines. Team members tend to be more sensitive about deadlines toward the latter part of the project life. Deadlines do not seem to have the same impact at the early stages of the project. Maintaining steady progress at all stages of the project development life cycle therefore poses a challenge for the project manager. Monitoring progress through milestones is an effective approach that enables the project manager to link team member performance and accomplishments with the initial commitment. The work breakdown structure defines work units in terms of deliverables and constraints that include deadlines.

As described earlier, the involvement of team members in estimating time and cost for each work unit helps not only to obtain estimates but also to create commitment. Important milestones should be highlighted by the project manager, and the team that accomplishes any of these milestones should be rewarded. In other words, the project manager must make the following clear:

- Monitoring project progress is a continuous process and
- Milestones are used as yardsticks for measuring the progress.

Team members must be challenged to adhere to the deadline they helped to establish for milestones and within the timeframe that they helped to define.

---

### 9.6. Interview With a Project Manager

What skills do you feel are necessary in becoming a successful project manager?

"About 90% of the projects I am called in to salvage are not due to technical problems—most are "people problems"—so my response needs to be interpersonal skills: understanding personalities, defining roles/responsibilities, dealing with conflict, etc. These "soft skills" are often put down by most IT professionals as not important. Perhaps this is why the Gartner Group/Standish Group studies show that the majority of IT projects fail because of schedule/budget challenges."

Our course textbook also mentions that more and more companies are starting to require new positions for project managers to have project management certification. Studies have shown certified project managers perform better and have better leadership skills than those who are not certified. From what you have seen in the field so far, would you agree with this study?

"I agree that the trend is to require certification (yes, I am certified), but certification does not, by itself, produce an excellent PM—it is the result of practical experience, which, unfortunately, can only come through the experience of working on both good and bad projects. . . . To me, the PMP certification is not a necessity to work in this business and only shows that the PMP has the initiative and has a baseline understanding of PMI's terminology."

What are some of the tools and software programs you currently use at work?

"They include email, Excel, MBWA (Managing By Walking Around), teleconferences, Web, document repositories, brainstorming, sticky-note parties (for WBS creation and initial dependency analysis), etc. Scheduling tools: MS Project, Niku (ABT workbench), Primavera, and Artemis."

How often would you say projects typically start and finish on time?

"Most projects start on time and, from my observations, end late—probably 80% of them finish late due primarily to scope mismanagement or nonperformance."

Does the scope of a given project remain fairly consistent as unexpected problems and obstacles may occur during the project?

"Again, scope changes as a result of a poor initial definition. The client's scope definition (what they REALLY wanted doesn't change)—the IT folks either ASSUMED incorrectly or were not savvy enough to extract true requirements."

What are some techniques that you do to motivate other members in a project and keep everyone on track with projects?

"Keeping the eye on the ball (objective). Partitioning the project such that a product is produced quickly. Keeping each development phase of the SDLC from 6 to 12 weeks (produce a sense of accomplishment). Humor is essential in all aspects and really is the No. 1 motivator. Respect for performance; ability to remove a nonperformer; short, productive team meetings; and having team "traditions and rules.""

How much do politics in an organization play a part in new projects getting the OK to proceed, raise necessary funds, and/or terminating a project that some upper management people would view as a waste of time?

"Politics are part of everything that project managers do and are most essential in the initiation phase of the project when the project is authorized, stakeholders are analyzed, allies are groomed, and managers are contacted regarding resource commitments. Politics should be reduced as an active sponsor is identified. One of the roles of the sponsor is to manage politics."

Involving users in the implementation phase of a new system helps users and everyone else involved accept the new system. Do you feel people actually like being involved in this process and that their opinions matter?

Absolutely. In fact, it is essential. After all, the client is the custodian of the project's product and must "live" with it long after the project is completed. The key stakeholder role of the client is "ownership."

What is the most important skill that a team member must have?

The most important skill as a team member to have is being able to communicate early and often so everyone knows what's going on. You must stay focused so if there are problems it can be resolved early and efficiently."

What do you expect the demand for IT project managers to be 3 years from now?

"I believe the PM industry will continue to grow, but not exponentially, as it has in the past 10 years; perhaps 5% a year. The demand for GOOD project managers will never be satisfied, as it is a combination of hard and soft skills that tends to be a rare combination in the individual."

## 9.7. Chapter Summary

The project team is the key to project development and implementation. Team members must function as a team and must collectively feel responsible for the project's success or failure. For a project team to succeed in accomplishing project objectives, it must exhibit *synergy* and demonstrate that team members can work together. Forming the project team is one of the first responsibilities that the project manager undertakes. The project manager must create a sense of camaraderie among team members by providing the team with a common vision. The project manager should select individuals carefully who are technically competent and demonstrate traits that are important for teamwork, such as interpersonal skills, communication, analytical skills, tolerance, a "can do" attitude, and the like.

The project manager should also make sure that the talent of each team member is carefully matched with assigned tasks. Each member should be formally appointed for the duration of the project and should understand how their performance is reviewed and appraised. Responsibility and authority should be assigned and communicated to key members. Individual team members should be clear about their tasks and how they might communicate their concern, opinion, feedback, and so on. Team members should be clear about the extent of their commitment, when this commitment starts, and when it is expected to end.

The project manager should provide a forum for team members to interact with each other early in the developmental process. This could be accomplished through a meeting where project objectives are described, ground rules are defined, and ideas are exchanged. This is part of a systematic approach to forming and developing a project team. Project managers are well advised to spend time and effort up front to carefully select a team that functions as a team and accomplishes project objectives. Project managers should assess carefully the tradeoff that may exist between technical competencies on the one hand and interpersonal skills on the other. It is also important to realize the difference between knowing how things work and making things work.

## DISCUSSION QUESTIONS

1. This chapter argues that an effective team exhibits a sense of trust among members as well as between members and the project manager. It argues that a sense of trust enables team members to openly discuss their ideas and their mistakes without fear of being penalized. As a project manager, what would you do to create a sense of trust among team members?

2. This chapter describes several characteristics for an effective project team. Describe three of these characteristics that you feel are most important and suggest ways of obtaining them.

3. It is suggested in this chapter that highly interactive and communicative management styles will inform and stimulate team members on the one hand and inform and collaborate with functional managers on the other. It is argued in this chapter that to accomplish these objectives, the project manager must become the conduit for a two-pronged communication channel. What is meant by a two-pronged communication channel?

4. Sometimes individuals from functional areas work on a project for a short period of time and as a result continue to report to their functional managers and are evaluated by them for the work they do on the project. This will result in a situation where some team members are selected and appraised by the project manager and some are appointed and appraised by functional managers. Discuss issues that such situations will raise for the team and the project manager.

5. Assume you are the project manager preparing for your first meeting with your team of 25 members. Discuss (a) how you would prepare for your meeting, (b) what the main items are that you plan to discuss in your meeting, and (c) what you would hope to accomplish in this first meeting.

6. Comment on the interview with a project manager presented in this chapter. What do you think of the interviewee's comment about PMP certification? What is your opinion about this response?

## EXERCISES

1. Interview an information systems project manager to obtain her or his comments and opinion of the list of characteristics described in this chapter for an effective project team. Your interview should confirm or revise (add or delete) the current list.

2. Sometimes projects fail primarily because the team does not function as an effective unit despite the fact that there are sufficient resources, a good plan, a clear scope statement, and so on. It is important that the project manager spends time and effort up front to select individuals with appropriate characteristics to function as a team. Create a table with two columns. In the first column, list what you think are appropriate characteristics of project management team members. In the second column, describe your rationale for each entry.

3. An effective team exhibits a "can do" attitude that sometimes compensates for deficiencies such as inadequate skills, difficult schedules, and so on. Describe three situational examples that tell you there is an attitude issue within your team and explain what you will do to address these situations.

4. Assume you are the project manager for an information systems development project that is authorized to integrate your organization's inventory system with several of your vendors. You have selected a team of 25 individuals from across the organization to work with you. Draft an email to your team members to attend the first project team meeting and provide them with an agenda for your meeting.

5. Look again at the interview with the project manager in Section 7.9. Having now read Chapter 9, what would you advise him to do as preparation for his next project?

## APPENDIX TO CHAPTER 9: THE SARBANES–OXLEY ACT

### Preamble

The United States Congress passed the Sarbanes–Oxley Act to protect investors from potential fraudulent accounting activities of corporations. The Sarbanes–Oxley Act was signed into law by President George W. Bush on July 30, 2002.

Compliance with the requirements of this act requires direct and significant support by information systems function within organizations. Information technology plays a critical part in a corporation's ability to comply and to demonstrate how and to what extent its management and processes adhere to the requirements of this act. Several sections of this act clearly suggest the role and importance that information technology can play in successful compliance: Section 302 requires corporate CEOs and CFOs to confirm that their company's financial statements are accurate; Section 404 calls for proper audit attestation and reporting on management's assessment and the effectiveness of internal controls; Section 406 defines formal written code of ethics; and Section 906 requires all companies to include the certification and signatures of CEOs and CFOs in their reporting documents.

Information technology helps organizations and their management establish and demonstrate controls for data accuracy, security, privacy, and the like. The implications of this act influence firms' practice within and outside the United States, including outsource offshoring practices. The act also has implications for different aspects of information security, including infrastructures for cybersecurity, virus definitions, firewall, and wireless security. The implications for corporate accounting, audits, and reporting are so critical that there has been a growth in specific consulting practices in this area, including the development of commercial Sarbanes–Oxley Act software solutions.

### An Overview of Sarbanes–Oxley Act

Sarbanes–Oxley was named after a Democrat senator Paul Sarbanes and Republican congressman Michael Oxley. This act amended U.S. securities law and other laws related to conducting ethical business within the United States of America. The reason for enacting this statute was the forced declaration of bankruptcy of firms like Enron, Global Crossing, and WorldCom. Public press and media provided details of extensive violations by these and other major U.S. corporations. These violations pointed to fraudulent accounting practices. Even accounting firms that provided services to these corporations were at fault and in fact were considered partners to these violations. They presented wrong financial figures on their balance sheets and income statements, thus misleading their shareholders and investors as to the actual profit margins. As a result, investors in stocks of these companies lost a lot of capital as well as trust in the U.S. securities markets and business opportunities.

The Sarbanes–Oxley Act was passed by the Congress to protect current and potential investors from future fraudulent accounting activities by corporations. This act calls for a "reasonable assurance" that information provided to the public by corporations about their financial figures is truthful and sufficient. The act calls for improved accuracy and reliability of corporate disclosures and is intended to deter and punish corporate and accounting fraud and corruption. It also ensures penalty for wrongdoers. The Sarbanes–Oxley Act pertains to all U.S. and non-U.S.

public companies that have registered securities in one of the U.S. security markets. The act is organized into 11 titles. Below we look at sections 302, 404, 406, and 906, which have implications for information technology application and development.

## Section 302

This section of the act requires CEOs and CFOs to confirm that their company's financial statements are accurate. The certification for this section has to be filed under the Exchange Act. Corporate executives are now personally liable for any and all financial mistakes that affect company's stock price or even reputation. This means that all top level managers' evaluations must exhibit "evidential matter," which includes but is not limited to proper documentation, improved internal controls, and executive signatures on all reports. The design of internal controls, whether it is the formulation of special control committees or other committees responsible for making sure that all financial figures are true and correct, is now a necessary component of all publicly traded companies. This design must be accompanied by sufficient documentation of all accounting practices, proper and adequate cost and revenue breakdowns, and executive management signatures on all accounting-related exhibits. Those who violate these requirements and provide false information to the public and Security and Exchange Commission (SEC) are both professionally and personally liable and can be imprisoned or severely penalized.

## Section 404

This section of the act calls for proper audit attestation and reporting on management's assessment. It measures the effectiveness of internal controls. Auditors have to be members of independent audit organizations, such as Public Company Accounting Oversight Board (PCAOB); they can't be hired internally by firms. Auditors are required to work closely with the management, and they have to coordinate their audit processes to best examine proper corporate internal controls, such as documenting and testing of financial information. PCAOB's responsibility is mainly to protect the interests of investors. In addition, this board has been given the power to investigate financial fraud and oversee the correct use and enforcement of Sarbanes–Oxley Act and Exchange Act rules and business conduct procedures in all public companies. Under this section the company has to inform the auditors about any material weaknesses that the company might be facing at each specific reporting period.

## Section 406

This section of the act pertains to financial officers' code of ethics. All reporting companies have to disclose whether they have a formal written code of ethics for the company's employees, partners, and all others involved in conducting business with such firms. It is not required for all publicly traded companies to have a written code of ethics; it is more beneficial for them to have one. The reason for this is that a company that does not have clear written guidelines as to behavioral and moral conducts has to explain to SEC why there is no such written code. The SEC and Sarbanes–Oxley Act promote ethical and behavioral compliance with the business law, regulations, and procedures. They also encourage reporting any illegal or unethical behavior, which is referred to as whistle-blowing.

*(Continued)*

(Continued)

## Section 906

This section of the act amended the U.S. criminal law and states that now it is required for all periodic statements that contain any kind of financial information to include the certification and signatures of CEOs and CFOs, which also have to be filed under the Exchange Act and are subject to civil responsibility. Both executives have to make sure that the reports and information contained in them comply with the Exchange Act rules and exhibit all required documentation and financial entries. The certification for this section is only required in periodic reports that hold financial testimonials. Anyone who knowingly certifies and signs false periodic reports can be fined up to $1,000,000, imprisoned up to 10 years, or both. Moreover, anyone who knowingly certifies any statements that accompany periodic reports which are filed under section 906 can be fined up to $5,000,000, imprisoned up to 20 years, or both. In both cases, such violations are considered as violations of Exchange Act rules and are to be treated as criminal violations.

## Management Information Systems Responsibilities

Information technology and system principles are critical to a variety of business functions, including planning, directing, scheduling, staffing, organizing, and controlling. Information technology investments are infrastructural in nature and affect all departments across the boundaries of the firm. Staff members of the information system function are required to support and manage corporate information relative to technological products and services utilized by the company. They are responsible for carrying out plans for future development of company's information system needs and infrastructure, stay current with technological advancements and innovations, and support and maintain technical equipment throughout the company. Information system personnel are also responsible for application development, system design, and systems integration in a way that closely ties with the specific needs, including reporting needs, of the company.

It is often difficult for executives to appreciate information technology investment because of its role as a support for all functions within the firm and because of its infrastructural nature. Many non-IS executives have traditionally been skeptical of the true added value to the bottom line of information systems investments. With the advent of the Sarbanes–Oxley Act, however, firms have developed new appreciation for the support that they can receive from information systems services. As a CFO of a large firm noted, they now feel they need the CIO to be with them when they attend board meetings. Senior executives are now more supportive of investment in information technology infrastructure and services.

## IT Support for Compliance With the Sarbanes–Oxley Act

The Sarbanes–Oxley Act has implications for the information technology management because information system support is critical to the corporation's ability to comply and to demonstrate how and why the management believes they are in compliance. For corporations to effectively comply with Sarbanes–Oxley, they will need reliable information systems. The sections of the act that require the companies to tighten internal controls, provide better documentation, and promote ethics, security, and awareness suggest the need for proper integration of corporate information systems. The act does not specify the use of information technology in accomplishing the required objectives, the extent, or the timeliness of the reporting requirements. But it is difficult to imagine how those objectives can be achieved without the use of effective information systems.

Information systems function can also influence compliance through risk assessment, employee training, education, and ethics. Further, corporations involved with offshore outsourcing practices need to monitor and report their financial statements more carefully. The company is responsible for the accuracy and sufficiency of financial statements whether they are internal or external. Security infrastructure is a key component for compliance. Network security and protection against unauthorized access and malicious virus attacks have become strategic concerns of modern businesses. Because of the increased Web application and online commerce, network security and reliability has assumed new importance. Moreover, the use of wireless technologies such as remote access points and VOIP services require proper security and controls as well. All of these matters and issues are important to compliance with Sarbanes–Oxley and an important part of information system function.

## IT Governance

The Sarbanes–Oxley Act calls for controls to ensure data accuracy and security and a process that excludes the creator of the data approving the same data. This is where IT governance comes into play. It sets a framework for firms to link their business strategies and objectives with IT processes and resources. There are many tools available that support the IT governance with Sarbanes–Oxley Act compliance. Companies can obtain advice or consult with the Information Technology Governance Institute (ITGI), the Information Systems Audit and Control Association (ISACA), the Committee of Sponsoring Organizations of the Treadway Commission (COSO), Control Objectives for Information and Related Technology (CobiT), and the Information Technology Infrastructure Library (ITIL). All of these organizations are able to tailor to individual corporate needs and provide control guidelines and tests that help demonstrate compliance effectiveness.

The Web site address for the ITGI is www.itgi.org, for the ISACA is www.isaca.org, for the COSO is www.coso.org, for CobiT is www.isaca.org/cobit.htm, and for the ITIL is www.itil.org/itil_e/index_e.html.

## Issues of Corporate Ethics

When referring to corporate ethics in relation to information systems use, the principles apply not only to executives and managers but also to employees and entities that do business with firms. The ethical rules call for appropriate role definitions, proper training of employees and sometimes even subsidiaries, and for correct policies. All employees have to be aware of the Sarbanes–Oxley Act. They have to know what their limits are when using the company's computer equipment for retrieving emails, using instant messaging, or even opening electronic attachments on corporate computers. These activities, if not done with caution, can infect corporate systems with malicious viruses and thus destroy important data within the systems that are necessary for compliance with the act.

It is the information systems department's responsibility to acquaint all employees with the rules and regulations that a company has for the use of the firm's computer equipment. For example, all employees have to be advised of the benefits of using antivirus and anti-spyware software on all workstations. They also should be provided with special training programs that

*(Continued)*

will make them aware of harms that such malicious pieces of codes like computer worms and viruses can have on networked systems.

All employees should be informed that all emails sent and received through corporate networks can now be opened and read by designated staff members due to increased information leakage problems as well as to prevent any illegal activities within the company. Now, upon being hired, employees are often required to sign policies that pertain to cyber-security, information confidentiality, and use and proper care of corporate-owned hardware and software. All employees also should be informed about types of IT controls their company has. They have the right to know what is monitored, when, and where. They don't have to be informed about all the details of such controls, but they have to be aware that such controls exist and are put in use. Moreover, they also should be informed of the reasons why such controls are put in place, because the more the employees are concerned with legal business tactics, the easier it will be for the company to comply with the Sarbanes–Oxley Act.

The IT staff also should establish proper relations with the upper management, because now every piece of data that comes through corporate networks goes through IT. IT staff members have the responsibility of backing up all important information. Therefore, clear guidelines must be established that indicate who is responsible for what information or what tasks in regards to electronic records. The executives and managers, to better fulfill Sarbanes–Oxley Act requirements, should periodically hold meetings with the IT managers to learn about the latest threats in the IT world and the prevention tools used in the company and to be acquainted with the IT processes in general.

This responsibility goes both ways. Information system managers also have to better understand the financial reporting processes of their corporation in order to improve the firm's accurate reporting ability and be able to aid compliance with Sarbanes–Oxley. The Sarbanes–Oxley Act has given the IT department more power but also more responsibility for keeping all ends of corporate networks secured, all employees involved and informed, and communication among corporate levels more effective and accurate.

## APPENDIX TO CHAPTER 9: DISCUSSION QUESTIONS

1. For each of sections 302, 404, 406, and 906 of the act, answer the following questions: What are direct and indirect implications of this act for information systems development? What are direct and indirect roles for information systems in assisting corporate executive responsiveness to this act?

2. Would some of the failure stories discussed in this text, such as One.Tel, have turned out to be success stories if all concerned had followed the requirements of the Sarbanes–Oxley Act?

## BIBLIOGRAPHY

Berkun, S. (2005). *The art of project management.* Sebastapol, CA: O'Reilly.

Cadle, J., & Yeates, D. (2004). *Project management for information systems.* Harlow, UK: Prentice Hall.

Edum-Fotwe, F. T., & McCaffer, R. (2000). Developing project management competency: Perspectives from the construction industry. *International Journal of Project Management, 18.*

Lee, D. Trauth, E., & Farwell, D. (1995). Critical skills and knowledge requirements of IS professionals: A joint academic/industry investigation. *MIS Quarterly, 9*(13).

# 10

# Assessing Project Risk

**Themes of Chapter 10**

- ❖ What are the risk factors for IS projects?
- ❖ Which risk factors are more or less serious?
- ❖ What are the consequences of each?
- ❖ Why do risks occur?
- ❖ How can project managers plan for risks?
- ❖ Can all risks be identified?

**A**ny information systems project involves risks. Some risks are more serious and result in outright project failure, and some lead to budget overrun, delay, or quality issues. Some risks are inherent to information systems and their growth. Risks may also occur because of organizational, individual, or procedural reasons. Experienced project managers know that they cannot avoid risks but that they can plan for them and in the event that something goes wrong, have some contingency plan ready. Inexperienced project managers may prefer to pretend that there is no risk or prefer not to think about them. Project managers must identify possible risks, determine the likelihood of some failure happening, make provisions, and plan to respond. Not all risks are possible to identify. Some risks are difficult to imagine. To the extent possible, project managers must identify what might go wrong and be prepared to respond in the event that something does go wrong. A history of similar projects and individual experiences are often the best sources for identifying project risks. This chapter will describe the importance of identifying and managing risks for information systems projects. This chapter also describes ways of identifying and planning responses to project risks. This chapter ends with an interview with an information systems project manager. But we start with Exhibit 10.1, in which we discuss the decision about when and where we may (or may not) take the risk.

**Exhibit 10.1    Whether to Take a Risk . . . or Not**

Big ideas carry high risks. Project managers can make significant contributions to their organization with their ideas and innovations. In fact, they are increasingly expected to propose new applications and put forward new ideas to help reengineer business processes. However, they need to be prepared for potential risks that come with their ideas and innovations. In fact, they need to be prepared to explain their contingency plans for potential risks associated with their ideas. You do not have to be certain what the outcome might turn out to be, but you must be certain that you have a plan if they don't turn out as hoped.

Project managers should not be afraid of risks but be afraid of not being prepared to respond. There are *two key elements* in risk management: (1) how to anticipate it, how to forecast it, how to determine the likelihood of it happening, and (2) what should the response be in the event that something goes wrong, who should do what, who will be in charge to respond, what is their responsibility and authority, what is at their disposal. It is critical that these two elements are carefully considered and assessed for every potential risk.

The benefits of effective risk management are *twofold:* (1) the psychological preparedness of team members and their realization of management insight about risk occurrence and risk planning and (2) the estimation and preparation of resources necessary to alleviate the consequences of a risk. People living in hurricane- and tornado-prone regions are aware of the risks of natural disasters—they do not like it, but they prepare for it and respond accordingly. That is, they are psychologically prepared and have the resources ready in the event that they are needed. People are not as afraid of a disaster as they are afraid of being caught off-guard when it happens. Therefore, both these factors are critical to the outcome of any response to risks.

Risk avoidance is not necessarily an appealing trait of information system professionals and executives, but neither is obvious risk seeking. Of course, there are situations in which a project manager does not need to take a risk, but those situations are rare. Risk is a part of any decision-making process: personnel, hardware, or software; internal or external; and formal or informal. The real question is not whether to avoid risk or embrace it but how to anticipate and plan for it. In fact, risk-taking behavior has been on the rise in recent years due to increased competitive pressure to benefit from new technologies. Technology can offer major benefits, but at the same time it could present significant risks.

Risks occur all the time, and still people are surprised when problems arise. Some people have an excuse for not being ready when a significant risk arises because that is not what they usually expect. Information systems projects are different: They often involve risk. Project managers cannot be excused for not planning for risk. Risk is a part of every project, and the responsibility to respond to risk rests with the project manager. That does not mean that the project manager must personally respond when problems arise. That means they must have a plan to respond and identify people who will be responsible for carrying out specific tasks in the event that a problems arises. It is the discipline of planning, communicating, and monitoring, and that is part of the project management skill set.

Project risk management fosters the culture of openness and responsiveness on the part of team members. Individuals will not hesitate to come forward with ideas when they know there are plans to avoid serious consequences if necessary or if their project backfires. Furthermore, when individuals propose new ideas they will also think of potential risks associated with their ideas as well as how they might respond in the event that problems arise. In other words, project managers must encourage the culture of openness and innovation so long as it is combined with responsiveness; you can take a risk, but you must be prepared.

Finally, it is worth mentioning that many project managers tend to put off risk assessment and risk planning, arguing that it sends the wrong message to team members and it might be looked upon as a less optimistic way to start project activities. It's a "why talk about what may go wrong rather than what can go right" kind of argument. That is an excuse. Responsible people must behave responsibly. Risk planning and risk management are responsible ways to approach the goals of the project, team members, and the organization. Risk management is good for project managers, their projects, their team members, and their organizations. They should get into the habit and build the discipline for it.

## 10.1. Sources of Information Systems Project Risks

Project risk management involves understanding potential problems that might occur during a project and how they might impede project success. Project risk management helps project managers to *identify, evaluate, and respond* to potential project risks and increase chances of project success. Risk management is often overlooked, but it can help improve project success and protect the project manager and team members.

We take risk to gain opportunities that can result from the risk taking. High-tech organizations provide ample examples of risk-taking behavior that have resulted in significant payoffs. Some individuals or organizations tend to take higher and more frequent risks. They are often referred to as "risk takers." Some individuals or organizations tend to avoid risks and are very cautious when making decisions. They are often referred to as "risk avoiders." There are those who are in between and tend to take risks infrequently when they feel it is necessary and hard to avoid. There are arguably more people in this last group than the other two.

The sources of information systems project risks can be broadly grouped as internal or external. Important internal sources of risks include the following factors shown in Exhibit 10.2.

---

**Exhibit 10.2   Internal Sources of Information System Project Risk**

- Continued management support
- Top management style
- Alignment with organizational needs
- User skill and technology acceptance
- Shifting goals and objectives
- Developmental expertise and talent pool

The goal of project risk management is to increase the chances of project success and to protect organizational resources. Effective project risk management involves several steps: (a) **identify risk**—determine the type and the level of potential risks for a project; (b) **quantify risk**—evaluate the range of possibilities that could affect project outcome for each risk that is identified; (c) **prepare risk response**—describe the steps to be taken and the resources to be used if a problem occurs; and (d) **monitor risk response**—make sure appropriate actions are taken in a timely manner in response to something going wrong and report on potential problems that could arise throughout the project development life cycle.

Arguably, the most important risk that could make or break an ongoing project is associated with the *continued support of top management.* This is particularly true when a project is behind schedule, over budget, or perceived as having little strategic value. It is crucial that the project managers maintain top management support for the project. It is also critical to assess the risk that such support will be discontinued. Management style and whether it supports the application of technology provide clues for future support. Volatile and changing *management style* poses a risk, especially for projects with expected delays.

Effective communication and demonstration of a project's contribution to *organizational goals and objectives* is an important responsibility of the project manager. As described in Chapter 2, the need for the project and its outcome must be continually reinforced in the context of organizational goals and objectives. The project manager must be able to assess the likelihood or lack of continued support for the project at the outset. Assessing the risk of discontinued top management support depends on the following factors:

- The relationship between the project manager and top management
- The management's perception of the importance of the project
- The project's integration (how may departments within the organization are affected by the outcome)
- The progress expectation (how reliable are estimates that will influence timely completion of the project within budget).

Lack of *technology acceptance* within an organization can also be a particular risk for information systems projects. Technology acceptance is influenced by organizational culture and management style. Some organizations aggressively seek technology development and implementation. They provide extensive user training and support. They take chances with new technologies and maintain support when delays happen. These organizations are proactive and accept new and innovative ideas and thus pose less risk of reducing or even pulling support from an ongoing project. Some organizations behave differently and are more conservative with their support for the applications of technology. Project managers should evaluate the organizational attitude toward technology and assess the risk of losing support for a project that is innovative, new, or involves uncertainty. Experience is the best source of evaluating project risks in such organizations.

The usage of an information system and ultimately its success depend on user acceptance. Information technology applications have the potential to create change in the work process, quality of work, work planning, customer service, management expectation, and the like. Because of the uncertainty that it creates, users often react cautiously and at times negatively to change. *Shifting organizational goals and objectives* often enhances this negative response from information systems users. Users' negative response is a potential risk for any new information systems project. Project managers need to evaluate the risk that is associated with users' reaction to a new system. User involvement is often suggested as a means of increasing user acceptance and user satisfaction for new systems. Project managers must assess the impact of user involvement arrangements and use it to improve the quality of outcomes and to increase acceptance and use of an information system. User involvement is discussed in a number of contexts in this book because it is such a crucial success factor for project management and it also affects customer satisfaction.

*Individual expertise* and the talent pool within an organization are important resources for information systems development. The lack of such resources poses a risk as well as other challenges, such as dependence on external resources, and it raises security issues. The development of strategic information systems often involves sensitive information flows that require additional caution. Project managers are normally reluctant to draw upon external expertise for such information systems.

Internal expertise is also essential for end-user training, implementation, and information systems support, especially for integrated systems that affect a great number of users across organizational functions. A major drawback for information systems outsourcing is argued to be the loss of in-house know-how. Professional expertise and in-house know-how are developed at a great cost and over a long period of time. Organizations that lack internal expertise are forced to rely on external resources with all of the potential cost and security issues that this entails.

External sources of information systems project risk are associated with a number of issues including those shown in Exhibit 10.3.

---

### Exhibit 10.3    External Sources of Information System Project Risk

- Vendors
- Consultants
- Contract employees
- Market and change fluctuation
- Government regulation

---

External *vendors* are essential for most information systems development. It is critical that they are reliable, follow deadlines, deliver products according to specification, and adhere to the terms of the contract. The history of interaction with a vendor provides a good basis for the project manager to assess reliability and effectiveness. Outside *consultants* are often recruited to develop unique and specialized systems when internal expertise is inadequate. A great deal of effort goes into preparing these contracts to protect the interests of the organization and define the specifics of the required information system. Sometimes the company goes even further: to **outsource** and/or **offshore** developmental work. These pose even greater risks, and we devote the whole of Chapter 11 to outsourcing and offshoring.

Contracts will specify the type and extent of internal information that should be made available to consulting firms. Project team members of the consulting firm will visit with users and developers within the organization to gather information in order to design the specification. Some of this information may be sensitive and confidential. The contract with the consulting firm must be prepared so that the integrity of the information and its confidentiality is protected. Organizations often continue working with vendors and consultants with whom they have had good experience. First time vendors and consultants pose greater risks to project development. Project managers must consider this risk as they set deadlines for project activities that depend on external resources.

Large projects often involve *contract employees* to work for the duration of the project. Project managers must keep records of performance for these employees and refer to them when hiring. As the number of contract employees involved in a project increases, the level of risk increases. This risk is higher when there is no prior experience or record for contract employees. Risk sources include access to company systems, facilities, files, client information, and proprietary code and loss of key personnel or clients to outside contractors.

Organizations often support training for their users and internal personnel to get them up to speed with project activities and responsibilities. However, they are reluctant to do the same for external employees who are expected to be skilled and ready to make contributions toward the project's success. This poses a risk in cases where external employees do not have adequate skills.

Some of the external risks are difficult to control, in particular, *government regulation* and *market and exchange fluctuations.* However, it is important to assess such occurrences and plan for them. Project managers need to stay current with news about possible new regulations that may affect technology development or use. The usage of information systems may be influenced by new regulations, especially for aspects that relate to security and privacy. Sometimes extended user training programs may be necessary in response to a likely risk, hence the requirement to provide contingency funds and additional time for project development activities.

One general risk in information systems is sometimes referred to as the *adopter's dilemma.* This refers to the question about when is it best to adopt new technologies. We need to be critical of fads and fashions in IS, and managers are largely disappointed with "silver bullets" (the technology that is apparently the answer to all our problems). But project managers need to be aware of the realistic potential of new technologies. This means that they need to understand the innovation in terms of how it might support the project and then decide whether and when to adopt the innovation and make a resource commitment. Adopting early can bring considerable gains, not least of which is competitive advantage to the firm, but technical know-how will be limited and expensive and the project risky. Adopting with the majority will give competitive parity and be less risky, as know-how will be more easily available if costly. Adopting late loses some opportunities but is much less risky in terms of know-how and cost.

## 10.2. Identifying Information Systems Project Risks

As described above, there are multiple sources of risk for information systems project development. Sometimes these risks interact and create new and more complex risks associated with project development activities. For example, developments such as new regulations or market fluctuations will more readily influence conservative leaders who at the best of times tend to provide only cautious support for technology development. This makes the task of risk analysis more challenging. Good planning is the best response to the issue of project risk. In fact, poor planning by itself is a risk to the success of information systems projects.

Risk assessment should be done for every task. Probably around 80% of tasks are low risk and the project manager will assume team members will do these tasks competently. The project manager needs to identify and then spend 80% of his or her time working on the 20% of the high-risk tasks. A serious concern for the project manager occurs when a high-probability risk has a potentially high impact on the project. Thus project managers need to focus on the areas where they might have a problem.

Project managers must ask themselves important questions that help them identify risks and assess the level and extent of those risks. Such questions should include those in the following four categories shown in Exhibit 10.4.

During the project planning phase of the information systems development life cycle, the project manager is expected to benefit from the involvement of key team members (if not all members) for estimating activity duration, identifying the talent pool, deciding on project milestones, defining the project scope statement, and so on. Team members or key team members (in the case of large projects) can assist the project manager in identifying project risks.

The project manager could use a **brainstorming** approach for identifying potential risks. Brainstorming is a team activity aimed at generating a cross-stimulation of ideas. It is used in a semiformal setting to generate ideas, where the ideas of one person serve as a stimulus to generate further ideas from other people, which in turn serve as a stimulus for further ideas, and so on. Judgment on the usefulness or validity of the ideas is "suspended" until the brainstorming session is completed. The aim is to get a free flow of ideas. We looked at how software can help this process in Section 5.8. It may be feasible to produce a hierarchy of risks so that each type of major risk identified (technological, relationship, resource, and so on) has within it various examples of that general risk. Thus a *risk breakdown structure* is produced rather similar to the work breakdown structure discussed in Chapter 4.

Team members can also help to assess the level of importance for each risk and to help create a priority list. Assume that there are five key team members who are helping the project manager to plan the project and identify risks. Once all possible risks are identified through the brainstorming session, a list can be prepared for priority allocation. This list is first used to obtain the collective assessment of the likelihood that a particular problem will arise. The planning team members are asked to assess the probability that each problem may arise. The average of all responses can be used as an indication of the overall likelihood for any risk. Table 10.1 provides an example of this where five assessments are used to generate likelihoods for four potential risks.

---

**Exhibit 10.4  Questions to Identify and Assess the Level and Extent of Risks**

## Top Management Support

- Is there a risk that top management would discontinue support for the project?
- What are the circumstances that may trigger such a response by top management?
- How likely is the occurrence of those circumstances? What are possible responses to them?
- What is the possibility of management turnover?
- How extensive could the turnover be, and what would be the impact on the project?

## User Acceptance

- Is there a risk that users would not accept the new system?
- What might be their main concerns?
- Is there a way to address those concerns ahead of time?
- What are planning actions that would address user issues?
- Are there conflicting user needs that may create acceptance problems at the end?
- Can these conflicts be clarified at the planning phase?

## Supplier Problems

- Is there a risk that vendors or suppliers would fail to deliver necessary products on time?
- How much do project team members need to interact with vendors and external resources?
- How important is this interaction between project team members and outside providers?
- What is the risk of losing internal talents to external providers?
- Can that be avoided through contractual agreement?
- What is the risk of communication failure with suppliers, and what is the risk of that for the project?

## Employee Problems

- Is there a chance that employees would go on strike before the project is complete?
- Are conditions right for such an event?
- How much would that affect the project team, and is there an alternative plan if that happens?
- Are there any new regulations formulated that will affect this organization or this industry?
- Are there any environmental laws that may be affected by new system development?

---

The same list of risks can then be used to obtain the collective assessment of the importance for each event. The planning team members are asked to assess the importance of each risk to the successful completion of the project by assigning a number between 1 and 100 to each risk. Again, the average of responses for each risk can be used to indicate the level of importance for that risk. Table 10.2 provides an example using the same list of risks. It is also a good idea to calculate the variance for the numbers to gauge how closely team members have assessed each risk. To reduce the variance, it is reasonable to drop extreme numbers for each risk. This is more practical where a large number of members assess each risk.

❖ Table 10.1 Assessment of Risk Likelihood by a Five-Member Team

| Risk | Member 1 | Member 2 | Member 3 | Member 4 | Member 5 | Overall likelihood |
|---|---|---|---|---|---|---|
| Management support | 0.25 | 0.3 | 0.28 | 0.32 | 0.41 | 0.31 |
| User acceptance | 0.4 | 0.38 | 0.32 | 0.45 | 0.5 | 0.41 |
| Vendor timely delivery | 0.15 | 0.21 | 0.25 | 0.2 | 0.22 | 0.21 |
| Employee strike | 0.1 | 0.12 | 0.15 | 0.18 | 0.15 | 0.12 |
| Other | . . . | . . . | . . . | . . . | . . . | . . . |

❖ Table 10.2 Assessment of Risk Importance by a Five-Member Team

| Risk | Member 1 | Member 2 | Member 3 | Member 4 | Member 5 | Overall importance |
|---|---|---|---|---|---|---|
| Management support | 95 | 90 | 88 | 98 | 94 | 93 |
| User acceptance | 85 | 82 | 90 | 88 | 90 | 87 |
| Vendor timely delivery | 50 | 60 | 55 | 65 | 80 | 62 |
| Employee strike | 98 | 95 | 96 | 91 | 95 | 95 |

It is important in project planning that alternative views and representations of any given situation are ascertained. There are a variety of associated models, and the need to select that view that is the most appropriate to the particular circumstance is important. In the following paragraphs we discuss approaches to find out what are the various views, in particular, scenario planning, SWOT, and case-based reasoning.

One of the main concerns of the project manager is to ensure that the system they are leading will be suitable for the organization in the long term. We know that we cannot assume that the conditions of today will prevail in the future. Therefore we cannot assume that the system we build today for today's situation will be appropriate for the future. There are a number of techniques that can help us plan for future change. An obvious technique is forecasting, where we base our understanding of the future on present trends.

However, sometimes the future cannot be planned in this way—it is much more uncertain—and it is then that the project leader may turn to the *scenario planning* approach. Michael Porter defines scenario planning as *an internally consistent view of what the future might turn out to be—not a forecast, but one possible future outcome*, whereas Gill Ringland suggests that it is *that part of strategic planning which relates to the tools and technologies for managing the uncertainties of the future.* Assuming, then, that we cannot easily predict the future, how can we identify possible future outcomes?

One scenario-planning technique for obtaining group response is the *Delphi* method, which uses an iterative and interactive approach to generate consensus among a group about a topic. This technique is used to solicit expert opinion (sometimes anonymously) and to generate consensus among a panel of experts. A Delphi approach might be used so that experts see the views of other experts and some general consensus is achieved. In the Delphi approach, people in turn give their views so that the next person can build on the previous assertions. Sometimes experts might suggest two or three possible scenarios. Some of these cannot be said to be "expected," but they might be plausible and worth planning for.

*Morphological approaches* identify a number of future states built on different assumptions. These assumptions might relate to expected states for the economy, depletions or findings of natural resources, changes in people's values or lifestyles, or changes in the political persuasion of a new government. Scenario analysis might consider different combinations of values for these key factors. The spreadsheet package Excel has a scenario manager tool that can show these different scenarios side by side. For each of these different scenarios, their implications can then be discussed. In Figure 10.5, we use Excel to assess the impact of doubling the cost of advertising and halving the cost of materials on the income forecast for 2008. We see that doubling expenditure on advertising has a negative effect on overall income in this example, whilst the reduction in materials costs has a major positive impact.

*Cross-impact approaches* identify potential events, trends, and conditions that affect the decision and each other. Sometimes probabilities are assigned to each of them so the likelihood of these impact factors can be estimated.

Having agreed on possible scenarios, the organization then needs to assess the implications of present actions and alternative future decisions based on these scenarios. Scenario planning may also provide early warning and guidance so that potential problems can be detected and avoided before they occur. Further, strategy formulation can be proactively devised by considering the present implications of possible future events. Aspects of possible or desired future scenarios can also be seen and appropriately dealt with. Such scenario planning can ensure a greater likelihood of the information system being appropriate in the longer term, despite environmental change.

A *SWOT* analysis is another well-known technique that is often used for planning and could be useful in identifying project risks and challenges. SWOT is an acronym for **Strengths, Weaknesses, Opportunities**, and **Threats**, and those that apply to the project are identified. It can be used for a quick, "back of the envelope" assessment or an in-depth, highly researched analysis. It is usually used as a group technique, rather

❖ Table 10.3  Using Excel to Create Different Scenarios

| 2008 Forecast | | | |
|---|---|---|---|
| **Gross Receipts** | | | |
| Sales | 90,700 | | |
| Distribution | 11,444 | | |
| Total | 102,144 | | |
| **Costs** | | | |
| Materials | 38,760 | | |
| Transport | 799 | | |
| Misc | 187 | | |
| Total | 39,746 | | |
| Gross profit | 62,398 | | |
| **Expenses** | | | |
| Advertising | 3,555 | | |
| Commissions | 5,677 | | |
| Rent | 980 | | |
| Elec/Water | 258 | | |
| Insurance | 255 | | |
| Telephone | 266 | | |
| Office Supplies | 278 | | |
| Interest | 3,560 | | |
| Total | 14,829 | | |
| **Income** | 47,569 | | |
| Scenario Summary | 2008 Forecast | Double Cost of Advertising | Halve Cost of materials |
| **Changing Cells:** | | | |
| Sales | 90,700 | 90,700 | 90,700 |
| Transport | 11,444 | 11,444 | 11,444 |
| Materials | 38,760 | 38,760 | 19,380 |
| Shipping | 799 | 799 | 799 |
| Advertising | 3,555 | 7,110 | 3,555 |
| **Result Cells:** | | | |
| Income | 47,569 | 44,014 | 66,949 |

than something performed by an individual, and it is frequently employed initially in high-level brainstorming sessions.

*Case-based reasoning (CBR)* formalizes the process whereby managers make decisions based on their previous experience. A case reveals knowledge in its natural context. It represents an experience that teaches a lesson relating to the goals of the practitioner. This lesson can be useful in understanding a new project. Therefore, we may use this learning from previous cases to understand more the potential risks surrounding the project. For example, CBR may help us understand a solution that does not quite fit, warn of possible failures, and interpret a situation. CBR can therefore help solve what might be perceived as very new and difficult problems. It may speed up problem solving by reducing areas of difficulty and help in new domains. Experience gained in previous cases can help in evaluating solutions, interpreting open-ended and ill-defined aspects of the project. Further, by drawing on less successful cases, the practitioner may prevent repeating mistakes of the past.

## 10.3. Evaluating Information Systems Project Risks

The information in Tables 10.1 and 10.2 can be used to generate a ranked list of potential risks. Table 10.1 gives the probability of a risk happening, and Table 10.2 suggests the importance for each risk. The two numbers for each risk can be multiplied to generate a priority list of possible events. Table 10.4 provides this calculation. The last column suggests how contingency funds and resources should be allocated in response to identified risks. Note that while management support has a very high importance, the likelihood of losing this support is lower than the failure of users to accept the new application, which ranks first in the last column. Thus, the combination of likelihood and importance determines the position of a risk on the list. This list can be used by the project manager to plan for adequate response in the event that a risk event occurs.

There are other methods of risk analysis. For example, the same process described above can be carried out using the three levels of *high, moderate,* or *low.* In this method, again, each risk is assessed by team members for likelihood and for importance. To arrive at numeric results that can be used to generate a ranked list, the three levels can be weighted as 3, 2, and 1 for high, moderate, and low, respectively. The sum of the team's assessments can then be used to assess the likelihood and importance for each risk. Tables 10.5 and 10.6 illustrate this method using the earlier list of risks. Table 10.7 shows how this information is used to generate a rank ordered list.

High scores in the priority column (Table 10.7) warn project managers to plan for potential risks. Some organizations may have a cutoff point beyond which a risk may

❖ **Table 10.4**   Risk Analysis and Ranking for an Information Systems Project

| Risk | Likelihood | Importance | Priority | Rank |
|------|-----------|-----------|----------|------|
| Management support | .31 | 93 | 28.83 | 2 |
| User acceptance | .41 | 87 | 35.67 | 1 |
| Vendor timely delivery | .21 | 62 | 12.40 | 3 |
| Employee strike | .12 | 95 | 11.40 | 4 |
| Other | . . . | . . . | . . . | |

❖ **Table 10.5**   Assessment of Likelihood Using High, Moderate, and Low

| Risk | Member 1 | Member 2 | Member 3 | Member 4 | Member 5 | Overall likelihood |
|------|----------|----------|----------|----------|----------|--------------------|
| Management support | L | M | L | M | M | 8 |
| User acceptance | H | M | H | H | H | 14 |
| Vendor timely delivery | M | M | M | M | H | 11 |
| Employee strike | L | L | L | L | L | 5 |
| Other | . . . | . . . | . . . | . . . | . . . | . . . |

❖ **Table 10.6**   Assessment of Importance Using High, Moderate, and Low

| Risk | Member 1 | Member 2 | Member 3 | Member 4 | Member 5 | Overall importance |
|------|----------|----------|----------|----------|----------|--------------------|
| Management support | H | M | H | H | H | 14 |
| User acceptance | M | H | H | M | H | 13 |
| Vendor timely delivery | L | M | M | M | H | 10 |
| Employee strike | H | H | H | M | H | 14 |
| Other | . . . | . . . | . . . | . . . | . . . | . . . |

warrant contingency planning. For example, if a cutoff point of 150 is used for risks identified in Table 10.7, user acceptance will be considered a high-risk event for this project. In this case, the project manager may need to consider arrangements that are expected to increase user acceptance. For example, user involvement may need to be increased or user training may need to be planned.

❖ **Table 10.7**  Risk Analysis and Ranking Using High, Moderate, and Low

| Risk | Likelihood | Importance | Priority | Rank |
|---|---|---|---|---|
| Management support | 8 | 14 | 112 | 2 |
| User acceptance | 14 | 13 | 182 | 1 |
| Vendor timely delivery | 11 | 10 | 110 | 3 |
| Employee strike | 5 | 14 | 70 | 4 |
| Other | . . . | . . . | . . . | |

As shown in Exhibit 10.5, experienced project managers usually evaluate potential risks based on project characteristics that might contribute to risk.

---

**Exhibit 10.5  Project Characteristics That Could Contribute to Risk**

- Estimated project duration
- Estimated number of people involved in developmental activities
- Number of users of the final product
- Number of departments for the final product
- The level of external resources involved
- Number and type of technologies involved

---

Large projects may involve hundreds of people at different stages of developmental activities and are expected to affect a great number of users (large projects are seldom developed for a small number of users). As a result, a great deal of planning and communication is required among the stakeholders—for example, sponsors, developers, users, and vendors. As the number of stakeholders increases, the risk for miscommunication and misunderstanding will also increase. The project manager must plan carefully for effective interaction and consider potential risks associated with large and complex projects. Extensive vendor involvement and the need for external resources may also increase project risk. The application of cutting-edge technologies, technologies that may not be mature at the time of application, is also associated with higher levels of risk. Experienced project managers are able to evaluate these risks and plan to respond accordingly.

Finally, it is important that the project manager keeps a record of events and activities as they progress or are completed. Project progress reports can provide valuable information to the project manager and stakeholders about events that happened in the past as well as what might happen in the future. If part of a project is completed ahead of or behind schedule, or over time, or with poor quality, then it is important to analyze reasons for that outcome and plan possible responses to and the impact on other portions of the project. Reasons for unsatisfactory outcome may relate to technology, people's expertise, project scope, external resources, and the like. It is important to record the frequency and the extent of these problems. These records must be accurate, consistent, and comprehensive. They provide significant help to the project manager in planning adequate responses.

## 10.4. Responding to Project Risks

Identifying and assessing risks have little value unless they lead to a plan of action. The most effective response to risk is to plan for it. Information systems projects are considered high risk compared with construction projects, for example, that over the years have developed well-defined standards of measurement, practice, and control. In planning a response to risk, project managers must consider the *potential impact*, the *likelihood of occurrence*, and the *difficulty of response*.

Some risks may occur more often but are easier to address. For example, a poorly designed system may be less problematic if design issues are addressed in a timely manner even though it will take additional resources. An analogy for this can be made with building a house. It is very easy and costs next to nothing to add an additional telephone outlet in a room at the planning stage when the blueprints are prepared or when wall structures are being put in place. However, such a minor modification to the original plan is costly and time-consuming if it is to be done at later stages when that room is built and decorated. Therefore, timing is crucial to some modifications.

Some risks may occur very infrequently but are more costly and it is more difficult to determine an adequate response. A poorly designed, developed, and implemented system is likely to result in sunk costs; it cannot be addressed through contingency funds. In such cases, a new project may be initiated with a new design, budget, schedule, and management. Consider again the above example of building a house. It is more costly and time-consuming to alter floor plans or modify dimensions of a room once building has started. More difficult modification yet would be if you decide to alter view orientation so that, for example, bedrooms get more sun during the winter. It might be less costly to plan a new house in that case.

Preparing a response for risks that are imprecise or difficult to evaluate is challenging. For example, lack of agreement among experts on whether something will or will not go wrong creates a challenge for the project manager from two perspectives. One is to determine whether to plan a response for this risk and the other is to obtain additional support. A divergence of opinion makes it difficult to convince management. In such cases, it is prudent to obtain more expert opinions about risks.

The project manager must make sure that risks are defined clearly and accurately and that assessment methods are appropriate. Some experts may be thinking about risks from different perspectives or may have a different understanding of potential risks based on their experience. It might be a good idea to ask experts to define each risk as they perceive it before assessment. It is also useful to brainstorm risks and the likelihood of failure in a group setting. Interactive sessions provide opportunities for participants to clarify and define what they are evaluating.

## 10.5. Implementing Responses to Risks

Once risks are identified and ranked, the project manager must plan to mitigate and reduce the effect of each risk leading to problems. Additional resources are usually required, depending on the nature and extent of the potential risk. Contingency plans suggest the extent that the project manager and team members are prepared to respond to risk. Reasons for contingency planning include the following:

- *What action* is necessary when problems occur?
- *Who is responsible* for handling the situation?
- *What resources* are available?
- *Who is authorized* to release contingency funds?
- *How do you document* progress and file reports?

For example, if delay to a particular activity is likely, the project manager should review the work breakdown structure and PERT diagrams to determine whether that activity is on the critical path or has slack. If the activity is on the critical path, then the project manager must determine whether the risk can be eliminated through overtime or additional human resources. If the activity is not on the critical path, then it must be determined whether the slack for that activity is sufficient. If a risk is associated with external vendors, the project manager must consider the possibility of using other vendors. Contracts with external vendors must be carefully drawn to include provisions for using other vendors in these and some other circumstances.

Response to risk must be based on impact on the project and thereby on the stakeholders. In other words, risks with high impact (significant cost and inconvenience) must take priority even when they are less likely to occur. Low-impact risks are more tolerable even when they are more likely to happen. It is important that contingency plans are considered only when it is necessary. In other words, contingency funds are provided for out-of-the-ordinary situations. *They are not provided to make up for bad management, poor performance, or inadequate control.* Repeated poor judgment, control, and performance may jeopardize a project manager's credibility and support of the project by top management. The authorization to release contingency funds is usually held by top management rather than the project manager.

Once a risk leads to some failure, the responsible person must be supported with the necessary resources. The responsible person in turn must mitigate, monitor, and document progress. Documenting risks is useful to identify the sources of risks and effective approaches to them. Sometimes, it might be possible to transfer risks but not risk impact. For example, it might be possible to transfer risks associated with equipment or fluctuating prices to external vendors. In such cases, terms of the contract may include additional charges to provide for risks and vendors understand that they are responsible for controlling and mitigating risks. However, it might not be possible to mitigate the impact of all risks on the project.

There are potential problems with risk analysis. For example, it will be difficult to identify all the activities and risks and estimate (accurately) the probabilities of risks leading to failure. However, there is no limit to the amount of time that could be spent attempting to analyze risk and plan reactions to it! Indeed, complexity and uncertainty may be so great that any analysis of risk might in some circumstances be simplified. Analysis consumes resources, and this may lead to choosing the option that identifies "general responses" to several problems rather than identify in detail every source of risk. This reduces effort in dealing with uncertainty, and general responses are a natural first line of defense in coping with "unforeseeable" threats or opportunities. An important result of more detailed risk analysis is that decision makers can gain an understanding of the tradeoff between expected risks and costs of different alternatives, giving a firm basis on which to make and compare decisions.

## 10.6. Focusing on the Benefits

Most of our previous discussion has focused on such risks as not achieving our project goals within time and within budget, with user cooperation and acceptance of the new system. In this section we look more at the benefits side. Sometimes an "over-budget and over-time" scenario, although undesirable, can be offset if important benefits are achieved. Here we look at critical success factors as a way of identifying the key benefits of the project and a benefits realization program to ensure these key benefits are achieved. The first job is to identify the key benefits.

*Critical success factors* (CSFs) are the set of factors that can be considered critical to the success of the project (in our case, they can relate to the organization or department or even a role, such as that of the CIO). It is best if only a limited number of factors are identified as critical; if too many are identified, they are probably not all critical and at too low a level. The focus is on the relatively few areas where things must go absolutely right to ensure the project's success. The process thus includes a fundamental assessment and prioritization of factors. Where possible, CSFs should be measurable, indeed, not only measurable but actionable, and linked to perceived value. Strictly speaking, CSFs themselves should not be prioritized or ranked because, as the term implies, they are all critical and thus equally important. If they can be ranked in terms of importance, as is sometimes seen, it implies that they are probably not all critical.

CSFs are used in our context to help ensure that the information systems projects in an organization support the overall business strategy. A typical CSF approach might first analyze the goals and objectives of the project for the organization and then identify the factors critical to achieving each of those objectives. About four to six CSFs might be identified for each major objective of the project. So, using the CSF technique helps identify those relatively few things that must absolutely be achieved to ensure success at a strategic level. Then it can be cascaded down to specific lower-level activities or elements that contribute to the achievment of the overall CSFs. From the project manager's point of view, it is important to ensure that the overall CSFs embody the major requirements of the key stakeholders.

*Benefits realization programs* are a means of ensuring that these CSFs have the highest possibility of being satisfied when the project is operational. It is important to distinguish here between provision and use in such programs. The project may be deemed only a partial success, if at all, if the new information system provides all the information required but the information is not used. The recipient needs to understand not only the nature of the information provided but its potential and therefore needs both to recognize and value the improvement and change behavior in some positive way as a result. This might be achieved, for example, by existing customers buying more services or by not transferring their allegiances elsewhere or for the improved service to attract new customers. Customers or potential customers must first be aware of the change and second perceive it as an improvement over the service that they currently use. So, the benefit realization process comprises at least two stages: first, the provision or implementation of the project to provide benefit, and second, the effect of that benefit on the wider environment and any resultant behavior change; it is only after the second is achieved that benefits will be realized. Many of the considerations discussed earlier, such as training and education of stakeholders and top management support, are therefore vital to benefits realization.

The fact that there are two stages to the process unfortunately provides greater opportunities for the potential benefits to get lost or become dissipated and makes the evaluation of such effectiveness projects difficult. In the case of cost displacement, the organization is more in control of the realization of benefits, whereas in the improved services case (i.e., effectiveness justifications) the organization is in control of achieving the first stage but not the second stage. This is the impact on others—for example, suppliers, customers, and potential customers. This second stage is the area where miscalculations are frequently made; for example, it is often assumed that the move from Stage 1 to Stage 2 is a logical and deterministic process: that an improved service will lead to more people buying that service, or that better information will lead to better decision making.

One of the main uses of a benefits realization program is that projects that are going wrong can be identified earlier because it will be evident that benefits will not be achieved following the present path. The appendix to this chapter describes an e-government project that was failing. This failure was recognized and it was then possible to turn the project around. Similarly, the appendix to Chapter 8 described an ambulance allocation system that failed but was turned around successfully in the follow-up system. Edwin Bennatan argues that projects are rarely impossible to turn around, and he suggests ways in which failing projects can be turned around in a process he calls the **disentanglement process**. This is shown as Exhibit 10.6.

**Exhibit 10.6    The Disentanglement Process (From *Catastrophe Disentanglement*, by E. M. Bennatan, 2006, Boston: Addison-Wesley)**

1. **Stop:** Halt all project development activities and assign the team to support the disentanglement effort.

2. **Assign an evaluator:** Recruit an external professional to lead the disentanglement process.

3. **Evaluate project status:** Establish the true status of the project.

4. **Evaluate the team:** Identify team problems that may have contributed to the project's failure.

5. **Define minimum goals:** Reduce the project to the smallest size that achieves only the most essential goals.

6. **Determine whether minimum goals can be achieved:** Analyze the feasibility of the minimum goals and determine whether they can reasonably be expected to be achieved.

7. **Rebuild the team:** Based on the new project goals, rebuild a competent project team in preparation for restarting the project.

8. **Perform risk analysis:** Consider the new goals and the rebuilt team, identify risks in the project, and prepare contingency plans to deal with them.

9. **Revise the plan:** Produce a new high-level project plan that includes a reasonable schedule based on professionally prepared estimates.

10. **Install an early warning system:** Put a system in place that will ensure that the project does not slip back into catastrophe mode.

---

### 10.7. Interview With a Project Manager

What specific roles in your opinion are important to a project manager?

"It varies, but a great manager has three major roles to play. They are a planner, a provider, and a protector. As a planner, a manager has to take a long-term view; indeed, the higher you rise, the further you will have to look. While a team member will be working toward known and established goals, the manager must look further ahead so that these goals are selected wisely. As a provider, the manager has access to information and materials that the team needs. Often he/she has the authority or influence to acquire things that no one else in the team could. Last, as a protector, the team needs

*(Continued)*

(Continued)

security from the vagaries of less enlightened managers. In any company, there are short-term excitements that can deflect the workforce from the important issues. The manager should be there to guard against these and to protect the team."

What procedures and or tools do you use in order to keep team members informed and moving forward on the project?

"I have weekly status updates, and make sure the information in the meeting is documented. If I cannot physically meet with my team due to distance constraints I use Net Meeting, which is a Web-based software program that allows me to host my meetings. In the meetings, I usually discuss where we are in the time scope and detail progress and future tasks. If someone is responsible for a certain task prior to the next meeting, I will make sure to log a reminder in Microsoft Outlook so I can give that person a follow-up call. Without Outlook I wouldn't get anything done! Organization is crucial for successful project management."

Which phase of the project life cycle would you consider to be the most important?

"Concept is the most important; if any problems arise they can all be rooted back to the source, which is the concept. Without a clean, concise, understood concept there will probably be problems during the project."

What do you feel is your biggest challenge when working on a project?

"The accessibility to resources and resource allocation are the biggest challenges. Almost every project manager that I have worked with, myself included, have complained about not having access to certain resources."

How do you feel project management for IT differs from project management for other industries?

"Well, since I've only been exposed to IT project management it is difficult to say. As I think about it, though, it shouldn't be that much different. Project management boils down to managing people to achieve a goal. The 10 basic steps should be involved, which are define work, build work plan, manage work plan, manage issues, scope, communication, risk, documents, quality, metrics."

What do you believe to be the most important skill of a successful project manager?

"Organization and communication are the most important."

How critical is it for you to have programming/networking/database skills?

"If you have a logical mind, you could pick up programming; everything is helpful but not necessary. For example, I had a project that consisted of programming in Java and my little knowledge of Java helped me to communicate with my other team members. It helps to understand every area, but it isn't necessary."

Given that you enjoy working as a project manager, what is the most rewarding part of the job?

"Seeing a project go through its life cycle and seeing its goals accomplished. Getting to see people use and benefit from the project."

## 10.8. Chapter Summary

All real-world information system projects involve risk. It is important to recognize that risks can happen and that there are ways of mitigating and preparing for them. Project managers are responsible for anticipating risks, assessing risk likelihood, evaluating risk impact on the project, and finding effective ways of responding to risks.

Project managers must consider risk management as a *cost saving exercise* that if avoided might result in significant budget overrun and delay. At the same time, risk management is a *costly exercise* and involves careful planning, assessment, resource allocation, monitoring, and control.

The most effective way to respond to risks is to *plan for them*. Even for risks that are difficult to define, evaluate, and ultimately plan for, it is beneficial to brainstorm them and be aware that they may arise. It is important that team members are sensitized to the possibility of risks and are prepared in the event that risks are revealed.

Project managers and team members must consider risk analysis and risk management *as an integral part of system development activities* because of the impact that potential problems may have on the outcome of the project. Because of the negative impact that certain issues will have on a project outcome, the information systems project development team and the project manager must continually monitor and control for potential risks.

Risk-management planning and contingency fund plans are two important outcomes of risk management exercises. The *risk-management plan* describes what might happen, what the likelihood is that a risk might arise, what mitigating actions are feasible, who is responsible for implementing mitigating actions, and how to control and monitor the risk-management plan. Risk-management planning must describe whether a risk can be avoided, transferred, or reduced.

*Contingency funds* are predetermined and are released only when a risk event occurs. Their use must, therefore, be properly defined. Contingency funds must be directly linked with the significance of a risk and the likelihood of an event happening. Project managers usually initiate the need for contingency funds, but the authorization to release these funds usually rests with general managers.

*Internal sources* of risk relate to top management support, organizational needs change, user acceptance, and the talent pool. Projects closely aligned with organizational goals and objectives have a greater chance of continued support and acceptance. *User involvement* in systems development activities is considered an important way of improving the likelihood of user acceptance. Training programs are also critical for user support and to improve the talent pool.

*External sources* of risk relate to vendors and providers, consultants, contract employees, government regulation, and market fluctuation. Probably the most critical source of risk is *vendors*, and experience is the best resource for assessing that risk. *Documentation* and past records could prove useful to the project manager in evaluating risks associated with consultants and contract employees. Project managers must stay current with regulations that may affect information systems design, development, implementation, and use. A good example of this is the impact of the law on communication between countries.

Some risks are easier to *quantify*, such as loss of software or equipment. Some level of risk is appropriate to evaluate *qualitatively*, such as the strength and level of the internal talent pool, interorganizational communication and relations, top management style, and top management attitude toward new technology. The appropriate use of methods and approaches is important to project managers in *justifying* their assessment and recommendations.

## DISCUSSION QUESTIONS

1. What methods other than the ones described in this chapter would you suggest for identifying information systems project risks? What other methods would you use to assess those risks?

2. Which group of risks (internal, external) described in this chapter is more critical to an information systems project? Why? What is the most critical risk for any information systems project?

3. Read and comment on the interview with a project manager presented in this chapter. What question or which response do you find interesting and why?

## EXERCISES

1. This chapter describes two methods (probability and high, moderate, low) for identifying and assessing information systems project risks. In your opinion, what are the advantages and disadvantages of each method?

2. Ask an information systems project manager (a) how they identify project risks, (b) how they prioritize risks, and (c) how they respond to risks.

3. Assume you are the project manager for developing a large information system that involves different functional areas. How would risk management and assessment be different in this case compared with a system that is developed for a single department? Describe differences in your risk-management plans for these two projects.

4. Search and find out more about the Delphi technique and assess its advantages and disadvantages for identifying information systems project risks. Can you use it to assess the importance of each risk?

# APPENDIX TO CHAPTER 10: HOW TO TRANSFORM A FAILING PROJECT

The case looks at an issue that has bedeviled information systems projects for many years. It concerns the situation when a project seems to be failing and it is vital to get the stakeholders to somehow change direction to a more positive course. This is particularly difficult because the norm is for the "ball to run on in the same direction" even if it is the wrong direction. It is difficult enough to stop the project but even more difficult to restart it on a different and more successful course. Yet IS projects are complicated and tend to have frequently changing requirements, even as the project develops, that cause the project scope to change frequently. Projects that exhibit such volatility are especially difficult to manage and control. Organizations frequently react by investing additional resources in failing IS projects in an attempt to make them work, and consequently these "runaway" projects are continued even though it may make more economic sense to stop them. Here we discuss aspects of an electronic government application in a local UK metropolitan borough council, where the project was out of control originally but was turned around to be a successful project. A similar example that illustrates this is the baggage-handling system at Denver International Airport, a troubled IT project, which was 16 months behind schedule and close to $2 billion over budget but was eventually turned around. Actions to turn such troubled projects around might include redefining the project, improving project management, changing the project leadership, and adding and/or removing resources.

This case study concerns a UK municipal borough that has an elected council that serves a local population of 221,000 residents and provides a large range of services. The idea of e-government originated from the UK central government's 1999 white paper, *Modernizing Government*, which challenged all public sector organizations to achieve "citizen-centered services," by integrating policies and programs, "joining up" delivery, harnessing the power of IT, and getting the best out of staff. The white paper committed the government to the "use of new technology to meet the needs of citizens and business and not trail behind technology development." The overall champion for the e-government initiative was the cabinet deputy of the council, who was assigned a special post known as the "E-envoy." His main responsibility was to propel the e-government initiative and he had several key responsibilities: to deliver the existing Cabinet Office target for electronic service delivery (e-government agenda), to define and drive implementation of a government-wide IS strategy to support the public sector reform agenda, and also to provide leadership and guidance for the e-government initiatives.

In 2000, there was a need to revamp the existing purchasing function to meet the target set within the e-government strategy plan that 100% of the goods purchased by the council had to be purchased electronically by 2005. Besides that, there were other considerations for the council to implement the e-procurement system. These reasons included improving purchasing efficiency, setting up a cost-control mechanism, and a strong desire to be the first local council in the United Kingdom to purchase goods and services electronically. The council head gave full support for the project, and the 12-month project was launched in January 2001 with an initial estimated cost of £150,000 (U.S. $300,000). The project was headed by the IS manager, who was supervised by an e-procurement committee formed by a group of senior managers within the

*(Continued)*

(Continued)

council. An external software vendor, selected through a bidding system, helped to develop the software. Other key stakeholders included the internal users of the system, such as the chief procurement officer, corporate service manager, corporate affairs manager, technical service manager, and the e-business manager. External users would include goods and services suppliers.

The project faced several problems during its early stage of development. The main problem concerned conflicts among the IS project manager, the users, and the IS contractor over design issues. On the one hand, internal users complained about the low quality of the software prototype and the failure of the contractor to understand their requirements. On the other hand, the IS project manager and the IS contractor were dissatisfied with the indecisiveness of the users and pinpointed their frequent requests for design change as the main reason for delaying project development. The project initially stalled because of a disagreement between the users and the IS contractor. It started when the IS contractor demanded an additional £150,000 for "redesigning the software again." Their reason was that, because the contract price was "fixed," any changes to the software after the users signed off the earlier versions of software prototypes were chargeable. The reason the IS contractor asked for 100% of the original cost for the cost of redesign was that it had anticipated the users making many more rounds of modifications to the requirements. However, the users disagreed with their claim because they viewed those changes as alterations resulting from the contractor's mistakes, rather than additions requested by them. Eventually, the e-procurement steering committee intervened and agreed to make the additional payment.

After the committee's intervention, the project continued for another 2 months before it finally collapsed. The same problems resurfaced, and the users refused to continue participation in project development. Instead, they proposed the purchase of e-procurement packaged software. At the same time, the IS project manager seemed to lose control of the project and was busy haggling with the IS contractor over the issue of what requests were categorized as "additions" or "alterations." Despite this dire situation, the e-procurement committee did not intervene directly, except for insisting to the users that the project had to be continued. However, they did promise more resources. While the users were resolute about project abandonment, the IS project manager insisted that they should continue. He explained, "How could we give up? With all the resources invested, the option of reverting to buying packaged software was unimaginable." At that stage, the project had already exceeded £300,000 and was 6 months behind schedule. Apparently, the IS contractor was billing for changes made on an ongoing basis plus the fees for engaging a subcontractor who specialized in system integration.

Refusing to continue with the troubled project, one of the users decided to "blow the whistle" on the project by reporting to the E-envoy. She explained why she blew the whistle: "I believed the involvement of the E-envoy would resolve the entanglement. The committee and the project manager were too optimistic and irrational from my perspective." In December 2001, the E-envoy was informed and was surprised at the problems facing the project. He explained why the news came as a surprise to him: "I had delegated the project manager and the e-procurement steering committee to lead the project. Besides, even at the bimonthly management meetings over the past few months, the committee members did not inform me of any problem arising."

Immediately, he delayed the development project indefinitely until a decision had been made. To resolve the problems, he gathered relevant internal and external stakeholders, who include the council cabinet representative, the strategic management director, the head of IS services, and the project development team consisting of the IS project manager, an IS analyst, users representing several business functions, the goods and services suppliers, and the IS contractor.

The E-envoy had to send emails to these stakeholders requesting them to attend the meeting. In some cases, he even had to convince them the importance of the meeting by conducting numerous rounds of telephone conversations. To reconfirm his commitment to the project, he stated a strong desire for the project to be continued rather than abandoned and was very confident of a project turnaround. He commented, "It was important for everyone to understand my standpoint, especially in that state of confusion. Besides, those problems could be easily resolved as long as everyone was committed to turn the troubled project around."

Once everyone had agreed to continue the troubled project, the E-envoy organized a focus group meeting with the e-procurement steering committee, the IS project manager, the user managers, and the IS contractor to reexamine their previous problems. With the E-envoy's presence and participation, everyone showed great enthusiasm in the meeting. At the beginning of the meeting, the E-envoy delivered a speech to explain the significance of the meeting: "I simply assured them that no individuals would be punished in this project. I also stressed that turning around the failing project was our utmost priority in order to salvage our reputation and the confidence the external stakeholders had in us."

The assurance from the E-envoy was well received by everyone present in that meeting, as they began to discuss their differences openly. They were unafraid of highlighting their mistakes. In that meeting, several problems were identified. Sensing the E-envoy's determination to succeed, all relevant stakeholders arrived at a multilateral consensus to attempt to turn the project around. The IS project manager explained the change of attitude: "Basically, he [the E-envoy] banged all our heads together. All he wanted was to try to get the cohesion of the team back. We promised him that we would get together and work out the differences." Despite the successful turnaround of the attitudes, the IS project manager did admit that it was a very difficult phase: "We felt relieved that the E-envoy accepted our apologies for the earlier mess, and it also took several of us quite a while to restore our confidence that a turnaround was indeed possible." Furthermore, it was also discovered later that any packaged software would need a large degree of customization, which supposedly might take up to 6 to 9 months. The chief procurement officer admitted, "It was unsuitable for the council as the customization process would be too long for the project."

Having identified the problems, the whole team started to explore alternative courses of action. For the first time, with the participation of the E-envoy and the e-procurement steering committee, the three groups (the user managers, the IS project manager, and the IS contractor) started to cooperate and work toward a common goal. Sensing the E-envoy's determination to succeed, all relevant parties arrived at a multilateral consensus to draw up a list of turnaround tactics. The team proposed the adoption of a partial abandonment strategy, which was to reduce the original scope of the project without causing significant changes to its original specification. For that reason, three user departments were short-listed as the pilot sites, hence allowing the IS project manager to deal with the needs of only three user departments rather than eight departments as formerly. Furthermore, the project had been separated into three stages. Instead of

*(Continued)*

implementing full-scale procurement functions all at one go, the first stage would now focus on the "front purchasing process," which included ordering, issuing of purchase orders, and delivery of items.

In February 2002, the E-envoy ordered a stakeholder analysis before carrying out the action plans. The purpose was to find out whether relevant internal and external stakeholders fully supported the devised turnaround strategies. The new stakeholder analysis was seen as necessary because actors involved in the development process could still be strongly committed to the prior failing course of action. The e-procurement steering committee members carried out the stakeholder analysis. Many project members and users still had doubts, but because the E-envoy was personally involved in the turnaround effort, they did not put up a strong resistance for fear of upsetting him. The E-envoy and the committee members had spent considerable effort to convince the project group and the users. Project members were also encouraged to discuss among themselves to see if the exit strategy was the best available option.

All the changes were implemented immediately, and they produced remarkably encouraging results. The corporate service manager commented positively, "This time, we started to thrash out what the problems were with the IS contractor and found out what we needed. We drew up a timescale and everybody had to stick to it. The turning point was that we were able to communicate with the IS contractor directly. Everything was so easy after that." The IS project manager also commented, "With fewer users, things seemed to progress smoothly and quickly. I would think that every one of us was determined to make this work. Even the IS contractor came to meetings two or three times a week. The new team seemed to show more enthusiasm and responsibility. In addition, the E-envoy's close monitoring kept all of us on our toes."

When the first phase of the e-procurement system finally went "live" in August 2002, the project was 8 months behind schedule and close to £500,000 (US $950,000) over its original budget. However, the relatively smooth implementation after the adoption of the new strategy meant that the crisis concerning the project was finally over.

SOURCE: This case study is adapted from "Escalation and De-escalation of Commitment: A Commitment Transformation Analysis of an E-government Project," by G. Pan, S. L. Pan, M. Newman, and D. Flynn, 2006, *Information Systems Journal, 16*(1).

## APPENDIX TO CHAPTER 10: DISCUSSION QUESTIONS

1. Why do you think it is particularly difficult to turn around projects that seem to be heading for failure?

2. Do you think the problems were put right by getting the "people problems" or the "technical problems" solved or a mixture of both?

3. Discuss the role of the E-envoy as "champion" for the project.

4. Search the Web for references to the Denver International Airport project and discuss similarities and differences with this case. Was one of the users ethically correct to "blow the whistle" on the project?

5. Was one of the users ethically correct to blow the whistle on the project?

# BIBLIOGRAPHY

Avison. D., & Fitzgerald, G. (2006). *Information systems development: Methodologies, techniques and tools* (4th ed.). Maidenhead, UK: McGraw-Hill.

Barki, H., Rivard, S., & Talbot, J. (1993). Toward an assessment of software development risk. *Journal of MIS, 10*(2), 203–225.

Bennatan, E. M. (2006). *Catastrophe disentanglement*. Boston: Addison-Wesley.

Boehm, B.W. (1991). Software risk management: Principles and practices. *IEEE Software, 8*(1).

Chapman, C. (1997). Project risk analysis and management—PRAM, the generic process. *International Journal of Project Management, 15*(5), 273–281.

Checkland, P. B. (1981). *Systems thinking, systems practice*. Chicester, UK: Wiley.

Dhillon, G., & Torkzadeh, G. (2006). Value-focused assessment of information systems security in an organization. *Information Systems Journal, 16*, 293–314.

Ewusi-Mensah, K., & Przasnyski, Z. H. (1991). On information systems project abandonment: An exploratory study of organizational practices. *MIS Quarterly, 15*(1), 66–86.

Jiang, J. J., & Klein, G. (2001). Information system success as impacted by risks and development strategies. *IEEE Transactions on Engineering Management, 48*(1).

Keil, M. (1995). Pulling the plug: Software project management and the problem of project escalation. *MIS Quarterly, 19*(4), 422–447.

Keil, M., Cule, P. E., Lyytinen, K., & Schmidt, R. C. (1998). A framework for identifying software project risks. *Communications of the ACM, 41*(11).

Kliem, R. L., & Ludin, I. S. (1998). *Reducing project risk*. Aldershot, UK: Grower.

Lyytinen, K., Mathiassen, L., & Ropponen, J. (1998). Attention shaping and software risk: A categorical analysis of four classical risk management approaches. *Information System Research, 9*(3).

Porter, M. E. (1985). *Competitive advantage*. Basingstoke, UK: Collier-Macmillan.

Ringland, G. (2006). *Scenario planning: Managing for the future* (2nd ed.). Chicester, UK: Wiley.

Ropponen, J., & Lyytinen, K. (2000). Components of software development risk: How to address them? A project manager survey. *IEEE Transactions on Software Engineering, 26*(2).

Wyatt, R. (1995). How to assess risk. *Systems Management, 23*(10), 80–83.

# Outsourcing and Offshoring Information System Projects

**Themes of Chapter 11**

❖ What is offshore outsourcing of IS projects?

❖ What are the main differences between outsourcing and offshoring?

❖ What are the benefits of offshore outsourcing?

❖ What are the consequences of offshore outsourcing?

❖ Is information systems project offshoring different from other offshoring projects?

❖ Do all information systems projects benefit from offshore outsourcing?

❖ How can project managers plan offshore outsourcing?

Offshore outsourcing of information systems services has been growing rapidly in recent years and is likely to continue into the foreseeable future. The primary reason behind this trend is the apparent economic cost advantages gained by offshore service procurement. Offshoring is not unique to the information systems function. Manufacturing and online customer services, for example, have been outsourcing their work to Mexico, China, Ireland, and other countries for some time. Information systems *outsourcing* has been widely adopted for more than two decades, but *offshore* outsourcing of information systems services is a relatively recent phenomenon. The significant growth in communication technologies and the increased demand in recent years for information systems professionals in the United States and Western Europe have made offshore outsourcing of the information systems function an attractive option. In addition, the availability of an educated workforce in other countries, such as India and China, has made the offshore outsourcing of information systems services a reality. The offshore outsourcing of information systems services has implications for IS management. Information systems project management, in particular, is influenced by this trend in a variety of ways, including human resource issues, scheduling, relationships management, communication, quality control, risk, and evaluation. Information systems graduates need to be prepared for the challenges and opportunities presented by offshore outsourcing of the information systems function. This chapter will describe the origin of outsourcing and the reasons behind the offshoring of information systems services. This chapter further describes the impacts of outsourcing on the individual and organization, and the skills that are necessary for the management of offshore projects. This chapter ends with discussion questions that highlight the multifaceted nature of the offshore outsourcing phenomenon in terms of culture, measurement, quality and the like. But first in Exhibit 11.1 we look at potential problems that might arise when offshoring.

---

### Exhibit 11.1  Managing Diversity

Diversity is the essence of reality. It exists in any group or team that we are associated with: the family, work place, society, and the like. Successful enterprises have greatly benefited from the diversity of workforce, culture, and talent. The critical success factor in dealing with diversity is to understand the strengths and weaknesses in any situation. This assessment is more critical when we deal with global entities.

Success of international business depends to a large extent on the management of diverse relationships. The trend to *offshore outsourcing* information systems services is a new development. In a short period of time we have learned a great deal about opportunities and challenges that come with offshore outsourcing decisions. There is still a great deal that we do not know. We need to learn more about the management of diversity and the new relationship in vendor–client situation.

Peggy Zhu is a database administrator with many years of experience. For the past several years, she has been responsible for the management of a large integrated database system in a multistate utility company in the Southwest region of the United States. The database system is critical to the operation of this company. This utility company, like others, has been under competitive pressure in recent years to curb developmental, maintenance, and other costs of information systems services.

### Background

In recent years, there has been a rapid increase in demand for information systems professionals throughout the industrialized world, and that in turn has resulted in the increased cost of procuring human expertise in this field. Following a preliminary analysis, the utility company concluded that they must reduce their costs to remain competitive. It also became evident to them that a common practice for reducing costs was to seek talents internationally. In other words, outsource information systems services offshore.

The company carried out an investigation of how best to offshore their information systems services and decided to go with a large service provider in Bangalore, India. They decided to negotiate with the Indian company for maintaining a significant portion of their database services. Following a year of intense planning, communication, and transition, the bulk of database maintenance was contracted out to the service provider in India. Peggy Zhu was one of the people involved at different stages of this transition. As a result of this decision, her department and its resources were reduced by half. Several of the employees in her department decided to take an early retirement option that was offered by the company, and several others decided to relocate.

## Rationale

The logical deduction by Peggy Zhu was that the company will remain competitive and those employees that were retained will have more job security. Her job had become increasingly hectic in recent years due to frequent employee turnover and the difficulty of hiring experienced information systems professionals. She regularly put in extra time in order to maintain system up-time that the company needed for its routine functions. She realized she had been working 50 hours a week for several months. Given the situation, she did not mind the offshore outsourcing decision by the company. In a way she looked forward to a more normal pace of work and in being able to spend more time with her family.

After a long year of frantic arrangements with the offshore service provider, Peggy planned a 2-week vacation with her family in southern Nevada. She was looking forward to her vacation. She had accomplished what the company had planned to do and had successfully handed over to the new provider firm day-to-day responsibility of maintaining the database. She felt she really needed the time off.

## Panic Call

In her second day of vacationing, Peggy was having dinner with her family and a few friends when she received a panic phone call on her cell from one of her colleagues at work. The colleague apologized for calling her late in the evening and went on to explain that the system was down and that they had not been able to sort out things with the new provider as to what caused the problem and how they should respond to it. The colleague said that they recalled a similar problem a couple of years ago that Peggy had managed to diagnose and bring up the system quickly.

Peggy had feared that this would happen. She was afraid that even though they had outsourced responsibilities of maintaining their system, the company would find it easier to reach out to internal expertise. After all, she was the expert on troubleshooting. She was not happy about her intuition being so right so quickly. She expected something like a list of things that needed sorting out when she returned from her vacation but not a panic call from her colleagues.

Peggy apologized to friends and family and went to a quiet corner to deal with the problem. After a long conversation with the colleague over the phone, she realized that (a) it was difficult to clearly identify the source of the problem and (b) it was unclear which party, the provider or the client, was responsible for fixing the problem.

*(Continued)*

(Continued)

**Questions**

She returned to the table where her cold dinner was waiting for her. As she picked through her plate, a series of thoughts went through Peggy's mind. Did they not plan this right? Was the vendor the right choice? Was the communication a problem? Did they cover all issues in the contract, and did they cover them clearly? Are they protected by the terms of the contract? Should they expect more of this to come?

Peggy realized they were sailing on new waters and that they needed to know a lot more about how to map a new working relationship and how to manage that relationship. She also realized they needed to know more about the people they planned to work with, about their culture, their language, their habits, their values, and everything else. She thought about offshoring phenomenon as a whole and realized if they could not avoid it they should learn to gain from it.

## 11.1. Outsourcing IS Activities

Outsourcing may be viewed as a natural step in the evolution of a business. In the early days of computers large firms developed and maintained their information systems. Gradually, as hardware and software costs declined and as universities and colleges developed more programs and graduated more information systems professionals, companies of all sizes developed and maintained their information systems; they owned their systems. With the rapid growth of computer and communication technologies on the one hand and the increased innovation in technology use on the other, the need for information systems grew at a faster pace than ever before. As a result, the IT industry outran other industries and overexpanded itself to the point that it created a scarcity of talents. Hiring and retention of information systems professionals became a serious challenge for the management of technology. Outsourcing became an option.

*Outsourcing* occurs when information systems activities are carried out by a provider outside the organization. Outsourcing is not unique to information systems services. Other industries such as manufacturing and services have outsourced their product and services to outside providers for some time. In the early part of the 20th century, car manufacturers made all parts for a car, assembled, and sold it. In other words, the manufacturer carried out all tasks, from design to production to sale of a car. Gradually, manufacturing of certain parts such as the windshield and seats were outsourced to other companies that could produce them more cost effectively. Parts produced by these outside providers were often of higher quality because they focused on the core competencies. With the positive returns in cost and quality, auto manufacturers increased their outsourcing to the point that the majority of parts for a car were produced by outside vendors. Today, the primary focus of car manufacturers is assembling cars for distribution.

The outsourcing trend continued and was expanded by others, such as the airline industry, finance companies, and online service providers. Kodak outsourced its information systems services in 1989. Information systems outsourcing began with the hiring of external consultants to aid in areas where companies did not have sufficient internal expertise. Soon, every information systems task was a candidate for outsourcing, and vendors such as Electronic Data Systems (EDS) could provide information systems services of all types to companies of all sizes.

Information systems is going through similar sourcing phases as manufacturing did previously. The outsourcing of IS began with the hiring of external consultants to aid in areas where companies did not have sufficient skills to accomplish the range of necessary IS activities. As early as 1963, EDS contracted with Blue Cross of Pennsylvania to handle its data processing. In 1989, Kodak outsourced most of its IT to IBM and two other vendors. This was a large, prominent, and comprehensive outsourcing contract that involved the hiring of many of Kodak's IS personnel by IBM. From that point, IS/IT outsourcing became very visible, grew rapidly, and has evolved to include offshore outsourcing. Clearly, advances in communication and computer technologies in recent years have made this option more viable, and offshoring opportunities more feasible, particularly in the service domain.

Just as auto firms began outsourcing to achieve cost efficiencies only to find that quality, and eventually delivery time, also improved, some argue that the same scenario will be played out in offshoring IS. Already, some companies that have outsourced call-center operations to India report that customer satisfaction has increased. Overall, the quality gap appears to be closing rapidly. Many software development teams in India use Six Sigma approaches to quality management that are equivalent to those in use in world-class firms. This is a set of quality practices originally developed by Motorola but inspired by Edward Deming's methods (see Section 12.2) to systematically improve processes by eliminating defects. Given the abundance of skills at offshore sites as well as pressure on executives to drive down costs, there is little doubt that this trend to offshore will continue, and even increase, for some time, even if some firms have decided to return to home-based call centers as a result of some customer complaints.

While cost savings is often a primary reason for offshoring and the expectations are that significant savings will occur, the level and extent of these savings remains the subject of considerable debate. Quantifying costs and benefits may be complex even in the simplest case of manufacturing and assembling a physical product.

It is well recognized by academics and professionals that firms must focus their resources on their *core competency*—that is, they must spend their resources promoting the major aspects of their business. For example, if a firm is a retail business, its core competency will be the procurement and sales of products that they want to be known for. A company that is in the business of manufacturing certain household goods must develop its core competency for producing and selling that product. A company in the music business must be competent in signing up artists and producing and distributing music. While these organizations need information systems for their operation, they do not need to be expert in developing and maintaining hardware and software. They can outsource these non-core services to outside providers.

The reasons organizations outsource their information systems services are varied. Some of the more important factors behind outsourcing information systems are shown in Exhibit 11.2.

---

### Exhibit 11.2   Outsourcing Factors

- Cost economics
- Inadequate internal expertise and talent pool
- Rapid technology change
- Poor chargeback systems for information systems services
- Emphasis on core competency
- Top management discomfort with technology
- Management innovation
- Management imitation
- Changing goals and objectives

---

Today, almost all organizations outsource in one way or another to produce and provide services. Some companies are primarily responsible for "warehousing" their outsourcing decisions. These companies do not produce any product or provide any services themselves; they manage communications and relationships and outsource all other operations. For example, a book publisher may only agree to the contract with the author internally and outsource the rest—editing, printing, binding, distribution, organizing copyright protection, and reprint management—to outside providers. High bandwidth and sophisticated computing facilities have made virtual organizations a reality. We can accomplish more in less time, with less cost, and with better quality.

While many organizations outsource their information systems activities, there are many others that decide on the in-house development option. For example, Wal-Mart, the giant American retailer, develops and maintains all of its business information systems projects internally. They rely on internal expertise and management for the full range of information systems tasks, from coding to process reengineering to e-commerce applications. Every year, thousands of information systems projects are developed and maintained centrally by Wal-Mart employees. Wal-Mart's unprecedented success in the retail industry is credited to a large extent to their innovative and aggressive use of information technology. (A similar story is reflected by the Tesco retail chain in the UK.) The success of their supply-chain management processes is primarily due to state-of-the-art technology application. Clearly, Wal-Mart considers information systems function as a critical success factor, too important for their operations to be outsourced. Other firms are less convinced by the arguments for keeping the IT and IS provision internal to the organization.

Although outsourcing has been practiced for a long time, there is still an *emotional reaction* to the phenomenon within and outside organizations. This is partly due to the way that the popular press and public officials have treated the outsourcing phenomenon.

Reactions to information technology outsourcing have been extreme: Some have considered it to be a panacea, others a source of all ills. Neither position is correct. Many of the earlier predictions about outsourcing and its consequences turned out to be premature. The numbers of information systems jobs went through unprecedented growth and contributed significantly to the economies of the United States and Western Europe even during times of high outsourcing development.

There has been a great deal of interest on the part of academics and practitioners to understand issues of *whether* and *how* to outsource information systems services better. The sourcing issue is said to be among the top five agenda items for information systems executives. This is understandable, since more than 50% of American firms used outsourcing in 2006. We need to understand socioeconomic impacts of outsourcing better, on the individual and on organizations. The potential impacts are real, and organizations need to practice outsourcing with a clear understanding of what it implies to their short- and long-term objectives. As described in Chapter 2, the need for the project and its outcome must be continually reinforced in the context of organizational goals and objectives.

Information systems managers and professionals continue to have the highest opportunities and challenges in modern organizations. In the 1990s it seemed like information technology had provided us with all that was possible. Yet, technology has continued to surpass expectations, and users have continued to explore new potentials and frontiers not imagined before. Information systems executives and professionals are afforded unprecedented opportunities for value-added offerings. Organizations of all sizes can reach out and benefit from talents beyond national borders. The economic and business logic of outsourcing is extended to include offshore sourcing of information systems services. There are many information systems providers in many nations. In effect, information systems activities can be outsourced to providers outside the company and outside the country.

## 11.2. Offshoring IS Activities

While outsourcing was caused by the emphasis on organizations sticking to their core competencies, offshoring was caused by scarce resources. *Offshore outsourcing* occurs when products and services are procured from locations in other countries. Offshore outsourcing of information systems services is, arguably, the most significant phenomenon to occur in recent decades. American Express has been offshoring their back-office processing services in India since 1994. GE Capital opened its GE Capital International Services (GECIS) in India in 1997. Given the abundance of skilled professionals at offshore sites as well as pressure on executives to drive down costs, it is very likely that this trend will continue and even increase for some time, despite negative public reaction.

Many of these outsourcing vendors are "offshore" in large part because of the lower costs that can be attained outside of countries in the industrialized West. This exploitation of international cost differentials has been termed "global arbitrage," as it is an extension of the classic economic arbitrage strategy.

Factors influencing offshoring decisions are somewhat different from outsourcing, as a comparison of Exhibits 11.2 and 11.3 shows.

---

**Exhibit 11.3  Offshoring Factors**

- Bandwidth growth and telecommunication
- Scarce human expertise
- Increased demand
- Available global talents
- Routine tasks
- Changing goals and objectives
- Innovation
- Imitation

---

Offshore outsourcing of information systems activities is broadly accomplished in one of two ways. *First,* the client or offshoring organization sets up units in other countries and hires local talent to develop, maintain, and provide services. In this case, the company maintains responsibility for training, supervision, quality control, and the like. These responsibilities can be managed locally or remotely. *Second,* the client or offshoring organization contracts out services to providers in locations in other countries. In this case, responsibility for hiring, training, supervision, quality control, and the like rests with the provider.

An Association for Computing Machinery report (listed in the bibliography at the end of this chapter) describes six varieties of work related to information systems that are often offshored: (1) programming, software testing, and software maintenance; (2) information systems research and development; (3) high-end jobs such as software architecture, product design, project management, information systems consulting, and business strategy; (4) physical product manufacturing—semiconductors, computer components, computers; (5) business process outsourcing/IT enabled services—insurance claim processing, medical billing, accounting, bookkeeping, medical transcription, digitization of engineering drawings, desktop publishing, and high-end IT enabled services such as financial analysis and the reading of X-rays; and (6) call centers and telemarketing.

While information systems outsourcing took jobs outside the organization, offshoring transferred jobs and services to locations outside the country. In the outsourcing case, the talent pool was limited to national boundaries, whereas with offshoring that limitation is lifted. Both client and vendors of services have access to the greater pool of global talent. The range of information systems activities that are offshored has increased to the point that all activities that were traditionally outsourced can now be offshored. The cost of information systems products and services provided by offshore vendors can be significantly lower, and the quality of product and services in some case has been considerably higher than through in-shore provisions.

Controlling information systems development and maintenance costs is necessary for an organization in general and the information systems function in particular. In the early days of computers, investment in hardware, software, and IS products and personnel faced little scrutiny. Information systems services were considered special, and organizations felt that they could not afford to fall behind in technology investment, even if they did not fully understand where the money went. Top management and senior executives readily provided and supported information systems investment. Today, information systems activities are still considered important to short- and long-term objectives of organizations, but their costs and investment proposals are more carefully scrutinized. At the same time, expectations of information systems continue to rise.

Information systems stakeholders often develop and hold expectations of technology deliverables that are not always realistic. For example, there is a common perception that computers can do anything and everything. There is also a common perception that computers are responsible for whatever goes wrong in a workplace or in serving customers. These unrealistic expectations present a challenge to information systems executives who need to continually seek funding support from top management. The extent and quality of systems use is influenced to a large extent by users' competency and self-efficacy.

Technology in and of itself does not create value. Technology users create value in the fusion of doing and learning. In other words, value is generated by human–computer interaction. These inherent characteristics of computer and information technologies have posed and continue to pose challenges and provide opportunities for management. The offshoring phenomenon expands the scope for interaction, and this adds new dimensions. Top management and information systems executives see in offshoring opportunities to reallocate resources and focus on innovative and new services that were not previously available or affordable. While many tasks are offshored, others are retained and expanded, and this may give firms a new edge.

## 11.3. Risks in Offshore Outsourcing IS Activities

Any business decision involves risks, and that risk is greater in situations when there is increased *change* or *uncertainty*. The best option, however, is not to avoid decisions or to wait and see what might happen elsewhere. The pressure on CEOs and CIOs to reduce costs is real, and there is no sign that it will be lifted any time soon. Good management practice suggests careful assessment of potential risks for any decision. Although offshore outsourcing of information systems services has been going on for some time now, our understanding of its impact is still evolving. The trend in offshoring has been rapid, and there is little doubt that it will continue in the foreseeable future. It is critical that offshored projects are carefully studied and cost–benefit analyses are carried out to make sure benefits overweigh costs beyond a margin. Only significant cost benefits will warrant offshore outsourcing of information systems services. With only a marginal cost benefit of say 10–15%, most organizations are better off retaining their information systems activities in-house or in-shore.

The offshore outsourcing of information systems activities is primarily based on *transaction cost economics*. That rationale is narrowed down to the *cost of labor* to a large extent. There is an extant discourse among academics, professionals, and business leaders as to the exact nature of this cost advantage. In many cases, this cost advantage is evident. However, there is a risk in (a) overestimating the cost saving,

(b) underestimating the overhead costs that are necessary to get to the cost saving stage, and (c) discounting non-cost factors that influence offshore outsourcing outcome. The *tangible* transaction-cost economics of offshore outsourcing is more readily measured by economics and cost accounting models. The *intangible* costs or benefits of offshore outsourcing include issues of organization, behavior, morale, social, strategy, and the like, and these require acute management skills and insight.

These issues, it can be argued, relate to most organizations, whether or not they practice offshore outsourcing. However, in the case of offshore outsourcing in general (and offshore outsourcing information systems activities in particular), these issues take new dimensions and importance. For example, **organization intelligence** is a critical and volatile asset, particularly as it relates to activities such as new ventures and research and development. Organizations are highly protective of such information. Organization design, intelligence, and decision making have been formed and influenced by such information content. It is inconceivable to think that a large multinational corporation can function without timely, accurate, and relevant information. Decisions to offshore outsourced information systems activities must be carefully deliberated for their potential impact on current and future operations of a firm. In this section we will review important potential risks associated with offshore outsourcing decisions.

A recent study at the Johns Hopkins University surveyed senior IT managers in North America and Western Europe to identify the benefits and risks associated with offshoring IT activities. Risks to offshoring, these managers believe, stem from "the political situation in a host country" (political unrest, wars, confiscations, nationalizations, terrorism); "enforcement of intellectual property rights" (legal processes, loss of intellectual property rights, propitiatory design features, piracy, trademark infringements); "information vulnerability and security" (lack of regulation, different work ethics); "immature business environments" (volatile exchange rate, weak national currency, high tax rate, high tariffs on imports and exports, rigid customs laws, technological infrastructure); and "sociocultural problems" (misinterpretations, population attitude toward entrepreneurship).

Bill King and Yogesh Malhotra also identified a number of generic risks associated with IT outsourcing as compared with performing IT activities within the firm. They indicate that there is a growing awareness of the difficulties that are inherent in offshoring, pointing out that hidden structural, cultural, legal, and financial risk and costs can easily be overlooked.

Offshore outsourcing risks of information systems activities stem from the factors shown in Exhibit 11.4.

One of the potential risks of offshore outsourcing information systems services relates to **employee morale.** The reaction to information systems offshoring by individuals has been greater than that of outsourcing. This is despite our experience with outsourcing of information systems services that ultimately resulted in the increased application and use of computers. It is difficult to assess and measure the risk related to employee morale. The impact can broadly be grouped in terms of reduced employee *loyalty* and diminished *work quality*. Individuals tend to explore job opportunities elsewhere as soon as it is apparent that services might be offshored. Skilled and

---

**Exhibit 11.4  Risks of Offshore Outsourcing**

- Decline in employee morale
- Loss of innovation and know-how
- Public reaction to corporate citizenship
- Regional instability of host country
- Quality control and standards
- Communications and culture

---

valuable employees will find jobs more quickly, and their departure will affect the quality of work and services. This poses great challenges for the project manager.

Human expertise and innovation is the greatest asset that any organization can develop and retain. Thus, loss of *innovation and know-how* in applying technology due to offshore outsourcing of information systems services can pose the greatest risk to an organization. Many successful businesses, such as Federal Express, American Airlines, Wal-Mart, American Hospital Supplies, and United Parcel Services, owe their competitive advantage to the creative use of information technologies. It takes longer and costs more to develop savvy business employees who are technically competent. It is very expensive for a firm to build up its human expertise if it decides later to revert to in-house services; it is difficult to rehire skilled employees who have taken up positions with other firms, possibly with the competition. It is difficult to buy back lost loyalty.

Public loyalty to a firm and its goods and services is influenced by how people perceive the role of a firm as a corporate citizen. Corporate CEOs and other senior executives cannot ignore *public reaction to corporate citizenship*. As mentioned earlier, there has been a greater reaction by the public to offshoring practice compared with outsourcing. This is partly because of the way that the popular press has treated offshore practices, as mentioned earlier, and partly because computer and information technologies have been considered one of the greatest innovations ever to affect U.S. and Western European economies. In other words, the offshoring of information technology activities is considered more than sending jobs abroad. Some of the big corporations, such as IBM and Oracle, have been secretive about their offshoring practice and have at the same time increased publicity about their community and society contribution.

All this suggests the potential risks of a negative public reaction to offshore outsourcing. *Regional instability of the host country* is another risk associated with offshore outsourcing practice. For example, the threat of major disruptions arising from political upheaval or war in an offshore host country could pose a major risk to service continuity. A politically stable region with higher wages is a better host site for business planning. It is difficult to evaluate labor economics when issues of potential instability are present. Businesses need to examine the long-term effect on their business plans from short term-gains in wages carefully. Backup sites outside the region and careful security checks on contractors are sometime necessary and are added costs of doing business in locations in other countries.

Inadequate *quality control and standards* is another potential risk associated with offshore outsourcing of information systems services. Reliability and quality of services are crucial to computer and information systems. System downtime affects all operations of a business and its competitive strength. Customer service and customer satisfaction are directly influenced by the reliability and timeliness of information systems services. At the end of the day it is the responsibility of the information systems function in a firm to ensure steady and reliable services in support of operations. Compliance with standards and enforcement of quality may reflect the vendor's goals rather than the client's needs. Project managers must ensure that provisions of quality and standards are clearly outlined in contracts with offshore vendors and that they align with the goals and objectives of the client.

The role of *communication and culture* in the successful delivery of information systems services through offshoring cannot be overstated. Success of information systems project development in remote sites is heavily influenced by effective communications and clear understanding of local culture. Information systems project failure has often been associated with inadequate needs analysis resulting from poor communications. This can be more of an issue in offshore outsourcing practices. Understanding organizational culture has also been a factor in the success of information systems projects. Communications are more complex and culture is more diverse for offshore development projects. There is a risk that project development teams may take these complexities too lightly in the interests of time and cost and as a result adversely affect the quality and timeliness of information systems services.

## 11.4. Opportunities and Challenges

Information systems is an evolving discipline with unique opportunities and challenges for the management of this function. These opportunities and challenges are closely linked with management strategies and responsibilities for the information systems function. Important responsibilities are listed in Exhibit 11.5. Information systems project management has also been evolving over time in response to the growing needs for enterprise-wide systems. Organizations invest in and expect from information systems a great deal, and that in turn brings about tremendous responsibilities. Contract management adds important new dimensions to project management. These include negotiation, monitoring, and communications infrastructure. Managing cultural diversity is another important dimension added to project management. These are discussed in Section 11.5.

The long-term view of economic theorists suggests greater returns for offshore practice. Several important factors affect offshore practice decisions, including where to offshore, infrastructure at vendor site, business conditions, and potential risks. However, *low-wage* and *skilled labor* have been the overriding factors influencing decisions to offshore information systems services. So far, offshoring white-collar jobs to low-wage regions of the globe provides significant cost advantage to firms in the United States and Western Europe. These gains may not be permanent.

The adverse effect of offshore outsourcing information systems services has been primarily on the current job market. However, this effect is more complex than

## Exhibit 11.5 Responsibilities

- Develop a vision for the role and contribution of technology in the organization.
- Define an overall hardware and software architecture to include platforms and communications.
- Coordinate developmental activities across the organization.
- Develop and implement security plans.
- Develop and implement contingency plans.
- Manage technology transfer and infusion.
- Manage vendors.
- Rationalize funding and manage expectations.
- Manage turnover.
- Promote innovation.
- Support users.
- Provide guidelines for information systems use and application.
- Develop and mentor IS expertise.
- Ensure alignment with organizational goals and objectives.
- Ensure regulatory compliance.
- Ensure security and privacy of personal information.

simply jobs leaving the United States and Western Europe to other regions of the world. While some jobs currently held by information systems professionals will be lost to offshore destinations, new jobs that require different skills will be created in response to the increased demand for information systems services. Savings will enable firms to invest in newer technologies and innovative use of information services. This in turn will generate new higher level jobs and higher turnover. New jobs will require greater expertise in *business knowledge, systems analysis, communication, integration, team work, quality control, risk assessment, and contingency planning*. As described in various chapters of this book, effective project management requires these skills.

There has been a great deal of discourse about the short- and long-term effects of offshore outsourcing practice in academic and professional publications. Some of this discussion relates to the overall effects of offshoring, while others, more specifically, discuss these effects in terms of core competency, firm size, and organization culture. Yet, others discuss these effects relative to the information systems job market or national employment (see also Section 7.8). These future trends and consequences have been summed up by Stephanie Overby in an article that incorporates comments by several senior information systems executives, listed below in Exhibit 11.6.

There is little doubt that information technologies and those who know how to manage them will continue to play an important role in the success of modern organizations. The key is to retool and stay current in order to be able to respond to new and evolving business needs. In this chapter and throughout this book, we have tried to describe and provide the kind of skill sets that are needed to prepare our information system graduates for new and challenging jobs.

---

**Exhibit 11.6    Effects of Offshoring on U.S. Jobs (Stephanie Overby)**

1. IT jobs will be lost to offshore companies.

2. U.S. IT staffing levels will never return to their previous highs.

3. IT work that remains will be more important to the business.

4. Firms will continue to offshore application development, legacy maintenance, call-center operations, and the like.

5. American companies will keep work that requires close contact with the business, such as strategy development, business process improvement, and actual application of IT, in the business.

6. IT will become a core competency and economic engine in emerging economies, and these emerging economies will complement the U.S. IT industry.

7. American IT executives look beyond the possible short-term offshore savings to the long-term impact on the nation's ability to remain innovative.

8. The higher-level IT positions that remain will require new skills.

9. American IT degree programs should move more toward broader business education.

10. The IT cohort of the future has to be a good technologist but also be a savvy businessperson, a hybrid and versatile person.

11. Issues of infrastructure, security, communication, and project management are important to onshore jobs.

12. There is a need to protect intellectual capital, especially when IT is integrated in business processes.

---

Looking at the U.S. situation in particular, information systems is the third largest corporate expense category, and about 50% of U.S. capital expenditures by businesses are in IS/IT. This suggests that the potential for offshore outsourcing is huge. However, information system offshoring is only one small part of a much broader phenomenon that has enormous implications for Western industrialized countries (whose firms are typically the offshoring clients) and for developing nations (whose firms are typically the offshoring vendors).

In an article (*Foreign Affairs,* March/April 2006), Princeton University economist and former Federal Reserve Board vice chairman Alan Blinder identified the impact on the West by saying

> The world is now in the early stages of a third Industrial Revolution—the information age. The cheap and easy flow of information around the globe has vastly expanded the scope of tradable services, and there is much more to come. Industrial revolutions are big deals. And just like the previous two, the third Industrial Revolution will require vast and unsettling adjustments in the way Americans and residents of other developed countries work, live, and educate their children.

In saying this, Blinder suggested that we must understand the growing offshoring phenomenon better and develop management practices that are appropriate for this new environment. It will not be possible to manage IS as we have done in the past, and it will be necessary for information system professionals to develop their skill sets that are commensurate with managing in an offshoring-intensive context. Information systems offshoring is expected to expand the global use and application of information technologies. As described in this chapter, there are opportunities in this new era of global IT growth, and information systems professionals need to prepare in accordance with the new realities to better position themselves for the evolving job market.

Given this understanding, the nature and structure of information systems application and use in firms will change drastically in the future. The information systems function will shrink in many firms in the industrialized economies. The significance and the role of information systems in business will, however, remain strong. The type and level of information systems services will continue to proliferate and grow. Some information systems jobs will return onshore. Only a small fraction of total service jobs in the industrialized economies will go to offshore vendors. Information systems curricula will be revamped and information systems programs will produce necessary cohorts for the new challenges. The service industry in the United States and Western Europe will grow, and trade surpluses in services will increase.

Given this reality, information systems professionals need to learn to cope with the accelerated pace of job change and turnover. This also means that information systems jobs will remain competitive and out of the reach of non-skilled workers. The use of technology has increased over the years due to more user-friendly software tools and applications. The scope and nature of jobs for information systems professionals has also changed in spite of the increased role and responsibilities of the end-user. The changes created by the offshore outsourcing phenomenon will not diminish the role and significance of information systems services or of those with the know-how to manage it.

# 11.5. The Management of Offshore Information Systems Projects

The offshore outsourcing phenomenon has had a wide-ranging effect on the management of the information systems function. The first wave of offshore outsourcing practice reduced hardware costs and in turn increased demand for software. The new surge in offshore outsourcing has reduced software costs and in turn increased demand for information systems applications and services. The international value chain has made information technology more affordable to firms of all sizes and types. It has expanded the global application and use of information systems and created opportunities for information systems professionals to respond to the specific needs of businesses.

Offshore outsourcing of information systems services has added new dimensions to duties and responsibilities of project managers. Systems that are developed at remote sites in different countries are more difficult to manage due to differences in *culture, language, time zone, labor law, work habits*, and the like. These issues are relevant even to cases when a firm operates its own offshore practice. This section will describe specific sets of skills required for the successful management of offshore projects. These skills are listed in Exhibit 11.7 and discussed below. It is important to realize that many of these project management responsibilities are not new, but that they assume increased importance in the era of offshore outsourcing.

---

**Exhibit 11.7   Skills Required for the Successful Management of Offshore Projects**

- Contract negotiation and management
- Relationship management
- Risk assessment and management
- Planning and integration
- Business process redesign
- Enterprise needs analysis and testing
- Security and privacy planning

---

Project managers are often involved with *negotiation and management of contracts* with international vendors for the delivery of information systems services. Many firms have their legal division draw and finalize these offshore contracts. However, project managers play a crucial role in identifying and outlining information needs for these offshore contracts. In this process, project managers often interact directly with offshore vendors to negotiate and clarify responsibilities. Communication skills and clear understanding of the culture and language of offshore vendors are essential to successful negotiation.

Project managers are responsible for the development and *management of relationships* between their team members and offshore service providers. Routine and effective collaboration and interaction between client and vendor teams is heavily influenced by relationship management. While it is necessary to have responsibilities outlined in a contract, it is essential to establish a good relationship to facilitate effective collaboration. Relationship management is influenced by a clear understanding of culture, language, and the habits of offshore providers.

Chapter 10 described the importance of risk assessment and management for information systems projects. Section 11.3 above outlines and discusses potential risks associated with offshore outsourcing of information systems activities. *Risk assessment and risk management* of offshore projects is especially difficult. For example, risks associated with local politics, natural disaster, and communication and network infrastructure in offshore locations are more difficult to assess and manage. Project managers must plan for disaster recovery and backup provisions in locations outside the vendor country.

Systems *planning and integration* also takes a new dimension in offshore outsourcing practice. This may turn out to be a critical problem if the outsourcing firm reduces internal expertise to the point that planning and integration of information systems services becomes dependent on outside vendors. Project managers must carefully assess and retain internal expertise in order to plan and integrate information systems needs in alignment with organizational goals and objectives. This includes expertise to *redesign business processes* to reap the benefits of offshore provision. Information systems innovation inherently requires careful analysis of business processes and often leads to the redesign of these processes.

Chapter 2 describes how important it is for project managers to realize and understand business goals and objectives. As mentioned earlier, there is a need to retain, mentor, and manage employees that are business savvy and have technical competency. That skill set is always needed for *enterprise needs analysis and testing* of information systems that are developed by vendors outside the organization. Some information systems needs analysis requires intimate knowledge of business operations and intelligence. Firms are sensitive about their business knowledge and intelligence, and the cost of retaining internal expertise for needs analysis and testing is well justified in the long term.

*Security and privacy* continues to be an important issue for the individual and organization. Issues of security and privacy have assumed greater importance in recent years on priority lists of information systems executives and project managers. These issues continue to pose challenges for management because the technology continues to grow and information systems applications continue to expand. That is true even in cases where a firm develops and maintains its entire information systems services. Offshore outsourcing of these activities will amplify challenges to secure the information systems and keep private personal information.

As mentioned earlier, the effect of offshore outsourcing information systems activities is wide ranging, for both the individual and the organization. The range of effects for the individual includes *career, skills, relationships, privacy*, and other considerations. The range of effects for the organization includes *intelligence, knowledge, human expertise, security*, and the like. A great deal of offshore outsourcing that has already taken place has been to English-speaking countries such as India. However, a common language does not mean common culture, habit, procedure, law, environment, and the like. Communications consist of a great deal more than language. Firms and organizations have begun to realize that a common language does not eliminate communication difficulties. That is why it is critical for management to develop and retain individuals who clearly understand the business and are competent in technology application.

In a recent article published in the *Journal of the Association for Information Systems* (cited in the bibliography at the end of this chapter), Gordon Davis and colleagues suggest that management must always retain the ability to anticipate and monitor technological change. These changes are because of technology growth or those that a vendor makes to the technology applications. Many organizations have realized after offshoring their information systems practices that they need to monitor changes in technology and to evaluate new developments in hardware and software independently. Appraising new developments becomes more difficult as a firm increases its offshore practice and salespersons redirect their marketing and promotional efforts toward outside vendors. Salespersons have traditionally been a useful outside source for providing information about new developments in hardware and software. These outside links will gradually disappear because the offshoring client is no longer a potential customer.

Many of the issues associated with offshore outsourcing were not initially apparent to the management of information systems services. The opening case in this chapter illustrates some of the nuances presented by offshore outsourcing practice. The offshoring phenomenon is still at its early stage. Management must continually monitor and observe experiences gained by the firm and by others outside. Information systems professionals have long realized the need for ongoing improvement and self-learning. Management must encourage and support self-learning by employees.

Information systems curricula at universities increasingly emphasize the need for "learning to learn." It is not possible to learn everything about technology and its management in the classroom or through a degree. Information systems graduates need to continue developing their technical and managerial skills after graduation. Continual improvement and self-learning provide opportunities for career enhancement. Information systems professionals must be able to retool quickly to take advantage of new developments and add value to their organization. Demand for skilled information systems people has been and continues to be strong. Exhibit 11.8 lists a few simple but practical hints in this respect.

---

### Exhibit 11.8    Hints for Career Enhancement

- Make self-learning a hobby.
- Observe to learn.
- Listen to learn.
- Ask others for input.
- Learn from mistakes.
- Take time to review your work.
- Develop network.
- Learn about diversity.

---

### 11.6. Interview With a Project Manager

What specific factors in your opinion are important to offshore outsourcing of information systems activities?

"We need more time up front to study whether we want to go this route and then whom we might want to go with. If you end up outsourcing those applications that have taken your people a long time to get the kinks out and to get the users to be happy with, you may have a job on your hands. If you ask five different project managers about their experience with offshoring, you probably will get five different responses, and that is because not all applications that have been outsourced are the same and not all providers are the same. When we outsourced our computer applications it took us some time to get our communications straightened with the outside vendor. Now it will be a lot more complicated to outsource our applications to a vendor in another country. That is what I mean by putting time up front to make sure you know what you are doing."

What are the implications of offshoring for internal information systems skills and know-how?

"The first thing you will notice is that there are rumors among your staff that jobs are going to be lost and people are going to be let go, and that is a problem. Some of the people will start looking for other jobs. Your skilled and experienced people will find jobs quickly. You may end up with a serious problem when you lose your experienced and skilled people. For example, if you plan to keep 50% of your people, you may end up keeping the 50% you don't want."

What is in your opinion the best strategy to avoid that kind of personnel problem? What is the best strategy to avoid losing good people in a situation like that?

"I don't know about the best strategy. Your skilled people are the most valuable resource that you have, and you must do what you can to protect and keep them. Timely and truthful communication always helps. You need to let people know what decisions are being made and why those decisions are important to the long-term goals of the information systems division. You also want to let people that you want to keep know that in the event that some jobs are offshored, you intend to keep them. It all depends on how extensive your organization's offshore plans are."

What are the legal and procedural challenges posed by offshore outsourcing of information systems services?

"There are a lot of details in writing a contract with outside vendors, and it is best to leave that to legal people in the organization. As a project manager, you should be aware of the principles involved and you should be clear about responsibilities. You want to be clear about responsibilities of your team and those of the vendor. That should be clear in the contract. Once we had a contract with an outside vendor and every time we had an issue and needed clarification from the contract it was difficult. Our main problem was about user support responsibilities. We lived through the contract terms but revised it next time it was renewed. It is important to keep records of issues as they come up."

Do you think your users will blame offshore providers for information systems problems?

"That depends on how much the users think the outside provider is responsible for. That is why it is important to make things clear in the contract and also to let users know who is responsible for what. Ultimately, there are some responsibilities that you don't want to offshore. Whatever you pick up that others do not will gain you support among users."

What are those responsibilities that you do not want to offshore? Can you give an example?

"Those are the kind of responsibilities that involve intelligence and the internal workings of the organization. For example, if your internal communication and information sharing is primarily done by email, you may not want to offshore your email services. People tend to say a lot by email, and it accumulates."

What in your opinion are important differences in the evaluation of offshore versus in-house services?

"The evaluation of offshore services is linked to the terms of the contract. You want to make sure what is contracted is delivered in good time and with quality. There is also the quality of interaction with employees of the offshore service providers. Development and management of those relationships are important, and it is up to both sides to make it work."

## 11.7. Chapter Summary

Offshore outsourcing of information systems activities is based on transaction-cost economics. Firms have always looked for ways to reduce costs of producing goods and delivering services. Although some information systems costs such as hardware, software, and communications networks have steadily declined over the years, other costs such as human expertise, maintenance, and security have gradually increased. This has resulted in a net increase for the overall cost of information systems services. In response to cost pressure, firms have in recent years adopted two important strategies: (1) Outsource information systems activities or in some cases the entire function, to national vendors, and (2) offshore information systems services to global vendors.

The outsourcing and offshoring phenomena have had important effects on the management of technology in general and on project management in particular. Probably the most important impact of outsourcing and offshoring for information systems professionals has been on the job market and skills. The outsourcing trend resulted in significant employee turnover. In most cases, laid-off employees were hired by vendors in need of skilled workers. Ultimately, outsourcing increased the demand for information systems services and thus professionals. The need for information systems professionals grew to the point that there was a shortage of skilled workers in the United States and Western Europe.

The offshoring trend, on the other hand, has affected the job market and skills somewhat differently. Information systems jobs as well as services have been offshored to vendors in locations outside the United States and Western Europe. Many of the more routine information systems activities have been offshored, and the number of current jobs has been reduced. The jobs that remain in the United States and Western Europe require higher skills: increased business knowledge, systems analysis, project management, communication, and the like. As with outsourcing, offshoring has made information systems more affordable, once again increasing the overall demand for information systems services.

While outsourcing and offshoring have similar characteristics, they differ in several ways. Probably the most important distinction between outsourcing and offshoring stems from the role of culture in vendor nations. Understanding local culture as well as labor law, work environment, habits, and the like are important to the success of offshore projects. Negotiation and relationship management are important new responsibilities for information systems executives and project managers. Team development, communication, quality control, risk analysis, planning, and security and privacy assume a new emphasis in the project development process.

Offshoring has replaced many of the previous job and career opportunities with new ones, making it necessary for information systems professionals to retool in order to take advantage of new possibilities. Self-learning and ongoing improvement that have been important traits of information systems professionals assume even greater importance. Information systems professionals must quickly adapt to changing realities in order to add value to their organizations. The "learning to learn" idea has become more important than ever for information systems programs and students.

In summary: Efforts to reduce costs will continue; many current jobs will be lost to offshore locations; higher paying new jobs will be created that require higher skills; value-added principle continues to be the key; new realities require new thinking and new expertise; negotiation, innovation, business knowledge, communication, analysis, relationship, and diversity management assume greater importance. Global need for information systems services will continue to grow, creating opportunities and challenges for the information systems profession.

## DISCUSSION QUESTIONS

1. This chapter has argued that technology, in and of itself, does not provide value and that human–computer interaction generates value. What do you think of this assertion? Would offshore outsourcing of information systems services alter the effect of human–computer interaction as we know it?

2. Discuss the role and impact of offshore outsourcing on organization innovation and know-how. Take a long-term view of this issue and describe the role of management in the outcome.

3. The provision of information systems services continues to provide unique opportunities and challenges to the management of these technologies. Organization and user expectations are said to pose challenges and provide opportunities at the same time. Discuss how you would reconcile this apparent conflict. In what ways does offshore outsourcing of information systems services alter these challenges and opportunities?

4. Search the Web to find out more about some of the more successful offshore vendors such as Wipro, Infosys Technologies, and Tata Consultancy. Prepare a short summary of your findings for class discussion.

5. Assume you are the project manager responsible for the development of an integrated corporate-level database system. Top management in your company is concerned about your proposed costs to develop this system and has suggested that you consider offshore outsourcing some of the activities. Describe specifically what developmental activities you would offshore and what activities you would not.

6. Consider the opening case to this chapter. What specific suggestions would you offer Peggy Zhu in her current situation? What is the first thing she should do? What changes should she make in her daily work? How should she go about measuring the success of their offshore decision?

7. What risks other than the ones described in this chapter would you suggest might affect the offshore outsourcing of information systems projects? What methods would you use to assess those risks?

8. Is user involvement important to the success of offshore outsourcing information systems activities? How would you involve users in the design and development of offshored information systems projects?

9. Consider the following scenario. You are the project manager for the development of a corporate-level system such as the one mentioned above under Question 5. You were not

in favor of the decision to offshore those activities, and neither were your information systems personnel. The contract is final and you have been asked by the top management to facilitate user involvement with the development of this project. Describe your plans for doing that. With what activities, if any, would you involve the users and why?

10. This chapter suggests that common language does not mean common culture, habit, procedure, law, environment, and the like. It argues that communication is a great deal more than just the language and that common language does not eliminate communication difficulties. Discuss.

## EXERCISES

1. A widely used method of measuring information systems success is that of user satisfaction. You have recently contracted the development of one of your projects with an offshore provider in India. You need to identify factors that are important to users of that system. Identify critical success factors that you see as important to the users of that system. What is a good method to (a) identify those factors and (b) verify them to make sure they are important?

2. Schedule an interview with a project manager who has been involved with offshore outsourcing of information systems projects. Prepare a set of questions that include expected and unexpected difficulties, risks, personnel issues, quality control, and user response. Ask this project manager what is the one thing that he or she would do in any future offshore projects.

3. Search and find an article that argues in favor of offshore outsourcing information systems services and one article that argues against such decisions. Based on your reading of these two articles, prepare a table to compare and contrast the points in favor and against offshore outsourcing of information systems activities.

4. Refer to the interview with a project manager at the end of this chapter and list two points that you strongly agree with in the interview. Is there a point that you strongly disagree with in the interview?

5. As described in this chapter, Wal-Mart, the largest retailer in the world, runs its information systems operation entirely in-house. They also have an extensive training program that helps them develop and retain human expertise. Search and find information that describes Wal-Mart's information systems training strategy. What is unique about their training? How does it help them retain their information systems experts?

6. Offshore outsourcing of information systems services could potentially affect human expertise and organization know-how. To what extent can organizations afford to lower internal expertise? This chapter suggests that human expertise in planning and integrating information systems must be retained internally. Search and find articles that support or oppose that contention.

# APPENDIX TO CHAPTER 11: BELTECH INCORPORATED

## Background

Beltech Incorporated (BI) is a small firm that develops global positioning system (GPS) devices. BI's last year's sales were $3.1 million with a profit of $200,000. BI has a market share of 1% in a fiercely competitive market. BI's strategic goal is to gain an additional 2% in market share over the next 2 years. Like their competition, all of BI's products are proprietary in nature, using both proprietary software and hardware.

## Management

The firm has 18 employees with a small team of highly skilled engineers who develop the hardware and software for their products. Many of the functions of the firm such as payroll and marketing are outsourced to other firms who have the professional knowledge to support BI. BI is committed toward developing high-quality products. This is a necessary requirement due to strong competition from larger firms. BI promotes innovation and looks for ideas from all team members.

## Potential Opportunity

Recently, one of the employees presented an idea to management to use nonproprietary equipment for the basis of an innovative GPS product. The idea is to use common small, handheld computers as a medium for GPS hardware. This would provide an advantage because, for the most part, the software and hardware is already developed. This would also provide opportunities for a less expensive GPS and perhaps a quicker development cycle.

## PM Assignment

BI has assigned their project manager (PM) the responsibility to complete a feasibility study of the suggested product. The PM will need to perform research in order to complete the feasibility study. The PM will also need to coordinate within the company as well as their outsourcing partners to gain enough input for a comprehensive feasibility study. Additionally, some research will need to be performed to see how well the firm could utilize industry standard equipment and which firms would best welcome a partnership with BI.

## PM Research

The PM has found that there is a mature Personal Digital Assistant (PDA) market with a small computer that would be ideal for BI to base a hybrid device on. There are several good hardware manufacturers willing to partner with BI. There are two very good operating systems (OS) available for PDAs from which to choose. One OS is provided by Microsoft and is well supported. The second OS is just as robust and possibly the dominant PDA OS, which is provided by Palm. Both of the OSs are very mature with strong support from their prospective companies, who are both willing to partner with BI. The PM has also determined that the product can be developed in

*(Continued)*

(Continued)

about 20% of the time a usual product requires. This indicates significant development savings. The device's projected retail price will also be cost effective in comparison to current GPS products and will offer additional functionality above the standard GPS. An additional bonus has been found in the fact that there is strong potential for third-party programmers to develop applications for the new hybrid device, allowing unprecedented opportunities for software development and growth. The major obstacle is the potential that the new product may cause significant loss of sales to their current product line. To accomplish BI's strategic goal toward market share, BI will need to be willing to gamble away their current product line for the new hybrid product. There is also a concern that BI's competitors may be working on a similar product.

## Management Decision

The PM has identified several opportunities for a new product to facilitate strategic growth for BI. There is high risk involved. However, there is also good potential in exceptional success of the new product. The risk of erosion to the current product line is found to be acceptable. There is also the risk that BI's competitor may be working on a similar device. BI needs to be first on the market with a hybrid device or face the possibility of being forced out of business.

In summary, BI's management has decided to move forward with the project. Management is willing to support a new integrated PDA/GPS device, even at the risk of strong erosion of their current product line. It is anticipated that BI would gain strategic market share in the GPS market if they are first to market a quality hybrid device.

## APPENDIX TO CHAPTER 11: DISCUSSION QUESTIONS

1. Did the project manager perform sufficient research for the feasibility study to complete the assignment?

2. Should Beltech's management have used a larger project team and gather more information because of the impact the project could have on the company's core competency and products?

3. What do you think are the project manager's tools for conducting this important assignment?

4. Should the project manager have created and delivered more documents than the feasibility document mentioned?

5. Present cases for (a) in-house development, (b) outsourcing, and (c) offshoring some or all of the company's technology activities.

6. Role-play a discussion between the project manager with an outsourcing supplier and an offshoring supplier who both wish to "get the contract."

7. Search the Web for information about the Palm versus Microsoft operating system for the products mentioned. Provide a table of comparison.

# BIBLIOGRAPHY

Aspray, W., Mayadas, F., & Vardi, M. Y. (Eds.). (2006). *Globalization and offshoring of software: A report of the ACM job migration task force.* New York: Association for Computing Machinery. Available online at http://www.acm.org/globalizationreport

Association for Computing Machinery. (2005, March). ACM task force sharpens focus on IT globalization. *Member Net,* (4), 1.

Blinder, A. S. (2006, April/May). Offshoring: The next industrial revolution? *Foreign Affairs, 85*(2).

Carmel, E., & Agarwal, R. (2002, June). The maturation of offshore sourcing of information technology work. *MIS Quarterly Executive, 1*(2).

Davis, G. B., Ein-Dor, P., King, W. R., & Torkzadeh, G. (2006). IT offshoring: History, prospects and challenges. *Journal of the Association for Information Systems, 7*(11).

Dibbern, J. (2004). Information systems outsourcing: A survey and analysis of the literature. *DATA BASE for Advances in Information Systems, 35*(4).

Djavanshir, G. R. (2005, November/December). Surveying the risks and benefits of IT outsourcing. *IT Pro* (published by IEEE Computer Society), 32–37.

Hirschheim, R. A. (2004). Information systems outsourcing: A survey and analysis of the literature. *ACM SIGMIS Database, 35*(4).

Hirschheim, R. A., Heinzl, A., & Dibbern, J. (Eds.). (2006). http://www.amazon.com/Information-Systems-Outsourcing-Perspectives-Challenges/dp/3540348751/ref=sr_1_2/104-8528252-2507904?ie=UTF8&s=books&qid=1178014569&sr=1-2. Heidelberg, Germany: Springer.

King, W. R. (1994, Fall). Strategic outsourcing decisions. *Information Systems Management, 11*(4), 58–61.

King, W. R. (2004, Fall). Outsourcing and the future of IT. *Information Systems Management, 21*(4).

King, W. R., & Malhotra, Y. (2000, September). Developing a framework for analyzing IS sourcing. *Information and Management, 37*(6), 323–334.

King, W. R., & Torkzadeh, G. (2008, June). Information systems offshoring: Research status and issues. *MIS Quarterly, 32*(2), 205–225.

Matloff, N. (2004, November). Globalization and the American IT worker. *Communications of the ACM, 47*(11).

Overby, S. (2003). The future of jobs and innovation. *CIO,* December 15.

Rottman, J., & Lacity, M. (2006, Spring). Proven practices for effectively offshoring IT work. *Sloan Management Review, 47.*

Wang, T. G. (2002). Transaction attributes and software outsourcing success: An empirical investigation of transaction cost theory. *Information Systems Journal, 12.*

# 12

# Ensuring Project Quality

### Themes of Chapter 12

- ❖ What is the importance of system quality?
- ❖ What is the impact of quality on information systems developers?
- ❖ What are the principles of quality management?
- ❖ What is the role of quality standards?
- ❖ Who are the quality pioneers, and what is their contribution?
- ❖ What is the role of quality-control techniques?
- ❖ How can we evaluate system quality?

Quality matters, and information systems project managers must plan for it. Expectations of software quality have significantly increased over the recent years. Gone are the days that computer application users would accept software problems and system bugs as normal. Users expect the system to work! Information systems project managers are responsible for not only delivering the product on time and within the budget but also *with expected quality*. Information systems quality is defined in terms of user needs and system applicability. Quality must be in the mind of the project manager throughout the project. Users want information systems that help them carry out their tasks easily and effectively. They want information systems to help them save time rather than spend time managing them. This chapter will describe the importance of quality issues, emphasizing software quality, as it is an exemplar of quality issues associated with information systems as a whole. This chapter also describes ways of identifying such quality issues and planning for them. But we start with Exhibit 12.1, which discusses issues relating to choosing a computer system.

### Exhibit 12.1    What Do You Want From a Computer?

People treat stereotyping with contempt, but it seems they cannot resist it. We easily group people in terms of "what they wear" or "what they eat" or the "type of car they drive" or the "kind of work they do" or some other genre. We do the same when it comes to technology. For example, we group people as "gadget users," "high-tech people," "technophobes," "Internet addicts," and so on. You probably can add several new ones to the list.

People also seem to have their minds made up when it comes to computer attributes. There are those who seem to care only about "speed." For example, the first thing they ask you about your computer is "what is the speed?" There are others who seem to care only about "memory" size. For example, the first thing they ask you about your computer is "What's the gig on your computer?" Then there is the group of people who will first ask about software on your computer—audio, video, games, and the like. How did that happen?

In the early days of computers, information systems textbooks often used "speed" and "memory" to group computers into three categories of "mainframe," "mini," and "micro" computers. For example, a computer with so much speed and so much memory would be considered a mainframe, mini, or a micro computer. Of course this caused difficulty as computer speed and memory increased rapidly; soon a personal computer would have the same or even more speed and memory than earlier mainframe computers had. So describing computers in those terms was like hitting a moving target.

The same happened with computer software and applications. Increasingly, newer, more stable, more powerful, and more user-friendly software applications were developed at a lower cost. Thus the question of speed, memory, software application, and the like became less of an issue from the perspective of the individual user. At the same time, software companies came up with applications that did not exist before and marketed their product in terms of new and better features, usually as a turnkey system. In fact, most features imbedded in new software or computers are rarely if ever used.

Parallel to this, users grew more knowledgeable and less afraid of trying computers. Using a computer required less and less programming skills. Online as well as in-house computer training programs prepared an increased number of users who could use a computer to tackle basic tasks. The combination of powerful hardware, user-friendly software, declining prices, and savvy users created exceptional demand for computer and information systems. This all happened in a matter of a couple of decades.

It is difficult to predict where technology might take us next. Expert predictions about technology trend in the past have been by and large incorrect. We know that the technology will change and we know that those changes will affect our work life, but we do not know the nature and the extent of that change. It is remarkable how quickly we adapt to new technology and how fast we apply it to our benefit. Some will argue that technology is developed to meet our needs. Others will argue that technology maps its own trend and we adapt what is offered to our needs.

The reality is that both sides have compromised. Technology has been developed to meet our needs, and we have learned to take advantage of what it offers. Most people think deductively—that is, they are good at defining a problem then seeking a solution for it. Others think inductively—that is, they see a tool then look for problems it might solve. The latter approach to using technology has produced higher rewards as well as higher risk because it leads to the development of applications that are outside the usual boundaries.

People need a machine that is easy to use, is reliable, and is inexpensive. What they get out of it, by and large, depends on their skill, their innovativeness, their willingness to experiment, and their level of motivation. Concerns about megahertz or gigahertz and megabytes or gigabytes are to a large extent irrelevant. The technology has matured to the point that its potential is limited only by the aptitude of the individual user. The bottleneck is our creativity, not the power, speed, or memory of the computer.

## 12.1. Quality Matters

In the past, many information technology products were developed with little or no consideration for software quality control. Information technology project managers were primarily concerned with deadlines and resource constraints; they were inundated with requests for application development. New software products were expected to have "bugs." Networks were expected to fail several times a day. Users were expected to cope with software quality issues until a new version was introduced. New software versions would remove old bugs only to introduce new ones. People joked about computer programs and blamed computer systems for all their problems, even those that had nothing to do with computers. There are many examples in the news about quality-related problems; indeed, we have reported on many through the exhibits and case studies presented in this book.

Increasingly, software quality has become a critical success factor, and developers have significantly increased their attention to it. Sponsors of information systems expect to see quality control as part of project development plans. Information technology project managers are responsible not only for delivering product on time and within the budget but also according to quality standards. Software quality, for example, must be:

1. Supported by all management

2. Planned for during the design phase

3. Understood and followed by all stakeholders, especially project team members

4. Monitored continuously throughout the project development life cycle

5. Documented for accountability and reference

The advent of the end-user computing environment changed the dichotomous relationship that existed between information systems developers and end-users, giving the latter more opportunity regarding technological decisions, including software ones. End-users became more directly involved with the applications of information technology and in describing their expectations of the product. Increasingly, user satisfaction with information systems products was recognized as an important measure of success. Users had a greater role in determining whether a computer application was successful. Users are concerned with content, accuracy, format, usefulness, ease of use, and timeliness, amongst other factors.

The American Society for Quality defines quality as follows:

> **Quality** is the totality of features and characteristics of a product or service that bears on its ability to satisfy stated or implied needs.

Ideally, one would like to define and measure information systems quality in terms of the product outcomes as perceived by the user. That means different groups will define quality differently. However, most people will agree that quality information systems follow the criteria shown in Exhibit 12.2.

---

### Exhibit 12.2   Quality Criteria for an Information System

- It is developed in accordance with a written or stated specification.
- It meets industry standards.
- It includes characteristics that correspond to user needs.
- It is user friendly and can be used effectively by user groups.
- It provides users with accurate output.
- It is robust and reliable.
- It is compatible with a network of information systems components—that is, it is easy to integrate with related applications.

---

Information systems professionals—for example, software designers and developers—must believe that quality is important to their careers. It is important that designers and developers buy into the idea of quality and that they practice it throughout the project development life cycle. Emphasis on product quality has several advantages:

*Financial:* Quality control reduces the need for rework and maintenance, and that translates to financial gain. It costs more in the long term to produce inferior products than to spend on quality control. Doing things right the first time is always more beneficial.

*Operational:* Quality control streamlines processes and creates discipline in teamwork. Software rework is often uninteresting for programmers and systems developers. Maintaining information systems is normally less interesting than creating new ones.

*Legal:* Quality control reduces liability charges that may arise from inaccurate information, security, or privacy violations. In the long run, the organization, as well as team members, is better protected by developing quality information systems.

*Contractual:* Quality control ensures compliance with contractual terms with suppliers and customers. The idea that poorly developed information systems will increase demand for professionals and ultimately jobs is a mistaken belief. Quality systems increase demand.

*Customer relationships:* Quality control reduces customer complaints and helps build working/professional relationships. Customer relationship management systems are effective only when they are properly designed and developed to address the unique needs of the customer in their entirety. Poorly developed information systems are likely to affect customer relationships adversely.

*Reputation:* A firm's reputation is inevitably linked to the quality of its products. Information technology is a highly competitive industry, and computer users want bug-free software products. Inferior products damage a firm's reputation, which takes a long time to build. It is difficult to repair a bad image.

*Morale:* Quality control enhances team morale. Team members respect and value what they do and they want others to respect and value their work. They can relate to quality value for the customer. Individuals want their names associated with a quality product that can help their careers. Being involved with many information systems gives team members experience. Being involved with well-developed information systems also enhances their reputation.

*Appraisal:* Quality can be a good measure of performance evaluation for team members. The ultimate success measure for any information system relates to how well it supports customer needs. Teams that produce quality information systems directly help success of the information system and customer satisfaction and thereby the business.

## 12.2. Quality Management

Quality is primarily a management issue. If management does not believe in and support quality, it is unlikely that others within the organization will. But quality management must be planned for, implemented, and monitored. *Planning* means identifying and applying appropriate quality standards to the project. It is important to design for quality and communicate important factors that directly contribute to meeting the customer's requirements. The design of experiments helps identify which variables have the most influence on the overall outcome of a process. Many scope aspects of IT projects affect quality, like functionality, features, system outputs, performance, reliability, and maintainability. *Implementing* quality management means ensuring that the system performs in accordance with the appropriate quality standards. Quality implementation includes all the activities related to satisfying the relevant quality standards for a project. Another goal of quality implementation is continuous quality improvement. Benchmarking can be used to generate ideas for quality improvements. Quality audits help identify lessons learned that can improve performance on current or future projects. *Monitoring* means making sure that specific project results are consistent with appropriate quality standards. Monitoring system quality is a continuous process throughout the system development life cycle. Monitoring may result in reworking and process adjustments as the system development progresses. There are many tools, described in this chapter and elsewhere, for monitoring system quality and project progress.

The quality pioneers have provided practical guidelines that can help software developers and information systems project managers. Edward Deming was one of the founders of the quality management principle. He was highly influential in helping the Japanese industry build quality into their products. The Japanese have established a quality award named the Deming Prize. Deming believed that the ultimate responsibility for quality must rest with management, and that the importance of product quality must be recognized at the top. Deming suggests that quality must be considered at the design phase and must be built into the process rather than controlled for at the end. He proposed guidelines that are broadly accepted and used by manufacturing industry and have become part of its quality standards. Deming's 14 points on quality are presented in Table 12.1.

❖ **Table 12.1**   Edward Deming's 14 Points on Quality

| Point | Statement |
|-------|-----------|
| 1 | Innovate and allocate resources to fulfill the long-term needs of the company and customer rather than short-term profitability. |
| 2 | Discard the old philosophy of accepting nonconforming products and services. |
| 3 | Eliminate dependence on mass inspection for quality control; instead, depend on process control, through statistical techniques. |
| 4 | Reduce the number of multiple-source suppliers. Price has no meaning without an integral consideration for quality. Encourage suppliers to use statistical process control. |
| 5 | Use statistical techniques to identify the two sources of waste: system faults (85%) and local faults (15%); strive to constantly reduce this waste. |
| 6 | Institute more thorough and better job-related training. |
| 7 | Provide supervision with knowledge of statistical methods; encourage use of these methods to identify which nonconformities should be investigated for a solution. |
| 8 | Reduce fear throughout the organization by encouraging open, two-way, non-punitive communication. The economic loss resulting from fear to ask questions or reporting trouble is appalling. |
| 9 | Help reduce waste by encouraging design, research, and sales people to learn more about the problems of production. |
| 10 | Eliminate the use of goals and slogans to encourage productivity, unless training and management support is also provided. |
| 11 | Closely examine the impact of work standards. Do they consider quality or help anyone do a better job? They often act as an impediment to productivity improvement. |
| 12 | Institute rudimentary statistical training on a broad scale. |
| 13 | Institute a vigorous program for retraining people in new skills, to keep up with changes in materials, methods, product designs, and machinery. |
| 14 | Create a structure in top management that will push every day for continuous quality improvement. |

In the United States a quality award was named after a former secretary of commerce and is called the Malcolm Baldrige National Quality Award. Several companies, including Texas Instruments, Xerox, and Motorola, have won this award. Other quality management pioneers include Genichi Taguchi, Philip Crosby, Joseph M. Juran, and Kaoru Ishikawa. Taguchi and Crosby argued that the benefits of quality are far greater than its costs. Taguchi believed that quality should be considered in the design of a product and must be part of the process of product development. Crosby argues that what costs organizations is the lack of quality, not the cost of quality. Juran believed in top management involvement in quality management and implementation. He argued that management must continuously seek quality and ways of rewarding it. Ishikawa proposed the *fishbone diagram*, which describes the cause-and-effect relationship between quality problems and responsible units (see Section 12.6).

Each of these quality pioneers has provided useful guidelines and methods for controlling and improving product quality. They provide a rich source of information for addressing quality issues. While these quality guidelines were developed and proposed primarily for other industries, particularly manufacturing and operations, they can be of great help to information systems project managers and professionals. Exhibit 12.3 lists important principles of quality management.

---

### Exhibit 12.3  Principles of Quality Management

- *Provide leadership for quality control:* Top management involvement and support are critical. Quality must be an organizational concern. Memos and email messages alone do not ensure quality performance. The workforce must see evidence of management commitment to quality.

- *Start at design phase:* Quality must be a part of the design. It is more costly to instill quality later in the project development life cycle. The later system quality is addressed, the costlier it will be.

- *Make it part of the process:* Quality control must be present at each stage of the project development life cycle.

- *Keep it continuous:* The continuous improvement principle is critical to quality management. Developing products within the limits of "acceptance" is a short-sighted approach; obtaining the highest standards must be the target.

- *Empower team members to manage quality:* Plan for quality as part of the developmental process and assign individuals to monitor it and report. Empowering individuals helps quality control at the level where the task is being performed.

- *Train team members for quality control and assessment:* Ensure understanding of the quality principle. They need to know what is meant by quality management, how to ensure quality, how to measure quality, how to respond to quality problems, and how to record it.

- *Reward teams for quality performance:* Project deadlines and budget constraints have traditionally been used as criteria for performance appraisal. It is equally important to merit quality of performance. Individuals understand reward systems that affect them.

- *Promote free and open communication:* Eliminate compliance through fear. Explore avenues to promote a willingness to manage quality; promote an environment that supports quality work.

---

## 12.3. International Quality Standards

International trade and global competition has made quality a worldwide issue. In 1987, over 90 countries including the United States collaborated and produced a series of standards known as *ISO 9000.* The purpose was to facilitate international trade by providing a single set of standards that is recognized and respected by all countries.

ISO 9000 is increasingly recognized as the most important quality standard worldwide. Over 100 countries have adopted ISO 9000. It is applied to all types of products and services and is used by large and small firms as well as public and private ones.

The International Organization for Standardization also established an environment management standard called *ISO 14000*, which specifically deals with the five areas of environmental management: management systems, auditing, performance evaluation, labeling, and life-cycle assessment, along with environmental aspects in product standards. Information technology has played a significant role in bringing world markets closer. Products that include information technology elements—that is, information systems—will need to follow international standards for quality and compatibility. Following international standards will also result in reduced liability and increased customer satisfaction. Multinational firms benefit from standard applications that are easy to integrate with their existing systems. (The Web site www.iso.ch provides more information on international standards.)

## 12.4. Capability Maturity Model (CMM)

In most of this chapter we refer to the quality of the information system as a product. However, the capability maturity model (CMM) refers to the maturity of the organization that produces the software. The implication is that a company that is more mature (measured on a scale of 1 to 5) is more likely to produce quality software. Thus the capability maturity model is a framework for evaluating processes used to develop software projects. The CMM classifies the maturity of these processes in an organization into five levels, with Level 5 being the most mature. The CMM framework specifies the characteristics that the various levels should have rather than prescribing any particular processes. It also provides advice and guidance relating to the improvements necessary to move from a lower maturity level upward. However, the CMM, although being a maturity framework and not prescriptive, does embody a certain philosophy concerning the way information systems and software should be developed.

CMM was created by the Software Engineering Institute (SEI) at Carnegie Mellon University for the U.S. Department of Defense to help assess the software engineering capability of their suppliers and subcontractors. Its original goal was to "advance software engineering practice" in the light of the increasing dependence of the military on software and the increasing recognition that software was problematic in terms of its delivery, escalating costs, and customer dissatisfaction. It now aims to ensure the development and operation of systems with predictable and improved cost, schedule, and quality.

According to Mark Paulk and his colleagues at SEI, CMM

> provides software organizations with guidance on how to gain control of their processes for developing and maintaining software and how to evolve towards a culture of software engineering and management excellence. The CMM was designed to guide software organizations in selecting process improvement strategies by determining current process maturity and identifying the few issues most critical to software quality and process improvement.

Since these early days, SEI has defined a number of other capability maturity models, based on the success of the original CMM for Software, that relate to wider areas and other issues than just software engineering—for example, they defined a People model (P-CMM), a Software Acquisition model (SA-CMM), and a Systems Engineering model (SE-CMM), among others. More recently they have focused their attentions on defining a new model that integrates these previously separate and individual models. This model is known as the CMMI (capability maturity model integration). This work attempts to integrate the existing models into a common meta-model with common terminology, processes, and activities.

The SE-CMM is designed to help organizations improve their software processes by providing a path for them to move from ad hoc development through to more disciplined software processes in a staged approach. The CMM framework in general provides a context in which policies, procedures, and practices are defined and established that enable good practices to be repeated, transferred across groups, and standardized. CMM has five maturity levels shown in Figure 12.1 and characterized as follows.

**Initial: Level 1.** Development is characterized as ad hoc or possibly chaotic. Processes are generally not defined, and success or failure depends on the capabilities of the individuals involved. Typically development lurches from crisis to crisis, software is frequently delivered late and over budget, and there is little effective management and control.

**Repeatable: Level 2.** Policies for managing software development are identified and established based on experience. Project development is characterized by being practiced, documented, enforced, trained, measured, and able to improve. Management process and controls are also established for planning, estimating, and tracking costs, schedules, functionality, etc. Project standards are defined and followed. For an organization to be in Level 2, software projects and processes are essentially managed and under control with realistic plans based on performance of previous projects.

**Defined: Level 3.** The standard software engineering and management processes are documented and form a coherent, integrated, and standard approach to software development for the organization as a whole. The process is well defined, relatively stable, and recognized as the organization's approach to software development. There should exist a group responsible for maintaining and improving these standard processes and an organization-wide training program for communicating and imparting knowledge and skills concerning the process. Overall, management should understand and be in control of quality and technical progress on each project.

**Managed: Level 4.** Quantitative quality and productivity measures are established for key software development activities across all projects and goals set that will help ensure consistency, understanding, and improvement of the processes. The level is characterized as measured and predictable.

**Optimizing: Level 5.** The whole organization is focused on continuous process improvement on a proactive basis. The ability to identify strengths and weaknesses, to

❖ **Figure 12.1**   Capability Maturity Model

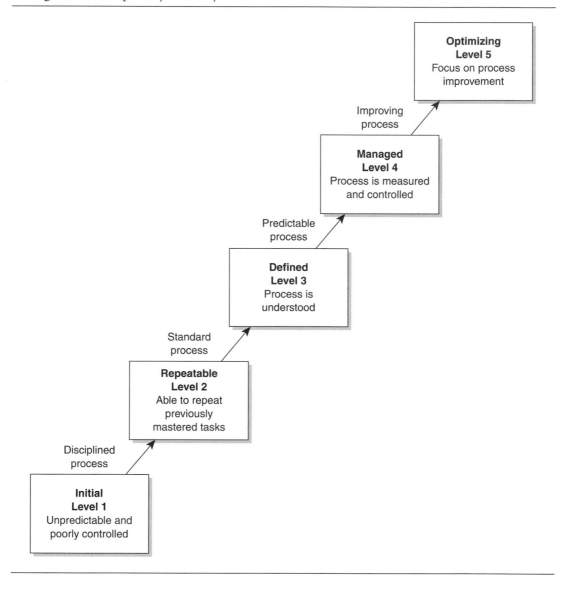

assess new technologies and process innovations, and take action to improve things on this basis is in place. The level is one of continuous process improvement on a planned and managed basis as a standard activity.

Each maturity level (except Level 1) contains a number of *Key Process Areas* that need to be focused upon in order to achieve a particular capability maturity level. These are shown in Table 12.2.

❖ Table 12.2   Key Process Areas Grouped According to CMM Level and Process Category

| Process categories | Management | Organizational | Engineering |
|---|---|---|---|
| Levels | Software project planning, management, etc | Senior management review, etc | Requirements analysis, design, code, test, etc |
| Optimizing: Level 5 | | Technology change management Process change management | Defect prevention |
| Managed: Level 4 | Quantitative process management | | |
| Defined: Level 3 | Integrated software management Intergroup coordination | | Software quality management |
| Repeatable: Level 2 | Requirements management Software project planning Software project tracking Software subcontract management Software quality assurance Software configuration management | Organizational process definition Training program | Software product engineering Peer reviews |
| Initial: Level 1 | Ad hoc processes | | |

## 12.5. Quality Planning

Quality should be planned for and not seen as an afterthought. Project managers need to identify those attributes of the system that relate to quality so that they can be measured conveniently when the information system is up and running. Discussion with the stakeholders will have identified particular attributes of the system that are seen as key features. These may relate to the functionality of the system. Is the information content produced by the system that which was expected (and that was promised) in terms of detail and range? In other words, the information system should conform to requirements. One aspect of this will relate to accuracy: Is the information produced accurate (or at least accurate enough for the particular users)? Is the performance of the system as predicted? In other words, are data throughput as expected, in the hoped-for volumes, loaded on the technology as predicted, and is the information produced in a timely fashion? Other sets of issues relate to fitness of purpose—for example, is the interface suitable? Are there different screen options for users with different levels of sophistication with technology? Does it therefore have a flexible interface? Do the users find the outputs easy to interpret? In general terms, is the system easy to use? Is the system reliable so that maintenance will not be a major problem and the users believe the system will not fail frequently?

The quality plan should be a written document and provide the above measurements and details within the context of sections on requirements, project organization, responsibilities, quality control techniques, a timetable showing when the quality tests will be made, and so on.

The above suggests some of the quality features that the project manager should plan for ensuring that data is collected about them during the system's testing phase and following the implementation of the information system. Much will depend on good relationships with the users, customers, and other stakeholders so that key features can be identified and be given measures of quality that can be used as markers. Quality-control techniques can help the process of planning quality control, measuring the required standards, and assessing the quality of the information systems product.

Achieving quality does cost the organization, and there are a number of types. Some costs are for **prevention**: the cost of planning for quality throughout the system development life cycle to ensure that the software product meets acceptable standards. Some costs are for **evaluation**; the cost of testing and evaluating the product and the process throughout the system development life cycle. Some costs occur **before release**: the remedy cost to correct imperfection in the product before it is released. Some costs occur **after release**: the remedy cost for post-release or after-sale problems caused for the customer. Some costs are for facilities: the cost of procurement and maintenance of testing equipment and facilities. However, the cost of nonconformance or taking responsibility for failures or not meeting quality expectations can be great to the organization.

## 12.6. Quality-Control Techniques

### Fishbone Diagram

The fishbone diagram, or *Ishikawa diagram*, helps to identify the source of quality problems. It is called a fishbone diagram because entities that influence quality are connected in a way that resembles the skeleton of a fish. This method is also called a cause-and-effect diagram, because it helps link quality problems with the responsible sources. Figure 12.2 shows an example of a fishbone diagram. Quality problem sources for each heading (hardware, software, team, vendor) are identified by arrows. For example, possible sources of quality problems that relate to hardware such as memory, platform, and power are identified by arrows pointed at the heading labeled "hardware."

Once a problem is identified it is possible to work backward and trace the sources of the problem. Fishbone diagrams enable us to focus our effort and resources on a relatively smaller area rather than having to evaluate all possible sources of a problem. You could also consider the work breakdown structure as a tool that enables information systems project managers to narrow sources of quality issues.

❖ Figure 12.2   Example of Fishbone Diagram

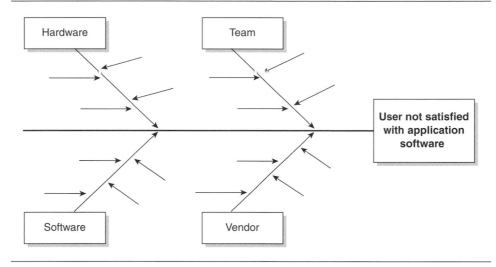

## Pareto Charts

Pareto charts or diagrams are useful in organizing and *prioritizing* problem areas. Nineteenth-century economist Vilfredo Pareto developed these charts. As quality-management tools, these charts readily identify problems that have the greatest effect on the success of an application. Juran suggests that 80% of the problems stem from 20% of the possible sources. Pareto charts help us identify those few causes that result in most of the quality problems in an information system.

To create a Pareto chart, the frequency of events is used to draw histograms to show how often a problem occurs. For example, assume user complaints for a newly installed information system are grouped into the five categories of "content," "accuracy," "interface," "ease of use," and "timeliness." For each problem area, Table 12.3 provides the number of complaints collected over a period of time. In grouping user complaints, it is important to capture the real source of dissatisfaction and to use labels that can be linked to information systems functions. In other words, it must be possible to link user complaints to system attributes. For example, complaints about system accuracy are expected to relate to data collection, data entry, or data analysis.

Table 12.4 provides a cumulative percentage of user complaints for the newly installed system. This tally of user complaints suggests that nearly 74% of the problems are caused by system "interface" or "ease of use" aspects. This is close to the *80–20 law* (sometimes referred to as the *Pareto optimum*) mentioned above. In the case of the newly installed information system, the project manager must focus remedial efforts on making the system easier to use and to improving the interface with the information system since these two problem areas account for the majority of the complaints. This does not mean that the project manager should ignore other quality

❖ Table 12.3   Statistics for User Complaints of a Newly Developed Application

| Problem category | Frequency of complaints | Percentage (%) |
|---|---|---|
| Accuracy | 4 | 4.3 |
| Content | 12 | 13.0 |
| Ease of use | 40 | 43.5 |
| Interface | 28 | 30.4 |
| Timeliness | 8 | 8.8 |
| Total | 92 | 100 |

❖ Table 12.4   Cumulative Percentage of User Complaints

| Problem category | Percentage | Cumulative % |
|---|---|---|
| Accuracy | 4.3 | 100.0 |
| Content | 13.0 | 86.9 |
| Ease of use | 43.5 | 43.5 |
| Interface | 30.4 | 73.9 |
| Timeliness | 8.8 | 95.7 |

problems raised by the user. All these problems must be checked. However, it is a way of prioritizing so that dealing with ease of use and interface aspects, in this case, enables the project manager to address the majority of complaints quickly.

The project manager must also consider the nature and type of each problem. Sometimes, you may get very few complaints about a particular feature of the information system, but that might be because very few users use that feature. Some problems are serious even though few users complain about them. Consider, for example, the problem with accuracy. Although the number of complaints for accuracy problems is only 4 out of 92, it still requires attention because of the nature of the problem. Given the small number of people complaining about information systems accuracy, the project manager might well interview those individuals to understand the nature and severity of the problem more fully.

It is possible that complaints about the information system are due to a deficiency in user skills rather than system features. If so, it might be more effective to plan a user training program to address these problems. In other words, it is important to identify the real source of a problem. But that may not always be easy because sometimes a user's description of a problem may be misleading, vague, or inaccurate. In such cases, the project manager must try to understand the true nature of the user's concern rather than discard it as inaccurate or irrelevant. The ultimate test of a good system is closely tied with user satisfaction and how well it can help users accomplish their tasks.

## Control Charts

Quality-control charts help project managers to see the pattern of change in product quality. These charts describe occurrences rather than detect quality problems and therefore they help the project manager control for quality. Control charts show whether events progress in a normal trend. In a normal situation, quality problems occur randomly, rather than in a pattern. *If events occur in a nonrandom fashion, then there is a quality problem.* So the project manager needs to determine therefore whether events happen randomly or if there is a pattern. Further, the project manager needs to determine a range within which an event is considered *normal*. For example, if past experience suggests that testing a software application should take between 8 to 12 hours then any case outside that range can be considered out of the ordinary. The acceptable range is usually built around the mean score for the events. For our example, the mean score for testing a software application should be around 10 hours, and we consider "acceptable" 2 hours above or below the mean.

Therefore, the main question that control charts provide answers for is whether events regarding information systems development happen within an acceptable range and, if not, whether irregularity is a random occurrence with no particular pattern. Plotting the values for occurrences shows whether events happen outside the "acceptable" range as well as the pattern of these violations. The *seven run rule* suggests that if events happen in the same direction (upward or downward) for seven times in a row, then there is a problem. You may also determine a range around the mean for events to be considered *normal*. If events occur too far from the mean, upward or downward, then a violation has occurred that requires recording and attention.

## Benchmarking

Benchmarking happens when the project manager uses a standard (a case) as a guide and compares productivity, accuracy, timeliness, cost, and other indicators of quality with that standard. The selected standard provides a target for the project manager to work toward. It is similar to having an ideal case that you would want to repeat. Consider an information systems project that has been completed within budget, within time, and has earned the best possible response from the users. In other words, everything about this project went smoothly and according to the plan. This project can be considered a target or an example for the project manager and the team to repeat. Therefore, benchmarking is about comparing our performance with something we have done before or something others have done before. As shown in Exhibit 12.4, benchmarking has a number of issues associated with it.

---

**Exhibit 12.4. Benchmarking**

- The target project must be comparable with the current project to avoid comparing "apples and oranges."

- Technology used in the target project must be comparable with what is needed for the current project to make the comparison realistic.

- The target project must have been developed under normal conditions; exceptional circumstances do not provide appropriate examples.

- Recent projects are more appropriate as targets since major changes may occur in developmental tools and methods.

---

### Testing

Whereas many IT professionals think of testing as a stage that comes near the end of IT product development, testing should be done during almost every phase of the IT product development life cycle. There are different levels of testing—for example, a *unit test* is done to test each individual program module to ensure it is free of bugs; *integration testing* is necessary to test how well a group of programs are integrated and how well they work as an integrated system; *system testing* is an overall system test for all components included; and *user acceptance* tests how well potential users in the organization perceive and accept the new system.

## 12.7. Statistical Quality Control

Decisions are made based on a **qualitative** or **quantitative** analysis of a situation. Sometimes a combination of these two approaches is used. A qualitative approach relies primarily on the analysis of intangible and subjective factors. A case study might be an example of a qualitative approach. A quantitative approach, on the other hand, involves data analysis. A survey design is an example of a quantitative approach. There are pros and cons to each of these approaches. Some decision makers are better at the qualitative approach, while others are more comfortable at using the quantitative approach. Further, some decisions are better supported using a qualitative approach, and some decisions are better supported through data analysis. Not all situations provide an opportunity for data collection, and not all situations can benefit from a subjective approach.

An effective qualitative approach requires *intuition, impartiality, consistency, broad knowledge* of a given situation, and the *ability to synthesize* findings. An effective quantitative approach requires the knowledge of *statistics*, study *design skill*, the *ability to use an analysis tool*, and the *ability to interpret results* and relate them to the original decision problem. The important question about the appropriateness of an approach is directly linked to the effectiveness of the results and the confidence that the decision maker has in those results. There is little value in results that are not understood.

*Statistical quality control* is based on the analysis of data that are collected about specific situations. Statistical quality control is frequently used to set standards as well as to detect and correct errors in product development. When possible, data must be collected and analyzed to help decisions regarding quality and performance. Mean score and standard deviation are used to determine the range for quality acceptance. Occurrences outside an acceptable range are detected and actions are taken to remedy the situation. *The accuracy and reliability of statistical analysis and results are directly linked to the quality of data collected.* The project manager must, therefore, pay close attention to what data are collected and how they are analyzed.

The reliability of data analysis results depends also on the sample size. A sample size that is too large will be more costly and time-consuming. A sample size that is too small may result in inaccuracy. One approach is to select a certain percentage (for example, 5%) of the total population. While a percentage approach may work for some problems, it may not be appropriate for all situations. For example, for a population of 100, a sample of 5 may be too small, whereas for a population of 1,000, a sample of 50 may be good. Therefore, a constant percentage may not work in all cases.

A more popular approach to determine sample size is based on the following:

- The degree of confidence we want to have in the outcome
- The number of errors we are prepared to tolerate
- The standard deviation of the population

As you can see, this sample size selection approach relies heavily on variance rather than the size of the population.

The *level of confidence* frequently used corresponds to 1, 2, or 3 standard deviations about the mean. Standard deviations of 1, 2, and 3 cover 90%, 95%, and 99.7% of the area under the normal distribution curve, respectively. The higher the confidence level, the greater the areas under the normal distribution curve. Standard deviation is represented in statistics by the Greek symbol $\sigma$ (*sigma*). The *z value*, or *confidence factor*, for 1, 2, and 3 standard deviations is 1.645, 1.96, and 2.96, respectively. See normal distribution tables for other values. The information for these three levels of confidence are:

| Confidence level | Standard deviation ($\sigma$) | z value |
|---|---|---|
| 90% or 0.90 | 1 | 1.645 |
| 95% or 0.95 | 2 | 1.96 |
| 99.7% or 0.997 | 3 | 2.96 |

Figure 12.3 provides the standard distribution curve table.

The *error factor* that we are prepared to tolerate can be determined by creating a range about the mean. Assume that your company has leased a broadband communication

❖ Figure 12.3   Standard Distribution Curve Table

## Areas of the Standard Normal Distribution

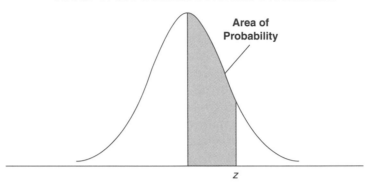

Entries in the table give the area under the curve between the mean and $z$ standard deviations above the mean. For example, for $z = 1.25$ the area under the curve between the mean and $z$ is 0.3944.

| z | 0.00 | 0.01 | 0.02 | 0.03 | 0.04 | 0.05 | 0.06 | 0.07 | 0.08 | 0.09 |
|---|------|------|------|------|------|------|------|------|------|------|
| 0.0 | 0.0000 | 0.0040 | 0.0080 | 0.0120 | 0.0160 | 0.0199 | 0.0239 | 0.0279 | 0.0319 | 0.0359 |
| 0.1 | 0.0398 | 0.0438 | 0.0478 | 0.0517 | 0.0557 | 0.0596 | 0.0636 | 0.0675 | 0.0714 | 0.0753 |
| 0.2 | 0.0793 | 0.0832 | 0.0871 | 0.0910 | 0.0948 | 0.0987 | 0.1026 | 0.1064 | 0.1103 | 0.1141 |
| 0.3 | 0.1179 | 0.1217 | 0.1255 | 0.1293 | 0.1331 | 0.1368 | 0.1406 | 0.1443 | 0.1480 | 0.1517 |
| 0.4 | 0.1554 | 0.1591 | 0.1628 | 0.1664 | 0.1700 | 0.1736 | 0.1772 | 0.1808 | 0.1844 | 0.1879 |
| 0.5 | 0.1915 | 0.1950 | 0.1985 | 0.2019 | 0.2054 | 0.2088 | 0.2123 | 0.2157 | 0.2190 | 0.2224 |
| 0.6 | 0.2257 | 0.2291 | 0.2324 | 0.2357 | 0.2389 | 0.2422 | 0.2454 | 0.2486 | 0.2518 | 0.2549 |
| 0.7 | 0.2580 | 0.2612 | 0.2642 | 0.2673 | 0.2704 | 0.2734 | 0.2764 | 0.2794 | 0.2823 | 0.2852 |
| 0.8 | 0.2881 | 0.2910 | 0.2939 | 0.2967 | 0.2995 | 0.3023 | 0.3051 | 0.3078 | 0.3106 | 0.3133 |
| 0.9 | 0.3159 | 0.3186 | 0.3212 | 0.3238 | 0.3264 | 0.3289 | 0.3315 | 0.3340 | 0.3365 | 0.3389 |
| 1.0 | 0.3413 | 0.3438 | 0.3461 | 0.3485 | 0.3508 | 0.3531 | 0.3554 | 0.3577 | 0.3599 | 0.3621 |
| 1.1 | 0.3643 | 0.3665 | 0.3686 | 0.3708 | 0.3729 | 0.3749 | 0.3770 | 0.3790 | 0.3810 | 0.3830 |
| 1.2 | 0.3849 | 0.3869 | 0.3888 | 0.3907 | 0.3925 | 0.3944 | 0.3962 | 0.3980 | 0.3997 | 0.4015 |
| 1.3 | 0.4032 | 0.4049 | 0.4066 | 0.4082 | 0.4099 | 0.4115 | 0.4131 | 0.4147 | 0.4162 | 0.4177 |
| 1.4 | 0.4192 | 0.4207 | 0.4222 | 0.4236 | 0.4251 | 0.4265 | 0.4279 | 0.4292 | 0.4306 | 0.4319 |
| 1.5 | 0.4332 | 0.4345 | 0.4357 | 0.4370 | 0.4382 | 0.4394 | 0.4406 | 0.4418 | 0.4429 | 0.4441 |
| 1.6 | 0.4452 | 0.4463 | 0.4474 | 0.4484 | 0.4495 | 0.4505 | 0.4515 | 0.4525 | 0.4535 | 0.4545 |
| 1.7 | 0.4554 | 0.4564 | 0.4573 | 0.4582 | 0.4591 | 0.4599 | 0.4608 | 0.4616 | 0.4625 | 0.4633 |
| 1.8 | 0.4641 | 0.4649 | 0.4656 | 0.4664 | 0.4671 | 0.4678 | 0.4686 | 0.4693 | 0.4699 | 0.4706 |
| 1.9 | 0.4713 | 0.4719 | 0.4726 | 0.4732 | 0.4738 | 0.4744 | 0.4750 | 0.4756 | 0.4761 | 0.4767 |
| 2.0 | 0.4772 | 0.4778 | 0.4783 | 0.4788 | 0.4793 | 0.4798 | 0.4803 | 0.4808 | 0.4812 | 0.4317 |
| 2.1 | 0.4821 | 0.4826 | 0.4830 | 0.4834 | 0.4838 | 0.4842 | 0.4846 | 0.4850 | 0.4854 | 0.4857 |
| 2.2 | 0.4861 | 0.4864 | 0.4868 | 0.4871 | 0.4875 | 0.4878 | 0.4881 | 0.4884 | 0.4887 | 0.4890 |
| 2.3 | 0.4893 | 0.4896 | 0.4898 | 0.4901 | 0.4904 | 0.4906 | 0.4909 | 0.4911 | 0.4913 | 0.4916 |
| 2.4 | 0.4918 | 0.4920 | 0.4922 | 0.4925 | 0.4927 | 0.4929 | 0.4931 | 0.4932 | 0.4934 | 0.4936 |
| 2.5 | 0.4938 | 0.4940 | 0.4941 | 0.4943 | 0.4945 | 0.4946 | 0.4948 | 0.4949 | 0.4951 | 0.4952 |
| 2.6 | 0.4953 | 0.4955 | 0.4956 | 0.4957 | 0.4959 | 0.4960 | 0.4961 | 0.4962 | 0.4963 | 0.4964 |
| 2.7 | 0.4965 | 0.4966 | 0.4967 | 0.4968 | 0.4969 | 0.4970 | 0.4971 | 0.4972 | 0.4973 | 0.4974 |
| 2.8 | 0.4974 | 0.4975 | 0.4976 | 0.4977 | 0.4977 | 0.4978 | 0.4979 | 0.4979 | 0.4980 | 0.4981 |
| 2.9 | 0.4981 | 0.4982 | 0.4982 | 0.4983 | 9.4984 | 0.4984 | 0.4985 | 0.4985 | 0.4986 | 0.4986 |
| 3.0 | 0.4986 | 0.4987 | 0.4987 | 0.4988 | 0.4988 | 0.4989 | 0.4989 | 0.4989 | 0.4990 | 0.4990 |

line from an outside vendor to link your financial applications to a remote server. Your outside vendor has guaranteed that this communication line will be up 99.97% of the time. This means the system will not be down for more than 43 minutes in a given day [24 x 60 x .03]. To determine whether the system is as reliable as your vendor suggests, you want to collect data on the *system reliability*. You have determined that the total error in predicting the system downtime should not exceed 5 minutes. That means if the population mean for down time is 43 minutes in a day, you want to select a sample size (*n*) that assures you the downtime mean is in the interval between 38 and 48 minutes [43 – 5 and 43 + 5]. In other words, the error factor that you are prepared to tolerate for this experiment is 5 minutes.

The third component you need to determine for your sample size is the *standard deviation* of the population. You need to estimate the variation in the population. This can be accomplished through a pilot survey based on, say, 3 weeks of observation. You can monitor the system and collect downtime data for 3 weeks to calculate the standard deviation. You could also use the mean score of this survey to determine your error factor described earlier. Assume you have conducted a pilot survey based on 3 weeks' data and have found the sample standard deviation to be 7.5 minutes. You can use the following formula to determine sample size *n* for your study:

$$n = \text{sample standard deviation x (confidence level/error factor)}^2$$

or

$$n = [(z \times \sigma)/e]^2$$

where

$n$ is the sample size

$z$ is the z score associated with the confidence level

$\sigma$ is the standard deviation of the sample

$e$ is the error factor

Using this formula, sample size *n* for our problem will be:

$$n = [(2.96 \times 7.5)/5]^2$$

$$n = (4.44)^2$$

$$n = 19.7 \text{ (or 20 days)}$$

Notice that 2.96 is the *z* value or confidence factor associated with 99.7% guaranteed up-time. The sample size of 20 days may or may not provide the project manager with the estimate of true mean of downtime for the new communication line with plus or minus 5 days. This is because the standard deviation of sample size is an estimate; we do not know the true variance of the population. However, this approach is often used to determine the sample size for survey studies.

## 12.8. Interview With a Project Manager

In Exhibit 8.1 (Chapter 8) we recalled a conversation with a student in which the student suggests different reasons why he wants to extend the deadline date for coursework, whereas the professor seems to be sticking to her guns. We have previously interviewed project managers in business, industry, and not-for-profit organizations. Here we interview a professor of information systems about his experiences of supervising student projects over many years.

How many student projects have you supervised?

"Hundreds! The most common are undergraduate projects. In order to achieve their qualifications there are lots of examinations, but I feel the most important assessment is the project as it is truly the student's own work. It simulates what they might do in their future work. It can last for anything up to a year and normally carries the equivalent marks of one course of 3 hours per week throughout the year. The student does some empirical work (often including software development) and produces a written project report. And normally the student enjoys doing the project. Often it is the sole extended topic of conversation between a student and his potential future employers."

Are there other sorts of student projects?

"Of course. There is normally a practical project as part of a master's program, and this may be connected to a company requirement. Then of course there is the much more demanding PhD project, which can take 3 years or more to complete. There are also group projects in some universities, similar to conventional projects but carried out by a group of four to six students."

From the point of view of the professor, which are the best students?

"Well teachers differ, as do students, but I like students who are enthusiastic about their project, are well organized, do not need to be told about planning (and their plans are realistic), and see me when they have a genuine question to discuss (not simply either to say hello or ask 'what is the next thing I should do?'). With good students we have conversations, not question-and-answer sessions, and I am enthusiastic and interested at the end of meetings. They give me some notice—at least a few days—to read material beforehand. They always turn up on time (I expect them to inform me if they cannot make it—and of course I will inform them if I will be late or unavailable). They write well and talk well. Meetings with project students enable me to discuss other issues with them, including general progress on the course as a whole and their integration in university life. And, one more thing, they are polite, pleasant, and interesting to be with. You will be surprised, perhaps, that many students (but not all of course) conform to this apparently idealistic picture."

How often do you meet your students?

"For most projects, either once a week or once a fortnight. As I said, I prefer it if there is an agreed-upon topic for the next meeting, be it to address a particular student's concern, to discuss a chapter that the student has written (for use of English as well as content), agree that the student's plan is appropriate, or discuss a paper that the student has read."

What are the most important lessons for the student?

"Most universities lay down 'house rules' for the project report. They concern things like the maximum and minimum number of words, styles for layout, ways of referencing, and so on. It is surprising how many students don't follow them. This is stupid as it is sacrificing marks and sometimes may actually lead to a project mark of 0. Secondly, there is no substitute for good planning—and some gaps should be left in the plan in case things do go wrong (they inevitably do). Allow time especially for revising the drafts. Most students don't like writing and find it difficult. They are less practiced at it. But they need to communicate their work and their ideas, otherwise, what is the point? Also, if students have a genuine problem, discuss it with their supervisor as soon as possible—don't leave it, as it won't go away and it will be easier to solve earlier on. Surprisingly, as most projects are challenging, the least problematic aspect tends to be the empirical work, as students tend to love doing the practical work and feel confident about it."

You put a stress on problems that they have with "writing up." What guidelines have you to help the student?

"The structure of the report—which could consist of a variation on the following: title page, abstract/executive summary, table of contents, introduction, literature review, research method, research completed, results, conclusion, references—is sometimes 'dictated' by the 'house rules' but is always important. The number of words is usually a problem. At the beginning, the student thinks 'how can I write 20,000 words (or whatever)?' At the end, the student thinks 'how can I write only 20,000 words about this?' So the student must be very selective, choosing only those aspects that are directly relevant to the project in hand. Sacrifice those papers you have read and things that you have done, which are not directly relevant. The material may be organized in different ways—for example, by chronological ordering (by time the data was collected); order by space (describing each part in turn and the relationship between the parts); by increasing importance, which adds weight to the most significant findings; general to particular...oh, there are lots of ways, but choose an appropriate one and be consistent. Oh, and very important: Don't cheat! Always acknowledge your references. Copying material—for example, from the Internet—can be spotted. The reader notices changes of style, uses of English, and terminology. Further, there are organizations, which many universities use, that will look for examples of copied material in projects. The penalties can be very high, including immediate expulsion from the university."

You have said that the structure of the report is important. Can you give more details?

"OK, this is what I tell my students, but I also say this can be varied according to the particular project. First, get the title right. Make it less than 10 words. To do that, write down every word related to the topic then select a minimum number that gives the essence of your report. It must be accurate, must capture the true essence of the report, must be easy to understand and easy to remember.

In the abstract you tell your readers about your report in a nutshell. Make it in one paragraph if possible, expand the title and state early why this study is important, state what you did and what you found. Point out why your findings are useful, mention follow-up opportunities, make it attractive for the reader to continue, and remember, busy people—for example, the external examiner—may only read the abstract.

*(Continued)*

(Continued)

In the introduction you establish that this topic is important and it needs to be addressed, what has been done in this area and what you know about it, what has not been done in this area that needs to be done, and what this study does that links to the above. Tell the reader what to expect in your report.

In the background chapter give a thorough review of the literature on this topic, relate to prior works in this area and describe how the prior cumulative work helped the current study, identify the gap that exists in our current understanding for this topic, provide the rationale for the current study, and don't promise what you cannot deliver.

In the methods chapter, describe fully the methodology used in the study, present your methods in a logical sequence and think about how appropriate they are, and provide evidence that other similar studies successfully used the same methods.

In the analysis and results chapter, describe your analysis with every result that you plan to give, sequence the results for a cumulative effect, use tables and figures and refer to them in your text, make tables and figures self-explanatory by providing headings and labels and be factual, minimize opinions on results, as your opinions can come up under discussions later.

In the discussions and conclusions chapter, outline the contributions of your work, interpret results as you see them, discuss your results in the context of other findings, describe opportunities for follow-up studies, describe the limitations of your work, and describe what else you would have liked to do but could not under the current study design.

In the bibliography, house rules may well apply, but whatever format or style you use, be consistent. Make sure the information is complete. Include only references that you used and cited in your report. Make the source (journal) clear—use italics—and list all authors names.

As I say, this is general advice and can be adapted according to the house rules of a particular university or project."

## And use of English?

"You are not writing a literary masterpiece. You are communicating what you have done in your project! So keep it simple—short sentences, short words (unless a technical term is appropriate), avoid flowery language, one topic per paragraph, avoid vagueness, and take care with spelling, punctuation, and grammar. All obvious things! Use illustrations to break up the text and make it easier for me (the reader) to enjoy reading your project. Make the report look good with a consistent layout.

## Many thanks for discussing your experiences with me.

Allow me to add something else. I am sometimes disappointed by the behavior of students during seminars, in terms of their attendance and listening span, and in their examination performance, where they seem to be confused or forget the most basic material at times, and I cannot pretend that every project supervision experience has been wonderful nor every project groundbreaking. However, during many years as a project supervisor I have never failed to be amazed by the quality of so many projects each year. Frequently I am surprised by what has been achieved in so short a time, the quality of the student's presentations. Some report writing has been of outstanding quality, indeed publishable in a good journal or conference. Supervising project students has been the highlight of my academic life."

## 12.9. Chapter Summary

Quality matters, and project managers are responsible for it. Information systems quality was often compromised in the past because of high demand for information technology applications. Growth of the end-user computing environment and easy-to-use information systems development tools enabled users to be more directly involved with design and development of information systems and in influencing the quality of system outcome. Quality information systems are developed when the project manager, team members, and users understand and apply quality throughout information systems development life cycle. Quality must be:

- Supported at the organizational level by the top management
- Planned for at the design phase of system development
- Understood and adhered to by all stakeholders
- Monitored continuously
- Documented for reference and accountability

Information system quality saves costs in the long run because it reduces rework on the system and its maintenance. It helps organizations with standards and reduces legal problems due to security and privacy as well as compliance with contractual agreements. The most important benefit of quality information systems development relates to customer satisfaction and relationships. A poorly developed information system damages the reputation of the project manager as well as the team. It takes a long time to build a good reputation. A damaged reputation adversely affects individual morale, reducing enthusiasm and interest. Measures of information systems success and customer satisfaction inherently include quality appraisal.

Quality pioneers include Deming, Juran, Crosby, Ishikawa, and Taguchi. They provide relevant guidelines and suggestions for management and professionals to improve quality. International standards include ISO 9000 to help trade and global competition worldwide. Another international standard is called ISO 14000, which deals with specific areas of auditing, performance evaluation, labeling, life-cycle assessment, and environmental management.

Important quality-control techniques include the fishbone diagram, which helps to identify the source of quality problems; Pareto charts, which help to organize and prioritize problem areas; control charts, which help to see the pattern of change in product quality; benchmarking, which provides the project manager with a model for comparison; and statistical quality control, which uses data analysis to detect and analyze problem situations.

## DISCUSSION QUESTIONS

1. Describe three factors that influence quality. How would you plan for quality control? Does statistical quality control make sense in all situations? Do you find quality charts useful to your monitoring of quality? Does the seven run rule make sense to you?

2. Discuss the relationship between information systems speed and quality. Is there a tradeoff between speed and quality? Are faster computer systems more effective?

3. It is suggested that quality control is different from inspection. Discuss whether this statement is true or not and why. What do you consider to be important quality issues for any information system?

4. Information systems development has grown in terms of volume and complexity over the last couple of decades. Quality has traditionally been an issue for information systems development. Yet the demand for new systems continues to grow. Why do you think that has been the case? What is the role of the project management in this regard?

5. What did Taguchi believe about quality? Crosby? Juran? Ishikawa?

6. Describe how quality information systems might lead to reduced costs.

7. Which 5 points of Deming's 14 points do you feel are most important to quality information systems development?

8. What would you say are the three most important principles that nearly all quality pioneers described in this chapter recommend?

## EXERCISES

1. Review Deming's 14 points on quality and describe how these points may help the quality of information systems products. These guidelines were originally developed to help the manufacturing industry. However, the concepts behind many of them apply to all products. Do you agree?

2. Figure 12.2 shows an example of a fishbone diagram, which enables you to trace back quality problems to their causes. Four variables are described as the main causes of quality problems for customer dissatisfaction with an application. For each arrow suggest a title that describes the cause of the quality problem.

3. Use a spreadsheet to plot numbers provided in tables 12.3 and 12.4. Use a histogram to depict the frequency for each of the five quality problem areas. On the vertical axis, give information about the number of complaints as well as the cumulative frequency for them.

4. Chris Hong, the network manager at a state university, feels flooded by the number of complaints he receives about a new system that was installed about 6 months ago. The following table shows the type of complaints that he received within the last 6 weeks. Use a Pareto chart to analyze his data and make recommendations.

| Week | Response time | Downtime | Unwanted mail | Web connectivity | Ease of use |
|------|---------------|----------|---------------|------------------|-------------|
| 1 | 9 | 2 | 33 | 12 | 15 |
| 2 | 8 | 3 | 30 | 11 | 13 |
| 3 | 6 | 3 | 25 | 9 | 12 |
| 4 | 7 | 4 | 34 | 11 | 11 |
| 5 | 9 | 3 | 32 | 12 | 10 |
| 6 | 10 | 2 | 28 | 11 | 8 |

5. Draw a quality control chart using hypothetical numbers. *Make sure there are seven run rule violations.* Comment on your results.

6. The Office of Computer Services and Facilities at your university has asked you to help them determine how many computer workstations to study. There are 4,200 computers on the campus and CSF wants to estimate the average hard disk capacity for these computers without having to check every one. Hard disk capacity for these stations range from 10 to 100 gigs. The CSF wants the mean score to be calculated within plus and minus 5 gigs of the population mean. They also want you to use .95 degree of confidence. The standard deviation of a small survey they carried out is 25 gigs. How many workstations should be surveyed?

7. Describe the pros and cons of each quality-control technique described in this chapter.

## APPENDIX TO CHAPTER 12: IT PROJECT MANAGEMENT AT A-BANK (PART 1)—IMPLEMENTATION

This case is an example of how things can go wrong if the proper steps are not taken during a project. This is a real case about a "receipt imaging system" at a midsize credit union bank in the United States. However, anonymous names are used throughout the case to protect the identity of the firm and individuals. This case is presented in two parts: Part 1 (implementation) and Part 2 (evaluation), which is found in the appendix to Chapter 13. In this two-part case, specific emphasis is placed on project selection, project portfolio management, project plan development, interorganizational relations, leadership, project risk management, project scope, and post-project audits.

A breakdown of A-BANK's corporate history as well as some of their IT projects will be described. In-depth analysis will be done on one of these projects—namely, their *receipt imaging* implementation project. This analysis will include information on how the project was chosen, resources were allocated, implementation was handled, and follow-up evaluations were done (Part 1). A detailed hindsight evaluation will then discuss what was done well and what could have been done better. With this in mind, recommendations will be given on how A-BANK, and other organizations, can improve their project management in the future (Part 2).

*(Continued)*

(Continued)

## Background

In the early 1950s a feeling of general dissatisfaction with banks was spreading across the United States. The root of the problem was that banks put stockholder satisfaction ahead of customer satisfaction. They were making business decisions based primarily on their financial bottom lines without giving much consideration to how their customers felt. In addition to not being very service oriented, banks had to pay high corporate taxes and substantial dividends to stockholders. These expenses led to higher loan rates and lower dividend rates, exactly the opposite of what their customers wanted. As a result of these factors, a large credit union movement was started. Credit unions functioned much like banks but were organized and owned by their members and paid no taxes. This opened the door to better customer service and more favorable interest rates. A-BANK is one of these credit union banks established in 1951. It now has more than $350 million in assets and over 30,000 members. It serves its customers through five branches and 30 ATMs. From the day they were organized, their mission has been to help their members earn and keep more of their own money. To achieve this mission, they strive to give their members the best possible service at the lowest possible price.

## IT at A-BANK

As could be expected in the 1950s, A-BANK ran their business through a general ledger book in the beginning. However, throughout their history they consistently implemented any cutting-edge technology that their board of directors deemed cost beneficial using payback analysis. In general, if a project could pay for itself within 2 years through lower expenses or higher productivity, it was approved. One of these IT implementations was a revolutionary mainframe-based accounting and transaction system implemented in 1981 by outsourcing supplier EDS. This system served as their main IT system until 1990 when a new information system replaced it. This new system offered several important new modules, including a collection system and loan-approval system. It was also capable of working with several powerful third-party software products.

Big changes came once again during the technology boom in the late 1990s. Adding to the power and flexibility of their system, they replaced all of their dumb terminals with PCs. This expansion allowed users to continue to do everything they could do before and a lot more. It opened the door to using Microsoft Office products, Internet applications, email, paperless reporting, and much, much more.

Today A-BANK continues to be innovative while keeping their expenses very low. One of the reasons for their success is that they continue to implement only IT projects that will pay for themselves in a short period of time. For example, in early 1999 A-Bank was faced with having to build additional offices to house their growing phone centers. To counter this huge expense the CIO proposed that they implement a remote-access system that would allow remote connection to both their computer network and phone system. This would enable phone-center employees to work at home. Although this was a very expensive proposition, it was over a million dollars cheaper than building new offices. This "out of the box" idea was accepted by the board of directors and implemented with huge success. Workers liked the flexibility of working at home, and the new offices were never built. Other technology implementations that have been very successful at A-BANK include an Internet banking and bill-payment system, in-house debit/ATM card production system, document imaging system, integrated phone/fax/email system, real estate document system and many more.

## Receipt Imaging

In late 2000 there was a buzz regarding receipt imaging. The concept was simple. When a receipt was printed for a member, an image of that receipt and the member's signature would be captured and stored in a database. During the capture process certain parts of the receipt, such as name, account number, and date, would be not only captured but converted into searchable index fields in the database. This database could be readily accessed later via a search engine and a copy of a receipt and signature printed from the previously captured image.

At the time, most credit unions, including A-BANK, used multipage carbon receipt forms and stored physical copies of every receipt. Boxes of these receipts would be organized by date and stored in warehouses. Research under this system was extremely slow. In order to find a specific receipt, an employee would have to sift through a day's worth of receipts. If it was not known exactly what day a transaction took place, the search could take weeks. With a database searchable by dates, teller IDs, transaction amounts, and names, this search time could be reduced to seconds. In addition, because all of the data were captured electronically, only a single form receipt for the member would need to be printed at the time of the transaction. The imaging solutions had the potential to increase productivity and drastically cut storage and research costs.

Because A-BANK had a reputation for being on the front end of the technology curve, several venders of receipt imaging systems approached them. Some even wanted A-BANK to beta test their products. As a result, the CIO and other executives decided to analyze the idea to determine if it was right for A-BANK. Information systems personnel, lead tellers, service center managers, and all the executives were consulted in the process, and a report of pros and cons was produced.

It was concluded that a receipt imaging system would fit perfectly within the business process of A-BANK and would have several positive effects. First, it would reduce research times for past transactions from days to seconds. In the case of divorce or suspected fraud, it was not uncommon for A-BANK to get requests or subpoenas for all signed receipts on a given account for a specific time period. These requests could take weeks to fill. For example, suppose a subpoena was received for copies of all signed transaction receipts on an account for the last year. The first step would be to create a list from the host database of all the transaction done on the account over the last year. Then a request would be sent to the warehouse to retrieve the daily box of receipts for every day a transaction was done. This could be dozens of boxes. When the boxes were received, they would be sifted through until all the receipts were found. Photocopies of these receipts would be made and the boxes would be returned to the warehouse. Assuming the same scenario under a receipt imaging system, a single query could be run on an account and images of all signed receipt copies could be pulled and printed in minutes. This would obviously be a major step in turnaround time, as well as a reduction in labor costs.

Second, it would eliminate organizing, packaging, warehousing, and the destruction of receipt copies. This step currently required a great deal of coordination and effort from several departments. Tellers would bundle all of their receipts at the end of each day, bag them as a branch, and send them to headquarters. Back-office personnel would then sort the bags by branch and box them up. These boxes were labeled and stored in-house for 2 months. At the end of 2 months, vault workers would ship the boxes to a warehouse. They would be ware-

*(Continued)*

(Continued)

housed for a minimum of 7 years. After 7 years they were destroyed. The cost of organizing, packaging, shipping, warehousing, and destroying these receipts was very high. All this would be eliminated under a receipt imaging system.

Finally, because multiple copies of receipts are not needed under a receipt imaging system, it would not be necessary to use multipage carbon receipt forms and impact printers. This would allow A-BANK to use cheaper receipt forms and laser printers. Currently, dot-matrix impact printers were being used. These printers were old, loud, temperamental, and expensive to fix. It had been the desire of the IT staff for some time to eliminate the impact printers in favor of laser printers. Receipt imaging would allow such a conversion to take place.

The only apparent negative to implementing a receipt imaging system was the need to train employees on yet another new system. Because of the many IT changes that had taken place in the past few years at A-BANK, this was not a huge concern. It was believed that the employees would adapt to this system quickly, much as they had done with all the other recent IT changes.

## Receipt Imaging Vendor Selection

Although no specific comparative analysis was done, in light of the many benefits that would come with a new receipt imaging system, the project was moved to the top of the priority list. Therefore, the CIO had to decide quickly which vendor had the best product, the best value, and the best ability to work with his project manager for implementation. In addition, before approval would be given, he would be required to present a favorable cost–benefit analysis of the chosen product to the board of directors.

His search for the best system was quickly narrowed down to three companies: Vendor, Techsource, and Techlogic. The first company, Vendor, was an immediate favorite because A-BANK used them for their main transaction system. In fact, their receipt imaging solution was specifically designed to work with their existing infrastructure. This product had been heavily tested and would bring few, if any, implementation headaches. Because the same company would support both the receipt imaging and the transaction systems, support would be centralized. All problems would be filtered through Vendor's help desk. However, this solution carried a huge price tag—nearly double that of the other companies.

Techlogic operated as a third-party solution to Vendor's transaction system. A-BANK was currently using Techlogic for other document imaging such as checks and loan documents. They had been very reliable and user friendly. If they were chosen, the new interface would be blended with their existing imaging system. This would allow copies of receipts, checks, signature cards, and loan documents to be retrieved from the same place. However, they were in the very early stages of development of their receipt imaging system and their cost was rather high. The CIO was hesitant to jump in before Techlogic had implemented their product at a few more credit unions.

Techsource also operated as a third-party solution. However, they were by far the most established and inexpensive choice. They had a solid track record of success with nearly 100 credit unions already running their system. Their customer references checked out well and their price tag was very low. However, they had never implemented their software in conjunction with the host system at A-BANK. This was a huge concern for A-BANK, but they were assured that the system would need only minor enhancements to function well with the host system.

After doing a cost–benefit analysis on these three companies, Vendor was eliminated due to its high cost. Vendor did meet the board of director's criteria but was much more expensive than the other two companies. With Vendor out of the picture, a comparison of Techlogic and Techsource was done. It was determined that the only advantage to Techlogic was its integrated interface. Management felt that this feature was not worth the larger price tag. Therefore, it was decided that Techsource was the best choice. However, management was still not convinced that they should move forward. They were concerned that Techsource had never implemented their product with the A-BANK host system. Therefore, further investigation of Techsource Systems was done.

A-BANK obtained several Techsource references and followed up on them. All of the companies they spoke with were having a great deal of success with the Techsource's receipt imaging system. They were happy with the functionality and service and all but one reported no problems with the implementation. The bank that had a problem reported that after implementation some of their receipts were not recognized by the system. However, Techsource developers remedied the situation within 48 hours. Even with these references, there was concern about being the first to run this system with the A-BANK host.

Techsource assured A-BANK that working with a new host system was not a problem. It was simply a matter of configuring their software to know the format of a host receipt. This could be done in a short time by providing Techsource with a copy of each type of receipt. They would be able to make the modifications to their software in a short period of time. Under these assurances from Techsource sales representatives, A-BANK signed a contract with Techsource solutions. The nearly $110,000 balance of the contact was paid up front and a maintenance contract was signed for 5 years at $3,000 per month plus a nominal charge per receipt. The monthly billing was set to start immediately.

## Receipt Imaging Implementation

The CIO believed that the implementation project would deal mostly with installation of software and training of employees. Therefore, the CIO appointed Skippy Smith to be the new project manager overseeing the receipt imaging implementation. Smith was the network administrator at A-BANK, and his skills were primarily technical. However, he had successfully completed a real estate document system implementation recently and had shown a great deal of ability to work with other departments to complete the difficult project. Smith was instructed to coordinate the implementation with the other members of the IS team and assist HR in employee training. He would be given whatever human resources were necessary to complete the project in a timely manner.

Smith's first step in the implementation process was to provide Techsource a list of all Vendor commands that produced receipts. They also wanted copies of each type of receipt. He approached the vice president of service for assistance in creating this list. After a brief meeting they sent a list of 18 commands and a copy of each type of receipt generated by those commands to Techsource. This was extremely critical for Techsource because these receipts would be stripped

*(Continued)*

(Continued)

for data to populate their database. Therefore, the location of certain information on these receipts was critical.

Next, Techsource informed Smith that in order for the new system to work, each workstation had to have a static IP address. Currently, A-BANK used a DHCP server that would assign a temporary address every time a PC logged onto the network. Assigning static address to all the workstations at all the branches was a big job but not unreasonable. However, A-BANK had several people working at home via a virtual private network. Under the current setup, it was not possible to configure these people with static IP addresses because they were using standard Internet service providers to connect. They would all need to be upgraded to static connections. This was an expense and effort that was not planned for. However, it had to be done. Smith and his staff devised a system of address numbering and reconfigured all the workstations at all of the branches. His team also worked with local phone, DSL, and cable companies to get static IP addresses assigned to all workstations at employee's homes.

About 6 weeks after sending Techsource the list of commands, Smith received word that the receipt imaging software had been adapted for the system previously developed by Vendor and was ready for testing and implementation at A-BANK. Techsource generally sent out a specialist for 2 days to a site to do product implementation. One day was used for software and hardware installation and a second was used for training and "hand holding" during the first day of use. However, because this was the first time their software had been run with a Vendor system, Techsource agreed to have one of their developers accompany their specialist. In addition, the team scheduled an extra day so that testing could be done before training started.

Two days before the implementation was to take place, all of the impact printers at A-BANK were replaced with laser printers. The IT staff had a good reason to wait until the last possible time to make this change. In order to replace the multiform carbon paper, the laser printers had to be configured to print two receipts for every transaction until the imaging system was up and running. This would slow down the tellers and also be more expensive. However, since it would only be for 2 days, the impact was acceptable.

When the Techsource team arrived at A-BANK they immediately ran into problems installing their application server. The security of A-BANK's network was much more advanced than other credit unions they had worked with. It took them several hours to get the proper properties and permissions set so that their software could run on A-BANK's network. By late afternoon they had their server installed and their software loaded on the first client workstation. They began testing immediately.

Minutes after testing began, more problems occurred. There were at least 12 commands done by testing employees that were not on the original list provided to Techsource. The system did not recognize these commands nor the receipts that they produced. Therefore, the database was not being populated correctly. To make matters worse, it was soon discovered that the format of several receipts changed depending on how a command was executed. This was also news to Techsource and causing even more errors.

The Techsource developer immediately went to work trying to fix all of these problems, but the situation continued to get worse. Because the original list of commands was made with the tellers in mind, all of the accounting, collection, and real estate commands were not included in the original command list. By the end of the first day a list of 83 possible commands was compiled, far more than the 18 originally given to Techsource. The task was growing increasingly difficult, and after 2 full days of work, it was decided to postpone the implementation until all the bugs could be worked out. Since the developers did not have access to a Vendor system, Smith agreed to coordinate testing of any new versions of the software at A-BANK. Techsource would work on all the issues at their office and email updated software to Smith for testing.

The A-BANK staff and the Techsource developers worked for several weeks to perfect the software. Because the Techsource developers had many other projects besides this one, they did not work on the project as much as Smith would have liked. Finally in early September they were ready to try again. However, just as they were scheduling a time to do the implementation, Smith received word that a Vendor system upgrade would be coming in the next few months. This upgrade would change the current format of their receipts. This was yet another blow to the implementation. All of the formats for the 83 different command types would have to be revised and tested.

The upgrade to the Vendor system was done in early December and by the end of February Techsource was once again ready to start testing. A-BANK employees began testing the software and found several issues of concern. A few of the commands still didn't work when executed in certain ways, and occasionally the built-in balancing function didn't work properly. Using the same system as before, A-BANK emailed Techsource with descriptions of the problems, Techsource worked on them and sent back updated versions of the software.

Several issues slowed this process down to a crawl. The developers at Techsource were very frustrated about how the project had progressed, especially with the fact that they had been given incorrect information about the number of Vendor system commands. They also had several other demanding clients to worry about. Therefore, they were reluctant to spend a lot of time debugging A-BANK's software. It was also obvious that Smith's counterpart at Techsource was not entirely dedicated to the project. She constantly tried to press for a final implementation, even with a substandard product, just so that she could move on with her other clients. Employees at A-BANK were also frustrated that so many things had gone wrong. Therefore, they were being very critical of the software and refused to allow another implementation attempt until everything was perfect.

Eventually progress came to a halt. Both organizations were working on other projects and blaming delays on the other company. In November of 2005, Smith's employment at A-BANK came to an end and a new project manager, Matt Bond, was assigned. Like Smith, Bond had a great deal of technical experience. However, in addition to his technical expertise, he also had accounting and business experience. He had managed several IT projects successfully and was well respected by the management of all departments at A-BANK. Bond was hesitant to except this project because he felt that much of it was out of his control. He agreed to do it with the understanding that the project would be terminated and the contract with Techsource broken if implementation were not successful in less then 3 months.

Bond began improving the spirit of those involved with the project at A-BANK. He promised them that it would all be over soon, one way or the other. In order to help with

*(Continued)*

(Continued)

motivation to succeed, Bond received approval for monetary bonuses for his team if the project was completed successfully. Soon, everyone at A-BANK was ready to try again and Bond began to pursue results from his counterpart at Techsource aggressively. Within 2 weeks, he began to hit major roadblocks. Due to lack of cooperation from Techsource, the project was getting bogged down again. Bond made several phone calls to senior management at Techsource and informed them that if things didn't change soon, A-BANK would pull out of their contract. Within days, a few employees at Techsource were terminated and new people were assigned to the project.

With a detailed project plan in place and a new level of confidence and teamwork, both sides worked over the next few weeks to perfect and test the product. Although several issues arose, solutions were reached quickly and a final attempt at implementation was scheduled in a few weeks. Throughout the intervening period, every employee that would be using the product went through a full day of training. Not only did this prepare the employee for the new system, but it helped to test the product thoroughly. More issues were discovered but all were fixed before the implementation date.

Finally, 2 years after the contract was signed, the first of A-BANK's branches began using the receipt imaging product. Because of the previous issues, nerves were high for everyone involved that day. However, the day went by with very few problems, and within 3 weeks all of A-BANK's branches were using the new system. Although the end result was a success, this had been the biggest fiasco in recent A-BANK history. The project, which was supposed to take less than 2 months to complete, had taken over 2 years. In addition, they had been paying $3,000 per month in maintenance without realizing any benefits. Therefore, the payback period that should have already been realized was at least 2 and half years away.

## APPENDIX TO CHAPTER 12: DISCUSSION QUESTIONS

1. What did the first project manager, Smith, do that was correct, in your view? What were his main mistakes?

2. What did the second project manager, Bond, do that was correct, in your view? What were his main mistakes?

3. How would you have done the task of generating a comprehensive command list for Techsource? What specific steps would you take?

4. Discuss (a) leadership roles at A-Bank, (b) employee morale at A-Bank, and (c) relationship building with Techsource throughout the project.

5. Assume you are the project manager at A-Bank responsible for developing a similar organization wide system. Looking back at the experiences with the "receipt imaging" system, summarize major lessons learned from that project and how you would benefit from them.

# BIBLIOGRAPHY

American Society for Quality. See www.asq.org.

Avison. D., & Fitzgerald, G. (2006). *Information systems development: Methodologies, techniques and tools* (4th ed.). Maidenhead, UK: McGraw-Hill.

DeMarco, T. (1982). *Controlling software projects: Management, measurement and estimation.* New York: Yourdon Press.

Deming, W. E., (1988). *Out of the crisis.* MA: MIT Press.

Fowler, A., & Walsh, M. (1991). Conflicting perceptions of success in an information systems project. *International Journal of Project Management, 17*(1), 1–10.

Juran, J. (1999). *Juran's quality handbook.* New York: McGraw Hill.

Kerzner, H. (2003). *Project management: A systems approach to planning, scheduling, and controlling* (8th ed.). Chicester, UK: Wiley.

Lackman, M. (1987, February). Controlling the project development cycle. *Journal of MIS.*

Lewis, J. (1995). *Project planning, scheduling, and control.* New York: Irwin.

Lyytinen, K., & Hirschheim, R. (1987). Information systems failures: A survey and classification of the empirical literature. *Oxford Survey of Information Technology, 4,* 257–309.

Oz, E. (1994). Information systems MIS-development: The case of star*doc. *Journal of Systems Management, 45*(5), 30–34.

Paulk, M. C., Weber, C. V., Curtis, B., & Chrissis, M. B. (1995). *The capability maturity model: Guidelines for improving the software process.* Harlow, UK: Addison-Wesley.

Phan, D. D., George, J. F., & Vogel, D. R. (1995). Managing software quality in a very large development project. *Information & Management, 29,* 277–283.

SEI, Software Engineering Institute, Carnegie Mellon University. See http://www.sei.cmu.edu.

Turner, J., & Cochrane, R. A. (1993). Goals and methods matrix: Coping with projects with ill defined goals and/or methods of achieving them. *International Journal of Project Management, IV*(2).

# 13

## Measuring Project Success

### Themes of Chapter 13

- ❖ How do we assess whether the project is a success or a failure?
- ❖ How do we assess the impact of a project on employee performance?
- ❖ How do we assess the impact of a project on the organization's competitive strength?
- ❖ How can we justify technology investment?
- ❖ Does the project empower or alienate staff?
- ❖ Does top management support the project?
- ❖ Are the above measurable?

nformation systems project managers have significant challenges and opportunities in modern organizations. Project managers and senior executives face the critical issue of assessing the impact and influence of information technology applications on employees' performance and the organization's competitive strength. Information systems are expected to empower employees to improve productivity, service quality, work planning, communication, and so on. Increasingly, information systems executives are expected to justify technology investment in terms of its impact on employees and their work. But the success or failure of an information system is not merely a matter of agreeing whether the project was on time and on budget. In this chapter, we discuss a number of factors that should be taken into account. To the extent that information systems empower end users to do their job more effectively and more efficiently, it can be considered successful. To the extent that a project outcome satisfies customer needs and accomplishes project specifications within time and budget, it can be considered successful. This chapter describes reasons for project failure and factors that influence project success. This chapter also describes widely used instruments in information systems to measure end-user satisfaction with a system, to measure the level and type of user involvement in information systems projects, and to measure impact and usefulness of information system project outcome. These instruments are useful tools that assist project managers in evaluating information systems success as perceived by the end-user. But first we look at Exhibit 13.1, which suggests that the issue of success and failure is more complicated than we may have thought! Most projects, like this one, are partial successes and partial failures!

---

### Exhibit 13.1  The Case of Sydney Opera House–Success or Failure?

**Point-of-View 1:** Of course the Sydney Opera House is a disaster. Building started in 1959, and by 1961 it was already 47 weeks behind schedule. Disagreement with a new government meant that Jørn Utzon, its original designer, left the project in 1966 due to a lack of payments and a lack of collaboration and he later famously described the situation as "Malice in Blunderland." The designs changed for the worse in terms of the cladding to the podium and the paving; the construction of the glass walls; and the interior where Utzon's plywood corridor designs, and his acoustic and seating designs for the interior of both halls, were scrapped completely. What a laugh–the major hall, which was originally to be a multipurpose opera and concert hall, became solely a concert hall, and the minor hall, originally for stage productions only, had the added function of opera to deal with and two more theaters were also added. This completely changed the layout of the interiors. More important, Utzon considered acoustics from the start of design. These designs were subsequently modeled and found to be acoustically perfect. As such the current internal organization is suboptimal with users' criticizing the acoustics. Surely a basic necessity, you might think! The plastic rings that hang from the ceiling in the concert hall are intended to improve acoustics, but sound is always a problem. Under Utzon's original design they would have not been needed. The opera house was formally completed in 1973, at a cost of $102 million. The original cost estimate in 1957 was $7 million. The original completion date set by the government was January 26, 1963. "On time, on budget!" What a joke! And it is not even to specification. What a disaster!

**Point-of-View 2:** The Sydney Opera House is one of the most distinctive and famous modern buildings and an excellent setting for the performing arts. It is one of the architectural wonders of the world, perhaps the best known building of the 20th century, with its design and construction involving countless innovative design ideas and construction techniques. It is an iconic Australian image and a major tourist attraction, yet is a superb venue with a concert hall, opera theater, drama theater, playhouse, and studio theater. The basic design of Jørn Utzon that was accepted in 1955 was fantastic, and the changes made have not detracted from this excellence. It was a wonderful logo and emblem for the Sydney 2000 Olympics. Surely nobody but the coldest hearts can deny that the Sydney Opera House is a most magnificent success.

## 13.1. Project Failure

It might seem odd to start a chapter called "measuring project success" with a section entitled "project failure." but not all projects are successful, and it is important to learn from failure to make it less likely in the future. In 1995, the Standish Group published a study entitled CHAOS, which has made a major impact on managers. Following a survey of 365 IT managers in the United States of over 8,000 projects, their study reported that only 16% of projects could be deemed successful. Success was defined as "on time and on budget." Further, 31% of projects were canceled before completion. Happily, a follow-up report published in 2003 suggested that project success rates had improved by over 50% and the number of canceled projects reduced to 15%. This "good news" still meant, however, that two-thirds of projects were unsuccessful even in 2002, when the survey was taken.

Project failure is rarely attributed to a single factor; often several factors interact and cause a project to fail. Some projects fail so badly that the company goes out of business. Some projects fail and hardly anyone in the organization notices it. In most cases projects are successful in some aspects and fail in other parts. We would hope that the successful aspects are greater and would overshadow the failed parts. A project is *normally* considered a failure if it runs over budget, if it completes beyond the projected time, or if it does not meet specifications. The easiest way of comparing the project plan with the project outcome is by checking that the measurable outcomes were achieved. Nevertheless, as we saw in Chapter 5, not all specifications are easily measurable.

Kalle Lyytinen and Rudy Hirschheim suggest four general categories of failure:

*Correspondence failure.* This is based on the idea that design objectives are first specified in detail and an evaluation is conducted of the information system in terms of these objectives. If there is a lack of correspondence between management objectives and evaluation, the information system can be regarded as a failure.

*Process failure.* This type of failure is characterized by unsatisfactory development performance. It may occur when the information systems development process cannot produce a workable system or when the development process produces an information system but the project runs over budget in terms of cost or time.

*Interaction failure.* Here, the emphasis shifts from a mismatch of requirements and the information system or poor development performance to a consideration of usage of a system. The argument is that if an information system is heavily used it constitutes a success; if it is hardly ever used, or there are major problems involved in using a system then it constitutes a failure.

*Expectation failure.* Lyytinen and Hirschheim describe this as a superset of the three other types of failure, as it is a more encompassing, politically and pluralistically informed view. They characterize correspondence, process, and interaction failure as having one major theme in common: a highly rational image of information systems development, which views an information system as mainly a neutral technical artifact.

In contrast, they define expectation failure as the inability of an information system to meet a specific stakeholder group's expectations. Information systems failure signifies a gap between some existing situation and a desired situation for members of a particular stakeholder group.

Following analysis of the One.Tel project discussed in the appendix to Chapter 2, David Avison and David Wilson suggested another type of failure:

*Business ethos failure.* This type of failure is defined as the inability of an information system to meet requirements because of organizational culture. This may reveal itself, for example, in the lack of standards such as an audit, a development methodology, formal documentation, and specifications. This lack of formalism is seen in some companies as very positive, to be lauded and championed as excellent examples of company ethos. But as the company grows, such values may be inappropriate. Thus the company ethos needs to align with the requirements of good information systems (and project management) practice. This suggests moving up a CMM level (Section 12.4).

The above shows that the issue of information systems failure and success is a much broader and more complex an issue than is sometimes assumed. Although failure is often *thought* to be caused by technological failure of some sort, *information systems failure is usually due to organizational and people factors, not the technology.* Indeed, a study by Anne Parr and her colleagues suggested that success and failure factors related to information systems can be due to numerous criteria and is frequently due to a fortunate or unfortunate combination of them. Some of these factors are listed in Exhibit 13.2.

---

### Exhibit 13.2 Potential Failure (and Success) Factors

- Availability of skilled staff
- Champion supporting the system
- Management support
- User satisfaction
- User participation
- Project management
- Understanding of corporate culture
- Communications
- Multi-skilled project manager
- Balanced team
- Methodology
- Appropriate training
- Commitment to change
- Project team empowerment

A useful technique that can be used at any stage of the project to ascertain views is the ***structured walkthrough*** (see also Section 4.7). This is a formal review of aspects of the information system and can be held at various stages of the life cycle. Structured walkthroughs are intended to be team-based reviews of a product but are not intended to be management reviews of individuals or their performance. If used at this stage, the overall quality of the information system and its impact can be assessed, although it is also used to assess individual deliverables at any stage. It is also an opportunity to inform if there have been hiccups in personal communications.

Structured walkthroughs have been identified as being of considerable value in the development of information systems, and they should be held on completion of certain phases of the development. It is impractical to hold formal walkthroughs too often, as it causes unnecessary administrative overhead. The best approach is to maintain the spirit of the concept by team members discussing all decisions with others without necessarily calling formal meetings. It is intended that the approach will normally promote discussion and exchange of ideas within the team.

As we have already suggested, it is noticeable that technology is rarely a major factor; indeed it might be the easiest type of problem to detect and put right. Contingency factors related to the cultural, organizational, and people aspects of information systems are much more important and fundamental than technological ones.

Further, successful information systems do not need to be at the leading edge of the technology nor necessarily related to any IT fashion but need to be appropriate for the customer. Success is related to the experience and knowledge of those undertaking the change and using this effectively in the context of the organization where the change takes place.

## 13.2. Evaluating Information Systems: A Broader View

The above discussion might give rise to a broader view of evaluating information systems. We have previously stressed the theme of "on budget and on time," but there are other ways to assess an information system. One of the concerns we have is that managers often take too narrow a view of costs and benefits. The risk is that managers rely on the measurable to make (or break) the case for and against an information system because otherwise it is seen as a nebulous decision—one based more on total guesswork than hard fact. This seems a sensible approach, but it is unlikely that information systems giving the organization competitive advantage will come from such a defensive strategy. Further, as we saw in Chapter 2, most gains have already been made from efficiency-oriented projects and the real potential is in effective-oriented projects. We suggest, therefore, that management may provide a multiple-perspective view on projects, using broader views of costs and benefits as well as the more traditional ones of dollar costs and benefits. These are briefly described in the following and some are developed later in the chapter:

***Impact analysis.*** The potential impacts of an information system are of many types and include effects on the operation of the organization, its finances, and its staff.

Approaches such as event logging, attitude surveys, and measuring the performance of the target systems, all of which assess the effects of an organizational change, are most helpful when used with periodic measurements or before/after comparisons. This would suggest that post-implementation evaluation and evaluation during system development should be carried out, as well as the more conventional feasibility study, and these should be pre-planned. This would be included in a benefits realization program (see Section 10.6).

*Measures of effectiveness.* A discussion of effectiveness implies that a system is expected to have some desired end outside itself. However, effectiveness is subjective and is seen differently by different people. Assessments of a system and expectations of it will differ, and it is not a directly measurable quantity. Substitute measures have included economic effectiveness, satisfaction of system objectives that will need to be taken into account, the extent of system use, and the opinions of system and information users.

*Objectives.* Assessment based on the extent to which the system satisfies its objectives has been widely accepted as a means of measuring system effectiveness. The setting of detailed objectives and attainment targets for a wide range of aspects of system quality is central to this approach and must be planned well in advance. Various stakeholder groups can have different objectives, and a range of measuring techniques will be needed.

*User satisfaction.* User assessments of information systems have been a popular surrogate measure of information systems effectiveness for some time, and user satisfaction derives from a match between the perceived importance of the factors assessed and the system's performance on these factors. The assessments cover a variety of subjects, ranging from opinions of individual output documents to satisfaction with supporting services and direct perceptions of system effectiveness and value. Emphasis can vary from the service provided by the information systems department to the features of the individual information system itself. But questions have been raised about the reliability of opinions as a measure of effectiveness.

*Usage.* The assumption here is that users will make greater use of an information system that is effective. The approach has limitations: The system must be optional, must take allowance of fluctuations in demand, and take no account of the importance of the function served by the system.

*Utility.* The concept of utility is taken from decision theory, where it represents subjective assessments of worth to a decision maker. Techniques such as hierarchies of weighted criteria and summing the results have been used in an information systems context. But this cannot take into account the value of different combinations of criteria. One approach to overcome the problem allows the decision maker to consider the utility value of each option, making any tradeoffs between criteria.

*Standards.* This systems-resource view is based on the achievement of satisfactory standards as opposed to the attainment of objectives. Standards are set to ensure quality, but they vary in type. For example, there must be a statement of requirements to assess software packages. or a defined set of procedures for an organization, formally imposed by legislation or relating more to "good practice."

*Usability.* System usability is an important area for assessment both during and after implementation, as deficiencies will affect users' opinions of the usefulness of the information system and their decisions about whether to use it, if this is optional. One model of usability is based on the correspondence between users' needs and expectations and the characteristics of the system. This includes physical requirements—for example, methods of input and output and their correspondence with users' skills and need for their control, provision of support facilities, and an appropriate learning environment.

*Flexibility.* This is variously used to describe the inherent properties of an information system, the nature of a change or implementation process, or a property of the information systems strategy. The term is also used in distinct senses, such as describing systems that can respond effectively to planned or unanticipated changes either where the response does not lead to changes in the nature of the system (flexibility is "designed in") or where the response involves the organization changing or transforming itself (a characteristic of an "organic" rather than a "bureaucratic" organization). Flexibility is nearly always seen as a "good thing." First, it improves the quality of internal processes in ways that may offer a variety of performance improvements. Advantages accruing might include higher staff morale. Second, it may give firms a competitive edge, for example, through the speed of response to an unexpected increase in sales orders, which other firms could not meet. Third, it is part of the "survival kit" of an organization. It may be that a measure of flexibility is necessary in a turbulent world: "Be flexible or cease operating." As a number of writers have noted, the acquisition of flexibility is not without costs, and these need to be compared with the likely benefits. In terms of information systems, real costs may include hardware, software, training, reorganization, and ongoing costs.

## 13.3. Causes of Failure

Every organization will have a profile of information systems projects. Table 13.1 provides a summary of some potential failure events for an organization.

Depending on the circumstances, some project failures may be more acceptable than others. For example, some projects are mission critical so the project manager can go slightly over budget to make sure it is done in time. The tradeoff here between extra cost and reduced time depends on organizational needs and management assessment. Having the new information system up and running 1 week ahead of schedule may be worth a lot more than the additional cost associated with quicker delivery. In situations like this, the project manager will work closely with the project sponsors, customers, and top management to determine the best decision for the organization.

A project may fail for a variety of reasons. Information systems specifications may change so rapidly that the developmental activities cannot keep up. Rapid turnover of

❖ Table 13.1   Failure Events Profile

| Project Event | Likelihood |
|---|---|
| Cancellation | High |
| Late delivery | Medium to high |
| Over budget | Medium to high |
| Quality problems | Medium to high |
| Vendor issues | Low to medium |
| Management issues | Low to medium |
| Employee turnover | Low to medium |
| Technical issues | Low |

key and talented team members can cause project failure, especially when recruitment cannot keep up with demand. This is a more challenging task for information systems project managers because of the high demand for talent and expertise in this area. Some projects fail simply because human expertise does not match project complexity. As the number of phases in a project increases, so does the complexity of the information system and its developmental activities. Large information systems involve complex testing that requires metrics for all possible test conditions. Testing by itself may become a major task. Even if a solution is correct, it must be demonstrated that it is correct; that is not always easy. As Exhibit 13.3 shows, there are many potential causes for information systems projects failure.

Project managers who have experienced different types of problems can readily come up with a possible solution for a given situation. Table 13.2 provides a list of typical problems and possible solutions. Often management can detect when a project might fail.

## 13.4. Project Success

Evaluating information technology applications is always a complex process, and multiple criteria are relevant. There are at least two perspectives for evaluating information systems:

> The first perspective calls for evaluating information systems relative to defined specifications or user needs. User satisfaction is typically defined as the extent to which the system meets the user's information needs. This definition assumes that user needs are accurately described, documented, and understood by the developing team. Even so, catering for situations in which user views differ (almost inevitable in large projects) will be difficult.

## Exhibit 13.3 Potential Causes for Information Systems Projects Failure

Human issues

- Employee turnover
- Conflict
- Motivation

Technical limitations

- Incompatible hardware and software platforms
- Limited bandwidth for data transfer
- Inadequate response time

Political game play

- By the individual to gain rewards
- By the team to create rivalry
- By the project manager to control

Funding issues

- Erroneous estimates
- Poor budgetary control
- Runaway costs

Leadership issues

- In dealing with people
- In dealing with technology
- In dealing with processes

The second perspective calls for performance-related evaluations and focuses on processes and activities. This perspective assumes that the project focus and work units are clearly defined and appropriately assigned to team members. Again, real-world situations tend to be more complex.

These two perspectives are related in that customer needs and satisfaction is linked with team effectiveness and performance. However, there are several important management and leadership skills such as communication, coordination, conflict resolution, and interaction that influence this relationship and the outcome of any project development activity. There are several critical success factors that influence both perspectives of user satisfaction and team performance and in turn the outcome of information systems projects. These critical success factors include user involvement, business knowledge, expectation management, and the management of changing requirements. Discussion of each of these factors follows.

### User Involvement

User involvement in the design and development of information systems projects is considered one of the essential principles of effective information systems development.

❖ **Table 13.2**  Examples of Problems and Possible Solutions

| Typical Problem | Possible Solution |
|---|---|
| Users cannot agree on business needs; usually happens in the early stages of the project development. | Document all communications. Use a prototype to allow users to see the impact of their decisions. |
| Users and team members do not communicate. | Provide guidelines for communication. Encourage open communication. |
| Users want a solution without fully understanding the ramifications. | Facilitate meetings to take users through various levels of the system. Share details with all parties to help understanding. |
| Stakeholders resist change. | Document changes and assign priorities for them involving stakeholders and continually monitor the change list. |
| Employee turnover, new hire with insufficient expertise. | Have team members learn skills. Provide training. Have technical "gurus" to go around helping. |
| Stakeholders have unrealistic expectations; they want to fulfill a dream. | Clarify project scope and avoid scope creep. Explain difficulties of making changes and the impact on cost and delivery date. |

End-users are an integral part of the information systems development process. Users must be involved in all phases of the information systems project development life cycle, especially during the specification and design phase of the project. User involvement is critical in design of input and output forms, creation and testing of prototypes, and the development of the human–computer interface, which can take many forms even in one project.

The project manager must ensure the involvement of users from the entire organization and include individuals that will directly or indirectly interact with the system outcome. The information systems literature and research studies suggest a strong relationship between user involvement and user satisfaction. One of the priorities of the project manager might be to establish a training and education program that involves a discussion of what information systems can and cannot do—that is, their limitations as well as their potential. In that way, it is hoped that user expectations will be reasonable.

User involvement in information systems development is expected to improve the quality of design decisions and resultant applications, improve end-user skills in system utilization, develop user abilities to define their own information requirements, and enhance user commitment to and acceptance of the resultant application. In situations where users are only consulted regarding their needs with no direct involvement, user satisfaction with the resultant outcome is less likely.

The user population is characterized by great diversity in skill and motivation. Some users enjoy getting involved while others, concerned about the complexity of the technology or their ability to contribute, show little interest. Sometimes it is argued that user involvement will delay information systems development because of the users' inadequate skills. This is a short-term outlook at information systems development and use. The project manager should create involvement arrangements that enable end-user input and contribution to the process of project development as well as assessment.

User involvement should mean much more than agreeing to be interviewed by the analyst and working extra hours as the operational date for the new system nears. This is "pseudo-participation," because users are not playing a very active role in decision making. With a low level of participation, job satisfaction is likely to decrease, particularly if the new system reduces skilled work. The result may be absenteeism, low efficiency, a higher staff turnover, and failure of the information system.

Enid Mumford (see also Exhibit 7.2 in Chapter 7) distinguishes between three levels of participation.

Consultative participation is the lowest level of participation and leaves the main design tasks to the technologists, but it tries to ensure that all end-users are consulted about the change. The systems analysts are encouraged to provide opportunities for increasing job satisfaction when designing the information system. It may be possible to organize the users into groups to discuss aspects of the new system and make suggestions to the analysts.

Representative participation requires a higher level of involvement of end-users. Here, the "design group" consists of user representatives and systems analysts. No longer is it expected that the technologist dictates the design of their work system to the users. Users have an equal say in any decision. It is to be hoped that the representatives chosen do indeed represent the interests of all the users affected by the design decisions made.

Consensus participation attempts to involve all user department staff throughout the design process, indeed this process is user driven. It may be more difficult to make quick decisions, but this form of participation has the merit of making the design decisions those of the staff as a whole. Sometimes the sets of tasks in a system can be distinguished and those people involved in each task set make their own design decisions.

Even with the best will of the project manager, individuals may be reluctant to get involved because it will take time away from jobs that they perceive to be more important to their career development. Individuals may also be reluctant to get involved because of their beliefs about the benefits and outcome of the system. They perceive little personal benefit for their efforts. The project manager must think of adequate rewards and incentives to facilitate further user involvement. Lacking motivation, user involvement may be dysfunctional for some individuals. Research studies suggest three involvement episodes that provide a useful perspective to the project manager:

- *Involvement equilibrium:* This situation exists where perceived involvement equals (or roughly corresponds) to the level of desired involvement. Thus, in this situation there is congruence between how much the user wants to be involved and the extent to which the user is required to be involved. Several factors may influence this equilibrium, such as individual skills and competency, career and promotional opportunities, and learning opportunity. Within this frame of reference, perceived involvement, whether low or high, is expected to have a positive effect on the end-user. In such situations, (a) involvement is viewed by users as a means of getting what they want from their environment, (b) end-users are more receptive to learning about the application, improving their understanding of how to use the system, and making suggestions that might improve system quality, and (c) involvement enhances trust and contributes to a sense of ownership and control, improving system acceptance and commitment.

- *Involvement saturation:* This occurs when an individual's perceived involvement exceeds desired involvement and the user's frame of reference regarding the value of involvement is altered. Thus, the individual desire or motivation to get involved plays a key role in creating the feeling of too much involvement or saturation. Other factors such as individual characteristics, opportunities for higher responsibility, and the nature and form of involvement may influence whether, or at what point, saturation occurs. In such situations, involvement may be viewed as a time-consuming interference with other activities, an impediment to other opportunities to enhance. The more valuable users regard their other activities, the greater the likelihood of saturation; involvement in project activities might be viewed as an imposition. Where users are more involved than they want to be:

> Involvement is unlikely to increase trust or sense of control.

> End users might be less receptive to learning about the information system, improving their understanding of how to use it, or making suggestions that might improve its quality.

> User satisfaction is less plausible as end users see little or no value in being involved.

- *Involvement deprivation:* This occurs when an individual's involvement substantially exceeds perceived involvement and the user develops a sense of alienation. Thus, the individual has a high level of desire and motivation to be involved in information systems development activities but does not get nearly enough chances of participating. Individuals in such situations feel either that there is little regard for their talents and energy or there is insufficient use of them. It is difficult to determine the exact point where an individual's perception regarding their level of involvement is altered to high deprivation. This might happen even when there is a level of involvement but the user perceives it as too little or of inconsequential effort. Users often expect meaningful involvement that gives them opportunities for self-expression, respect, influence, and contribution. Users may resent nominal involvement, considering it as an act of manipulation. In such situations:

> End-users are unlikely to be receptive to learning about the information system, improve their understanding of how to use the information technology, or make suggestions that might improve its quality.

> Resistance is increased and acceptance is reduced.

> User satisfaction is negatively affected.

These involvement episodes create opportunities and challenges for the project manager. Opportunities exist for identifying individuals who are motivated to be involved and providing them with the right level of involvement through appropriate arrangements. Opportunities also exist for avoiding dysfunctional situations such as creating high involvement deprivation or involvement saturation scenarios. Challenges exist for the project manager in evaluating the individual's competency, matching the individual's talents with task difficulty, creating appropriate involvement arrangements, and determining involvement rewards. Ultimately, individuals want to benefit from involvement arrangements and enhance their career opportunities.

The project manager must seek avenues providing user benefits through the involvement process and the organizational context. Research studies have suggested eight activities in which users may be involved in information systems projects. Table 13.3 provides these activities and suggests a five-point scale for measuring the user's level of desired involvement. The scale reflects a range from not at all (1) to a great deal (5). The project manager can use this survey instrument in preparation for selecting team members. This instrument also provides information on the type of involvement that the user may feel confident or prepared to undertake.

❖ **Table 13.3**   Measures of End-User Involvement

| Developmental Activity | Desired Involvement |
| --- | --- |
| 1. Initiating the project? | 1 ——— 5 |
| 2. Determining system objectives? | 1 ——— 5 |
| 3. Determining the user's information needs? | 1 ——— 5 |
| 4. Assessing alternative ways of meeting the user's information needs? | 1 ——— 5 |
| 5. Identifying sources of information? | 1 ——— 5 |
| 6. Outlining information flows? | 1 ——— 5 |
| 7. Developing input forms/screens? | 1 ——— 5 |
| 8. Developing output format? | 1 ——— 5 |

## Business Knowledge

Business knowledge and understanding is another critical success factor for information systems projects. There are at least two perspectives for this business knowledge.

The *first* perspective relates to the understanding of what the business is about, what the organizational mission is, and what its goals and objectives are. This perspective involves a focused understanding of the business over and beyond understanding of the industry. For example, while it is useful to distinguish clearly between the service and manufacturing industries or the healthcare and insurance industries, it is critical to understand the business of the organization within a given industry. The project could, for example, be developed for a business that is in the healthcare, insurance, or manufacturing sectors. Project managers must have a good understanding of the industry that their business is in and a really good understanding of their organization.

The *second* perspective relates to the understanding of the organizational culture and processes. Organizations are run differently even within the same industry, and much of that depends on the culture of the organization and top management decision-making style and viewpoint. The project manager must have a good understanding of effective ways for getting things done within the existing organizational culture. Two crucial questions are "What is the level of organizational understanding and appreciation for the technology?" and "How can good interorganizational relations be implemented in support of project activities?"

Sometimes, project managers find themselves in a situation where they might need to educate senior executives about potential and eventual benefits of technology applications. This approach can be quite effective in situations where top management is skeptical of technology benefits but open to learning. This approach may not work in situations where top management is not only unenthusiastic about the application of technology but unwilling to learn. The project manager must use discretion in deciding what approach to adapt in relation to top management support and have understanding of **technology transfer**—that is, how technology is diffused in the organization. The knowledge and understanding of organizational culture is an important factor in that determination.

## Expectation Management

Managing user expectation is a critical success factor for information systems projects. There are two levels at which this user expectation is influenced.

The *first* level relates to the congruence between the expectations of project owners, sponsors, and users on the one hand and those of the project manager and team members on the other. Project owners express their expectations through the project proposal and the initial interaction with the project manager and developers. Understanding business issues as well as communication skills is important to creating the necessary congruence between expectations of the sponsors and developers.

The *second* level relates to managing expectations relative to the original understanding between the project sponsors and developers. Project owners, sponsors, and users alter their expectations as the project progresses and as they learn about new technologies. The project manager must communicate expectations clearly to the project team and update sponsors and users through progress reports and periodic feedback. It is important that project progress is communicated with respect to the scope statement and in the context that the sponsors and users can see their original expectations realized. In other words, progress is expressed in terms of deliverables, milestones, and other indicators established through the project plan.

## Management of Changes in Requirements

Managing changes in requirements is also an important success factor for information systems projects. Such change can also alter outcome expectations. Some changes can be significant and as a result can alter the overall project outcome. This in turn may lead to change in the original expectations of owners, sponsors, and users. Project change may be perceived differently by different stakeholders. Some may see change as a useful development that improves the situation, and some may see change as having a significant negative impact on the outcome. Some changes are proposed primarily to improve the developmental process, while others are proposed with the intent to alter the outcome.

It is important to assess whether a change will alter the outcome of the project. It is critical to evaluate the effect of change on owners' expectations.

It is important that project managers establish and communicate regarding the change process. Forming a requirements change-management committee, as described elsewhere in this text, is an appropriate way to accomplish several objectives:

- To encourage useful and innovative change proposals
- To establish a review and approval process for change proposals
- To create a mechanism for administering approved changes
- To establish a communication channel for keeping stakeholders up-to-date with changes and progress

The requirements change-management committee can therefore become an effective means of managing expectations. The establishment of such a change-management process through an organization-wide committee has practical benefits that relate to receiving additional support to implement a change in requirements or to release contingency reserve funds. Expectations are often linked with due dates. Some change proposals may delay project completion. The requirements change management committee can play an important role in informing stakeholders about possible delays and in providing them with a rationale for such delays.

## 13.5. User Satisfaction

Ideally one would like to evaluate information systems in terms of their degree of use in decision making and their impact on productivity, innovation, customer service, management control, increased competitive advantage, and the like. In other words, information systems utility in decision making and problem solving reflects their benefits. However, this *decision analysis* approach is generally not feasible. End-user satisfaction is a potentially measurable surrogate for utility in decision making. User satisfaction is typically defined as the extent to which the system meets the user's information needs. An information system utility in decision making is enhanced when the outputs meet the user's information requirements and the system is easy to use. User friendliness or ease of use is especially important for voluntary use of the system by managers and individuals who are not technology savvy.

In a voluntary situation, information systems use can also be a surrogate measure of its success. In situations where information systems use is mandated by top management, perceptual measures of satisfaction may be more appropriate. Research studies have also shown that user satisfaction leads to increased information systems use, making it a critical factor for measuring success. Researchers in information systems have dedicated significant efforts to developing reliable and valid measures of user satisfaction. One of these instruments measures end-user satisfaction with different dimensions of information systems and is widely used in research and practice. This instrument measures end-user satisfaction with respect to *content, accuracy, format, ease of use,* and *timeliness.* These five factors capture features of information systems that are important to the end user and that influence user satisfaction.

Table 13.4 presents recommended measures for these five factors of user satisfaction. More than one measure is used to capture end-user belief about each factor. These factors collectively reflect the overall user satisfaction with a specific system. A five-point scale is also recommended for these measures, ranging from not at all (1) to a great deal (5). This instrument could be a useful tool for project managers in assessing end-user satisfaction with the resultant product. Mean scores of responses to these questions will provide the extent of satisfaction. This instrument is also helpful in determining areas of strengths and weaknesses for the system.

These five factors are intuitively appealing and seem relevant to the majority of information systems projects. However, additional questions may be added to these measures to evaluate unique features of an information systems project. For example,

❖ **Table 13.4**   Measures of End-User Satisfaction

| Measures of User Satisfaction | Satisfaction Level |
|---|---|
| **Content**<br>Does the system provide the precise information you need?<br>Does the information content meet your needs?<br>Does the system provide reports that seem to be just about exactly what you need?<br>Does the system provide sufficient information? | 1 ——— 5<br><br>1 ——— 5<br>1 ——— 5<br><br>1 ——— 5 |
| **Accuracy**<br>Is the system accurate?<br>Are you satisfied with the accuracy of the system? | 1 ——— 5<br>1 ——— 5 |
| **Format**<br>Do you think the output is presented in a useful format?<br>Is the information clear? | 1 ——— 5<br><br>1 ——— 5 |
| **Ease of Use**<br>Is the system user friendly?<br>Is the system easy to use? | 1 ——— 5<br>1 ——— 5 |
| **Timeliness**<br>Do you get the information you need in time?<br>Does the system provide up-to-date information? | 1 ——— 5<br>1 ——— 5 |

if an information systems project involves online database access through the Web, additional questions that relate to the communication channel and speed may be added to measure retrieval effectiveness. Similarly, one or more of these recommended factors may be dropped from a given survey if they do not seem to be relevant to the focus of the system.

This is a short and easy to use instrument that can be administered at multiple points in time to all users of an information systems product and to study the pattern of change in the level of satisfaction as well as the areas of concern. For example, the level of satisfaction for the ease-of-use factor may increase as users are better trained, while the level of satisfaction with content or accuracy factor may remain the same, suggesting the need for modification of the information system. In other words, this instrument can be used to compare end-user satisfaction with specific factors *across* projects. Multiple administrations of these measures at different times and for different information systems will provide a framework for comparative analysis.

In the following example, the sample data that were used to develop this instrument represented diverse information systems from 44 firms. The sample also represented a diverse set of applications for analysis, decision making, engineering, planning, and control from 618 respondents. This cross-organizational aspect of the sample and its characteristics made it appropriate for the development of tentative standards. Percentile scores for the 12-item satisfaction instrument are presented in Table 13.5. The possible total score for the 12 items is 60, given the 5-point scale used with this instrument. These statistics can be used as a benchmark to evaluate end-user satisfaction with a specific project outcome.

❖ **Table 13.5**   Percentile Scores for 12-Item Satisfaction Instrument

| Percentile | Value |
| --- | --- |
| 10 | 37 |
| 20 | 43 |
| 30 | 46 |
| 40 | 48 |
| 50 | 51 |
| 60 | 53 |
| 70 | 54 |
| 80 | 57 |
| 90 | 59 |

## 13.6. Perceived Usefulness

Information systems executives are increasingly required to justify technology investment in terms of its impact on and usefulness for the individual and his or her work. This perspective goes beyond design features to evaluate benefits in terms of outcome. The success of information systems from this perspective is measured through the impact on work at the level of the individual. The widespread use of information technology at all levels within organizations has increased its impact. Organizations that spend millions of dollars on information technology are primarily concerned with how their investment will influence organizational and individual performance.

Information systems researchers have shown increased attention to measures of information technology impact and usefulness. One research study has produced an instrument that measures perceived usefulness of information systems for the individual. It is argued that the effects of information technology are quite varied in their nature and their levels, not only across different types of settings but also across different computing contexts within comparable settings and even across different individuals. The set of questions presented in Table 13.6 relate to information systems usefulness through perspectives of *task productivity, task innovation, customer satisfaction*, and *management control*. A five-point scale was used to develop this instrument where 1 = not at all, 2 = little, 3 = moderately, 4 = much, and 5 = a great deal. The instructions for respondents should ask them to indicate the response that reflects their *current* belief rather than their expectation.

Individuals responding to these questions describe the extent to which an information system affects their work relative to these dimensions. This instrument enables the project manager to study a system's usefulness and the areas of concern relative to the four dimensions. There may be different levels of interest for each dimension depending on project focus. For example, if an information system is developed to help employees improve customer satisfaction then the factor that measures this dimension will be more relevant to measuring information systems success and may be given more weight when analyzing data. This instrument can also be used to compare perceived usefulness across time, across user groups, and across projects. The project manager can develop a frame of reference for comparing different project outcomes by administering these measures at different times.

By identifying unique aspects of the end-user perception regarding a project's outcome, the project manager can allocate human and other resources to improve project success more carefully. The two success instruments presented in this chapter for user satisfaction and perceived usefulness provide good tools to the project manager to gather data from the end-user and study strengths and weaknesses. The involvement instrument is also useful in assisting the project manager in assigning end-users as team members and the extent to which these end-users might be able to help with the project activities. The project manager can develop other measures that are more closely related to a specific project outcome. However, these instruments have been developed using widely accepted research methodologies for instrument development. They have high reliability and validity, which makes them appropriate

❖ **Table 13.6**   Measures of Information Systems Usefulness

| Measures of Usefulness | Level of Use |
|---|---|
| **Task Productivity**<br>• This application saves me time.<br>• This application increases my productivity.<br>• This application allows me to accomplish more work than would otherwise be possible. | 1 ————— 5<br>1 ————— 5<br>1 ————— 5 |
| **Task Innovation**<br>• This application helps me create new ideas.<br>• This application helps me come up with new ideas.<br>• This application helps me try out innovative ideas. | 1 ————— 5<br>1 ————— 5<br>1 ————— 5 |
| **Customer Satisfaction**<br>• This application improves customer service.<br>• This application improves customer satisfaction.<br>• This application helps me meet customer needs. | 1 ————— 5<br>1 ————— 5<br>1 ————— 5 |
| **Management Control**<br>• This application helps management control the work process.<br>• This application improves management control.<br>• This application helps management control performance. | 1 ————— 5<br>1 ————— 5<br>1 ————— 5 |

for decision-making analysis. The results of survey analyses can be documented for future reference as well as for communication with stakeholders. The use of instruments such as these suggests a systematic approach by the project manager in obtaining feedback from the end-users. The advantages of using a structured approach to evaluating project success such as a measurement instrument approach include those listed in Exhibit 13.4.

The above discussion assumes that these evaluation techniques will be used with individuals, most likely through the use of a questionnaire in a survey study. Interviewing individuals might be more revealing with a real opportunity to gain in-depth feedback, but interviewing a number of users separately will be much more expensive. An alternative approach is to interview people in *focus groups*. These do give an opportunity to develop concerns in more depth, although the project manager needs to be aware of the possibility of "groupthink," where all participants attempt to give the impression of a consistent view (which may not be held by all) or the domination of powerful participants (based on position in the hierarchy or other factors). Again this might give a misleading picture of what people actually feel about the information system.

A final question concerns when the evaluation of a project should occur. Many assume that it is a concern only at the end of a project. In fact, evaluation should

---

**Exhibit 13.4    Advantages of Using a Structured Approach for Evaluation**

- Provides historical data for comparative analysis
- Enhances confidence in stakeholders
- Provides confidence in the reliability of the results
- Provides ease of documentation
- Can be used as additional means of communication
- Helps user acceptance of the project outcome
- Provides evidence of project success
- Provides useful information to design training programs
- Provides useful information to evaluate team performance
- Maintains top management support

---

be a concern throughout the life of a project. Of course, evaluation starts to be on the agenda at the beginning of a project as we define our objectives and requirements. These form the basis of the evaluation process. Further, as we showed in Chapter 5, the project is justified on the basis that benefits exceed costs. But evaluation should also play a role during the development of an information system, as an integral part of the information systems development process, to ensure benefits are going to be met. This might form part of a benefits realization program (Section 10.6).

Predevelopment evaluation can take two forms: planning for information systems and as a feasibility study. Planning aims to ensure that information system provision supports the objectives and needs of the business. It includes some form of project selection process to identify the most suitable applications for development in terms of organizational objectives. Feasibility studies, in contrast, assess the needs of a single application area, identify the initial framework for the application, and propose alternative solutions. They will be assessed in terms of technical, operational, and financial feasibility. One of the feasible options is recommended. The project selection process and the feasibility study are two "filters" (course-grained and fine-grained, respectively) at the beginning of the information systems development life cycle. This is by far the most common evaluation practiced, and the literature abounds with the techniques and examples of their application.

Post-implementation studies are often confined to monitoring costs and performance, and feasibility decisions can be based on cost-justification, but as we have seen, the scope of evaluation can be much wider than this. Concentration on the economic and technical aspects of a system may cause organizational and social factors to be overlooked, yet these can have a significant impact on the effectiveness of the information system. Evaluation carried out following implementation may allow problems of various types to be identified and can provide input to long- and short-term planning. Opportunities to expand the use of the information system, or to gain further advantages through extending the facilities provided, may be identified. Other possible beneficial effects of evaluation are an improved understanding of the system, greater use of the information provided, and better communication between users and developers. In general, more favorable user opinions are likely. Valuable lessons for the future may also be learned and absorbed into the organizational culture. However, the measures for evaluation need to be appropriate.

---

### 13.7. Interview With a Project Manager

**What are job description and duties as it applies to project management?**

"Duties include the estimation and bidding of public and privately funded infrastructure projects. Upon award of work, duties include organization of materials and subcontractors and scheduling of work. Upon notice to proceed, duties include day-to-day office supervision of field operations, preparation of claims, updating schedules, etc."

**Please list any tools (computer programs, PERT, Gantt charts, etc.) that assist you as a project manager and describe their use to you.**

"I have utilized the Primavera Project Planner for scheduling and the Quest Estimator 5.0 for estimating. I generally rely on an Excel spreadsheet that I helped formulate some years ago for estimating most work.

**What has been your biggest challenge as a project manager?**

"My biggest challenge is to control my personal feelings on any particularly sensitive matter, and always take the best position for the company's future. There are many instances where a project manager must defend the actions of the company even though the company may not always be right."

**Please list (if any) other challenges regarding project management.**

"Project managers must be on call 7 days, 24 hours to handle emergencies. There have been times where I have worked 16-hour days, such as during the time I supervised recovery crews cleaning up the city of Homestead after Hurricane Andrew struck Florida."

*(Continued)*

(Continued)

Can you give me an example of how the quality of the work (from one of your projects) has directly affected your job as a project manager?

"I was involved in a project where the soil conditions were different than those that were indicated at time of bid. After a great deal of letter writing and meetings, the firm I represented was awarded a $300,000 change order."

How do you strike a balance in managing all the individuals on a project and trying to hold them together as a team?

"By delegating responsibilities and constantly giving credit and not taking credit, a project manager will gain the respect of the people who are involved with the project."

How do you keep people energized on a project that lasts for long time periods?

"By giving them different tasks. By challenging them to find a better way to do a task."

Reflecting on your own experience, what do you think are the best ways to train younger project managers?

"To have them start working under the guidance of a senior project manager who has the patience to teach and lead. They should also spend a lot of their time in the field in order to get the "feel" and learn to recognize the particularities of their work."

Any additional comments?

"In my opinion, there is nothing more satisfying than being able to proudly observe the finished project and marvel that you are the individual who was chiefly responsible for it's completion. As a project manager, you also unknowingly gain the foresight to handle your own personal activities in an orderly fashion."

## 13.8. Chapter Summary

Measuring information systems success has been and remains one of the challenges for information systems executives. Organizations increasingly evaluate information systems investments in terms of their impact on work at the individual as well as the organizational level. The project manager must consider project success from both perspectives. Experience suggests a high rate of failure for information systems projects in terms of cost, time, and focus. Projects fail because of human, technical, organizational, or leadership issues. Projects may also fail because user expectations are dramatically altered. The project's success is greatly influenced by issues of user involvement, user satisfaction, user expectation, business knowledge, and management of changes in requirements.

It is critical to evaluate and assign individuals carefully to tasks that they can best perform. It is equally important to evaluate and assess user expectations regarding the project outcome. User satisfaction as a surrogate to success must be carefully measured and assessed. Research studies have developed instruments that can be used to evaluate potential user involvement, user satisfaction, and perceived usefulness. These instruments are described in this chapter and can be used by project managers to gather data from information systems users in order to

Improve user involvement arrangements in information systems development activities

Understand better the extent and dimensions of end-user satisfaction with an information system

Evaluate the usefulness of information systems products as perceived by the end-user

The use of these instruments for data collection and analysis helps project managers in their problem solving and decision rationalization.

## DISCUSSION QUESTIONS

1. Regarding the Sydney Opera House, with which argument are you more sympathetic? Why?

2. Evaluating information systems success is a complex task that involves knowledge of *business* as well as *technology*. Information systems can be evaluated from the perspectives of the user or the developer. What are some specific success features from the developer's perspective? The user's perspective?

3. Review items of the end-user satisfaction instrument presented in Table 13.4. Why do you think there are multiple questions for each factor (content, accuracy, format, ease of use, timeliness)?

4. Review items of the end-user satisfaction instrument and propose additional factors that you think are important to end-users.

5. Review items of the user involvement instrument and discuss them in terms of project development life cycle. Do you see a pattern that fits the project development life cycle?

6. Review items of perceived usefulness and suggest additional factors that you think are important to improving work. Do you think that the recommended factors are applicable to most systems?

## EXERCISES

1. Studies of successful projects indicate several success factors:
   - User involvement
   - Top management support
   - Clear project mission

- Good project plan
- Good project change management
- Proper project schedule
- Clear scope and requirements
- Effective communication with stakeholders

How would you rank these? What other factors would you add to this list?

2. Discuss the role of project management in information technology development and success.

3. Complete the forms given in Tables 13.4 and 13.6 for an information system that you have used. Give reasons for the low scores and suggest ways to the project leader developing an improved system of addressing these weaknesses in the information system.

4. Conduct a survey using the form given in Figure 13.4 for an application that you all use in class. Present your results and discuss the strengths and weaknesses of the application as found in your results.

## APPENDIX TO CHAPTER 13: IT PROJECT MANAGEMENT AT A-BANK (PART 2)—EVALUATION

This case is an example of how things can go wrong if the proper steps are not taken during a project. This is a real case about a "receipt imaging system" at a midsize credit union bank in the United States. However, anonymous names are used throughout the case to protect identity of the firm and individuals. This case is presented in two parts: Part 1 (implementation) was discussed in the appendix to Chapter 12, and Part 2 (evaluation) is discussed here. In this two-part case, specific emphasis is placed on project selection, project portfolio management, project plan development, interorganizational relations, leadership, project risk management, project scope, and post project audits.

A breakdown of A-BANK's corporate history as well as some of their IT projects are described. In-depth analysis is performed on one of these projects—namely, their *receipt imaging* implementation project. This analysis includes information on how the project was chosen, resources were allocated, implementation was handled, and follow-up evaluations conducted (seen in Part 1). A detailed hindsight evaluation is now carried out showing what was done well and what could have been done better. With this in mind, recommendations will be given on how A-BANK, and other organizations, can improve their project management in the future (Part 2).

### Receipt Imaging Project Evaluation

The project to implement receipt imaging at A-BANK is a good example of how things can go wrong even when dealing with experienced IT teams, good managers, and established vendors. Until this point, A-BANK had an excellent implementation record. Prior to this, they had implemented several sophisticated information systems with very few complications. Techsource had implemented their imaging system at more than 100 credit unions with great success. Yet, this project was riddled with problems. To discover why so many things went wrong, a deeper analysis of several areas is done here.

## Project Portfolio Management

Although this project had several difficulties, a few things were done very well. For example, the project was in alignment with the organizational strategy of A-BANK. This was very important. Many companies see information technology as a solution to business issues rather than a tool to reach their overall business goals. This can result in companies implementing technology that is in direct conflict with their core competencies or out of line with their business strategy. Management at A-BANK considered the functionality and advantages of the new system to assure that it would fit well within the organization. As stated in their goals, A-BANK wishes to provide the best possible service at the lowest possible price. In general, a receipt imaging system would provide them with higher productivity, better service levels, lower costs, and more reliable equipment. Therefore, a receipt imaging system was an organizational fit at A-BANK, and it was very wise for the company to pursue one.

After determining that the project was a strategic fit, management followed up with a detailed cost–benefit analysis. Once again, this was extremely important. Technology systems have great appeal. Managers sometimes have a hard time looking past the glimmer of the functionality and advantages of a new system. If they do dig deeper, they might find that the costs far outweigh the benefits. The new project manager for the imaging system, Bond, believes that if a system is going to cost more money than it is going to generate or save, it should not be implemented. He suggests, given that technology changes at an incredible rate, A-BANK's guideline of a 2-year payback is very reasonable.

Even though the receipt imaging system project was a strategic fit and met their cost–benefit analysis, a better evaluation of its importance compared to other projects should have been done. Since no specific comparative analysis was done, it is possible that receipt imaging may not have been the most important project to devote resources to at the time. Limited capital and skilled resources should have pushed A-BANK to develop a project portfolio management system. As part of this system, a weighted analysis of all projects could be done using such criteria as: strategic fit, urgency, need for regulatory compliance, improvement to productivity, increase in customer service, and return on investment. Combined, these weighted factors would provide A-BANK with a prioritized project list. To be consistent, each project should be evaluated using the same list of criteria, regardless of which criteria are chosen.

The results of both the strategic fit analysis and the project prioritization analysis should be published at a location that all employees have access to, such as an electronic bulletin board. When results are published, individuals will know exactly why a certain project was accepted or rejected and the reasons for its prioritization. This information will show employees

*(Continued)*

(Continued)

that each project is analyzed objectively and no project idea is ignored. Therefore, this procedure will encourage people with project ideas to continue to present new ideas. Publishing results will also discourage political power plays. If individuals are aware that an objective analysis will be done and published, they will be less likely to push certain projects that play toward their own private agendas.

Not only should the results be published, project progress should also be published and the entire evaluation process should be reviewed on a consistent basis. Constant evaluation of the project selection and prioritization criteria will ensure that the project portfolio remains firmly in line with the goals of the organization. An open and evolving project portfolio system will encourage project involvement, promote feelings of project ownership, and prevent individuals from bypassing the system.

## Vendor Selection

To their credit, management at A-BANK did investigate multiple vendors for the same IT solution before making a decision. All too often IT managers will go with the vendor that has the best sales representative rather than do an objective evaluation of all of their choices. However, despite their vendor evaluations, A-BANK's selection process was flawed. Similar to project portfolio management, all vendors should have been assessed the same way with the same criteria. All the pros and cons of each vender should have been laid out in such a manner that they could be compared in all things. For example, it was a mistake to eliminate Vendor's product strictly on price. Although price should definitely be taken into account, it should not have been the only factor considered. All three of the final choices should have been evaluated against each other with criteria such as *functionality, compatibility with existing systems, stability, service, business fit*, and *price*. Although Techsource may still have been chosen with such a system, there would be far fewer questions as to why they were selected.

A better job of ascertaining system requirements of each system should also have been done before a vendor was chosen. For example, the static IP address requirement of Techsource's system was not considered in the initial feasibility or cost–benefit analysis. This might have made a big difference in the decision of which vender to choose. In the future, they should ask for detailed requirement specifications before choosing any system. A more in-depth analysis could also have helped them to foresee the potential problems that Vendor system updates could bring.

The CIO did follow up on Techsource's references. As with anything else, it is a good idea not to take a salesman's word on how good a product is. Much better information can come from a nonbiased source using the product. This is especially true in A-BANK's industry. Credit unions are not-for-profit organizations. They emphasize serving the public. Therefore, other credit unions are not looked at as being competitors. They are usually more than happy to share information with each other. However, since Techsource had never implemented their system in conjunction with a Vendor host system, these references had to be looked at as testimonials to Techsource's service and implementation history, not for their products' functionality at A-BANK.

Even after Techsource was chosen, there was still a high level of concern that their system would not function well with a Vendor host system. Therefore, A-BANK should have negotiated some kind of back-out clause in their contract. This would have given them more options if these concerns were realized, as they were. If a full, or even partial, refund could have been rewarded at anytime before successful implementation, A-BANK may have backed out at several different points. For example, they could have reassessed their commitment to the project after they realized the number of commands that didn't function or when they were told that they had to provide static IP addresses.

Given that hindsight is now available, A-BANK should have gone with a system that had a positive track record with their host system, even if it was more expensive. Instead, they chose to take a risk to save money, assuming that risk was not necessarily a mistake. However, A-BANK had done no risk planning up front and therefore were not prepared for the problems they faced. If a risk analysis had been done, a more educated decision could have been reached, contingency plans could have been made, and financial clauses could have been put into their vendor contract.

## Project Manager and Project Plan Development

Once it was decided to pursue this project, a project manager was selected. The appointment of a project manager is perhaps the most important decision that management makes. This project seemed very simple on the surface, and therefore a highly qualified project manager may have seemed unnecessary. However, management cannot hesitate to make changes when things go wrong. They waited almost 18 months to replace Smith as project manager even though he had made several crucial mistakes. For example, he provided an 18 item command list to Techsource when over 80 commands existed. In a matter of weeks it became obvious that he was frustrated with the project and was not dedicated to it. He should have been replaced much sooner.

Not developing a detailed project plan was one of Smith's biggest mistakes. Developing a detailed project plan and approving it with Techsource should have been his first item of business. A project plan with detailed time and cost estimates is fundamental to the success of a project. Such a process provides individuals involved with the project a way to measure accomplishments and milestones. The progress of a project plan should also be tracked carefully. This provides feedback to those involved with the project. It also helps with early problem identification and allows for quick correction. In addition, publishing project progress will improve communication and accountability with everyone involved in the project.

A-BANK would be wise to invest in some project scheduling software. Many software packages exist that are relatively inexpensive and do a great deal. For example, Microsoft Project is only a few hundred dollars per license and provides coordination, scheduling, and budgeting tools as well as Gantt charts, PERT diagrams, and progress reports. At a minimum, this type of software would help all involved parties know what is expected of them and information about the project's progress.

*(Continued)*

(Continued)

### Risk Management and Project Scope

Risk management lies at the heart of project management. In essence, most techniques in project management are related to risk management. Project selection techniques reduce the risk of taking on projects that will not contribute to the mission of the organization. Team building reduces the risk of social conflicts. Work breakdown structures hedge the risk of projects going past schedule or over budget. In actuality, all planning is part of risk management. Another element of risk management is planning for problems to arise. This is known as contingency planning. A-BANK had no contingency plans in place when this project began. Therefore, they were unprepared when they started having problems.

Contingency plans should be proactive and not reactive. If contingency plans anticipate potential problems, there will be fewer surprises when problems occur and less stress in fixing them. If proactive contingency plans are in place, projects will be more likely to finish on time and in budget. Although contingency plans require resources to set up and will most likely never be implemented, they will more than pay for themselves if problems do come about. This would have been the case with A-BANK.

Contingency plans can be simple workarounds or detailed step-by-step plans. In the case of A-BANK's receipt imaging project, plans should have been in place to counteract things they were anticipating. Management acknowledged their concern about the new system not working well with their Vendor host system. However, there were no contingencies in place when this concern came to fruition. In the future, they should address these types of possible problems before they start work on the project.

Another part of risk management is change management. On the surface this project appeared to be a simple software implementation. However, this was far from true. Much more than simple scope creep, the scope of the project shifted dramatically once it was determined that Techsource's software was not functioning properly with a Vendor host system. In reality, the scope changed from software implementation to software development, and A-BANK became a beta test site. At that point of significant change, the project should have been reanalyzed. The result of this analysis may have been to scrap the project completely or to develop an entirely new project plan. However, A-BANK had no contingencies for this scope change in place and made no effort to reanalyze the project. Therefore, different elements of the project became unmanageable, the timeframe extended indefinitely, and the employees involved with the project became very frustrated.

### Interorganizational Relations

According to Tim Arthur's article "The Five W's of Project Management," projects are 80% interpersonal. Therefore, interpersonal relationships are very important. Because many projects, including A-BANK's receipt imaging project, involve individuals from different organizations, fostering interorganizational relationships is critical. Before a project is started, significant time and effort should be spent to build relationships between those involved in a project. Procedures and provisions for dealing with problems should be agreed upon, and open lines of communication should be established.

One of the best ways to accomplish good working relationships is to find common goals. Although the underlying reasons were different, all parties involved in this project wanted to complete a successful implementation. By focusing on that end goal, all parties should have been able to find common ground to work on. However, the original project management from both A-BANK and Techsource struggled with this.

To handle interorganizational relationships better in the future, A-BANK should place more emphasis on its importance up front. Procedures to assess how well a partnering arrangement is working should be set up. Both parties should agree on escalation procedures for solving disputes in a timely manner, and provisions for risk sharing should be established. In so doing, A-BANK will be able to maximize cooperative efficiency in their joint project ventures.

## Project Leadership

Successful project managers know how to be good leaders. Project managers must build cooperative networks from many different types of people and must earn the trust of a variety of different stakeholders. They begin by identifying who the project's key individuals will be and they ascertain the nature of the relationships they must establish with these individuals. They go out of their way to build these relationships early so that those same key players will be ready and willing to help when their assistance is required. Finally, good project managers do all of this in a manner that promotes trust and respect. When a manager is trusted and viewed as a leader, team building will be much easier, employees will have better attitudes toward projects, and problems will be looked at positively.

These leadership skills were not present when Smith was managing the receipt imaging project. His attitude was poor, and he looked at the project as a nuisance rather than an opportunity. Bond, however, did a much better job. By establishing relationships of trust, he was able to get his team motivated and the project completed in a relatively short amount of time. One of the keys to his success was the bonus incentives he was able to set up for his team. This showed them that he valued their work and believed they could get the job done. It also provided them with motivation to make sure the project was completed on time.

## Project Audit

Learning from mistakes is a great way to progress. Although it is best not to make mistakes at all, once mistakes are made, it is important to learn from them, not pretend they didn't happen. A thorough evaluation of successes and failures should be done at the end of every project. A-BANK has the opportunity to learn a lot from the issues they experienced throughout that project. They should bring in an individual who was not involved with the project to do a project audit. This person will be able to look at all of the things that took place objectively and provide constructive feedback to those individuals involved in the project.

The project team members should be encouraged to share their perceptions on how the project went and should not feel threatened by sharing critical sentiments. Management must portray the ideology that constructive criticism breeds progression, not termination. This is much

*(Continued)*

(Continued)

easier said than done. Employees must feel secure in their positions, and an open line of communication must be established.

## Conclusion

Although A-BANK had a great history of successful IT projects, their receipt imaging project had several problems. When asked how he felt about the receipt imaging system implementation, the CIO of A-BANK said that if they "weren't making some mistakes, they weren't pushing hard enough." On many levels this is true. If an organization is not pushing the envelope a little, they can fall behind their competition and miss out on benefits that can come from new technologies. However, to make the same mistake twice is not wise. Rita Mae Brown said that "the definition of insanity is doing the same thing over and over expecting different results." With that in mind, if some changes aren't made, A-BANK can expect the same results again. The problems they faced during this implementation must be evaluated, and emphasis needs to be placed on the lessons that can be learned from them.

## APPENDIX TO CHAPTER 13: DISCUSSION QUESTIONS

1. Looking back at the experiences with the "receipt imaging" system, summarize major lessons learned from that project and how you would benefit from them. Assume you are the project manager at A-BANK. How would you go about developing a project portfolio management for information system application at your bank?

2. Given the hindsight evaluation of the receipt imaging system project, what were the most important steps missing from the management of that project? The least important steps that were missing?

3. Assume you are the development team leader at Techsource. What are the main lessons that you have learned from this experience?

4. Again, assume you are the development team leader at Techsource. What would be your priorities if you were to develop another system for A-BANK?

5. Discuss specifically the approach taken by the second project manager, Bond, to team management and personnel issues.

## BIBLIOGRAPHY

Avison, D., & Wilson, D. N. (2002). IT Failure and the collapse of One.Tel. In R. Traunmuller (Ed.), *Information systems: The e-business challenge.* Amsterdam: Kluwer.

Cash, C., & Fox, R. (1992, September). Elements of successful project management. *Journal of Systems Management,* pp. 10–12.

Davis, F. D., & Herron, D. (1989). Perceived usefulness, perceived ease of use, and user acceptance of information technology, *MIS Quarterly, 13*(3).

Doll, W. J., & Torkzadeh, G. (1988). The measurement of end-user computing satisfaction. *MIS Quarterly, 12*(2), 259–274.

Doll, W. J. and Torkzadeh, G. (1989). End-user computing involvement: A discrepancy model. *Management Science, 35*(10), 1151–1172.

Ewusi-Mensah, K., & Przasnyski, Z. (1994). Factors contributing to the abandonment of information systems development project. *Journal of Information Technology, 9,* 105–201.

Johnson, J., (1995). Chaos: The dollar drain of IT project failures. *Application Development Trends, 2*(1), 41–47.

Lyytinen, K., & Hirschheim, R. (1987). Information systems failures: A survey and classification of the empirical literature. *Oxford Surveys in Information Technology, (4),* pp. 257–309.

Lyytinen, K., & Robey, D. (1999). Learning failure in information systems development, *Information Systems Journal, 9*(2), 85–101.

Mumford, E. (1995). *Effective requirements analysis and systems design: The ETHICS method.* Basingstoke, UK: Macmillan.

Parr, A. N., Shanks, G., & Darke, P. (1999). Identification of necessary factors for successful implementation of ERP systems. In O. K. Ngwenyama, L. Introna, M. D. Myers, & J. I. DeGross (Eds.), *New Information Technologies in Organizational Processes* (pp. 99–120). Deventer, The Netherlands: Kluwer.

Torkzadeh, G., & Dhillon, G. (2002). Measuring factors that influence the success of Internet commerce. *Information Systems Research, 13*(1), 187–204.

Torkzadeh, G., & Doll, W. J. (1999). The development of a tool for measuring the perceived impact of information technology on work. *Omega, 27*(3), 327–329.

# 14

## Closing the Project

### Themes of Chapter 14

- ❖ When can we close a project?
- ❖ What happens if there has been premature ending of the project?
- ❖ What jobs do we do before closure?
- ❖ What is performance appraisal?
- ❖ How can we learn lessons toward organizational learning as well as individual learning?

**A** project formally begins with the approval of the project proposal and the appointment of a project manager. Developmental activities begin with scope definition and continue through implementation of planned activities until goals and objectives are obtained. A project must be administratively closed once its outcome product is successfully delivered to the customer. The scope statement describes when a project is expected to end. Administrative closure is necessary even for cases where there is a premature ending or a failure to complete the project. This chapter describes the importance of closure for information systems projects through three sets of activities: (a) administrative closure of contracts and accounts, personnel issues, documentation, and release or transfer of equipment and facilities, (b) performance appraisal and individual evaluation, and (c) conducting a project audit to review lessons learned and evaluate the overall project's success. This chapter provides guidelines for planning an information systems project closure and audit. But first we look at Exhibit 14.1, which discusses an issue that we may think simple: How do we tell people the project is done?

### Exhibit 14.1   How Do We Tell People the Project Is Done?

Project managers come up with creative ideas to alert everyone of the closing phase of the project and to make sure that everyone understands that it is coming to an end. Sometime they don't even need to mention closure. For example, often project managers organize a big party to "launch" a new software product and invite stakeholders and others to attend. This serves as a public announcement to everyone that the project they have been working on is complete and that they will be moving on to other projects.

When is a project complete? The simple answer to this question is that a project development is *not complete until it is closed* and until all stakeholders recognize that the process had ended and team members have moved on to the next project. This is not a trivial matter because it will affect the current schedule as well as the future projects. At some point, every project, big or small, must be properly closed and documented and team members must move on. Remember, *all projects are temporary.*

Some people on your project team as well as the user side will drag their feet and come up with all kinds of odd reasons to continue with the project. Some of your team members may drag their feet because of their *psychological involvement* with the project and because they have developed a *sense of ownership* for the project and they do not want to let go of it. The users and owners of the project may drag their feet because they want to add new features to the project or because they want the project to help them with other new tasks that were not there when the project was initially designed.

Regardless of whether these reasons are valid, the end result is likely to delay delivery. Project managers are responsible for handling the situation and keeping the project on schedule for delivery and, to the extent possible, maintaining a positive relationship with stakeholders. It is tempting sometimes to listen to the user and continue making changes to increase their satisfaction. That may not necessarily be a good idea for the project and the user group as a whole. It is important to realize that you cannot satisfy everyone all the time. The *project charter* acts as a contract between you and the user and in that sense defines the *boundaries of your responsibilities*, including the deadline for delivery. It is important that the project manager maintains focus and pursues key objectives of a project.

Project closure is important because it helps register with the user that they can take up *"full use"* of the system and realize that the team members have accomplished their task. That, in and of itself, could be a *source of satisfaction* to the user because it will tell them that the project team has completed what they agreed to do and has done what they could to bring the project to a satisfactory closure. Remember, users are often eager to have their system delivered since information systems projects are notorious for being late. We are not talking about projects that are dysfunctional or seriously mismanaged. That will obviously generate the expected dissatisfaction.

It is also important to realize that closure does not happen in a vacuum. It is not like the project manager wakes up one day and decides to close the project. Closure is a phase in the system development life cycle that begins at some point and ends at some point. The process of closing a project involves a *steady stream of communication* to key stakeholders as well as to the collective user. It starts well before the project ends; how long before depends on the scope and size of the project.

This communication must ultimately accomplish two objectives: (a) to provide information and *documentation* for the project development activities to act as supporting evidence of responsibilities being carried out and (b) to help develop a realistic *expectation* among stakeholders regarding the project delivery date. The project manager must ensure that the information is disseminated to all stakeholders using appropriate means such as email, memo, intranet, and so on. Not everyone uses email or reads memos. The project manager can reach the intended audience using a variety of communication modes.

Here are some effective *habits* that help your communication:

*Listening.*  A good communicator is a good listener. A good listener is a person who listens with the intent to understand the message. Words could inadvertently be misused and as a result may not convey the real intent. A good listener develops the habit to go beyond words to understand the real intent. Taking notes for later review is helpful.

*Observing.* A good communicator is also a good observer. A good observer is a person who notices small changes, moves, and gestures in a speaker or in an audience. Not everything can be put in words, thus the saying "a picture is worth a thousand words." A good observer benefits from what cannot be put in words or pictures.

*Reading.* A good communicator is also an avid reader. A good reader makes it a hobby to read and enjoys the learning process. Develop enthusiasm for reading by thinking of it as a hobby not as a task that you have to do. Develop the habit, and it will stay with you. It is also the best way to expand your vocabulary.

*Reaching.* Good communicators choose their words carefully. They show empathy for their listeners while at the same time get their points across. Keeping the right balance in this respect is a talent that is gained by habits of *listening, observing,* and *reading.* One word here or one word there can make a difference. Keep a proactive and responsive posture in your communication; avoid being reactive.

*Spanning.* Most people resent a "talk down" communication style where the subject matter is watered down, or as some would call it, "dumbed down." It is important to educate yourself about your audience—their background, their interests, their demographics. Use that information to outline the scope and the level of your message as well as to choose your words, your examples, and your tone. It is difficult to keep the right balance when you have a mixed audience; it is useful to let your audience know the situation and adjust their expectation.

*Timing.* New technologies like email have created the habit of hasty response. We tend to click on the *reply* and *enter* buttons too quickly. That may be OK in many cases, but there are times when we need to curb our *urge* for a quick reply—when we are emotional about an issue. In fact, most people will tell you after the fact that they should have waited—"count to three" before responding to a message. We are talking about waiting 1 day in most cases—"sleep on it" before rushing to respond. How many cases can you think of that could not wait a day?

Finally, you have read elsewhere in this book that for information to be effective it must be *timely, accurate,* and *relevant.* That applies to communication content as well.

You don't remind people that the project will be complete 6 months in advance; it is like reminding people to attend a department meeting 2 weeks in advance: It is not *timely* and it won't grab attention.

You don't conjure up a report or give fancy exhibits, graphs, and tables if the data you have used for your report are unreliable; it is not *accurate* and it won't be good.

You don't refer to a work breakdown structure when giving a progress report; it is like giving detailed computer printout to show the sales trend: It is not *relevant* and it won't help.

## 14.1. Administrative Closure

Three broad activities are carried out at the closing stage of the project: administrative closure of contracts and accounts, performance appraisal and individual evaluation, and project audit.

An information system project must be administratively closed once its product is successfully delivered to the customer. Even a failed project must be administratively closed. Sometimes the project is said to be deadlocked. This might be due to a drastic change of focus, support, personnel, executive decision, etc., and even here, the deadlocked project must be administratively closed.

The project manager is responsible for planning project closure, and the project closure plan must address the following activities:

*Project accounts closure.* Most information systems projects involve contracts with outside vendors, partners, information systems professionals, temporary workers, and the like. These accounts must be properly closed and contracting parties duly informed. This includes closing of accounts for the individuals and professionals who are hired for the duration of the project. It is also necessary at this point to evaluate outside participants. Vendors should be evaluated for responsiveness, reliability, service quality, adherence to contract terms, and the like. Partners and professionals should be evaluated for their conduct, relationships, competency, added value, and so on. Other outside individuals involved with the project such as temporary staff should be evaluated for professionalism, reliability, and the like. These evaluations are important sources of reference for future contracts and vendor management.

*Delivery acceptance.* There is a potential for information systems projects to continue adding new features, modifying existing features, providing new or additional training, and so on. Project customers often consider these activities to be a part of the original plan or their expectation. This is partly due to the nature of the information technology and its potential growth. As users learn about the technology and its capability, their expectations alter. While this is a positive development for the organization and should lead to better and increased use of information systems, it does provide a challenge for the project manager to conclude the project. Administrative closure of the project provides the project manager the opportunity to bring customer expectations and requests to a satisfactory ending. Formal acceptance of the project from the owner or the customer is necessary to accomplish that. The acceptance document should refer to the final product, the delivery date, and the end of the project.

*Equipment and facility release.* Once the project is delivered, equipment and facilities that are assigned to the project's activities must be released. These are resources that were allocated to the project for a specified duration. Sometimes, these facilities are in demand by other projects and their formal release will allow others to utilize them. If equipment and facilities are not released when their use is ended, others may unofficially start using them and that leads to inaccurate accounting. The timely release of project equipment will avoid that and suggests proper use of organizational resources by the project manager.

*Project personnel release.* Project team members must move on to other projects or go back to their departments once the project is completed. Like customers, team members sometimes develop a psychological link with the project and might want to continue their involvement with the project indefinitely. While this may suggest that the work on the project has been rewarding and enjoyable, it should not lead to resources being extended unnecessarily. Team members must realize that all assignments are temporary and will end once the project is completed. That also means performance evaluations should be done for that duration and for activities that relate to the project.

*Acknowledgements and award.* It is important to acknowledge and reward individuals, departments, or centers that supported the project and directly or indirectly influenced the success of the project. This provides the project manager an opportunity to build strong relationships for future projects while recognizing contributions. Considering awards for unique and significant contributions may be appropriate at the closing stage of the project. Organizing a social event provides the project manager with the opportunity to recognize and award individuals for their contributions and announce the project's closure. This social event can be formal and elaborate or informal and modest depending on the impact of the project outcome on organizational goals and objectives. Sometimes organizations use such events to promote and publicize new services and information systems for the benefit of employees or customers. Usually, information systems projects that are closely aligned with organizational goals and objectives are delivered through formal social events that also publicize the project's closure.

*Assigning individuals to carry out closure tasks.* Individuals must be assigned to carry out project closure activities. At this stage, the project manager is familiar with the competency and effectiveness of each team member. This knowledge can be useful to the project manager in assigning project closure tasks to individuals. The project closure plan should identify activities that are necessary for closing the project, timelines for each activity, and the individual responsible for carrying out each activity. Key individuals who help the project manager in team formation are good candidates for closure activities. While most activities can be delegated, the project manager must take the primary responsibility for performance evaluation. Activity and progress reports prepared by key individuals can be used by the project manager for performance evaluation.

*Monitoring implementation.* Once closure tasks are defined and individuals are assigned to carry them out, the project manager needs to plan for monitoring progress. Key individuals are good candidates to carry out these monitoring tasks. In many cases, the project manager monitors the implementation of closing activities. Given the fact that most information systems projects are over budget and behind schedule, the project manager must ensure timely closure of accounts, termination of contracts, release of personnel, and transfer of equipment and facilities. The project manager may want to develop a priority list for monitoring closure of high-budget items, such as personnel.

*Ending closure process.* Even closure needs an ending. The project manager must ensure that project creep does not happen in the closing phase of the information systems development life cycle. The customer or the end-user can still expect upgrades or changes since the project is not yet formally closed. The primary intent for ending the closure process is to communicate to team members and the customer when the post-closure date is. The post-closure date could begin with the social events when awards are presented and contributions are acknowledged.

## 14.2. Performance Appraisal

The closing stage is an appropriate time for performance evaluation of the project team members. The project manager is responsible for evaluating each team member for their contribution to the project. This is an important responsibility since it can influence team members' development and careers. The evaluation must be limited to activities that directly relate to the project and for the duration of that project. Most organizations have established standards for performance appraisal. These standards are helpful in guiding the project manager and providing consistency across individuals and over time.

Sometimes end-users are partially involved with the project while they continue working for their functional areas. The project manager is not in the position to appraise these individuals for work done outside the scope or duration of the project. In many organizations these individuals are appraised by their functional managers only. In that case, the project manager may be asked to provide input to the functional manager for an individual's performance on the project. As described in Chapter 9 on developing project teams, this approach may influence the loyalty of those members; people tend to respond to what influences their rewards. However, having a single source of performance evaluation simplifies the process. As seen in Exhibit 14.2, in appraising team members, the project manager must consider a whole range of criteria.

---

### Exhibit 14.2  Criteria for Appraising Team Members

- Innovation and creativity
- Responsiveness
- Teamwork
- Customer relations
- Learning and adaptability
- Adherence to the triple constraints of time, cost, and focus
- Overall contribution to project goals and objectives

The project manager must arrange a one-on-one meeting for each team member to discuss their performance. It is appropriate for the project manager to ask for a *self-appraisal* by the individual. This will give project managers the opportunity to compare and contrast their appraisal of a team member with the individual's self-evaluation. It will also help the project manager to prepare for the ensuing discussion with the individual; it provides a timely warning for the project manager in cases where significant differences exist between the two appraisals. The gap between the two appraisals is minimized when the project manager continually and effectively provides feedback to team members about their performance and the project's progress.

In this meeting, the project manager should limit the discussion to the individual's performance appraisal relative to communicated responsibilities, expectation, and standards and avoid comparisons with other team members. Such comparisons tend to be dysfunctional in these meetings. The project manager should deal with strengths and weaknesses of each individual relative to specific project activities. It is important for individuals to see their contribution or lack of in the context of the project goals. The project manager must be consistent in his or her appraisal; individuals become resentful when they find out different standards are used to appraise them. The project manager must also discuss ways in which individuals can improve performance and make progress toward their career goals.

## 14.3. Information Systems Project Audit

Project audits provide valuable feedback to the project manager and the organization. There are two types of project audits. One is an *ongoing audit* that is carried out during the project development life cycle. Another is an *end of the project audit* that is carried out during the project closure phase. In other words, audits are done during project development activities and after the projects are complete. There are similarities and differences in goals and objectives for these two types of audits. An ongoing project audit benefits the project management of information systems under development more directly while an end of the project audit benefits the information systems steering committee and subsequent projects.

Although there are stages in the project when control procedures and a formal audit are particularly stressed, control and audit should be seen as a continuing process and always in the mind of the project manager. A periodic project audit is necessary *during* the information systems development process in order to provide timely and necessary feedback to the project manager, the project team, and management. The outcome of such an audit must be a report that responds to three important questions regarding the project at that stage of the project development (see Exhibit 14.3).

The audit feedback helps the project manager to correct the course early in the process and avoid negative consequences. Early warnings can save significant time and effort in addressing problems that if ignored would later result in serious costs. A periodic audit also helps the project manager to assess other personnel and organizational issues that influence the ultimate success of the project (see Exhibit 14.4).

---

**Exhibit 14.3 Crucial Audit Questions**

- Are we doing the right thing? The audit can be at each milestone or at the completion of a phase such as requirements analysis or systems design.
- Are we doing it right? The outcome at the time of audit must be evaluated relative to specification and user needs.
- Are adjustments necessary? The outcome at the time of audit can be reviewed in terms of time, cost, and focus to see if improvement can be made.

---

**Exhibit 14.4 Assessing Organizational and Personnel Issues**

- Are we making adequate progress? Can performance be improved?
- Are stakeholders and top management still supportive of the project?
- Is the project team functioning as expected? Are there any major personnel issues?
- Are there significant issues of internal, external, morale, and the like that may affect the project's outcome?
- Have organizational priorities changed affecting project priorities? How serious are the changes? Is closure necessary now?

---

The audit report may provide complete or partial answers to these questions. For some of these questions, the audit report will provide a timely warning so that the project manager can address the issue. For example, a response to weakening support for the project may include increased communication with top management and improved relationships with functional managers. The audit report may provide an early warning about an issue that does not require any action but should be carefully monitored.

The outcome of an audit that is carried out *after* the project is complete must be a report that responds to the important questions shown in Exhibit 14.5.

Despite clear benefits, most information systems projects are not audited. Project audits require planning, take time, take resources, and influence individuals' behavior and emotions. However, if planned and implemented properly, project audits have short- and long-term benefits for the organization in general and for the project manager in particular. The audit plan is shown as Exhibit 14.6.

The idea of an audit creates anxiety in most situations and can lead to behavior change. However, such consequences are minimized when organizations have audits as a rule rather than as an exception. Every information systems project should have audits during and at the end of information systems development activities. The

**Exhibit 14.5    Questions to Be Addressed by the Audit Report**

- Was the project the right choice? How is the project outcome aligned with the organizational goals and objectives?
- Was the project developed right? How is the project outcome aligned with the original specifications?
- Did the project meet customer satisfaction?
- What are the lessons to be learned for future projects?
  - Leadership lessons?
  - Team interaction lessons?
  - Organizational lessons?
  - Top management support?
  - External entities, vendors?

- Did the project meet cost and time constraints? What were specific reasons for the project running over or under time and over or under budget?

**Exhibit 14.6    The Audit Plan**

- The scope—what can and cannot be audited.
- Tasks to be carried out—progress reviews for each activity in terms of time, cost, and specification. The content of the final report.
- Timetable—when the audit begins, how long it should take, when the final report is due.
- Audit team—most organizations have policies regarding membership of audit teams. These organizational policies provide consistency and must be followed. *Audit activities must be independent of project activities.* The project audit report must not be influenced by the project manager or team members; only external people should be involved with audit activities. The project manager and team members should be available to provide information for the audit process. Sometimes, specific team members or key individuals are appointed to cooperate with the audit team, especially for audits that are carried out during the project development.
- Audit leader—the success of the project audit depends to a large extent on audit leadership. Several individual characteristics influence the leadership of the project audit:
  - Independence
  - Integrity
  - Business knowledge
  - Information systems project knowledge
  - Understanding business processes

---

### Exhibit 14.7   The Characteristics of an Information Systems Project Audit

**INFORMATION SYSTEMS PROJECT AUDITS ARE NOT ABOUT**

- Finger pointing
- Who did what wrong
- Judging
- Retribution

**INFORMATION SYSTEMS PROJECT AUDITS ARE ABOUT**

- Prevention
- Learning from mistakes
- Continuous improvement
- Measuring project success

---

information systems project manager must welcome audits and prepare team members to understand their benefits. Exhibit 14.7 lists criteria on what these audits are (and are not) about.

The idea of the project audit must be a part of the information systems project plan and considered beneficial by team members for the successful completion of the project. Audits provide timely and important feedback to the project manager in monitoring and controlling progress. Audit reports have the potential to protect team members and enhance management support. For example, an audit report may reveal problems that relate to unclear definitions, poor decision making, poor coordination, low commitment, poor leadership, inadequate personnel, outside interference, lack of responsibility or accountability, tight schedule, staff turnover, and the like. An audit report of an ongoing information systems project provides timely warnings that enable management to address many of these issues in a timely manner. An audit report of a completed project provides relevant information that enables the management to prevent these problems from happening in future projects.

The audit plan can be seen as part of the toolkit of the *reflective practitioner.* The project manager needs to learn from what went right and what went wrong to guide future work. Similarly, an organization where its people learn from experience so that future projects are done better is a *learning organization.* It is obvious, but still worth stating, that reflective practitioners and learning organizations are likely to be stronger than ones that do not reflect and learn. Many organizations have a comprehensive database of project lessons learned, and the potential of this to support future projects is itself a critical success factor.

## 14.4. Interview With a Project Manager

What is the difference between a general manager and a project manager?

"Well, if we limit this to IT management, a general manager can be one of several things. For example, a general manager could manage a team that does more maintenance and enhancements of current systems and/or applications, or a general manager could manage operations like the print area or a large IT shop.

An IT project manager typically focuses on new IT initiatives or 'major' enhancements to a current system. A project manager may work with resources from many areas within an IT organization or in some instances may have a staff of dedicated resources reporting directly to him or her. Typically projects are managed differently than small enhancements in terms of structure and reporting."

What do you enjoy most about your position?

"What I enjoy most is that where I work I have total decision-making abilities and I am seldom questioned about the way I manage projects. Another piece of my job that I find very rewarding is to watch people under my direction grow and develop. I get a sense of accomplishment in knowing that I am helping others with their careers."

What is most challenging about your job?

"Well, there are several things, but I guess the main challenge I have is that I am not allowed to pick the technical or business resources for some of my projects (I do get to pick for some of them). I prefer to work with a very self-motivated, self-directed staff that is not afraid to provide input, very willing to share information, and a team with a good attitude and willingness to get the job done on time no matter what it takes. Sometimes I get stuck with much less than that."

What is unique about your job?

"Every project is different. For the projects I manage, each team is different, the technology is different, the project goals are different, etc. It is constant variety."

What are the tools that you use on a daily basis?

"MS Office (Excel, Access, Word, PowerPoint), MS Project or Project Central, Visio, and I use other tools since I have maintained a very technical background and assist in data modeling, design, and every once in a while still troubleshoot source code."

How do you motivate your team?

"Rather than have just a couple of technical leaders working on my projects, I actually assign everyone a leadership role—even if it is a small one. I also have a couple of people on the team maintain a project Web site, and I purchased a digital camera so that we can have a project photo album on the site. The site makes it easier to navigate and find technical documents, requirements, time sheets, etc.

*(Continued)*

(Continued)

I always give everyone a chance to provide input and generally reward those who come up with ideas that significantly benefit the project. Also, my team truly knows I care about them and try to help them out (particularly the ones that want to move on to positions that require added responsibility). Also, my team knows that I shoot straight and do not play the political games and hide information that some project managers do. You have to earn your team's respect, and you can't do it unless you are straightforward and sincere.

Also, I have events. For example, depending on the age and overall personality of the team, I pick from several things. One project team I am currently managing (this is a small team of 12 people) meets the first Monday of each month during the lunch hour. Sometimes we bring bag lunches, and sometimes we decide to all bring something like Mexican food. We scheduled on Mondays so that people would be able to put something together over the weekend if need be. Anyway, then we go to this conference room and play a game (Pictionary, Gestures, or something like that). Pictionary is great to break the ice with a new team. Someone on the project team coordinates the event each month (whether we are going to bring snacks or bring our own lunches, or order in from Quiznos or whatever) and which game we're going to play."

What keeps you motivated?

"I like what I do. I find my position very satisfying, and I have always been self-motivated. I guess my main motivation is I feel a personal sense of responsibility in ensuring that everything is running smoothly and quality work is being produced."

What is your typical day at work like?

"On any given week, I have vendors in to demonstrate something we are interested in, I have meetings with both my direct management and project status meetings with our executive management, and team meetings for projects. I also take time to visit with some of our stakeholders face-to-face each week. And I review the project constantly to see if one area is getting behind and determine the best approach to catching up. It's hard to describe a typical day, because every one is very different."

Would you consider this a position that you would be able to learn "on the job" or through an academic institution?

"I would never put someone in a project management position for an IT project that has not had years of hands-on development experience (actually coding experience) and a strong background in systems analysis. Our company does not have anyone in a project management role that does not have these two qualifications along with strong insurance industry knowledge and at least 2 years of management (systems maintenance management). I think you have to prove capabilities as a manager before you can prove yourself as a project manager. Some people disagree with this, but I network with project managers from many companies and have never found one willing to hire without several years of experience outside of project management."

What are some of the success factors that you would recommend?

"I can provide you with a 'top 10' list of success factors:

1. Keep an open mind: Things change, you may be wrong, so don't appear stubborn and unchangeable.

2. Listen to your team: This is an extension of the first point. If you can keep an open mind, your team will suggest improvements—knowing that they will not be fobbed off due to your inflexibility.

3. Do not take on a project for which you cannot understand, in detail, the technical components, technical architecture, and the business driving the project.

4. Read constantly—much of what we learn is through reading

5. Discuss constantly—courses can also help as can conferences through talking to colleagues with more experience. Talking to those with similar levels of experience can also be helpful as they can act as 'walls' to bounce ideas off.

6. Be meticulous and organized and bring structure to the projects you manage.

7. Be committed to quality, and be a role model for your project teams.

8. Document well. No one will know about your achievements if they are not communicated, and this includes documentation.

9. Keep everyone abreast of project information (do not think your team doesn't need to know things; they may want to know everything). Even when doing presentations for executive management distribute copies of the material to everyone on the project team.

10. Praise your team and your project—if you don't, no one else will!"

What advice would you give to a recent graduate who would like to pursue the position of a project manager in the near future?

"Expect a career in which you will not have a typical 8–5 workday. Gain some experience in general management—it's important before managing project teams. Also, if you ever plan to manage IT projects, then you will never have the respect of your technical staff if you do not have a technical background. Get one!"

## 14.5. Chapter Summary

Information systems project management includes administrative closure of the project and formal delivery of the final product to the customer. Project closure prevents scope creep. Primary activities at the closing stage for an information systems project include administrative accounts closure, performance evaluation of team members, and a project audit. Contracts and accounts must be properly closed, including those of professional employees hired for the duration of the project and equipment and facilities transferred for the project use. Team members must be appraised for their contribution to the project. The project manager must evaluate each team member with the intent to assess individual contributions to the project as well as to provide constructive feedback to the individual regarding career development. Project audits should be carried out during the information systems development as well as at the end of the project. Audits during the project development provide timely warning to the project manager to address potential problems and avoid serious consequences. Audits at the end of project development provide useful feedback for future projects and help management avoid costly mistakes. Project audits are not always carried out, and individuals sometimes react with anxiety to them. However, this anxiety factor is minimized when audits are carried out regularly and with the intent to learn and improve project outcome. All information systems projects must include project audits as part of their plans.

## DISCUSSION QUESTIONS

1. Comment on the following statement: "We cannot afford to terminate the project now. We have already spent more than 50% of the project budget."

2. It is suggested that project audits create anxiety among team members and may lead to internal politics among departments and in turn make the whole process dysfunctional. Describe the benefits of a project audit and suggest ways of implementing it that avoids these problems.

3. What are the main differences between auditing a marketing project versus auditing an information systems project? What are the similarities?

4. How would you justify cost, time, and efforts spent on auditing an ongoing project? A completed project? If you had a choice of only one, which audit would you think the most useful, during or after? Why?

5. Comment on the following statement. "You cannot manage what you cannot measure." Is this statement true in the case of information systems project management?

6. Why is it difficult to perform a truly independent and objective audit?

7. What personal characteristics and skills would you look for in selecting a project audit leader?

8. Do you agree with our project manager's "top 10" critical success factors for the role?

## EXERCISES

1. Design a survey questionnaire for measuring team performance. Include in this survey:

   Who should respond to your survey

   The instructions for respondents

   A scale

   Six questions

2. Describe your rationale for the way you designed your survey. For example, why you chose the scale that you did? Why did you choose the set of questions that you did? Hint: Use the reverse of the "input–process–output" model for designing your survey.

3. Prepare a table with two columns. In the first column, list four individual characteristics and skills that you would look for in selecting a project audit leader. In the second column, provide your reasoning for each individual trait.

4. Performance review of team members is an important activity that if done properly will improve member behavior and be a base for reward and promotion. List what in your opinion are important characteristics of an effective performance review. What would you not include in your performance review list? Things that in your view would be counter-effective?

5. Describe performance evaluation of information system projects from the following two perspectives. (a) You as a team member being evaluated. What approach would be most beneficial to you? What approach you would find least beneficial? (b) You as an information systems project manager evaluating your team members. What approach would be most practical to you? What approach you would find least beneficial?

## APPENDIX TO CHAPTER 14: REFLECTIONS ON IS PROJECT MANAGEMENT

The purpose of this appendix is to discuss the issues raised in this book. This has not been a conventional textbook that describes the "one way" of doing project management with the implication that all you need is to learn the material to be a successful project manager. If only project management were that simple! In truth there is no one approach that will be successful for all projects in all companies in all countries. In this book we have described the complexity of real-world project management. Along with the general material, we have achieved this especially through exhibits, which often suggest a contrary position to the conventional; interviews with project managers, which uncover real-world difficulties and challenges and different points of view; and case studies, which show that projects are rarely straightforward. As such, there are debates about the topics raised and we take the opportunity in this appendix to enable students to reflect on these issues and topics to enable greater understanding. We suggest that discussion of each of the following issues is carried out through an individual essay (or written examination question), group presentation, team debate, or even a team "playlet."

*(Continued)*

(Continued)

Debate 1: Is project management a sociocultural or technical subject? Qualitative or quantitative? An art or a science?

Hint: You may like to list the topics of the book that are in each category. For example, there are many human traits required of the various stakeholders, most of which will be sociocultural (people skills such as communication skills, negotiation skills, leadership skills, conflict management, using experience for estimating, etc.) but also many techniques (timeboxing, work breakdown structures, structured walkthroughs, payback analysis, CoCoMo, PERT, etc.) and software tools (*MS Project, ThinkTank, Crystal Ball,* etc.) described that are firmly in the technical domain. Which ones take on the greatest importance in project management? Which ones seem to be more important as you have perceived from the interviews and case studies (which were all drawn from real situations)?

Debate 2: Is the life cycle of an information systems project a realistic or unrealistic description of project development?

Hint: Describe the elements of the life cycle shown as Figure 1.6 first and then discuss whether projects always flow in such a fashion or whether they are not to some extent iterative. Do all projects display each of the elements in each step? Do they always occur as suggested? For example, is the project manager always appointed in the initiating phase, is the project scope always clear in the early planning phase, and so on? Reconsider the case studies and also cases that you find on the Internet. Did they follow this pattern?

Debate 3: Describe the job opportunities and career structures in project management.

Hint: The book discusses what is required of the project manager and each team member. It also raises issues such as ethical ones, which also relate to the debate. But you may also search the Web for information—for example, from the Project Management Institute (www.pmi.org), the British Computer Society (www.bcs.org), and also individual job advertisements (what experience was required, what was the salary level?). Discuss also how globalization, in particular outsourcing and offshoring, has affected job opportunities.

Debate 4: To what extent have ethical, political, and other issues led to a reinterpretation of the role of the information systems project manager in modern organizations?

Hint: First outline the traditional description of the project manager who "seems" to guide a rather mechanistic process from initiation through planning, developing, implementing, and closure of the project. Show how the "reality" might be different from this "ideal." Then you could add other dimensions to the role—for example, as it has been influenced by ethical issues, such as the codes of conduct discussed in the appendix to Chapter 1, and political and legal issues, such as the Sarbanes–Oxley Act outlined in the appendix to Chapter 9.

Debate 5: Discuss how the barriers to CRM success at MedicalCo (Chapter 5) might be generalizable to other industries.

Hint: You have learned in this book that while there is a lot that we can learn from past experience and other projects, every case will have values in and of itself. This is arguably more so when we cross industry boundaries. For example, health care information systems will have unique characteristics that may be different from those for the manufacturing industry. Therefore, in analyzing the customer relationship management (CRM) at MedicalCo, you need to consider how common each of those barriers is within and outside the pharmaceutical industry.

Debate 6: Discuss and describe critical success factors for the ERP system at NGC (Chapter 7)?

Hint: Again consider your response for different levels. The marketing, sales, and distribution of natural gas in some areas of the United States were altered by the 1997 deregulation. This means that NGC Natural Gas Company as a regulated utility company is governed by the area public utility service commission. To what extent would this affect the supply-chain management system and related information support systems? How would this influence user demand for system specifications and in turn the information system development process? Are critical success factors different for "regulated" industries? The company has decided to purchase and install ERP software modules for purchasing, inventory management, accounts payable, and employee expense reporting. Would these choices of modules be part of the critical success factors? You need to consider, in your analysis and response, how well these modules will support organizational goals and objectives. Discuss in particular the role of the consulting firm (ConsultCo). Comment on their statement of work, for example; does it contain too much or too little detail?

Debate 7: What were the main factors, in your opinion, that turned the London Ambulance Service case (Chapter 8) from a failure to a success scenario?

Hint: There is no hard-and-fast rule about any success story, and this case is no exception. This information support system was particularly affected by public and popular press involvement. That made decisions of budgeting and management somewhat political. This adds a new dimension of project management skills to those we have discussed in this book. This case is also affected by the law of England, which makes ambulance services to the London population of over 7 million people a duty. To what extent should the project management and leadership responsible for this project be influenced by these issues? To what extent did these factors influence the process and the outcome of this case? You need to structure your response so that you will cover issues of history and background, organizational culture, internal and external politics, management and technical competency, and other such factors.

Debate 8: Are information systems projects largely successful or unsuccessful?

Hint: You may first discuss what is meant by success and failure in this context (as projects are rarely 100% successes or 100% failures). Is the assessment largely based on whether the project is delivered on time and on budget or are there other factors to take account? How does the discussion on "quality" affect this? Note that we included many case studies that were failures (to some extent at least), as we feel that readers will learn more from these cases than ones in which "everything went right." We suggested in the AAHELP example (Exhibit 1.1) that "successes" are frequent but rarely get publicity, as failures are far more newsworthy. Do you think that is fair comment?

## BIBLIOGRAPHY

Arthur, T. (2003). *The five W's of project management.* Retrieved from www.projectmanagement .com/article/1,2462,91268,00.html

Gray, C. F., & Larson, E. W. (2003). *Project management: The managerial process.* New York: McGraw-Hill Irwin.

Jones, G., & George, J., (1998). *Contemporary management.* New York: McGraw-Hill Irwin.

Kerzner, H. (2003). *Project management: A systems approach to planning, scheduling, and controlling.* New York: Wiley.

Lemberg, P. (2003). *Seven ways to be unreasonable.* Retrieved from www.lemberg.com/ unreason7.html

Rankos, J. (1990). *Software project management for small to medium sized projects.* Harlow, UK: Prentice Hall.

# Index